## DATE DUE

| | | |
|---|---|---|
| | | |
| | | |
| | | |
| | | |
| | | |
| | | |
| | | |
| | | |
| | | |
| | | |
| | | |
| | | |
| | | |
| | | |
| | | |

# Oklahoma

A HISTORY OF THE SOONER STATE

# OKLAHOMA

## A History of
## The Sooner State

*By* EDWIN C. McREYNOLDS

NORMAN

UNIVERSITY OF OKLAHOMA PRESS

*By Edwin C. McReynolds*

*Oklahoma: A History of the Sooner State* (Norman, 1954, 1964)
*The Seminoles* (Norman, 1957)
*Missouri: A History of the Crossroads State* (Norman, 1962)
*Oklahoma: A History of the State and Its People* (with Alice Marriott
    and Estelle Faulconer) (Norman, 1961)

*International Standard Book Number: 0–8061–0302–7*

*Library of Congress Catalog Card Number: 54–10052*

*Copyright 1954, 1964 by the University of Oklahoma Press*
*Publishing Division of the University*
*Manufactured in the U.S.A.*
*First edition, 1954; second printing, 1956;*
*third printing, 1960; fourth printing (revised),*
*1964; fifth printing, 1969; sixth printing, 1972.*

*To My Wife*
*who made the task of writing every day*
*seem worth the doing*

───────────────────────────────

# Preface

This history of Oklahoma is intended for readers who desire a brief yet reasonably comprehensive account of the state's growth. The narrative goes back to the time of the Spanish *conquistadores,* as a balanced record of Oklahoma must do. At every stage an attempt is made to preserve the relation between events and conditions within the area and main currents outside of it. It is this connection of its people with the history of other regions that gives significance to Oklahoma's story.

It has been my good fortune to be in more or less continuous residence in the present area of Oklahoma since 1892. Thus at various stages of my life I have seen the unfolding of vital steps in Oklahoma history. From them I have firsthand information on such topics as the early rural and town schools of Oklahoma Territory, farm and ranch life in both of the Twin Territories, the A. and M. College at the turn of the century, and the University of Oklahoma two years before statehood. Newspaper reports of the Constitutional Convention in 1906 were preserved in my first conscious effort to gather historical data; but impressions of people and of society that was developing in Oklahoma began much earlier.

Some significant figures in the shaping of Oklahoma life, both in territorial days and after statehood, have been personal acquaintances or friends. For example, as a high-school boy I did the yard work at the residence of President Angelo C. Scott of the Oklahoma A. and M. College at Stillwater. The president was an educator who shared his philosophy with casual acquaintances among the youth of his town. The wages he paid were much appreciated by his yard boy; but the wisdom that fell from his lips became a treasure of inestimable value. A pioneer schoolman, he had the intellectual tastes of a patrician and the democratic simplicity demanded by his fellow citizens of the frontier. He could teach a class in English literature, sing a powerful bass in the college quartet, or preside over a faculty meeting, as the occasion required. So far as I observed, he never attempted to rope a steer or nail a shoe on a mule; but there was little doubt that he was capable of either task. He was a man who did what had to be done.

It must be admitted that acquaintance with a few educators, political leaders, editors, attorneys, businessmen, and physicians, along with thousands of other citizens, cannot be regarded as an adequate basis for the writing of a state's history. My view, like that of any historian, is imperfect and subject to the limitations of personal impression. But the intimate quality of firsthand acquaintances is, at least, a beginning of thorough understanding. The historian can only hope to harmonize the little he has learned about the lives of a people with material he has found in the records.

Most of the work for this volume was done in the University of Oklahoma Library, where the Phillips Collection is particularly useful in many phases of Oklahoma history. Research for specific points of information has taken me to the Oklahoma Historical Society collection at Oklahoma City, the Oklahoma State Library in the Capitol, the Library of Congress, and the National Archives in Washington, D. C.

Grateful acknowledgment is made to the many people who have given generously of their time in explaining points of difficulty. Professors Edward Everett Dale, Morris L. Wardell, Charles C. Bush, Jr., and Donald J. Berthrong have given valuable assistance. Dean Roy Gittinger was kind enough to read the entire manuscript with painstaking care, and his suggestions were most helpful. Acknowledgment is also made to those alert students whose critical discussions in the classroom have helped the author to appreciate values in Oklahoma history.

EDWIN C. McREYNOLDS

*Norman, Oklahoma*

# Contents

# Illustrations

xi

# Maps

# Oklahoma

A HISTORY OF THE SOONER STATE

# CHAPTER ONE

# The First Explorers from Europe

## SPANISH NEIGHBORS

"There are pearls and great riches on the coast of the South Sea," the Indian said to Alvar Núñez Cabeza de Vaca.[1] As he wandered across the plains of Texas, one of four survivors of a Spanish expedition to the Gulf Coast in 1528, Cabeza de Vaca heard the stories of rich treasure many times, repeated with endless variation—pearl islands off the South Sea coast, inland cities where utensils in common use were fashioned from gold, and houses built many stories above their stone foundations, with rich colors in their walls and with turquoise-studded doorways. The attention of Cabeza de Vaca sharpened at the mention of jewels, and the Indians shaped their talk to fit the interest of their guest. Out of the Spaniard's eagerness for precious stones and metals, an obsession shared by many of his countrymen, old stories of fabulous towns in the north were revived by the Indians, and the legendary Seven Cities of Cíbola became common gossip in the northern provinces of Mexico.

The men who tested the truth of the legends and, in the process, made the first explorations by Europeans in what is now Oklahoma were Spanish *conquistadores,* whose lives were filled with romantic adventure. There was Don Antonio de Mendoza, "the good viceroy," sent by Emperor Charles V, to rule over New Spain in 1535. It was Mendoza who sent out the expedition to search for gold. There was Francisco Vásquez Coronado, the dashing commander of Spanish cavalry, who came to Mexico with Mendoza and received a commission as governor of New Galicia, the frontier province in the north of Mexico. It was Coronado who

[1] George Parker Winship, ed., "The Coronado Expedition," Bureau of American Ethnology *Fourteenth Annual Report,* Part I, 350.

3

was sent north in 1540 with the army to conquer the Seven Cities of Cíbola.[2]

Father Juan de la Asunción had a part in the enterprise, since he made a preliminary journey to the north, probably as far as the Gila River in southern Arizona. Friar Marcos de Niza commissioned to go as a scout to the land of Cíbola, had a larger part. He was a man greatly respected by his fellow Franciscans, both for his services in the routine duties of his religious order and for his wide experience in American exploration. He was a native of Nice and was called a Frenchman by his companions. In 1535 he had been with Pizarro in Peru.

Niza, with a small band of followers, left Culiacán in the province of Galicia on March 7, 1539, on his advance expedition into the wilds of the region that is now Sonora and Arizona. One Spanish churchman, Friar Onorato, accompanied him for several days, but was forced to turn back by illness. Estevan, a Negro companion of Cabeza de Vaca ten years earlier, went with the expedition as its principal guide. Six natives of Arizona who had been taught the Spanish language were taken along as interpreters.[3]

After two weeks the party reached a point in central Sonora which Friar Marcos called Vacapa. Here he rested until April 6, while Estevan with a smaller band proceeded northward. The leader instructed Estevan to send back news as he penetrated the land of the pueblos. If he found evidence that there was vast wealth in Cíbola, he was to send a white cross the size of a man's palm—a larger cross if he desired to convey "very promising" news. If Estevan found proof that the country around Cíbola promised to be a greater find than New Spain, he was to send back a cross even larger. The message that he sent, after a few days, was a cross as tall as a man. He was still many rough miles short of reaching Cíbola, but obviously the stories that he heard from Indians who had been there impressed him greatly. Friar Marcos marched his party out of Vacapa, and on the journey north he eagerly ques-

---

[2] *Ibid.*, 382–93; 413–69 (Spanish text); 470–546 (English translation). Coronado was a native of Salamanca, Spain. His wife was Beatrice de Estrada, a cousin of Emperor Charles V. Her father, Alonso, was treasurer of New Spain, and Coronado received from him a valuable estate.

[3] *Ibid.*, 355.

4

tioned all the natives he encountered, concerning the fabulous cities of Cíbola. All of their accounts agreed with the symbol message sent by Estevan.

As a matter of fact, pueblos built by the Zuñi Indians of the Colorado Plateau had all the appearance of mansions when viewed by the natives of Sonora. The four-storied houses, whitened by gypsum water, presented a sharp contrast to the one-roomed huts of more primitive Indians. It is not remarkable that Spaniards, with credulity born of their ardent desire for wealth and appetites whetted by the marvels of golden treasure already found in Mexico, should misinterpret the stories told them by the Indians. A native of Cíbola, questioned closely by Friar Marcos de Niza himself, confirmed the message that Estevan had sent in the form of a large white cross.[4]

On May 9, Niza received news of Estevan's death. The natives of Cíbola had killed him, in spite of his efforts to convince them that he was a great magician, a medicine man in good standing with the Indians of the Texas plains. Unable to go into the region where his scout had been killed, Niza returned to New Galicia and reported to Coronado. Together, the two men went to the capital and placed the story of the preliminary expedition before the viceroy.[5] The towns of Cíbola promised greater wealth than New Spain, they said.

A second party, consisting of fifteen men under the command of Melchior Díaz, was sent out in November, 1539, to verify the reports of Marcos de Niza. Cold weather prevented an extended and thorough investigation. Apparently Díaz was quite skeptical concerning the wealth of Cíbola; but as his party returned to Mex-

---

[4] *Ibid.*, 358.

[5] The evidence on the report of Friar Marcos is somewhat contradictory. Andrés García, whose son-in-law was a barber and was acquainted with Niza as a customer, repeated his account of his journey, perhaps with added features to increase the interest of his listeners. George Parker Winship's opinion: "Friar Marcos undoubtedly never willfully told an untruth about the country of Cíbola, even in a barber's chair. But there seems to be little chance for doubting that the reports which he brought to New Spain were the cause of much talk as well as many sermons, which gave rise to a considerable amount of excitement among the settlers, whose old-world notions had been upset by the reputed glory of the Montezumas and the wealth of the Incas." *Ibid.*, 366. In a letter to Emperor Charles V, Hernán Cortés accused Niza of reporting as facts the wild rumors that he heard only from the natives.

ico he met Coronado and joined the expedition to the north. He was not allowed to give a discouraging report to the soldiers.[6]

## THE CORONADO EXPEDITION

Friar Marcos had returned from his first journey to the north in August, 1539. By the middle of October, Mendoza had taken steps toward the preparation of a great military expedition to Cíbola. He named Compostela, on the west coast, as the point for assembling the party. The Viceroy had in mind two advantages in starting the march from the Pacific port, rather than the capital: a larger part of Mexico would be relieved from the passage of an army; and troublesome young adventurers in Mexico City would be drawn into the service of Coronado, and thus the capital would be rid of them.[7]

On February 23, 1540, the force was assembled and ready to march north. It consisted of 250 mounted men, 70 foot soldiers, and 1,000 natives, armed with their customary weapons. The Spanish soldiers were fitted out more elaborately than any other band in the history of the Mexican conquest. The horsemen were dressed in coats of mail, with metal or bull-hide helmets, armed with swords and lances, and mounted on the best animals that the Mexican ranches could furnish. In addition to pack mules for spare equipment and light artillery, the force was supplied with herds of cattle, sheep, goats, and hogs to slaughter along the way. The extra horses numbered 1,000. Each foot soldier was armed with a harquebus or crossbow and carried a sword for hand-to-hand fighting, and each was supplied with a sturdy shield. Perhaps the spectacular trappings of this expedition are evidence of the Spaniard's predilection for showy splendor, but the army was about to prove that it could do more than parade. Coronado's men were a hardy breed of fighters.

Three ships loaded with additional supplies sailed along the coast of Mexico on the west, but turned back at the head of the

[6] *Ibid.*, 384.
[7] *Ibid.*, 377.

Gulf of California without making contact with Coronado's men. After receiving the report of Melchior Díaz concerning the scarcity of food in the barren land to the north of Culiacán, Coronado decided to divide his force at that place and push on rapidly with a diminished command. He selected eighty horsemen and twenty-five foot soldiers, and with Friar Marcos as guide marched northward along the coast from Culiacán on April 22, 1540. The main body of his force was ordered to follow, after a rest of two weeks, and to travel at a more leisurely pace.[8]

Coronado's party marched through rough, arid, inhospitable country. The difficulties and dangers of the trail were many. Pasturage for the animals was scarce, and the soldiers ate pine nuts to stretch out their own meager supply of food. Horses and Indian carriers died of exhaustion and lack of nourishment. The speed of the march gradually decreased, and occasionally Coronado called a halt for several days to rest the pack animals and to care for sick men. "In seventy-three days we reached Cíbola, although after hard labor and the loss of many horses and the death of several Indians, and after we saw it these were all doubled, although we did find corn enough" ran one of the chronicles of the memorable journey.[9] The natives assembled their fighting men to resist the invasion, but after a short battle the town was taken. The warriors of Cíbola fought with bows and arrows, clubs and rocks, and yielded only to the superior arms of the Spanish soldiers. On the day after the battle, in which Coronado himself was slightly wounded, the Spaniards learned that the people and their army had fled from all the towns. The first town to be captured, called Hawikuh by the natives, was renamed Granada by the conquerors.[10]

[8] *Ibid.*, 386.

[9] Anonymous account, quoted by Winship, from Joaquín F. Pacheco and Francisco de Cárdenas, eds. *Colección de documentos inéditos relativos al descubrimiento, conquista y colonización de las posesiones españolas en América* (42 vols., Madrid. 1864–84).

[10] Winship, "Coronado Expedition," Bureau of American Ethnology *Fourteenth Annual Report*, Part I, 389. The natives came out and fought an unequal battle outside of their town against the well-armed invaders and later defended their houses fiercely, fighting from house to house. Aganiez Suárez and three of the foot soldiers received arrow wounds, and many of the attacking force were hit by rocks. Coronado himself, whose shining armor marked him for special attention by the defenders, was twice knocked flat on the ground by heavy stones and disabled for several days. Apparently his well-designed helmet prevented more serious injury.

7

In their visible evidences of wealth, these precursors of present-day Zuñi communities fell far short of the reports Friar Marcos had heard, and perhaps of the impression he had conveyed to Mendoza and Coronado. There was none of the rich silver and golden treasure the Spaniards had found two decades earlier in the conquest of Mexico. In spite of some four-storied houses, to justify their description by humble Indians of Sonora as mansions, there was little in the way of movable property, and the people were quite primitive in most respects. In their disappointment over the poverty of Cíbola, the soldiers were very bitter towards their guide; and we may suppose that Niza was eager to go back when Coronado sent him with orders for the main army to join the advance force.

The pueblo towns which had been identified as the famed Seven Cities of Cíbola were near the border of the present-day Zuñi Indian Reservation in western New Mexico. In a straight line, Cíbola was nearly four hundred miles southwest of Black Mesa Butte in the northwestern corner of the present-day Oklahoma Panhandle, and six hundred miles due west of the present-day Oklahoma capital. Although they found no gems or precious metals, Coronado's men obtained a supply of food and settled down with the intention of waiting for the rest of the Spanish forces to arrive. There seemed to be ample supplies of beans, corn, and fowls. The Zuñi Indians also had a store of good salt, "the best and whitest I have seen in all my life," as one of the invaders wrote. Coronado sent an exploring party northwest along the Little Colorado, and for the first time Europeans saw the scenic marvel, the Grand Canyon. Another party marched east to the Río Grande; and when Coronado received their report, he decided to spend the winter at a place which the Spaniards called Tiguex, probably in present-day Sandoval County, New Mexico. The reunited Spanish army rested at Tiguex from December, 1540, until March, 1541.[11]

Relations between the natives and invaders were bad from the start. The young Spanish adventurers who were not welcome

---

[11] *Ibid.*, 390, 391, 489, 490. Don García López de Cárdenas led the party that explored the region between Cíbola and the Grand Canyon. Don Hernando Alvarado discovered the town which the Spaniards called Tiguex and explored a part of the Río Grande.

in Mendoza's capital because of their lax behavior could hardly be expected to establish friendly relations with the conquered people of Tiguex. A native revolt was put down by Coronado only after a prolonged siege of their town. The Indians were promised immunity from punishment if they would surrender; but after they had laid down their arms, it was discovered that Coronado had ordered his lieutenants to take no prisoners, and the captives were burned as a warning to others who might plan an uprising. With Spanish accounts as the only available records, it is clear that the invaders were generally inconsiderate, harsh in their demands, cruel in their suppression of resistance, and dishonorable in regard to solemn promises of pardon.[12]

In Tiguex the Europeans heard new rumors of cities that contained great stores of wealth. A native of a land to the north called Quivira, purchased by the Spaniards as a slave, gave the eager gold seekers a new dream to stoke the fires of their imagination. He said that all the people of his country ate their food from golden plates and carried their water in golden jugs. With the slave as their guide, the invaders set out early in 1541 for the land of Quivira. Northeastward to the Pecos River, then southeast for thirty-seven days they marched, probably following the course of the Brazos River to a point near the 98th meridian. Here their guide, "the Turk," as the Spaniards called him, admitted under severe pressure that he had led them on a wild march, not toward Quivira but far to the south of it. Ysopete, another native of Quivira who was with the party, had maintained from the start that the Turk was lying. The guide's purpose, obviously, had been to lure Coronado and his men away from Tiguex and to lose them in the vast level spaces of the southern Great Plains.

Coronado now divided his force, sending the larger party back to Tiguex and proceeding with thirty horsemen toward Quivira. For forty-two days the band traveled due north, marching entirely across Oklahoma and to the Arkansas River in south-central Kansas. Ysopete was their new guide while the Turk was taken along in chains. They found the Quivira Indians living in the valley of the Arkansas River. Their houses were round, grass structures, artfully fashioned to keep out moisture and wind, built upon designs used

[12] *Ibid.*, 392, 393.

by their Caddoan ancestors for many centuries and by their descendants for several more. Their houses were clustered together in villages, and the people lived from their crops of maize, beans, squash, melons, and other vegetables, supplementing their agriculture by hunting and fishing. They possessed no movable wealth other than buffalo robes, dogs, and a few simple implements and weapons.[13] This was the first European glimpse of the future Oklahoma. The Indian communities fell far short of Spanish hopes, with no evidence of the grandeur that Cortés had found in Mexico and no store of movable wealth to tempt the cupidity of the Christian monarch of Spain. It was chiefly an undeveloped land with virgin prairie soil awaiting the great events of a later century.

Although the Turk had long since admitted his guilt in regard to the location and condition of the Quivira Indians, the Spaniards found an excuse to execute him before they began their return journey.[14] On the march to Tiguex they crossed the Oklahoma Panhandle and the Texas Panhandle. Coronado's army spent the following winter in Tiguex and returned to Mexico in the spring of 1542.

Eyewitness accounts of the Coronado expedition, written largely by Pedro de Castañeda and Captain Juan Jaramillo, but with important details added by the letters of Coronado to Emperor Charles V and to Viceroy Mendoza, provide the earliest descriptions of the Southwestern Plains and the nomad Indian tribes.[15]

---

[13] *Ibid.*, 393–96.

[14] According to Jaramillo's account, the Turk conspired with the Quivira Indians, asking them to attack the Spaniards. "We learned of it . . . and strangled him that night so that he never waked up." *Ibid.*, 584–93.

[15] *Ibid.*, 504 ff. As Coronado's men moved southeastward from the Pecos River in the spring of 1541, they saw many thousands of buffaloes. Castañeda wrote: "After ten days more they came to some settlements of people who lived like Arabs and who are called Querechos in that region. They had seen the cows for two days. These folks live in tents made of the tanned skins of the cows. They travel around near the cows, killing them for food. They did nothing unusual when they saw our army, except to come out of their tents to look at us, after which they came to talk with the advance guard and asked who we were. . . . That they were intelligent is evident from the fact that although they conversed by means of signs they made themselves understood so well that there was no need of an interpreter. . . . These folks started off from here next day with a lot of dogs which dragged their possessions. For two days, during which the army marched in the same direction, . . . they saw other roaming Querechos and such great numbers of cows that it already seemed something

In the meantime eastern Oklahoma, a region distinct from the buffalo plains by reason of its timber and rugged surface, was also visited by its first European invader.

## THE DE SOTO EXPEDITION

Hernando de Soto was another Spanish adventurer who added greatly to European knowledge of North America, and in the course of his extensive travels covered a part of Oklahoma. De Soto was a very young man when he commanded his first ship in the Caribbean region in 1523. He was with Francisco Pizarro nine years later in Peru, as second in command. He returned to Spain in 1536 and married the daughter of Pedrarias Dávila. Soon afterward he sold all of his property in order to purchase supplies for a military party with which he hoped to effect the conquest of Florida. The Emperor made him governor of Cuba and Florida. On May 18, 1539, he left Havana with 950 soldiers in ten ships, bent upon the occupation of Florida, which he believed to be as rich in precious metals as Peru.

He had no strong opposition from the natives until his army marched into the interior toward the Mississippi Valley. At Mabila he fought a great battle with the Choctaws in which, according to the Spanish report, more than 3,000 Indians were killed. The Span-

incredible. . . . They came across so many animals that those who were in the advance guard killed a large number of bulls. As these fled they trampled one another in their haste until they came to a ravine. So many of the animals fell into this that they filled it up, and the rest went across on top of them."

Jaramillo, describing the region around Quivira, wrote in his report: "The country presents a fine appearance, than which I have not seen a better in all our Spain nor Italy nor a part of France, nor indeed in the other countries where I have traveled in His Majesty's service, for it is not a very rough country but is made up of hillocks and plains, and very fine appearing rivers and streams, which certainly satisfied me and made me sure that it will be very fruitful in all sorts of products. Indeed, there is profit in the cattle ready to the hand, from the quantity of them, which is as great as one could imagine. We found a variety of Castilian prunes which are not all red, but some of them black and green; the tree and fruit is certainly like that of Castile, with a very excellent flavor. . . . There are grapes along some streams of fair flavor, not to be improved upon. The houses which these Indians have were of straw, and most of them round, and the straw reached down to the ground like a wall."

11

iards lost 22 killed and 148 wounded, and among the wounded was De Soto.[16]

After resting his army for a period of four weeks, De Soto marched north into the Chickasaw country and eventually turned west to the Mississippi. On June 18 the Spaniards crossed the river, and during the following twelve months explored through the region now included in Arkansas, Oklahoma, and Kansas. In the records left by the De Soto expedition, Indian life in the wooded section of eastern Oklahoma is described in detail.[17] In the valleys of the Arkansas and Ouachita rivers, the Spaniards lived on small game, fish, wild fruits, nuts, maize, pumpkins, and beans—all of which were plentiful. On Wednesday, August 24, 1541, Rodrigo Ranjel wrote in his diary: "They slept in a burned village. The next day, Thursday, in another near the river, where there were many pumpkins and an abundance of corn." On the following day, Friday, August 26, he recorded: "In these swamps, or pools, there was no end of fish. . . ."[18]

Frequent reference is made to the killing of "wild cows" by the Indians and to their use of "cow skins," which were De Soto's names for wood buffaloes and the hides which were put to many and diverse uses. Many of the Indian towns were protected by elaborately constructed stockades. At one place, probably in the valley of the Illinois River, the Spaniards gathered baskets of dry sand, strained water through it, "and there came out a brine that they boiled down, and let harden, and in that way made excellent salt, very white and of very good flavour."[19]

On the way back to Florida, De Soto died and was buried by his followers in the Mississippi River. In chronological order, the principal events of the Coronado and De Soto expeditions were as follows:

March 7, 1539      Marcos and Estevan left Culiacán to find the Seven Cities.

May 9      Friar Marcos entered the wilderness of Arizona.

[16] Edward Gaylord Bourne, ed., *Narratives of the Career of Hernando de Soto,* II, 123–28.

[17] Rodrigo Ranjel, De Soto's private secretary, wrote the narrative of the Spanish expedition in some detail in his diary. *Ibid.,* 47–149.

[18] *Ibid.,* 146.

[19] *Ibid.,* 148.

| | |
|---|---|
| May 21 | Friar Marcos learned of the death of Estevan. |
| May 25 | De Soto landed on the coast of Florida. |
| September 2 | Friar Marcos reported to Mendoza and certified to the truth of his report. |
| February 5, 1540 | Cortés stopped at Havana on his way to Spain. |
| February 23 | Coronado and army left Compostela for Cíbola. |
| March 28 | Reception for army at Culiacán, on Easter day. |
| April 22 | Coronado, with select force, depart from Culiacán. |
| July 7 | Coronado reached Cíbola and captured the first town. |
| July 11 | The Indians retired to their stronghold on Thunder Mountain. |
| August 25 (?) | López de Cárdenas started to explore the canyons of the Colorado. |
| August 29 | Hernando de Alvardo marched eastward to Tiguex. |
| September to January, 1541 | The army reached Cíbola and marched to Tiguex for winter quarters. |
| April 23 | Coronado started from Tiguex in search of Quivira. |
| May | De Soto reached the Mississippi River. |
| June 18 | De Soto crossed to the west side of the Mississippi. |
| June | Coronado turned north toward Quivira, where he arrived after forty-two days. |
| October 2 | Coronado returned from Quivira to Tiguex. |
| 1542 | Coronado and army returned to New Spain, starting from Tiguex in the spring and reached Mexico probably late in the fall. |
| May 21, 1542 | De Soto died at the mouth of Red River.[20] |

## THE NATURE AND EXTENT OF OKLAHOMA HISTORY

From the story of Spanish exploration before the middle of the sixteenth century, it may be seen that the actual recorded events of Oklahoma history reach back more than four hundred years. In the excavations of burial mounds and other material remains of native inhabitants, many facts of even earlier date have

[20] Winship, "Coronado Expedition," Bureau of American Ethnology *Fourteenth Annual Report*, Part I, 341-44.

been uncovered. All of these interesting discoveries are a part of the background of Oklahoma history. In a broad sense Spiro Mound, a great repository of early Indian materials in eastern Oklahoma, is a vital part of the record. From this storehouse of early Indian civilization, a variety of specimens have been recovered—cleverly shaped objects in quartz, jade, and agate; beaten copper vessels with arresting designs; textiles of fine quality, including laces; ceremonial objects; and ceramics fashioned with skill in the images of human beings, beasts, and birds. These evidences of developing Indian civilization belong to a period earlier by three hundred years than the western voyages of Christopher Columbus.

In some respects the story of Oklahoma is unique. No other section of the United States has the same basis of Indian culture as Oklahoma. Pre-Caddoan civilization, glimpsed in the material remains of Spiro Mound, extended over a wide area which included the wooded sections of the state. Nomadic and semi-nomadic tribes in the west, practicing their primitive agriculture and finding a major food supply in the buffalo herds that roamed the plains, contributed their peculiar traits to the native culture.

Into this geographic area, with its human elements already complex at the beginning of written history, new factors were to be introduced, gradually at first and then with increasing speed. The land was to be claimed in succession by Spain, England, and France. Although the first journeys of discovery by Spanish adventurers were more than sixty years earlier than the British settlement of Jamestown and the French province of Quebec, the Stuarts of England and the French Bourbons were soon laying claim to the region explored by Coronado and De Soto.[21]

The eighteenth century, filled with wars for empire between these rival powers and by coalitions formed by them, was to answer important questions of ownership. France was to be defeated and driven out of North America. In the process of stopping her principal rival, England was to make powerful enemies, thus laying the groundwork for loss of her thirteen American colonies. At the

---

[21] King James I's charter of 1609 for Virginia is an example of the Stuart view of British possessions in America. The text of the charter is printed in W. Stith, *History of Virginia.*

outset of the nineteenth century a new independent confederation of commonwealths, the United States of America, was to gain possession of the vast territory west of the Mississippi and thus to settle permanently the political status of Oklahoma.

As a territory of the United States, the land west of Arkansas, south of Kansas, and north of Texas was to be set aside as a permanent location for American Indians after the first quarter of the nineteenth century. The Cherokees and Creeks of Georgia, Choctaws and Chickasaws from Mississippi, Florida Seminoles, Texas Kickapoos, tribes from Kansas, Ohio, Missouri, Nebraska, and Idaho, along with many others, were to be concentrated in the Indian Territory. The area was to become the home of native Americans in a peculiar sense.

Thus, the decline of Spanish imperial power, the defeat of France in the struggle for colonial leadership, defeat of England in the revolt of her own colonies aided by France, and finally the complete dominance of Spain by Napoleon Bonaparte, were all prerequisite to the acquisition of Louisiana Territory by the United States in 1803. Hence, the history of the southwestern outposts of Louisiana, the Red River and Arkansas River valleys, is directly concerned with the story of the European contests for empire.

## Oklahoma before the Coming of Europeans

The land area within the boundaries of the state of Oklahoma is approximately 69,000 square miles in extent. Thus, it is larger than any state east of the Mississippi River and smaller than any of the western states excepting Iowa, Missouri, Arkansas, Washington and Louisiana. Each of Oklahoma's fifteen largest counties is more extensive than the state of Rhode Island, and the total area of its seventy-seven counties is greater than that of all New England.

Variety is the most striking feature of the Oklahoma landscape. Elevation ranges from 4,700 feet above sea level in the extreme northwest to 350 in the southeast. The high, level plains of the Panhandle and other portions of the west side present a sharp contrast to the heavily wooded hills in the eastern part of the state.

Before Europeans visited Oklahoma and for many years following the earliest exploration, the level plains of the west were a natural pasture for the vast herds of buffaloes that roamed from south to north and back to the south again, between the Rocky Mountains on the west and the forests of the Mississippi Basin on the east. Travelers who made extensive visits to the "buffalo plains" during the sixteenth century—Friar Marcos de Niza, Cabeza de Vaca, Captain Juan Jaramillo, and many others—were much impressed by the thousands of these great animals, standing six feet high and measuring ten feet in length, roaming the prairies and feeding on the coarse grass that grew there in abundance.[22]

The prairie buffaloes, like migratory birds, had a tendency to move southward with the coming of winter and northward as the weather grew warm. Unlike the winged travelers, the buffaloes were not moving to and from breeding grounds, primarily, but were simply following the growth of pasture northward from Texas and the Oklahoma plains in spring and coming back to the land of natural winter pasturage when deep snow covered the region of present-day Alberta, Montana, Wyoming, and the Dakotas. Many of the Plains Indians regularly followed the herds northward and southward, traveling on foot and taking with them their families, dogs, shelters, and such weapons and utensils as they possessed. Other tribes had more or less fixed habitations, and at the same time hunted the buffaloes at frequent intervals. Siouan tribes, such as the Osages, Kansas, and Crows; Caddoan bands, including Wichitas and Pawnees; Kiowas, Comanches, and many others subsisted in part on buffalo meat and regarded the Arkansas, Cimarron, Canadian, and Red River valleys as their homeland.[23] Some of these tribes were peculiarly dependent upon the buffalo herds not only for food, but also for clothing and shelter and for many items of lesser importance. One of the Comanche bands in the Canadian Valley was known as the Kotsotekas, or buffalo eaters.

[22] Winship, "Coronado Expedition," Bureau of American Ethnology *Fourteenth Annual Report*, Part I, 505 ff.; Herbert E. Bolton, ed., *Spanish Explorations in the Southwest, 1542–1706*; Edward Gaylord Bourne, *Spain in America*, 149–174.

[23] The Comanche tribe came to the Southwest from the latitude of Wyoming and Montana, about the end of the seventeenth century.

Spanish introduction of horses among the nomadic tribes of the Southwest in the sixteenth and seventeenth centuries revolutionized their habits of travel.

The eastern part of the Oklahoma area was an attractive hunting ground for many tribes. Cherokees, Choctaws, and many other eastern tribes crossed the Mississippi River and ranged westward in search of game, unmolested so long as they avoided contact with the powerful and warlike Osages and other great tribes of the Plains. Probably many clashes occurred over the use of hunting grounds in Texas, Arkansas, Kansas, and Oklahoma long before the arrival of Europeans in the North American continent. Traditional hostility between tribes is apparent in the earliest records, and intertribal warfare was quite common in the period of written history. Early in 1807, for example, a hunting party of Choctaws led by Chief Pushmataha fought a battle against a band of Osages commanded by a French trader named Joseph Bogy, near the site of Tullahassee on the Arkansas River.

## French Exploration

France was relatively late in her bid for settlement and expansion in North America. In the period of the great discoveries by Christopher Columbus, the throne of France had been occupied by Charles VIII and Louis XII in turn. These two monarchs and their successor, Francis I (1515–47), were concerned mainly with policies of European expansion. Disorder and weakness in Italy, adjacent to France, aroused the desire of strong French kings to add the peninsula to their growing possessions. The resulting conflict with Spain was a powerful element in the growth of French national unity. The wars also drained French resources, preventing adequate financial backing for the American expeditions of Giovanni da Verrazano, in 1524, and Jacques Cartier, ten years later.

During the second half of the sixteenth century, French affairs were fashioned to a great extent by internal religious strife. Up to 1589, the period was characterized by monarchs of weak will and, in the case of Francis II, of brief tenure. During the reign

17

of Henry IV (1589–1610) France was ready, for the first time, to contest other European nations for control of overseas colonies. The slow beginning of French colonization in the West, the development of a powerful French monarchy under the Bourbons (1589–1791), and the contests of France and England for dominance in North America are directly related to possession of Louisiana Territory, including the area of present-day Oklahoma.

A foothold was established, after several failures, in the lower St. Lawrence Valley. Sieur de Monts and Samuel de Champlain founded a settlement at Quebec in the summer of 1608. Port Royal in Acadia became a permanent foundation after 1610. Champlain and Jean Nicolet paved the way by their explorations for a flourishing fur trade in the West, and Jesuit missionaries carried the Christian faith and the French flag to the upper Mississippi and beyond it.

Robert Cavelier, Sieur de la Salle, who explored the Mississippi River to its mouth in 1682, probably did more than any other Frenchman to advance the cause of his country in the American Southwest. His companion on the journey down the great river was Henry de Tonty, who later built a fort at the mouth of the Arkansas. In the meantime, La Salle went to France and urged upon King Louis XIV the wisdom of occupying the lower Mississippi Valley. His memoir on the subject, given in part below, traces in some detail the design of the great explorer for French empire in America.

"The principal result which the Sieur de la Salle expected from the great perils and labors which he underwent in the discovery of the Mississippi, was finding a port where the French might establish themselves and harass the Spaniards in those regions from whence they derive all their wealth. The place which he proposes to fortify lies sixty leagues above the mouth of the River Colbert (Mississippi), in the Gulf of Mexico, and possesses the advantages of excellent position and the favorable disposition of the savages who live in that part of the country.

"The right of the King to this territory is the common right of all nations to lands which they have discovered—a right which cannot be disputed after the possession already taken in the name of his Majesty, . . . with the consent of the greater number of its inhabitants. . . . A port or two would make us masters of this whole

18

continent—as the posts there are good, secure, and afford means of attacking an enemy or of retreating in case of necessity; . . . and the friendship of the savages toward the French, and the hatred which they bear toward the Spaniards, will serve also as a strong barrier.

"These Indians, irritated by the tyranny of the Spaniards, carry on a cruel war against them, without even the aid of fire-arms, which they have not yet had."[24]

The memorial shows some familiarity with Mexico and the Texas plains separating it from the lower Mississippi, and particularly with the difficulties the Spaniards would encounter in defending the great area. La Salle suggested that an allied army of fifteen thousand Indians might be brought to the aid of the French, besides some four thousand from the vicinity of Fort St. Louis, and the Negro, mulatto, and Indian slaves of the Spaniards.

The request of La Salle for further backing in Louisiana was granted by Louis XIV, and an expedition of four ships and four hundred men set out from Rochelle bound for the Gulf of Mexico on July 24, 1684. The story of the voyage and the disasters which followed it was written by M. Joutel, one of La Salle's company.[25] Missing the mouth of the Mississippi, the French ships sailed far to the west and made a landing on the Texas coast at Matagorda Bay. After several efforts to find the Mississippi River by marching overland, the French adventurers, seriously depleted by disease, desertions, and Indian attacks, fell into bitter dissensions among themselves. As the result of a dispute which arose over the distribution of two buffalo bulls killed by La Salle's Indian servant, a group of conspirators determined to murder their leader. The surgeon, Liotot, and two other disgruntled members of the party, Heins and Duhaut, killed the Indian servant and then murdered La Salle's nephew and his footman, smashing their skulls with axes as they slept. Afterwards they ambushed La Salle, and Duhaut shot him through the head. Thus, deep in the wilderness, the greatest of the French explorers lost his life. Fort St. Louis, on the Garcitas River near the Texas coast, was destroyed by the Indians, and all the settlers who were not killed withdrew to France. The death

---

[24] Benjamin F. French, ed., *Historical Collections of Louisiana*, I, 25 ff.

[25] *Ibid.*, "Joutel's Historical Journal," 85–193.

of La Salle and the neglect of his ambitious designs were basic reasons for the failure of the French in the long contest for control of Louisiana.

The occasional references to buffalo hides in early French chronicles of the lower Mississippi probably indicate direct commercial contact with the Plains.[26] It is likely that many *coureurs de bois,* French half-blooded trappers and hunters, pushed their canoes into the streams of Oklahoma before the beginning of the eighteenth century and before any written record was made of their exploits.

In 1718, Bernard de la Harpe received from a commercial company a grant of land on the Red River above the fort at Natchitoches, probably near the site of Texarkana. This grant resulted in no permanent settlement, but La Harpe left an account of his journey up the Red River, through eastern Oklahoma, and down the Arkansas. He made other expeditions through the valleys of the Red, Ouachita, Arkansas, and Grand rivers, and recorded interesting observations concerning the Indian tribes of the area. His account touches upon the lead mines north of the Arkansas River, Indian trade in metals with the Spaniards of New Mexico, Indian customs surrounding the peace conference, foods, and presents in the form of buffalo skins and a youthful slave.[27]

[26] The woods buffaloes, not found in numbers comparable to the plains herds at any time, were rapidly disappearing.

[27] Edward Everett Dale and Jesse L. Rader, *Readings in Oklahoma History,* 46–48. Henry de Tonty's "Memoir," in French, *Historical Collections of Louisiana,* I, 52–78, contains interesting contemporary notes on the Cadadoquis (Caddo), Osage, and other Indian tribes of the Red River Valley.

# CHAPTER TWO

# European Rivalry for the Mississippi

### England's Position in 1689

It was exactly two hundred years from the accession of James Stuart to the throne of England in 1603 to the purchase of Louisiana from Napoleon by agents of the United States during the administration of Thomas Jefferson. Throughout the seventeenth century, the great powers of Europe maneuvered for favorable positions, made claims of ownership that led straight toward war, and prepared their forces and treaties of alliance for a great conflict over colonies. In the eighteenth century England and France, each supported at times by powerful coalitions, fought their battles for North American empire. Ownership of Oklahoma was a part of the issue every time the two major powers clashed, although the region was never designated separately in the treaties of peace. The primary question was: Which of the contesting powers will dominate North America?

The Dutch lacked the resources for a long, exhausting contest over distant territory; but the British and French were ready, about one hundred years after the Spaniards had first established American provinces, to make their bids for overseas expansion. During the first three-quarters of the seventeenth century, the French monarchy established firm control of the St. Lawrence Valley and, as we have seen, in the last quarter took bold steps toward occupation of the Mississippi Basin. In the meantime, England made settlements along the Atlantic coast from Maine to Carolina, overcame Dutch competition in the Hudson Valley, and became the principal threat to both Spanish and French imperial claims.

Sea power was to be the basis of English colonial vigor. Fundamentally an agricultural nation at the end of the fifteenth century, when the discoveries of Vasco da Gama, Columbus, and John

21

Cabot had burst upon Europe's concept of world geography, England had been slow to found colonies. The fisheries of Newfoundland Banks, on the other hand, had proved an immediate and irresistible invitation to the coastal population. Development of fisheries and allied commercial interests had increased the demand for seacraft, and English shipbuilders had found the resources for expanding their industry. Safety, economy, and speed were required by the fishermen; and the new ships, even small vessels, were built for crossing the stormy North Atlantic. British shipbuilders and seamen, in meeting the requirements of their peculiar situation, became the most skillful of their kind in the world. Indirectly, the future of Oklahoma was determined by the gradual development of English sea power.

The real colonial contest was between France and England; and the prize, as the ardent expansionists of both nations viewed it, was nothing less than control of the North American continent. This French and British rivalry in the eighteenth century had a direct bearing upon the history of Oklahoma in the nineteenth and twentieth centuries. War may be deplored as a means of settling international disputes; but it cannot be denied that long-range problems of ownership and government have often been determined by armed power. In spite of Charles III's vigorous rule in Spain (1759–88), lack of homeland resources gradually reduced that nation to the status of a second-rate power in the struggle for empire. Before the French Revolution of 1789, Spain's military might had declined; although her colonies still occupied an impressive place on world maps, Spanish arms no longer brought terror to her enemies.

In England, during the brief reign of James II, a climax was reached in the bitter contest between the Stuart kings and the Parliament. The Revolution of 1688, startling enough in its immediate aspects, was far-reaching in its consequences. James II, who had been subservient to Louis XIV of France, was replaced by William of Orange, principal enemy of French expansion. As to the internal affairs of England, the changes wrought by the revolution were fundamental and permanent. Parliament won the long fight for recognition of its supremacy, and the crown assumed its modern position of responsibility to the legislative branch. In foreign affairs, England began the contest against France which was to continue more than one hundred years, with permanent effects in the Mediterranean, the Indian Ocean, the Gulf of St. Lawrence, and the Mississippi Valley.

## COLONIAL WARS OF LOUIS XIV

Four colonial wars between England and France during the period 1689 to 1763 effected important readjustments of territory in North America. Although the decisive battles took place outside of the Mississippi Basin in colonies of the Atlantic coast and on the high seas, the ultimate status of Louisiana was constantly among the objectives of the warring powers.

In 1689, Louis XIV of France began one of his great military struggles for dominance of Europe and, incidentally, for colonial expansion. The American colonists of each nation fought on the side of their monarch, and diplomats worked for alliances with the various Indian tribes. The Algonquian leaders of eastern tribes were generally inclined toward support of the French, while the Iroquoian tribes of the Mohawk Valley enlisted their forces on the side of the English. In the Mississippi Valley and the southwestern plains, at the beginning of the struggle, France regarded Spain as her principal competitor and formed her Indian alliances with the purpose of checking the advance of the Spanish colonists. At various times the French were allied with the Comanche, Wichita, Caddo, Osage, and other tribes who lived in Oklahoma or frequented the hunting grounds north of the Red River. The French explorers had given friendly attention to the Indian tribes, and *coureurs de bois* seldom gave occasion for Indian hostility. All the alliances of Europeans with the natives of the Southwest were complicated by traditional intertribal conflicts, such as those of the Osages with other Plains tribes and with eastern Indians who made expeditions to the "buffalo plains."[1]

[1] Herbert E. Bolton, *Athanase de Mézières and the Louisiana-Texas Frontier*, I, 22. In the "Historical Introduction," Professor Bolton states: "The Caddo and Hasinai, both divisions of the great Caddoan linguistic stock, were similar in culture and spoke nearly or quite the same language. . . . The traditional enemy of the Caddo

23

King William's War, as the colonists called the clash with France in 1689, was decided largely on European battlefields and in naval engagements.[2] William Phips, of Massachusetts, led a successful expedition against Port Royal, a French privateering center, shortly after the war began. There were notable English naval victories, also; and William III might have claimed Acadia in the peace settlement, but the armies of the Grand Monarch were still the best in Europe, and France was able to end the war, by the terms of the Treaty of Ryswick in 1697, without loss of territory in North America.

Five years later the war broke out again on a larger scale. The occasion was acceptance of the throne of Spain by Philip of Anjou, grandson of Louis XIV. The Grand Alliance, promoted by William III of England and Leopold I of Austria, included Holland, Hanover, the Palatine, Prussia, Portugal, and Savoy.[3]

In Europe, brilliant warfare was waged by England and her allies against the French and Bavarian forces of Louis XIV. The Duke of Marlborough, selected by Queen Anne of England to lead her troops, and Prince Eugene of Savoy were outstanding generals for the armies of the Grand Alliance. At Blenheim, after inflicting crushing defeats on the Bavarians at Donauwörth and elsewhere, Marlborough and Eugene led their combined forces against Marshal Tallard, Marshal Marsin, and their ally, the elector of Bavaria. The result was a complete victory for the British commander and his associates.[4] Blenheim was followed by other allied successes, and at last the great military machine of Louis XIV was halted.[5]

---

and Hasinai were the Osage of the Arkansas and Osage rivers, and the Apache of the West. Hostility between these groups continued to the end of the eighteenth century, and even later, and was a constant factor in the policy of tribal balance alike pursued by France and Spain."

[2] In Europe this conflict was commonly called the War of the League of Augsburg. The League of Augsburg included Austria, Spain, Sweden, and some of the minor German states. William of Orange, coming to the throne of England in 1689, brought the Dutch and English into the alliance against Louis XIV. See Carlton Joseph H. Hayes, *Political and Cultural History of Modern Europe*, I, 302.

[3] *Ibid.*, 306–309.

[4] For an account of events leading to the battle and the story of the military clash, see Edward S. Creasy, *The Fifteen Decisive Battles of the World* (New York, 1885).

[5] Prince Eugene defeated the French in Italy, Marlborough drove them out of the Netherlands, and a British fleet captured Gibraltar.

Only by a remarkable display of energy, backed by the united national spirit of the French, did the Grand Monarch save himself, at the end of his long career, from more severe losses.

In America, the English colonists, led by Samuel Vetch, again captured Port Royal and quickly dominated the entire Acadian peninsula. A combined attack upon Quebec by a land campaign through Montreal and a fleet which approached through the Gulf of St. Lawrence and the river failed miserably. But when peace was made at Utrecht in 1713, the gains of the Vetch expedition against Port Royal were recognized by awarding Acadia to Great Britain and confirming British rights in Newfoundland and Hudson Bay. Gibraltar, seized from Spain by a naval force, became a British stronghold. The French island of St. Kitts in the West Indies and the Spanish island of Minorca in the Mediterranean were also added to the British Empire. England had taken its first giant step toward colonial supremacy. The ultimate decisions on the status of Louisiana Territory, not clearly seen by any statesman of Queen Anne's England, were in the making at the conferences of Utrecht.

## The Nature of the Struggle in the Southwest

French exploration of the inland waterways from the St. Lawrence River and the Great Lakes to the Gulf of Mexico brought the imperial ambitions of France into sharp conflict with the designs of Spain. In three of the four colonial wars, European coalitions united Spain with France against the British; but colonial leaders of states formerly hostile found it difficult to adjust their plans to the volatile diplomacy of the period. After 1700 the Spanish throne was occupied by Bourbons, closely related to the French royal line; but the plains Indians did not keep closely in touch with family compacts in Europe.

The military projects of France and Spain on the plains of Kansas, Oklahoma, and Texas had little effect upon the ultimate ownership of Louisiana. However, the French and their Indian allies did much to set a northern limit to Spanish expansion, thus affecting decisively the boundaries of the territory. Certainly both France and Spain left indelible prints upon the character of the American Southwest.

In 1700, nine or more distinct Caddoan tribes lived along the banks of the Red River from the site of Natchitoches, Louisiana, up to the vicinity of present-day Idabel, Oklahoma.[6] The Osage tribe, a division of the Siouan family who lived farther north, were often at war with the Caddoes, as noted above, and with the Wichitas, Tonkawas, and other Red River Indians. The Wichitas, who were a division of the Caddoan family, lived in the Canadian River Valley at the time of the earliest European exploration. In the eighteenth century they had spread as far southward as the Trinity and Brazos Rivers. The Comanches, migrating to the southern Great Plains from the region of the upper North Platte in present-day Wyoming about 1700, contested the Apaches for control of the "buffalo plains" from southwestern Kansas to the Texas Panhandle. Eventually the Apaches were pushed southward and westward; and the wild Comanche tribes formed an effective barrier between the Spanish settlements and the Indians of the Red River country, who were in the main allied with the French.[7]

The French trading post established by Bernard de la Harpe in 1719, just six years after the War of the Spanish Succession ended, was a move to check Spanish expansion toward the Mississippi.[8] La Harpe's agent, Du Rivage, carried presents to the Tonkawas (Tancaoye) and the Wichitas on the upper Red River and soon French firearms were being exchanged for horses and mules stolen by the Comanches from Spanish settlements.[9] The Wichitas carried on a large part of the French trade, which included guns, ammunition, and other goods. They often bartered for Apache Indian slaves captured by the Comanches, and these slaves ultimately found their way to the slave markets of Louisiana. Apparently the

---

[6] Bolton, *Athanase de Mézières*, I, 21, 22.

[7] *Ibid.*, 24, 42, 43.

[8] Pierre Margry, *Découvertes et établissements des français*, VI, 243–306. For a short selection from the "Relation du Voyage de Benard de la Harpe," see Dale and Rader, *Readings in Oklahoma History*, 46–48.

[9] Margry, *Découvertes et établissements*, 278.

principal slave market on the Red River was near the site of Ringold, Texas, in the Taovayas settlement.[10]

The Comanches were a barrier not only to Spanish expansion northward but also to the penetration of French trade into the Texas Panhandle. Up to 1746, Comanche policy was to prevent the Apaches from obtaining arms; but after these enemies to the Comanches had removed farther southwest, a treaty with the French opened the Arkansas River as a trade route to Santa Fé and other points in the Southwest.[11]

## British Victory, 1744–1763

King George's War was the American portion of the conflict that arose in 1740 over the succession to the Austrian throne. In Europe the war involved many allies, and was fought in Silesia, Italy, Bavaria, and the Netherlands. In naval warfare and the colonial struggle, England was usually successful, although her victories were local and not of such nature as to leave France or her allies in a helpless condition. At the Treaty of Aix-la-Chapelle in 1748, both powers restored territory taken during the war. Madras in India, captured by the French in 1746, was returned to the British; Louisbourg in North America, taken when Governor William Shirley of Massachusetts sent out an expedition under Colonel William Pepperrell in 1745, was returned to the French.[12]

The Treaty of Aix-la-Chapelle proved to be a truce of short duration. Within six years the governors of New France and Virginia had taken up arms against each other over occupation of the Ohio Valley, and two years later a general war had broken out in Europe, India, and on the high seas. A revolution in diplomacy threw England into the role of financing Frederick II of Prussia

[10] Bolton, *Athanase de Mézières*, 48.

[11] Alfred Barnaby Thomas, *Forgotten Frontiers*, 59. The reference of Professor Thomas to the Jumano (Wichita) tribe along with the Comanches indicates the close connection of the two Indian groups in trade relations.

[12] Hayes, *Modern Europe*, I, 340–42, 406–407. For an interesting account of the colonial wars between France and England, see George M. Wrong, *The Conquest of New France*.

against Maria Theresa of Austria, with France taking the opposite side, against her traditional enemy.[13] Again the diplomatic arrangements of powerful European states were connected, indirectly but decisively, with the future of Oklahoma. The final decisions regarding the title of Louisiana Territory were growing closer.

The English colonists of North America, confronted by French claims to the valley of the Mississippi in direct contradiction of their own sea-to-sea charters, entered into the contest with enthusiasm. This time England aided their efforts more promptly than Queen Anne's government had supported Samuel Vetch, and far more quickly than the ministers of George II had come to the assistance of Governor Shirley in the late war. But in spite of British regulars marching with the colonials and British fleets operating along the coasts, the allies of Frederick the Great were doomed to several years of bitter disappointment. The armies of the Prussian king, supported by British wealth, suffered defeat. The early campaigns in distant India furnished only bad news to send back to the mother country. In America, George Washington's Virginians were repulsed, General Edward Braddock's British forces were decisively beaten, Shirley and Pepperrell were turned back, and important British frontier forts fell to the French commander, the intrepid Louis Joseph de Montcalm. Even the British fleets suffered reverses, and the French captured Minorca in the Mediterranean.

In 1757 the elder William Pitt astonished and electrified the British Parliament by his announcement that he was prepared to organize the forces of the empire for certain victory. Within a year of his selection as a member of the ministry, the vastly extended war effort of the British was showing a new spirit of confidence and vigor. The French fort at the forks of the Ohio was captured, English forces gained control of the Lake Champlain area and of western New York, and Louisbourg on Cape Breton Island was taken.

Furthermore, in 1759 the victorious British regulars and colonial veterans, supported by naval action, went on to take Quebec from Montcalm's forces, thus striking at the very heart of the

[13] Hayes, *Modern Europe*, I, 342–45, 407–13; Wrong, *Conquest of New France.*

French colonial empire in America. Four years later when peace terms had been arranged, France held but little to show for her one and one-half centuries of colonial effort in North America. Fishing rights in Canadian waters and a minor position in the West Indies were the only items she had been able to salvage—a far different status from that envisioned by Sieur de la Salle and Marquis Jean Baptiste Colbert a century earlier. French imperial hopes in the Far East had been considerably dimmed, too, by the victories of Robert Clive and other British leaders in India. England was in a definite position of leadership among the imperial states of Europe; and its unbroken series of successful colonial conflicts had raised up powerful enemies on every side. Also, departure of the French monarch's armies from North America brought a new tone to the demands of the American colonies for their rights as Englishmen.

In the Treaty of Paris (1763), the powers agreed that Louisiana Territory should belong to Spain. The Philippine Islands and Cuba, seized by British naval action during the war, were returned to Spain, and that nation's only loss was Florida. Great Britain was awarded the St. Lawrence Valley and the Great Lakes, together with all the trading posts to the north. She also held the territory east of the Mississippi River, with the exception of the Isle of New Orleans.

It was rather remarkable that the Comanche, Wichita, and Caddo Indian allies of the French in 1758, just two years before Spain also entered the war as an ally of France, laid the Colorado Valley mission of San Saba in ashes, killing a number of Spaniards, including two Franciscan friars. Spanish reports declared that Don Diego Ortiz Parilla attacked the Indians in a fortified camp which contained French defenders when his army marched to the Red River to retaliate for the massacre of San Saba. Parilla was driven off, his retreat in the face of heavy odds being so hasty that he lost his baggage and cannon. The site of this engagement was near the present-day town of Ringold, Texas, a short distance south of the Red River.[14]

The transfer of Louisiana Territory from France to Spain in the peace settlement of 1763 brought a considerable change in

14 Bolton, *Athanase de Mézières*, 49.

Spanish colonial policy. The frontier moved from the Sabine and the Red to the Mississippi River, where Spain faced England, a more dangerous rival than the French. The missions and garrisons of the Texas border were moved back to San Antonio, and steps were taken to build up the strength of St. Louis and other posts adjacent to the British.[15]

The Spanish governors of Texas also became aware of a new danger from the North: British alliances with the Plains Indians. These alliances would mean British firearms in the hands of Comanche, Tonkawa, and Wichita Indians, who had usually been allied with the French, and others, such as the Osages, who had generally pursued a more or less independent policy. Before Spain had the time to deal adequately with this new threat from the Red River country, two rapid changes were made in the ownership of Louisiana Territory, and the whole nature of the Spanish colonial problem was altered greatly.[16]

## THE AMERICAN REVOLUTION AND ITS EFFECTS IN THE WEST

Prominent among the causes of opposition to British policies in America, so far as the people of the Thirteen Colonies were concerned, was the attempt of England to restrict these citizens to the eastern seaboard. The interest of the Americans in the Ohio and its tributaries, north and south, was perfectly apparent after the French wars. The Vandalia settlement had the powerful backing of such well known men as Benjamin Franklin, of Philadelphia, and William Johnson, of Connecticut. Wheeling and other communities on the upper Ohio grew rapidly, and these were matched farther south by settlements in the Watauga Valley in 1769. The rapidity with which frontiersmen pushed into the bluegrass region of Kentucky by the spring of 1775 suggests strongly the existence of a tendency that foreshadowed "manifest destiny," even before the Revolution.

[15] *Ibid.*, 66, 67.
[16] Napoleon Bonaparte acquired Louisiana in 1800 and sold it to the United States in 1803.

After the beginning of the war against England, the Americans found a commander, George Rogers Clark of Virginia, to uphold their claims in the west. Clark was a frontiersman by birth and training. At twenty years of age he had been a mature leader in frontier affairs, accustomed to responsibility and able to meet emergencies common to the life of raw western settlements. In 1772 he led an expedition down the Ohio River to the mouth of the Kanawha. During the next year he explored the vicinity of Fish Creek, and with one companion pushed on a total distance of three hundred miles from Pittsburgh. During Lord Dunmore's War against the Shawnee Indians in 1774, Clark served as a captain in the Virginia militia. The campaigns against Chief Cornstalk were in the portion of the upper Ohio that the young Virginia surveyor had recently covered; and immediately after hostilities ceased, Clark was employed by the Ohio Company to survey lands on the Kentucky River. His biographer James A. James credits him with thwarting the attempt of Judge Richard Henderson to set up a proprietory colony, Transylvania, in the Boonesborough region. According to the same authority, Clark obtained, through Governor Patrick Henry, a grant of five hundred pounds for the protection of Kentucky settlers against British-supported Indian war parties. With materials of war thus provided, the Kentuckians repulsed Indian attacks at Boonesborough, Fort Logan, and Harrodsburg.

In June, 1778, Clark started on the campaign which made him famous. He was twenty-six years of age, and his new commission gave him the rank of lieutenant-colonel. In appearance Clark was a vigorous six-footer with a rugged, muscular frame, red hair, clear black eyes, and an habitual expression of good humor. In his character there was an ample supply of iron, but it did not take the form of grim solemnity. With 175 militiamen he left Fort Massac on the Ohio River near Louisville, and marched for six days through the wilderness of southern Indiana and Illinois.[17] The party was without food during the last two days of the march. On July 4 they attacked the British garrison at Kaskaskia and captured it. The French inhabitants of the community were won to Clark's cause by his frankness and hearty good humor, and many of them en-

[17] *Dictionary of American Biography,* IV, 127–30.

listed as volunteers in his frontier army. He was soon able to move against Cahokia on the Mississippi and Vincennes on the Wabash and to supply each of the captured posts with some armed protection.

Henry Hamilton, British commander at Detroit, descended upon Vincennes with 175 British troops and more than 300 Indians while Clark and the main body of his forces were in the west. The weak garrison surrendered; and if Hamilton had pushed his victorious troops forward, taking full advantage of his initial success, he might have regained control of the entire region north of the Ohio. He was stopped by the difficult winter trails and swollen streams of the sparsely settled area, however; and while he was resting at Vincennes, Clark marched 180 miles and attacked him there, on February 25, 1779. Half of Clark's force of 170 men were French volunteers. Most of Hamilton's Indian allies had departed, but 79 of his men surrendered with the fort. During the rest of the war, Clark guarded the western territory against recapture and defended Spanish St. Louis against British attack. Colonel Bird's threat of Kentucky invasion was thwarted, and the Shawnee allies of the British were generally kept under control. Fort Nelson, established by Clark at the falls of the Ohio, became the center of his operations. In retaliation for the Shawnee victory at Blue Lick over the Kentuckians, a force under Clark came out of his stronghold and beat the Indians in a punishing, bloody encounter at Chillicothe. At the end of the war, occupation of the western territory was a vital factor in the American claim to the Mississippi River as the western boundary of the new republic.

George Rogers Clark was a prominent figure in the French schemes, after the war, for recovery of Louisiana. In 1793 and again in 1798 he planned expeditions against the Spaniards. Washington, in his capacity as president of the United States, checked the first of these projects by a vigorous protest and by his request for the recall of Charles Genêt as French minister. John Adams took a similar attitude in the later attempt. Under President Jefferson, Clark served as land commissioner and on occasion as the government's agent to treat with the northwestern Indians.

By provisions of the Treaty of Paris in 1783, the new United States of America extended from the Atlantic Ocean and the St.

Croix River on the east to the Mississippi River on the west.[18] The northern boundary was described as extending, "from the northwest angle of Nova Scotia . . . along the . . . highlands which divide those rivers which empty themselves into the river St. Lawrence, from those which fall into the Atlantic Ocean, to the northwesternmost head of the Connecticut River; thence down along the middle of that river, to the forty-fifth degree of north latitude; from thence, by a line west on said latitude, until it strikes the river Iroquois . . .; thence along the middle of said river into Lake Ontario, through the middle of said lake . . . along the middle of (the) communication into Lake Erie, through the middle of said lake . . . thence . . . into Lake Huron; thence through the middle of said lake to the water communication between that lake and Lake Superior; thence through Lake Superior northward of the Isles Royal and Phelipeaux, to the Long Lake and the water communication between it and the Lake of the Woods, to said Lake of the Woods; thence through the said lake to the northwesternmost point thereof, and from thence on a due west course to the river Mississippi; thence by a line to be drawn along the middle of the said river Mississippi until it shall intersect the northernmost part of the thirty-first degree of north latitude . . . ."

The southern boundary, along the thirty-first parallel for more than half the distance to the Atlantic, separated the United States from Florida, which was turned over, in the final settlement, to Spain. Louisiana Territory, also, was retained by Spain, the recent ally of the United States in the war.

## Spain and France at the End of the Eighteenth Century

The great upheaval of the French Revolution occurred during the decade following 1789. For sixteen years thereafter, France was under the dominance of Napoleon Bonaparte, who became master of western Europe and made his influence felt in

18 William M. Malloy, ed., *Treaties, Conventions, International Acts, Protocols, and Agreements between the United States and Other Powers*, I, 586 ff.

33

every continent. The regions most completely drawn under Napoleon's will were France, the Low Countries, the Italian Peninsula, the Iberian Peninsula, and the German states. In the first four of these he ruled directly or appointed the rulers. In Austria and Prussia he dominated through military power, reshaping governmental institutions at will in the lesser German states and dictating terms of peace to the greater ones.

The re-establishment of France's empire in North America was one among Napoleon's many ambitious schemes, for a time. He studied the map, considered previous French holdings in the new world and the probable influence of the French population, and determined upon Louisiana as the heart of his American enterprise. As a means of protecting the river entrance to the great valley, he took steps to regain a foothold in the West Indies from which naval operations might be conducted in the Caribbean and the Gulf of Mexico. Marshal Leclerc, the husband of Napoleon's younger sister, Marie Pauline, was sent to Haiti with an army to begin the difficult task of reducing the island to order and re-establishing French control.

Charles IV, who had inherited the Spanish throne in 1788, was one of Napoleon's weak neighbors who made the work of building the French empire less difficult than it would have been in normal times. The king of Spain was the second son of Charles III, an elder brother having been barred from the succession as an epileptic and imbecile. King Charles IV was married to his first cousin, Maria Luisa of Parma. Physically, Charles was large and powerful but he lacked the intellectual vigor and the interest in statecraft to make him an effective king. Maria Luisa was the mistress of her husband's principal minister, Manuel Godoy, who in a large measure determined Spanish policies and ran the state. The king devoted a large part of his time and energy to hunting, a sport from which he could be diverted only by the most extreme emergencies. Now and then he asserted himself on a public question, showing flashes of determination to have his own way. He was so lacking in knowledge of statecraft, however, and so erratic in his views of Spanish interest, that his excursions into politics were not likely to result in needed reform of the administration.[19]

[19] *Encyclopaedia Britannica* (11th edition), V, 926.

34

In 1800, Charles IV made an agreement with Napoleon at San Ildefonso by which the Louisiana Territory was ceded to France in return for a supposed advantage for Spain in Italy.[20] Actually, the establishment of Charles IV's son-in-law as king of Etruria had little significance; Napoleon required a puppet on the throne of the Italian kingdom. Godoy had not been consulted before this bargain was reached, and apparently he was much pained by the casual manner in which Charles disposed of a vast and potentially priceless realm in America. It is difficult, however, to see how Spain would have been able to stand firm against the will of Napoleon Bonaparte in 1800.

Within a short time, the ambitious First Consul was to discover that the obstacle of British naval power was a decisive factor on all questions of French colonial expansion. It was essentially the same set of circumstances that had forced Napoleon to change his policy concerning Egypt and the Far East at the outset of his career. In the deadlock between Napoleon's ambitions in the Western Hemisphere and the hurdle of British sea power, the youthful United States of America was to receive one of the greatest bargains in real estate ever recorded in history.

[20] *Dictionary of American History*, V, 24, 25.

# CHAPTER THREE

# The Louisiana Purchase

## THE UNITED STATES IN 1800

At the opening of the nineteenth century, the sixteen American states and the public domain, stretching west of the Appalachian Mountains to the Mississippi River and south to Spanish Florida, contained approximately 800,000 square miles of land and about 5,000,000 inhabitants. The area was a little more than one fourth of the present United States, excluding Alaska, Hawaii, and all other outlying possessions. In westward expansion beyond the Mississippi and across the continent, Louisiana was the first major addition of territory, practically doubling the land of the nation. Thirteen states, with a combined area much larger than the original thirteen, were to be formed from this great acquisition.

Thomas Jefferson began his first term as president in the spring of 1801. At that time nine tenths of the American people lived in the states bordering on the Atlantic Ocean, and about nine tenths were rural, rather than urban, population. Towns on the seacoast and river settlements enjoyed the benefits of water transportation, which was slow but relatively safe and inexpensive. Roads, even between the larger towns, were poor; in many sections of the country, impassable in rainy weather. When a stream had to be crossed, the traveler found a shallow ford, if possible; and for the deeper crossings, ferryboats were in common use.

The principal American cities were on or near the Atlantic coast. Philadelphia was the largest with 70,000 inhabitants; New York, destined to become the first city within a few years, had 60,000 people; Baltimore and Boston each had fewer than half as many; and Charleston was a sleepy, straggling community of 20,000. There were a few river towns such as Albany on the Hudson, Trenton on the Delaware, and Hartford on the Connecticut, with access to the Atlantic ports. West of the mountains, Pittsburgh at the forks of the Ohio, with a port 1,800 miles to the southwest, at New Orleans, was a thriving trade center; and Cincinnati was just emerging as a frontier village community.

Large areas in the original states were still sparsely peopled. The western half of New York, the northern half of Pennsylvania, the western counties of Virginia, and the mountain section of North Carolina contained fewer than six persons per square mile. Georgia had only a small region in the northeast and a narrow fringe along the lower Savannah River where population was relatively dense. The District of Maine had few inhabitants outside of the coastal settlements of the southwest.

West of the Appalachian Mountains, population was concentrated in a few areas—the valley land in northeast Tennessee, the vicinity of Nashville on the Cumberland, the Kentucky bluegrass region, and the fringe of settlements north of the Ohio River below Pittsburgh. Roughly, one fourth of the land east of the Mississippi River contained six persons or more per square mile. The remaining three fourths of the land was practically unoccupied. Actual need of soil for our people to cultivate can be ruled out at once as a motive for the huge expansion of 1803.

There was room for growth of rural population, and there were vast resources in timber and mineral wealth which promised large returns to a people who were ready to grapple with problems of transportation, along with the difficulties of large-scale government. European wars, between the beginning of the French Revolution and the final defeat of Napoleon Bonaparte (1789 to 1815), created a persistent demand for American products. Sales abroad gave Americans cash with which to purchase European goods, and foreign trade as a whole increased substantially during the second half of the Federalist regime. Exports rose from $47,855,000 in 1795 to $93,020,000 in 1801; imports, from $69,756,000 to $111,-363,000 during the same period.[1] High prices for American wheat, corn, fish, pork, beef, pelts, and lumber expanded production of those commodities and brought prosperity to farmers, as well as to merchants and shippers. Only better means for hauling heavy

[1] Adam Seybert, *Statistical Annals of the United States of America, 1789–1818*, 93.

goods were needed to push the frontier line farther west. Vermont had entered the Union as the fourteenth state in 1791, Kentucky had followed a year later, Tennessee became a state in 1796, and Ohio was to achieve statehood in the middle of Jefferson's first term as president.

In addition to the obvious differences between the frontier and the older communities, another kind of sectionalism had appeared. From the settlements of Maine to the Delaware Bay, legal steps had been taken to abolish Negro slavery; in the region south of the Delaware, slave labor had become firmly planted. Growth of cotton culture in the South was to widen the differences between free and slave states to the breaking point during the next half century. The great addition of territory that was about to be made west of the Mississippi River was destined to play an important part in the sectional controversy, for part of it was in the South, where plantation labor could be carried on with profit to the owner, while part was in the North, where powerful sentiment against slave labor was gradually developing. The future of Oklahoma was to be involved in all the sectional issues, in a peculiar degree. With part of its territory in the latitude of South Carolina and other states of the deep South, it extended all the way north to the 37th parallel and bordered on Kansas.

## MARKET FOR WESTERN GOODS

In western states and territories, both north and south, good land was plentiful and cheap. As cotton and other money crops increased in total value, with improved transportation facilities, the price of land in Mississippi, Alabama, Ohio, and Indiana was to rise sharply. The country was filling up with people who came west to establish homes and build their fortunes in the new land. Many young families made their start in farming, lumbering, or running a store, beginning with small capital but great energy and enthusiasm.

The chief obstacles to material success in the West were distance and the mountain barrier, stretching between the infant settlements and their natural markets. Heavy goods could not be transported across the Appalachian highlands to Philadelphia, Boston, Richmond, or Charleston. Without markets, the western people could not develop their resources for wealth.

The eagerness of these people for access to the markets of the world is not difficult to understand. Since there were no available means of crossing the eastern mountains, they turned naturally to the great rivers that led to the Spanish port of New Orleans. The Ohio and its tributaries furnished an outlet for Tennessee, Kentucky, Ohio, and Indiana settlers. People who shipped grain, meat, and livestock, furs and peltries; lumber, whiskey, and other western products, made use of the right of deposit provided in the Treaty of San Lorenzo, negotiated by Thomas Pinckney in 1795. Every political maneuver which affected the conditions of river navigation was of immediate concern to the people of the West. Almost the entire money economy of the Ohio Valley was bound up in the trade through New Orleans. A small exception was the corn whiskey transported across the Pennsylvania mountains to the valley of the Susquehanna, mainly by means of pack animals. The independent attitude of the western settlers was shown during Washington's second administration as president by the agitation and violence of the Whiskey Insurrection.

Many of the western people were vaguely aware of the vast land that stretched away to the northwest along the course of the Missouri River, longer and potentially more important than the Ohio itself. The natural economic unity of the entire Mississippi Valley did not remain unnoticed by the western Americans.

## THE WEST AND THE POLITICAL PARTIES

The West was, in a peculiar sense, the home of democratic political activity. Ideas of universal suffrage, complete freedom in church affiliation, equality of eligibility to office, and all of the liberties that arise from the enjoyment of ample space, were common doctrines of the back-country people, most of whom were followers of Thomas Jefferson. In the West the principles of popular sovereignty, equality of opportunity, and personal liberty were practically universal.

The Federalist party was built upon somewhat different views. With its greatest strength among the commercial classes of the Atlantic seaboard and the aristocratic southern planters, perhaps it was natural that the Federalist organization should oppose development of the West. The mercantilist pattern of thinking, in which the function of provinces was to benefit the mother nation, was not entirely absent from American politics. The tendency is traceable in Federalist opposition to westward expansion and to territories west of the Appalachians. The opposition was to become more bitter over the admission of states west of the Mississippi River.

It was the growth of the West which gave the greatest impulse toward democratic development in the government of the United States. At the beginning of the nineteenth century, Jefferson's followers definitely advocated popular rights and more extensive participation of the people in government. Wider suffrage, equal eligibility to hold office, popular choice of presidential electors, and nomination by machinery under control of the voters were all principles advocated by the Republicans. The reforms came gradually, with the new states supporting every democratic step. Tennessee and Kentucky in the election of 1800, together with Ohio in the election of 1804, voted solidly for the candidates who advocated progress toward more popular government. All of the older states that contained large numbers of back-country people showed the same tendency. Eventually the Federalist party was to be completely overshadowed by the growth of western population and the admission of new states.

Jefferson's adherence to the doctrine of Jeremy Bentham, "the greatest good for the greatest number," met complete approval among the pioneers. The leader's bond of sympathy with western views is reflected clearly in his enthusiasm for exploration and expansion. Perhaps it was more than scientific interest which prompted him to encourage the explorations of John Ledyard and to give active support to the project of André Michaux for exploration of the Missouri Valley in 1792.[2] It was the "manifest destiny" of the young republic to occupy adjacent land on its west only because of men like Jefferson. Virginia, the state of Jefferson's birth and his youthful training, owes much to him in its progress toward modern ideas concerning church and state, public education, and democratic inheritance of property; but Oklahoma and Arkansas, Iowa and the Dakotas must regard him as their champion for membership in the federal union.

As president, Jefferson was confronted with the concrete problem of keeping the Mississippi River open to commerce for the settlers of the West, in order that they might reach the markets of the world with their growing surplus of goods. One immediate purpose was to obtain control of West Florida, as a guarantee of a river connection with Mobile, Pensacola, and other Gulf ports. Another purpose was to occupy the east bank of the Mississippi below the 30th parallel to insure people of the west a means of reaching a market for their products.

## CHANGE IN NAPOLEON'S IMPERIAL DESIGN

The interest of Napoleon Bonaparte in Louisiana Territory cannot be analyzed in detail here. As first consul and master of France he dominated the Spanish monarch and reorganized Spanish provinces, apparently without effective opposition from any quarter. In the secret Treaty of San Ildefonso on October 1, 1800, Spain agreed to cede the Territory of Louisiana to France. In exchange, Napoleon was to elevate the son-in-law of King Charles IV and Maria Luisa to the throne of Etruria in Italy, with a population of one million inhabitants for his enlarged estates.[3] Since one puppet king was very much like another to the First Consul, the bargain cost him but little and carried little advantage for Spain.

When the existence of this treaty became known, through hints dropped by diplomats over a period of many months, the President of the United States began to adjust his foreign policies to the change in the ownership of New Orleans. Since Thomas

[2] Thomas Jefferson, *The Writings of Thomas Jefferson* (ed. by Paul L. Ford), VI, 158, VIII, 192 n.
[3] Dale and Rader, *Readings in Oklahoma History*, 53, 54.

41

Pinckney's successful negotiation with Spain in the Treaty of San Lorenzo, in 1795, it had not been difficult to deal with the government of Charles IV for the export of American goods through the lower Mississippi; but with Napoleon in control of Louisiana and apparently ready to take over West Florida as well, the situation was alarming. President Jefferson considered the possibility of alliance with the British, calmed the fears of the western settlers, and concentrated upon the task of coming to a satisfactory understanding with France.

Napoleon's first move toward recovery of the French possessions in North America had been to send a military force to Santo Domingo, the great island that lies between Cuba and Puerto Rico —an excellent position for command of the Caribbean and the Gulf of Mexico. Here the Negro leader Toussaint L'Ouverture had headed a successful revolt against French authority in 1795, and was trying to maintain orderly republican government in the interest of the black population. It was Napoleon's purpose to regain control of Santo Domingo and then to proceed with occupation of Louisiana Territory.

Marshal V. E. Leclerc sailed from France with an army of ten thousand in November, 1801. The black followers of Toussaint L'Ouverture, aroused by rumors of the re-establishment of slavery, fought the invaders with unexpected determination. Yellow fever took a heavy toll among the French and conquest was slow. Within ten months, Napoleon sent twenty-eight thousand men and Marshal Leclerc was calling for new regiments—seventeen thousand soldiers was his estimate of immediate re-inforcement needs. Before the end of the year, Leclerc himself was among the victims of yellow fever.[4] This was the situation which brought about Napoleon's startling proposal to sell all of Louisiana Territory to the United States. Santo Domingo was costing him too much in soldiers and money needed by the military dictator of France for his European campaigns. War with England was an immediate prospect; and without undisputed control of Santo Domingo, Napoleon considered that French occupation of Louisiana would be precarious.

[4] Henry B. Adams, *History of the United States of America during the Administrations of Jefferson and Madison*, I, 418.

Robert R. Livingston, United States minister to France, had hoped only to buy the lower portion of the left bank—the Island of Orleans—and possibly the coastal area extending eastward from Lake Pontchartrain to Mobile Bay. It was Bishop Talleyrand, Napoleon's wily agent, who suggested to Livingston on April 11, 1803, that all of Louisiana might be purchased. The following weeks were occupied with negotiations as to price; obviously, Napoleon had decided to wash his hands of colonial empire in the West. James Monroe was appointed minister-extraordinary to France and Spain, and he arrived in Paris on April 12. It was Livingston, however, who came to an agreement with Marquis François de Barbé-Marbois, whom Napoleon appointed to complete the treaty terms. The sum agreed upon was 80,000,000 francs, of which 20,000,000 might be paid by the United States in settlement of its own citizens' claims against France.

Many questions arose, in America and Europe, concerning the legality of the Louisiana purchase. Clearly, Napoleon had agreed with the Spanish monarch that he would not turn the territory over to any country other than Spain. The French constitution did not give the first consul authority to sell territory. Furthermore, the agreement in regard to Etruria contained certain conditions which Napoleon had not met in full. The highhanded disposal of Spain's property was not popular in Europe, and more than one diplomat suggested, before long, that the whole affair was subject to international review. The British, in particular, were displeased with the vast addition of territory to the United States.[5]

President Jefferson himself had serious doubts as to his authority under the Constitution of the United States to negotiate the treaty for such a purpose. His first thought, upon receiving the offer from the French, was to seek a specific grant of power through constitutional amendment.[6] He went so far as to draft changes he wanted to incorporate in the Constitution, but Livingston was writing urgent letters on the necessity of closing the agreement while Napoleon was in the mood to sell. The need for haste determined the President. He submitted the treaty to the Senate,

[5] François de Barbé-Marbois, *Histoire de la Louisiane*, 282.
[6] Jefferson, *Writings of Jefferson*, VIII, 241–49.

and it was promptly ratified. Some portions of Jefferson's proposed constitutional amendment were directly concerned with the future of Oklahoma. If there had been time for his proposals to go before Congress, an Indian state with constitutional basis might have been provided in the Louisiana Territory.

Federalist party leaders held the purchase to be an abuse of the treaty-making function. It must be admitted that the President's views on strict interpretation of constitutional powers had undergone a drastic change; but his party opponents also had completely reversed their former position, and were now using some of Jefferson's earlier arguments to attack his new assumption of executive authority. The President and the Republican majority in Congress with him had readjusted their position concerning federal power in order that they might meet new and unexpected circumstances. In Edward Channing's words: "The Jeffersonian theory of strict construction was abandoned in the house of its friends."[7]

## LOUISIANA TERRITORY IN 1803

The exact boundaries of Louisiana were not to be found in the vague terms of the treaty.[8] When American commissioners called attention to the indefinite language of the purchase agreement, Barbé-Marbois admitted the truth of their comments and added, "If it were not indefinite, it would have been well to make it so."[9] The disputed limits of West Florida, variously placed at Lake Maurepas, the Pearl River, Mobile Bay, and the Perdido River, were included in the complex problem of Louisiana's boundaries. West of the Mississippi, too, the vast area west of the Sabine River and south of the Red was open to dispute. United States officials were inclined to regard the Río Grande as the natural boundary of the territory on the southwest.

French influence had been growing in some parts of the colony

[7] Edward Channing, *The Jeffersonian System*, 75.
[8] Dale and Rader, *Readings in Oklahoma History*, 55–58.
[9] Barbé-Marbois, *Histoire de la Louisiane*, 311.

for a century, slowly at first and later with increased volume. The settlement of Pierre Lemoyne, Sieur d'Iberville, on Mobile Bay in 1699, followed by a French post on the lower Mississippi and by the planting of New Orleans above the Delta in 1718, gave the French a start toward the realization of La Salle's ambitious designs. In the St. Lawrence Valley French settlement was well established, and to many of the French colonial leaders the plan of uniting northern and southern colonies by an unbroken line of fortified posts seemed feasible. Although there was some exchange of civil officers and, of course, military officers between the two colonies, considerable differences existed between Louisiana and Quebec, particularly with respect to land tenure. Individuals obtained land directly from the crown in Louisiana, with no semifeudal seigneurs in control of a peasant class. In another respect the Mississippi colony differed from the province on the St. Lawrence: in spite of La Salle's optimism in his report to Louis XIV, Indian relations in the southern colony were not so harmonious as the Algonquian and French connection in Quebec. Choctaw, Chickasaw, Natchez, and Creek Indians used their strategic locations to bargain for advantages from the French, Spanish, and British invaders alike. At times in the early history of Louisiana, Indian hostility became a threat to the colony's existence.

East of New Orleans, the Spaniards had planted a colony at Pensacola, and Spanish missions were making a feeble effort to educate the Florida Indians. Far to the west, Spanish settlements had been slowly developing on the upper Río Grande since the end of the sixteenth century. Juan de Oñate in 1598 had led a colony from Santa Bárbara, Mexico, northward to a spot on the river below the site of El Paso. Crossing to the left bank, these Spanish settlers had pushed upstream to found their outpost. Missions and ranches had kept the New Mexican province alive, and by 1680 there were about 2,400 persons in it. There was a marked tendency toward race mixture, which eventually led practically to absorption of the European stock.

Mexican ranchmen crossed the lower Río Grande and expanded northward to the valley of the Guadalupe. By 1720 stock raising and farming were well established near the site of San Antonio, and the missionaries were actively engaged in work

45

among the Apaches. For a time Spanish settlers contested the French for possession of the Sabine Valley, but before the middle of the century they had retreated westward. Spanish farming and stock raising continued to flourish in the Guadalupe Valley, and missions were established on the San Saba and Brazos rivers. The Comanche Indians were a major obstacle to expansion farther northward.

The French colony of Louisiana gradually added new items to its salable products. Indigo and sugar were introduced before transfer of the province to Spain in 1763, and cotton culture began about thirty years afterward. In 1802, Louisiana produced 20,000 bales of cotton, valued at $1,344,000.[10] Behind this leading product came sugar, with a value of $302,000; furs and hides, $200,000; indigo, $100,000; lumber, $80,000; molasses, $32,000; and all other articles, excluding livestock, corn, and lead, on which no records of sales are available, valued at $100,000. Naval stores, for the use of the Spanish and French governments, were also shipped in large quantities in Spanish and American vessels. Labor for the cotton and sugar plantations of Louisiana was supplied largely by the importation of Negro slaves from the West Indies or directly from Africa.

After Louisiana Territory was ceded to Spain at the end of the Seven Years War in 1763, there was little immediate change in the condition of the inhabitants. The Spanish *cabildo* was, perhaps, less representative of the people's will than the former French council, but both governments were strongly executive. Governor, *contador*, and intendant continued to serve as chief executive, revenue and commerce director, and treasurer, respectively. It cannot be said, however, that forty years of Spanish rule had left no permanent results in law and characteristics of Spanish blood.

## THOMAS JEFFERSON'S ADMINISTRATION OF LOUISIANA

The United States took official possession of Louisiana Territory on December 17, 1803, just seventeen days after Spain

[10] *American State Papers, Miscellaneous,* I, 354.

turned it over to France.[11] Congress gave the President immediate control, as a temporary measure. Afterward, the Territory of Orleans was organized, embracing most of present-day Louisiana.[12] The population of this southern portion of the purchase was about fifty thousand, including twenty-five thousand Negro slaves. William C. C. Claiborne was appointed the first governor, and the machinery of administration was set up without popular representative features, this lack of democracy being defended on the ground that the region was practically ready for admission to statehood and that elaborate territorial government was unnecessary.

An act of Congress forbade importation of slaves except from American states. Furthermore, slaves might be introduced only by actual settlers, and none imported into the states since 1798 might be brought to Louisiana. Planters in the territory petitioned Congress to drop these restrictions, and before Louisiana became a state, importation of slaves from other parts of the South was practically unchecked. The large per cent of Negroes in Louisiana who were new to slavery, together with the impressive strength of their numbers, created a dangerous situation.

A slave insurrection in 1811, starting in the region above New Orleans on the Mississippi and sweeping through the plantations toward the city, resulted in many deaths. Militia and regular troops succeeded in stopping the march of the five hundred desperate Negroes, maddened by the injustice of their new servile condition and resolved to slaughter as many of the hated master race as they could. Their leaders were captured and executed, after which their heads were pierced with sharpened poles and set up along the river bank as a warning to other slaves against revolt.

As originally organized, Orleans did not include the territory between the Mississippi River and the Pearl, south of the 31st parallel. This portion of West Florida was held very loosely by Spain. A revolt in 1805, intended by some of its leaders as the beginning of a movement for independence, was put down. Five years later a similar uprising resulted in the defeat of the Spanish military force at Baton Rouge and a declaration of independence by the inhabitants of the district. The leaders of West Florida tried to

[11] *American State Papers, Public Lands,* V, 708, 727; VII, 578.
[12] *United States Statutes at Large,* II, 283.

47

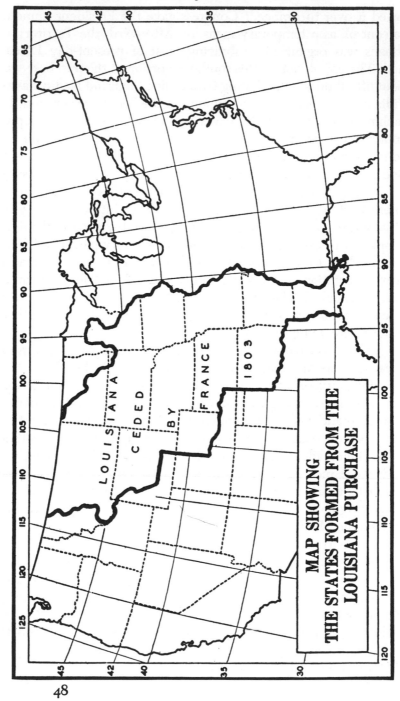

MAP SHOWING
THE STATES FORMED FROM THE
LOUISIANA PURCHASE

LOUISIANA CEDED BY FRANCE 1803

bargain with the United States for a loan, in exchange for secession from Spain and annexation by the United States. On October 27, 1810, President James Madison issued a proclamation in which he claimed for the United States all the territory to the Pearl River. This he did without reference to the proposal of annexation by John Rhea, president of the West Florida constitutional convention.[13] When Louisiana was admitted as a state, two years later, it came in with these enlarged limits. By the terms of its admission, the new state had agreed to federal control of all unappropriated land and to five tax-free years for all land sold by the United States. The Congress had agreed that 5 per cent of all public land sales should be devoted to road and levee construction.

In 1804, Upper Louisiana, the portion north of the 33rd parallel, contained approximately ten thousand population, resident for the most part in Missouri. Of these, about six thousand were immigrants from the United States—mainly from Kentucky, Virginia, and Tennessee—in many cases drawn by the offer of liberal land grants from the Spanish government.[14] A considerable number of Negro slaves had been brought in by these settlers, and a few by Spanish immigrants who had moved north from the lower Mississippi River after Louisiana was ceded to Spain to 1762. Many of the Illinois French settlers crossed the Mississippi into Missouri when it became known that England had acquired title to the Ohio Valley by the settlement at Paris in 1763. It was several years before it became generally known that Spain had come into possession of Louisiana.

The French residents of Missouri had a tendency to build their houses in compact villages, while the American settlers were more inclined to dwell separately, building houses on their individual homesteads. With the coming of the American settlers, an increase in land speculation, mining, and interest in politics began. Fur trade, long established by the French trappers along the Missouri and other tributaries of the Mississippi, continued to flourish

[13] John B. McMaster, *History of the People of the United States*, III, chap. 20; James Richardson, ed., *A Compilation of the Messages and Papers of the Presidents*, I, 480–81.

[14] *Encyclopaedia Britannica* (11th edition), XVIII, 612; XXIV, 24–27.

during the Spanish regime in Louisiana Territory (1762–1800).[15]

St. Genevieve, settled in 1735 between the site of present-day Cape Girardeau and St. Louis, was the first permanent French community in Missouri. Fort Orleans, above the Missouri River, had been established earlier, but its use as a garrison was not continuous. In 1764, Pierre Laclède Liguest, representing a French trading company which had been granted a monopoly of the fur trade in the Missouri area by the French crown, founded St. Louis as a post settlement. The French village already there, together with the trading post, was protected by a log stockade; and an era of great importance in the development of western fur trade began. By 1767 the community had about five hundred inhabitants, living in crude log cabins and devoting their attention, for the most part, to the fur trade. French-Canadian trappers from the upper Missouri frequented the new trading post and Missouri shipped lead and salt, as well as pelts, to New Orleans, Pittsburgh, and Montreal.[16] The river boatmen grew rapidly in number and added their unique language, garb, and customs to the picturesque village on the west bank of the Mississippi. Fur trade with the western Indians grew rapidly in importance; and by March 9, 1804, when Upper Louisiana was formally handed over to the United States officials, the St. Louis trading post had become the key to a considerable part of the economic development among Osages and other Indians who trapped along the streams of Oklahoma.[17] The population of St. Louis at that time consisted of river boatmen, Indian guides, fullblood Indians and mixed bloods, Spaniards, Frenchmen, and other Europeans, and Americans with a considerable number of Negro slaves. Probably the town and its supporting communities on both banks of the Mississippi contained six thousand persons.[18] By 1832, when Washington Irving visited St. Louis on his way to the Indian country, the population of the town

---

[15] Actually, Spanish officers did not take over administration of the province until 1771, because of hostility shown by the French inhabitants. Also, Spanish officials continued in office for more than two years after the signing of the Treaty of San Ildefonso in 1800.

[16] *Ibid.*, XVIII, 607–14; Reuben Gold Thwaites, *France in America*, 293.

[17] *Encyclopaedia Britannica* (11th edition), XXIV, 26; Victor Tixier's *Travels on the Osage Prairies* (ed. by John Francis McDermott), 97–185.

[18] Thwaites, *France in America*, 293.

alone had grown to about seven thousand, and the residents of St. Louis County numbered seventeen thousand.[19]

## THE LEWIS AND CLARK EXPEDITION

Two major expeditions were planned by President Jefferson to acquaint the administration with the vast territory purchased from France. The first of these was in the Northwest and affected Oklahoma only indirectly. Broadly, the settlement of ownership in the Northwest, through agreements with England, and in the Southwest, by means of treaties with Spain and Mexico, was a part of the general policy of western expansion in the United States. The second great expedition was concerned directly with the exploration of Oklahoma, among other portions of the Southwest. The boundary settlement of 1819 with Spain, in which two of the borders of Oklahoma were determined, was certainly influenced by the findings of Zebulon Pike and James Wilkinson.

For exploration of the Mississippi's greatest tributary, President Jefferson selected Meriwether Lewis, whom he had already engaged as his private secretary. Lewis chose William Clark as joint commander and placed him in charge of recruiting men for the expedition. It was to be a military party, Lewis holding the rank of captain in the United States Army and Clark the rank of first lieutenant. The forty-three men selected for the enterprise were enlisted as soldiers, and a fund af $2,500 was provided by Congress for supplies. The party assembled during the winter of 1803–1804 on the Illinois shore above the mouth of the Missouri River. Of the enlisted men none was older than Clark, who was thirty-three, and the majority were considerably younger. John Colter of Kentucky was a large, outdoor boy of sixteen years when the expedition started. The youngest man in the party, Colter was destined to become one of the most famous explorers of his time in such remote regions of the West as the Big Horn Range, the upper Yellowstone, and the Three Tetons. One of the three non-

[19] Washington Irving, *The Western Journals of Washington Irving* (ed. by John Francis McDermott), 80.

commissioned officers enlisted for the enterprise was Sergeant Nathaniel Pryor, who was to see active service later in the exploration and settlement of Oklahoma.[20]

William Clark, younger brother of the famous commander whose campaigns won the Northwest Territory during the American Revolution, was an able and experienced soldier. He had served in several Indian campaigns under various commanders— his brother, George Rogers Clark; Charles Scott, another officer of the Revolution, who moved to Kentucky, took part in the Indian campaigns, and eventually became governor of the state; and Anthony Wayne, the hero of Fallen Timbers and other Indian battles. In many respects, Lieutenant Clark's personal qualities were a supplement to the abilities of Captain Lewis. Clark was large of frame, red-faced and red-haired, easy in his social relations, affable, and good-natured. He was popular with the soldiers, knew how to approach the wild Indians of the Plains, and possessed a wholesome mixture of firmness and determination along with his suavity. Lewis was dour, hard-working, strict in discipline, resolute, and perhaps equally capable in comparison with Clark. Lewis was twenty-nine years old.

The party set out up the Missouri River in May, 1804. They traveled in two keelboats and a larger bateau. The fifty-five foot vessel, provided with space for storing supplies, presents for the Indians, and materials for recording scientific data, was moved upstream by means of long poles. The party was supplied with guides; and a herd of horses was driven along the river bank, during the early stages of the journey, for the use of hunters in supplying the explorers with game.

The officers of the expedition were charged with the task of recording information on physical geography, flora and fauna, Indians, white hunters, and any other persons whom they might meet on the great river, or near it. They did encounter an occasional trapper on his way to St. Louis with a boatload of furs. They visited Kaws, Otoes, and other Indians, holding council with the Otoes on August 3, near the site of Council Bluffs. They had covered 850 miles since their journey began, three months earlier.

As an interpreter for the Sioux Indians they employed Dorion.

[20] Jacob Fowler, *The Journal of Jacob Fowler* (ed. by Elliott Coues), 4, 5.

MAJOR RIDGE
*Leader of Cherokee Removal party*

CLERMONT

*Osage chief, with his war club and his leggings fringed
with scalplocks. From a portrait by George Catlin.*

**JOHN ROSS**
*leader of the Cherokees*

SEQUOYAH

Choctaw Indian ball player
*From a painting by George Catlin*

International Indian Council in session at Tahlequah in 1843
*Painted by John Mix Stanley*

WASHINGTON IRVING
*From the portrait by C. R. Leslie*

JOSIAH GREGG
*Redrawn from a photograph of an old daguerreotype*
*for reproduction in William E. Connelley's*
Doniphan's Expedition (1907)

Toussaint Charbonneau, a French half-blood guide, and his Shoshone Indian wife, Sacajawea, were encountered and picked up
on the way. The woman, who had been stolen as a child from the
Shoshone Tribe of the Northwest, proved to be a valuable addition
to the party through her skill as a guide, her knowledge of Missouri
Valley Indians, and especially her acquaintance with the leaders
of her own people. A son was born to Sacajawea in February, 1805,
while the party was in winter quarters at Mandan Village above
the site of Bismarck, North Dakota. When Lewis was ready to
resume the journey on April 7, Sacajawea was ready also to serve
as a guide, carrying the baby in an Indian "cradle" on her back.
The party advanced up the Missouri in six canoes which they had
constructed of willow poles and buffalo hides. The bateau, no
longer needed for hauling the reduced store of supplies, was sent
back to St. Louis in charge of thirteen of the men. Lewis entrusted
this returning band with a letter to President Jefferson, a package
of articles made by the Indians, mineral and other specimens, buffalo hides, a detailed report that he had prepared, and a copy of
William Clark's diary. Lewis and Clark continued up the Missouri
River and on July 25 reached the site of Three Forks, Montana.

The three branches of the river were named for Jefferson,
Madison, and Gallatin. Game had become extremely scarce and
the food supply was so low that the party was threatened with
starvation. In this emergency they were fortunate enough to encounter a hunting band of Shoshonean Indians whose chief was
Cameahwait, Sacajawea's brother. The Lewis and Clark journal
tells the dramatic story of the Indian woman's reunion with her
tribe and her kin. It gives an account of the gifts, including food
and other necessities, from the scant stores of the Shoshoneans.
The explorers crossed the divide to the Clearwater, with the aid
of guides and ponies supplied by their new friends. To the Snake
River they traveled, thence into the Columbia, and westward to
the Pacific. They spent the winter near the coast and on March 23,
1806, began the long trip home.

Traveling in two parties, one under each officer, they ascended
the Columbia and Snake rivers, crossed the Rocky Mountain divide, and reached the Missouri. It required nearly five months to
journey from the camp on the lower Columbia to Mandan Village,

where they had spent their first winter. John Colter remained there, to pursue his life of adventure in the unexplored West. Sacajawea and her infant son also left the expedition, which continued on its way back to the settled country. Borne by the powerful current of the Missouri, they took but forty days to complete the journey to St. Louis, arriving in the river town on September 23.

This expedition into the West, under able leaders, was in many respects a model for the other explorations of the Louisiana Territory. Meriwether Lewis, after a brief term as governor in the new territory, lost his life under somewhat mysterious and violent circumstances, on a trip to Washington in 1809.[21] His comrade William Clark was to live for many years in the land he had helped to explore. He served as an Indian agent, as governor of Missouri Territory from 1813 to 1820, and afterward as commissioner of Indian Affairs until his death in 1838.[22]

[21] *Dictionary of American Biography*, IV, 141–46.
[22] *Ibid.*, XI, 219–22.

# CHAPTER FOUR

# Exploration and the Spanish Boundary

## EXPLORATION IN OKLAHOMA BEFORE THE SETTLEMENT OF THE SPANISH BOUNDARY

Nearly three hundred years had elapsed since the expeditions of Coronado, De Soto, and the *conquistadores* across the plains and hills of the Southwest. Nevertheless, Oklahoma was in need of exploration by the Americans in 1806. The little information available on natural features of the land in Arkansas, Oklahoma, and Kansas, to say nothing of the wide expanse of territory west of their present borders, was in the hands of hunters, trappers, fur dealers, and Indian guides. One purpose of President Jefferson in exploring Louisiana before establishing definite boundaries was to give the United States an adequate basis for expansion. The Lewis and Clark expedition, as noted above, went beyond the Mississippi Basin and provided the nation with additional ground for claiming Oregon. In the Southwest, similarly, explorers were looking for information on tributaries of the Mississippi and on adjacent lands which might prove to be suitable fields for expansion.

Early in the summer of 1806, Lieutenant Zebulon M. Pike was sent on a journey into the unknown region south of the Missouri River. Lieutenant James Biddle Wilkinson, son of General James Wilkinson, of Maryland, was sent along as second in command. As in the case of the Lewis and Clark party, enlisted men made up the greater part of Pike's followers; with the twenty-three soldiers there were several civilians, including Dr. John H. Robinson, who had volunteered his services as physician for the expedition.[1]

Improvement of relations with Indian tribes of the Southwest

[1] W. Eugene Hollon, *The Lost Pathfinder: Zebulon Montgomery Pike*, 135 ff., 137 n.

was a secondary purpose of the expedition. A small band of Osage and Pawnee Indians who had been visiting in the East and were on their way home, accompanied Pike as a means of obtaining safe conduct through areas that might prove dangerous for them. Undoubtedly, these natives of the Plains were regarded as possible agents for the beginning of friendly relations between their tribes and the government of the United States.

Pike and Wilkinson traveled up the Missouri River to the mouth of the Osage, one hundred miles west of St. Louis in June, 1806. They followed the course of the smaller stream to the vicinity of present-day Lake of the Ozarks, where the Osage Indians were delivered to their kinsmen. Then the party moved northwest across the Plains toward the Republican River, where the rest of their wards were to be restored to the Pawnee tribe. At Pawnee Village, Chief Characterish (White Wolf) astonished the explorers by greeting them, *"bon jour,"* obviously a touch of European address picked up through contact with Jean Pierre Chouteau, or some earlier French trader on the western plains.

White Wolf agreed to replace the Spanish flag that was displayed in his village with a flag of the new American Republic furnished him by his visitors; but the Pawnees took a strong stand against further exploration of the Southwest by Pike and his followers. In order to create good will, the officers of the expedition purchased a number of ponies from the Indians, "miserable horses at exorbitant prices."[2]

The explorers traveled southward toward the Arkansas River and westward to the Great Bend. Lieutenant Wilkinson was not in good health, and by the time the party reached the Arkansas, he was so ill that it was decided he should return home, traveling down the course of the river. As Wilkinson began the return trip, accompanied by five companions, Zebulon Pike led the rest of the men farther west, pushing on through central Colorado, where they sighted the mountain that in the course of time came to be known as Pike's Peak.[3] After November 27, 1806, when he first

[2] Elliott Coues, *The Expedition of Zebulon M. Pike,* II, 542, 543.

[3] The name acquired general acceptance gradually. John C. Frémont called the mountain Pike's Peak in his reports of 1844 and also on his maps. Hollon, *The Lost Pathfinder,* 128.

caught sight of the snow-covered peak, Pike and his men wandered about in the Colorado highlands, trying to reach the headwaters of the Arkansas and hoping to discover a tributary of the Red River. For nearly two months the explorers suffered incredible hardships, enduring hunger and cold with gradually diminishing supplies of clothing and equipment. On January 14, 1807, Pike and thirteen of his followers marched southward into the Sangre de Cristo Mountains. Two men, disabled by badly frozen feet, were left behind in a rough stockade constructed for their protection. As the band pushed forward through the mountain range, three more had to be left behind in hastily constructed shelters. On January 27, Pike and ten of his men reached a narrow valley which they supposed to be the basin of the upper Red River. Actually, they had crossed into the valley of the Río Grande. About the end of January, the men erected a stockade and went into winter quarters on the stream which Pike still designated "Red River" on his maps.[4]

After a short time in their new camp, the Americans were visited by a young Spanish officer who suggested that Pike go to the governor of New Mexico, at Santa Fé, for aid in reaching the Red River. Pike agreed readily enough, and a few days later he and six of his men, ragged and unkempt, rode into the provincial capital. After looking over Pike's papers, Governor Alancaster decided to send the explorers to General Salcedo, at Chihuahua, for further questioning. Pike and his men were well treated on the journey into Mexico, through Albuquerque, El Paso del Norte, and 230 miles beyond that point to Chihuahua, the capital of Biscay. General Salcedo, after a careful examination of Pike's journal and other papers, decided to return the explorer and his followers to the United States, together with letters of protest to American officials. So the party was escorted back across the Río Grande, through San Antonio, and to Natchitoches in Louisiana, where they arrived on July 1, 1807.

While Zebulon Pike was engaged in this great expedition, Lieutenant Wilkinson and his five companions were making their way laboriously along the Arkansas River.[5] The winter of 1806–

[4] *Ibid.*, 133, 134.
[5] Coues, *Expedition of Pike*, II, 542–58.

1807 began early, and the little band was handicapped from the first by ice on the shallow water of the stream. On October 31 they abandoned their boats, but after two weeks of travel on foot, stopped for ten days to rest, to hunt for game, and to fashion new dugout canoes. Farther downstream, on November 28, one of the canoes was overturned in deep water, and most of the food supply and a part of the ammunition were lost. Two days later the party met a band of Osage Indians who were engaged in a hunting expedition. Wilkinson and his men camped with the Osages and gossiped with the elders while the young warriors hunted buffaloes to replenish the depleted meat supply. Lieutenant Wilkinson made a trip of twenty miles across the prairie and the wooded valleys east of the Arkansas to visit the camp of his friend Chief Tutta-suggy, who was a very sick Indian. The old Osage chief complained that the agent and trader, Auguste Pierre Chouteau, had ruined his influence among the people by cutting off his credit. Wilkinson did what he could for the sick man's comfort and went back to his camp on the Arkansas.[6]

Later, after the explorers had passed the mouth of the Grand Saline (Cimarron), they came to the camp of Big Track; and sixty miles up the Verdigris River they found the town of Chief Clermont, near the site of modern Claremore. In discussing the relations of Clermont and Pawhuska (Chief White Hair) in his journal, the explorer referred to the latter as a "chief of Pierre Chouteau's making," and remarked that neither Big Track nor Pawhuska was able to control the young men of the tribe.

On December 29, Wilkinson recorded, "I passed a fall of near seven feet perpendicular," evidently a reference to Webber's Falls on the Arkansas. It was here that the explorers were joined by a disabled hunter named McFarlane, who had been engaged in trapping on the upper Poteau.[7] He had come into conflict with the Osages, who had cut off both of his feet. Wilkinson continued his journey down to the Mississippi and thence to New Orleans. The journal of this first exploration of the Arkansas River by representatives of the United States government is a record of great historical value, with its many side lights on Indian society, diplomacy, and relations with traders and government agents.

[6] *Ibid.,* 550.　　　[7] *Ibid.,* 558.

58

The War Department sent an expedition to the Red River in 1806 under the command of Captain Richard Sparks. The intention was to make a thorough examination of the valley up to the headwaters of the Red River. In addition to its commanding officer, the party included Lieutenant Humphrey, Dr. Custis, nineteen soldiers, and a Negro servant. The journey began at St. Catherine's Landing near Natchez, Mississippi, the men traveling in small boats down to the mouth of Red River, which they entered on May 3, 1806. Navigation on the lower Red River was made very difficult by the log obstruction known later as the "Great Raft." After threading the numerous bayous of this region, Captain Sparks and his men came to a point above the site of Natchitoches, where they were met by a strong Spanish military party and ordered to go back to the place from which they came. Since Sparks had no instructions to contest Spanish occupation and since his little force was greatly outnumbered, he immediately turned back. He had expected to join Lieutenant Zebulon Pike and to make the return trip with him; but the complete exploration of the Red River was to be postponed for almost a half-century.[8]

In 1811, after James Madison became president, another important journey into Oklahoma was undertaken. The Osage Indian agent in Missouri, Colonel George C. Sibley, set out for the West to return a party of Osages to their homes. One of Colonel Sibley's purposes, as in the expedition of Pike and Wilkinson, was to promote friendly relations with the western tribes. After visiting the Platte River and making contact with the Osages there, Colonel Sibley turned to the south, crossed the Arkansas River, and continued into the portion of northern Oklahoma that came to be known as the Great Salt Plains. The party explored a part of Salt Fork in what is now Alfalfa County and left a description of the stream and the salt plains.

## SETTLEMENT OF THE SPANISH BOUNDARY

It will be recalled that the Treaty of Paris in 1783 gave Spain possession of East and West Florida, in addition to the wide

[8] Randolph B. Marcy, *Exploration of the Red River of Louisiana*, 32 Cong., 2 sess., *Sen. Exec. Doc. 54, 2.*

expanse of territory which the French called Louisiana. For thirty-six years thereafter, the United States and Spain disputed over various problems connected with use of the lower Mississippi River, the boundaries of Louisiana Territory and the Floridas, control of the Seminole Indians in the Spanish province, the problem of runaway slaves who took refuge in Florida, and a multitude of other questions. The agreement made with the Spanish minister by Thomas Pinckney at San Lorenzo in 1795 established a definite northern boundary for the Spanish domain east of the Mississippi River, but the purchase of Louisiana by the United States in 1803 created new boundary problems.

President Jefferson was inclined to regard the Perdido River, some thirty miles east of Mobile Bay, as the southeastern limits of Louisiana. Spain, on the other hand, claimed a fifty-mile strip of land along the Gulf Coast nearly two hundred miles west of the Perdido to the Iberville River. Through this disputed area flowed the Alabama, Tombigbee, Pascagoula, Pearl, and other streams important to the commerce of the interior. Backed by an appropriation of $2,000,000 for the purpose, President Jefferson made an attempt to purchase Florida, but was met by refusal on the part of Spain.[9]

Among the many revolts against Spanish authority in the Western Hemisphere after 1809 were the uprisings in Florida, East and West.[10] In addition to the Seminole Indians of East Florida, there were many other wild and restless elements in the population along the Gulf Coast. Runaway slaves over a long period, white and Indian refugees, and unscrupulous politicians from Tennessee and Georgia made an unpredictable combination. After the war against Great Britain in 1812, Red Stick Creek warriors were added to the Florida population from time to time; and with the passage of years, a younger generation of mixed bloods arose, more turbulent than their Indian, white, or Negro ancestors. In 1810, President Madison ordered Governor William C. C. Claiborne of Louisiana to take possession of West Florida to the Perdido River.[11] That year, in a secret message, he asked Congress to authorize

[9] Isaac J. Cox, *The West Florida Controversy, 1798–1813,* 69.
[10] Frederick Jackson Turner, *The Rise of the New West,* chap. XII.
[11] Cox, *West Florida Controversy,* 73.

seizure of East Florida, which was granted only in the event that a foreign power should attempt to gain possession of the territory, or in case the people of East Florida should ask for intervention by the United States. In 1812 a revolt south of the St. Marys River prompted Madison to send General George Matthews to Amelia Island with orders to take over the territory; but in 1813 the President reversed this policy and withdrew the troops. During the latter part of the war, both Floridas were regions of great disorder; smuggling was practiced at many points along the coast, acts of violence were common, piracy grew into a major activity, pillage and murder were hazards to be faced in all remote settlements.

In 1813 the Red Sticks, Tecumseh's Creek warriors, attacked Fort Mims on the Alabama River, killing nearly all the soldiers and the civilians who had taken refuge there. Seven months later, on March 27, 1814, Andrew Jackson surrounded the hostile Creeks with an army of frontiersmen at Horseshoe Bend, on the Tallapoosa River, and crushed their power.

After the war, disorder of many kinds continued in Florida. Negro Fort on the Apalachicola River, built by Colonel Edward Nichols of the British Army, served as a center for operations against territorial settlements at the north until an army came down from Georgia and destroyed it. After an exchange of letters with President Monroe, Andrew Jackson brought matters in Florida to a climax. Assuming that the President had authorized a drastic remedy for the disorder in Florida, Jackson marched two thousand men into the province and proceeded to the conquest. Among other actions, all without a declaration of war by the United States government, Jackson executed two Seminole raiders, seized and executed Robert Ambrister and Alexander Arbuthnot, subjects of Great Britain, captured the Spanish governor and sent him off to Cuba, and placed United States troops in control of St. Marks and Pensacola.

Jackson's highhanded dealing with the Florida problem caused a great deal of excitement in Washington. The British minister to the United States and Lord Castlereagh, the prime minister, were much concerned over the incident. Luis de Onís, representing Spain at Washington, entered a bitter protest. However, the negotiations of Secretary John Quincy Adams for the purchase of Florida moved rapidly to a successful conclusion, and in 1819 the agreement was reached.

By the terms of the Adams-Onís Treaty, Spain gave up her title to Florida, and the United States agreed to settle damage claims of her own citizens against Spain, amounting to $5,000,000. The treaty also provided a definite boundary between Spanish and United States territory in the West: along the west bank of the Sabine River from its mouth to the 32nd parallel; thence, due north to the Red River; thence, westward along its south bank to the 100th meridian; thence, north along that meridian to the Arkansas River; thence, up the south bank of that stream to its source; thence due north to the 42nd parallel; thence westward along that parallel to the Pacific Ocean. Thus, the United States gave up her claim to any part of Texas as a border province of the Louisiana Territory, and Spain abandoned her claims upon Oregon. Two extensive boundaries of the future state of Oklahoma were established by the terms of this treaty: the Red River boundary, and that along the 100th meridian which separates Oklahoma from the Texas Panhandle for a distance of 133 miles.

## TRADERS AND TRADING POSTS

Most important of the trading posts in early Oklahoma were those established by the Chouteau family and their associates. René Auguste Chouteau, with Pierre Laclède Liguest, founded a great fur industry in St. Louis, and after the death of Liguest in 1778, the junior partner became the wealthiest and most influential citizen of the Missouri town. His energetic younger brother, Jean Pierre Chouteau, acted as his agent for an extensive trade with the Osages, maintaining his headquarters in the upper Osage Valley near the site of present-day Nevada, Missouri. The Spanish government granted the Chouteaus a monopoly of the Osage trade from 1794 to 1802. After the formal transfer of Louisiana Territory to the United States on March 10, 1804, René Auguste Chouteau became one of the three justices of the territorial court, was named colonel of the Louisiana militia, and was elected chairman of the

St. Louis board of trustees. He also served the United States government as special commissioner to the Sauks, Foxes, and the Sioux Indians.

Jean Pierre Chouteau, company agent among Osage hunters who brought in pelts from an extensive area, contesting their hunting ground against eastern Indians in the Arkansas Valley, Kiowas farther south, and other Indians as well as a few white squatters, referred to his alma mater as "l'académie osage."[12] His biographer remarks, however, that he was able to quote Horace in the original, an accomplishment not often found among the Osage Indians of his time. When he was thirty-four years of age the Osage tribe gave him a tract of land as a reward for "his many years of service to them." When the Chouteaus lost their trade monopoly to Manuel Lisa in 1802, Jean Pierre Chouteau persuaded about three thousand of the Indians to go with him to Three Forks on the Arkansas, in the vicinity of present-day Muskogee and Fort Gibson, Oklahoma, where he had trading privileges. Later President Jefferson appointed him agent to the Osages and sent his son, Auguste Pierre Chouteau, to the new military academy at West Point.

It was Auguste Pierre Chouteau who established in 1817 the famous trading post near the site of Salina on Grand River, in the region that is now eastern Mayes County, Oklahoma. After his graduation from West Point, he had served briefly in the Army under the command of General James Wilkinson and had engaged in several hazardous missions to western Indian tribes. He was captain of a militia company during the War of 1812. On a fur-trading and exploring expedition to the upper Arkansas River in 1815 with Jules de Mun, he was captured by Spanish soldiers, lost all of his equipment and furs valued at $30,000, and spent some time in a Spanish jail. In 1817 he was back in the United States, and in that year he established himself on the left bank of the Grand River near one of the well-known salt springs of the Osages. He built his home there, described by one of his contemporaries as a "two-story log palace." He bought the trading interests of Brand and Barbour near the mouth of the Verdigris and maintained a shipyard and trading post there. From the vicinity of Three Forks he shipped an enormous volume of pelts and furs to New Orleans and

[12] *Dictionary of American Biography, IV.*

63

St. Louis. His cargoes in the eighteen twenties were made up of bearskins, deerskins, beaver, otter, wildcat, raccoon, and skunk hides, buffalo robes, and many other items. General Matthew Arbuckle, during his command at Fort Gibson, estimated the number of hunters in the vicinity of Three Forks at about two thousand. In addition to French trappers and other Europeans engaged in the business of taking furs and hides, there were many Osage, Cherokee, Delaware, Seneca, Shawnee, and other Indian hunters who packed their pirogues with furs and peltries and brought them downstream to Chouteau Trading Post.

Colonel "A. P." Chouteau, as he was called to distinguish him from his famous uncle, Colonel Auguste Chouteau of St. Louis, lived in a grand manner, entertained largely, and died with heavy debts standing against the title of his property. His wife was Sophie Labbadie, his cousin, who bore five daughters and a son. He also had an Indian wife, Rosalie, an Osage who was naturalized as a Cherokee; and there were Chouteau children by three other Indian women. The Chouteau house at Salina was known to many famous visitors in the Indian country, such as the great missionary, Isaac McCoy; Washington Irving, the writer, and Charles J. Latrobe, the English scientist and world-traveler; Sam Houston, distinguished in the history of the Texas Republic; and United States Commissioners Henry Ellsworth and Montfort Stokes.[13]

Pierre Chouteau, younger brother of Colonel "A. P.," served an apprenticeship in the fur business in his father's St. Louis store and in the course of his life engaged in a great variety of trading projects, including a partnership in the St. Louis Missouri Fur Company, another in Bernard Pratte and Company, and the western department of the American Fur Company, which was known as Pierre Chouteau, Jr., and Company. He also attempted the development of an iron mine in southeastern Missouri, ran a railroad

[13] Among the firsthand accounts of the Chouteau trading activities in the Southwest is the narrative left by Victor Tixier, translated by Albert J. Salvan, and published in English for the first time in 1940 by the University of Oklahoma Press under the title of *Tixier's Travels on the Osage Prairies* (ed. by John Francis McDermott). The *Dictionary of American Biography*, IV, contains an account of each prominent member of the Chouteau family: René Auguste Chouteau (1749–1829), Jean Pierre Chouteau (1758–1849), Auguste Pierre Chouteau (1786–1838), and Pierre Chouteau (1789–1865).

line east of the Mississippi, and a rolling mill in St. Louis. He became very wealthy as a result of his many business ventures.

Pierre Melicourt Papin, for many years resident agent for Pierre Chouteau's American Fur Company in the Osage village Nion-Chou (Neosho, in present Missouri), was the son of Joseph Marie Papin and Marie Louise Chouteau. He spent a large part of his life on the southwestern frontier and exercised a powerful influence among the Osages, Pawnees, Comanches, and other Plains Indians.[14]

## Exploration of Oklahoma
## after the Adams-Onís Treaty

The expedition led by Major Stephen H. Long, in 1819 and 1820, had important results in Oklahoma. The party left St. Louis in June, 1819, traveling up the Missouri in the steamer *Western Engineer*, and spent the following winter near the site of Council Bluffs, Iowa. In the spring Major Long with twenty companions —Captain J. R. Bell, Dr. Edwin James, Mr. Thomas Say, Mr. Seymour, Lieutenant Swift, three interpreters, and twelve soldiers —started out to travel by land up the course of the Platte River. Two of the men were noted scientific scholars: Dr. Edwin James, the botanist, and Mr. Thomas Say, who was distinguished chiefly for his studies in rocks and minerals. The principal purpose of the expedition was to explore the region between the Missouri and the headwaters of the Red River and to bring back scientific data on the area covered.

Major Long and his men marched to the vicinity of Pike's Peak, and five members of the party, including Dr. James, set out to explore the mountain. At the summit the observer recorded: "The Arkansa, with several of its tributaries, and some of the branches of the Platte, could be distinctly traced as on a map, by the line of timber along their courses."

Major Long divided his command, sending Captain Bell, Thomas Say, Lieutenant Swift, Mr. Seymour, the three inter-

14 Tixier, *Tixier's Travels*, 15, 100, 117n., 119n., 151, 259.

preters (Bijeau, Ledoux, and Julien), with five of the soldiers, down the Arkansas, while the commander himself with Dr. James and the rest of the men on July 24, 1820, traveled southward in search of the headwaters of the Red River. The ten men of this party took with them six horses and eight mules, "most of them in good condition for travelling."[15]

On the fourth day after the separation, Major Long and his companions crossed a stream which Dr. James later supposed to be "one of the remote sources" of the North Canadian, but which Reuben Gold Thwaites identifies as the Cimarron.[16] Suffering many hardships, including serious shortage of supplies, the band of explorers made their way farther south. On the night of July 29, Dr. James recorded, "Mr. Peale experienced an alarming attack of a spasmodic affection of the stomach, induced probably by cold and inanition." The thermometer had fallen from 70° to 47° F. within a few hours. On the next day Dr. James wrote, "Verplank, our faithful and indefatigable hunter, was so fortunate as to kill a black-tailed deer . . . and we once more enjoyed the luxury of a full meal."[17]

The explorers came to a creek which they supposed to be a tributary of the Red River, but which later proved to be a branch of the South Canadian. In his report, Major Long placed the blame for the error upon incorrect information given by a band of Kaskaskia Indians and upon the fact that no suitable guides could be obtained for the exploration south of the Arkansas River.

By August 17, Long's party had descended the Canadian all the way across the Texas Panhandle and reached the 100th meridian, which is the present boundary between Texas and Oklahoma. The travelers stopped at noon on the river, just north of the Antelope Hills, to hunt buffalo. While the mounted hunters rode after the big game, the rest of the men explored the vicinity of their camp and found a profusion of wild grapes, ripe and of excellent flavor. After eating all of the fruit they could hold, they threw themselves upon the clean sand in the shade and slept for several hours.

[15] Edwin James, *Account of an Expedition from Pittsburgh to the Rocky Mountains* (vols. XIV–XVII of Reuben Gold Thwaites, ed., *Early Western Travels*), XVI, 63.

[16] *Ibid.*, 80 n.

[17] *Ibid.*, 83.

The hunters killed a number of buffalo cows and the party at evening "assembled around a full feast of 'marrow bones;' a treat whose value must forever remain unknown to those who have not tried the adventurous life of the hunter."[18]

Dr. James noted the presence of black walnut trees in the vicinity, which, he thought, indicated a soil "somewhat adapted to the purposes of agriculture." He was impressed, also, by the fine growth of grasses, the abundance of plums, and the many varieties of birds and animals that lived in the region. Wolves and jackals, he observed, subsisted in part upon wild plums; while turkeys and black bears ate both plums and grapes. The herds of bison ranged over the hills, returning to the pools along the river bed, in dry weather, for water. Hunting was good as the party moved eastward along the Canadian, with daily sightings of "astonishing numbers of bison, deer, antelopes, and other animals." At one of the camps, a herd of wild horses came in during the night and "struck up a hasty acquaintance with their enslaved fellow brutes."

From time to time, smoke signals of the Plains Indians were observed, and the men speculated as to the disposition and intentions of the native tribesmen. On August 24 the supply of parched corn meal, carefully restricted to the fifth part of a pint per man each day, was exhausted. Fortunately there was an abundance of venison and turkey, as well as bison and bear meat. The hot, dry weather of August had its effect upon the Canadian River, and the party traveled many miles without seeing running water. For drinking, they sank shallow wells in the river bed and waited for water to collect in them; and because of the extreme difficulty of obtaining a meager supply of the precious liquid, the men passed over many days without washing themselves. For five days the interpreter, Adams, was lost from his companions, after returning several miles along the trail for the purpose of recovering his canteen. During the period before he was found, he managed to lose also his mule, to exhaust his ammunition, and to become thoroughly despondent over his chances of survival.

On September 6, Major Long and his followers passed the "falls" of the South Canadian, and on the same day reached the mouth of North Fork, "discharging at least three times as much

18 *Ibid.*, 134.

water as we found at the falls above mentioned."[19] Three and one half miles below the mouth of North Fork, the travelers found a tower-rock standing in midstream. Dr. James described it as being about fifty or sixty feet in diameter and about twenty-five feet high, with sides almost perpendicular.

On September 10, Long's party reached the Arkansas River, and discovered for the first time, with certainty, that they had not been traveling along the Red River but along the South Canadian. Three days later they arrived at Belle Point and were met by the commandant of Fort Smith, Major Bradford, and also by Captain Bell, Mr. Say, and other members of the Arkansas River party.[20] They had arrived at the fort on September 9 in good health but with a record of hardship, hunger, and privation similar to that of Major Long's band.

An interesting account of Bell's journey down the Arkansas was written by the scientist Thomas Say.[21] The party had reached Grouse Creek (called *Little Verdigrise* by Mr. Say) on August 18, nearly a month after the division into two bands at the headwaters of the Arkansas. The little stream flows into the river near the boundary line between Kansas and Oklahoma. Close to their camp on Grouse Creek, the men found a patch of Indian corn with watermelons growing among the stalks and helped themselves to both products. Game was scarce in the area, and for nearly a week the explorers suffered greatly from hunger. One day they greeted with great enthusiasm the killing of a polecat by Julien, the interpreter, and on the following day feasted on a "pittance of two ounces per man" of their dried bison meat, together with skunk soup and bread crumbs. During this period, one of the horses strayed away from camp in the night and was not recovered. Lieutenant Swift killed a "fine buck" on Saturday, August 26, and on the following day shot another deer. The venison thus obtained, together with a turkey and other game brought in by the hunters, relieved the situation for a time.

[19] *Ibid.*, 174.

[20] Major William A. Bradford, placed in charge of Fort Smith when it was founded, took a prominent part in the thorough exploration of the Arkansas Valley in the vicinity of Belle Point and southward to the Red River.

[21] Say's six chapters are included in the volume collected and edited by Thwaites, *Early Western Travels*, XVI.

The party's supply of tobacco was exhausted, and some of the men suffered greatly for the want of it. One of the soldiers led the others to suppose that he had still "a remnant of the precious stimulant" concealed about his person. When another of the party begged to be allowed a small taste of it, the soldier was overheard to answer: "Every man chaws his own tobacco, and them that hasn't any chaws leaves."

On a night when Bell and his followers camped at some distance from the Arkansas River, probably near the site of present-day Hominy, Oklahoma, the greatest disaster of the journey occurred. Nolan, Myers, and Bernard deserted and took with them the best horses, together with saddlebags containing clothing, presents for Indians, and a large part of the manuscript records of the expedition. In spite of the best efforts of Captain Bell and his remaining men, the deserters were never captured. Five manuscript books compiled by Thomas Say on the history, habits, and languages of the Indians, and on the animals of the area explored, together with a topographical journal of the expedition, were lost.

At Clermont's Village, the Osages informed Bell that the deserters had visited their camp and departed. Bell and his followers moved on to Glenn's trading house on the Verdigris, about a mile above the mouth of the stream, and on the day afterward, to Bean's Salt Works, located on a small tributary of the Illinois River at a distance of about seven miles from the Arkansas. Bean had occupied the spot since spring, had planted several acres of corn, and had constructed a "neat farm house." Livestock ranged about the place; and a beginning had been made in setting up necessary equipment for operating the salt works: a well near the springs for collecting salt water, a neat log shelter for the furnace, and two giant kettles, purchased but not yet in use.[22]

News reached the American frontier in 1821 that the revolutionary government in Mexico was ready to trade with neighboring states, with the restrictions of Spanish mercantilism lifted. Three trading expeditions were organized before the end of the year to make a bid for the Santa Fé market. John McKnight of St. Louis, with a trader named Thomas James, took a party south to the mouth of the Arkansas River and in May began the ascent of that

[22] Ibid., 286.

stream. At the site of present-day Tulsa the party turned west, following the Cimarron, probably to a point above the spot where Guthrie now stands. McKnight and James traded their boats for Indian ponies, journeyed overland to the Canadian, crossed the Texas Panhandle, and reached northern New Mexico. The McKnight traders were in Santa Fé by December 1, 1821.

Another party was led by Colonel Hugh Glenn, who operated a trading post on the Verdigris. A Kentucky surveyor named Jacob Fowler accompanied the expedition and recorded its adventures in a journal which combines unique spelling with a considerable gift for colorful narrative. The party left Fort Smith on September 6 and traveled west to the Bean and Saunders salt works on the Illinois River.[23] "Been and Saunders Has permission of the govern to work the Salt Spring—the Sell the Salt at one dollar per Bushil" —in the words of Fowler's *Journal*. In addition to Colonel Glenn and the author of the journal, the party of twenty men included the interpreter, Baptiste Roy, and Paul, a Negro servant belonging to Jacob Fowler. Another member was Nathaniel Pryor, who had served as a sergeant in the Lewis and Clark expedition. Lewis Dawson, who accompanied the party as a hunter, was fatally injured by a bear on November 13, 1821.

The explorers visited Glenn's trading post on the Verdigris, Chief Clermont's village farther north, and the region between the Caney and Verdigris rivers, where edible game was scarce, but wild horses were quite common. "Heare is one of the most delight full peace of Cuntry I have Ever Seen," recorded Jacob Fowler. Near the present boundary of Oklahoma at the north, the party turned across the Osage Hills toward the Arkansas River. They followed the stream westward to the Purgatory River, where they found the Kiowas, Cheyennes, and Arapahoes eager to exchange furs and pelts for goods carried by the traders. The party turned back at Taos. This expedition was an important step in the exploration of Oklahoma and the upper Arkansas, and it pointed the way for entrance of goods from Three Forks into the Santa Fé trade.[24]

The third expedition of 1821, that of William Becknell, had

23 Fowler, *Journal*.
24 R. L. Duffus, *The Santa Fe Trail;* Stanley Vestal, *The Old Santa Fe Trail;* Ray Allen Billington, *Westward Expansion*, 462.

far-reaching effects upon the subsequent development of south-western trade. Becknell traveled from the Missouri River to the Great Bend of the Arkansas, turned southwest across the Cimarron and the headwaters of the Canadian, and reached Santa Fé in the upper Río Grand Valley on November 6. Becknell's party consisted of four men besides the leader, and they carried their goods on pack animals. Becknell's route crossed the northwestern corner of the Oklahoma Panhandle and made little direct contribution to geographical knowledge of the region now included in the state; but his trading activities gave an impulse to the Santa Fé trade, which flourished until 1844. Becknell himself crossed the plains a second time in 1823, with a larger supply of goods in three wagons, in addition to the pack-horse loads. This party took a short cut across the Cimarron Desert.

During the following year a party of 80 men made up a caravan of 25 wagons and 150 pack animals in Missouri, with an investment of $30,000 in goods. Their profits on the exchange at Santa Fé amounted to $180,000 in specie, $10,000 in furs and pelts, and a substantial gain in livestock.[25] One member of this party was Jacob Gregg, an elder brother of Josiah, whose letters and journal constitute a store of information on the commerce of the Southwestern Plains a few years later. Josiah Gregg made four journeys out to Santa Fé, over a period of nine years, and recorded his impressions of everything he saw.[26]

In 1825 two important surveys were undertaken as the result of an act of Congress. One was from the newly established Fort Gibson on the Grand River to Little Rock in Arkansas Territory. The other was the Santa Fé Trail from the western border of Missouri, southwest through Kansas to the Cimarron River, and across the strip of territory that is now the Oklahoma Panhandle to Taos and Santa Fé.

The Santa Fé trade included a wide variety of goods: china, glassware, and mirrors; needles, buckles, locks, nails, tools, cutlery, and an assortment of utensils; silks and other textiles. At Santa Fé the traders could obtain silver, livestock, and furs, for which they found a ready market in the Mississippi Valley.

[25] Josiah Gregg, *Diary & Letters of Josiah Gregg* (ed. by Maurice Garland Fulton), I, 9.
[26] *Ibid.*, I, 19, 43–69.

The Kiowa and Comanche Indians raided a wagon train in 1828 and were a constant threat to the traders. Thereafter, without sufficient troops on the plains to furnish military escorts, the Santa Fé traders organized their expeditions in large parties, usually well equipped for defense against the Indians. Independence, Missouri, became the principal eastern terminal point of the trade. Conestoga wagons, pulled by five or more span of oxen and loaded with four thousand pounds of freight, hauled most of the goods to Santa Fé.[27]

## EARLY MILITARY POSTS

Between 1817 and 1842 the region that is now Oklahoma was transformed. The Indian tribes of Georgia, Alabama, and Mississippi were removed west of the Mississippi River, a process that will be described in a later chapter. As a means of keeping order among the new settlers in the West, the United States established military camps and a few permanent posts in the Arkansas and Red River valleys. A few eastern Indians had already built homes in the hilly, timbered area south of Missouri—Cherokees in the Boston Mountains and the White River country, Muskhogeans, south of the Arkansas. Plains Indians clashed with these newcomers over the occupation of choice hunting grounds, and on occasion white settlers and traders were involved. The first large party of Cherokees were removed to Arkansas in 1817, and in the same year Fort Smith was established.

Major Stephen H. Long selected the site for Fort Smith at Belle Point on the Arkansas, a spot of great natural beauty lying near the boundary line between present-day Arkansas and Oklahoma. Plans for blockhouses and barracks were submitted to Major William Bradford, who took charge of their construction and became commandant. The place was named for General Thomas A. Smith of Georgia.[28] Two forts were founded by Colonel Matthew Arbuckle in 1824. One, near the mouth of Grand River, was named

[27] Billington, *Westward Expansion*, 463.
[28] Thwaites, *Early Western Travels*, XVI, 187.

for George Gibson of Pennsylvania, a noted Revolutionary general; the other, built near the mouth of the Kiamichi 120 miles south of Fort Gibson, was named for Nathan Towson. He was the hero of Chippewa and other engagements of the War of 1812 who later saw action in the Mexican War and reached the rank of brevet brigadier general.

In 1825 surveyors marked off a road, fifty-eight miles in length, from Fort Smith to Fort Gibson, running approximately along the route of present-day U. S. Highway 64. This military road was the first to be surveyed in Oklahoma. Seven years later Robert Bean and Jesse Chisholm marked out a route from Fort Smith to Fort Towson. Another trail ran from southeastern Arkansas through Eagletown to Fort Towson, and was eventually extended to Boggy Depot, the Arbuckle Mountains, and westward. The road from Fort Gibson to Edwards' Store, on the South Canadian at the mouth of Little River, and from that point west to Camp Mason, near the site of Lexington, was occasioned by the march of General Henry Leavenworth's dragoons in 1834 and the resulting council with the Plains Indians at Camp Mason in 1835. Fort Holmes, established in 1834 across Little River and north of Edwards' Store, was a temporary link in an extensive plan for defense of the western frontier.[29] Near the site of Camp Mason, Colonel "A. P." Chouteau established a new trading post in 1835; and from this place his brother, Pierre L. Chouteau, and his nephew, Edward L. Chouteau, carried on an extensive trade with the Plains Indians. The little stream that flows past the site of the trading post is still called Chouteau Creek.

Generally, the military posts were provided with log barracks and one or more stockades for defense against Indian attack. Fort Towson was remodeled in stone during the year 1831. Fort Coffee, established in 1834 by Captain John Stuart, on the south bank of the Arkansas about ten miles above Belle Point, was intended to provide a working base for operations against the "whiskey-runners." Captain Stuart trained a small cannon on the river and

[29] General Edmund P. Gaines, commander of the Western Department, submitted a "Plan for the Defense of the Western Frontier," which received much attention in the War Department and in Congress. This plan covered the entire frontier from the mouth of the Sabine River to Fort Snelling, Minnesota. It proposed extensive developments at Fort Towson and Fort Gibson.

stopped all boats entering the Indian country; but his project was not entirely successful, because it was possible to bring large quantities of whiskey into the Indian nations without making use of river transportation. Fort Coffee was abandoned by the War Department after four years, but its buildings were later occupied by the Choctaw Academy for boys. Fort Wayne, with log barracks and two rows of stone pillboxes, was built in 1838 near the Arkansas boundary north of Siloam Springs. It was abandoned in 1846, but was occupied during the Civil War by Confederate troops under Stand Watie. Fort Washita, northwest of present-day Durant on the Washita River, Fort Arbuckle, ten miles northwest of the site of Davis, and Fort Cobb, west of Anadarko on the Washita River, were all established before the outbreak of the Civil War.

Among the numerous temporary posts were Camp Arbuckle, on the South Canadian below the site of Purcell and just north of the present-day town of Byars, Camp Mason, a mile north of present-day Lexington, mentioned previously as the location of the conference with the Plains Indians in 1835, and Camp Radziminski, in Kiowa County near the site of Mountain Park. Establishment and occupation of the various forts, the marking of military roads between them, and the constant movements of troops and military supplies led to the thorough exploration of a considerable part of Oklahoma.

## THE EARLY MISSIONS

The building of missions and schools in the western home of the Five Civilized Tribes resulted in further steady growth of information on the geography of Oklahoma. Union Mission, established for the Osages in 1821, near the west bank of the Grand River about twenty miles above its mouth, was active for two decades.[30] It was founded by the Congregational missionary, Epaphras Chapman, who served as its head until his death in

[30] Morris L. Wardell, *A Political History of the Cherokee Nation, 1838–1907,* 120; and, "Protestant Missions Among the Osages," *Chronicles of Oklahoma,* Vol. II, No. 8 (September, 1924), 285–97.

1825. Dwight Mission, a Presbyterian station established for the Arkansas Cherokees in 1821, was moved into the new Cherokee Nation eight years later by Reverend C. Washburn to a place that was called Nicksville. Major John Nicks and Walter Webber operated stores there; and before the western limits of Arkansas Territory were determined, the little community was the county seat of what was then Lovely County, Arkansas Territory. It lies north of present-day Sallisaw and approximately half way between Three Forks and Van Buren, on the old road joining those settlements. Samuel A. Worcester, who had been closely associated with the Cherokees in Georgia and Tennessee, came out to Dwight in 1835. Worcester brought the first printing press to the new Cherokee Nation and became publisher of the *Cherokee Almanac* at Park Hill, where he established another mission in 1836. Fairfield, founded by Dr. Marcus Palmer in 1829 near the site of Stillwell, and Old Baptist Mission, established ten years later near Westville, were other famous religious centers of the early Cherokee Nation in the West. Reverend Elizur Butler served as head of Fairfield after the retirement of Dr. Palmer and among the teachers at this frontier mission were Clarissa Palmer, Lucy Butler, Esther Smith, and Addie Torrey.

First among the missions for the Choctaws in Oklahoma was Wheelock, founded by Alfred Wright near the site of Millerton in 1832. The oldest church building now standing in the state was erected there of native stone, and in 1843, Reverend Wright opened a school for Choctaw girls at the mission.[31] Asbury Mission was established by the Methodists in 1847 at North Fork Town, near the southeastern border of the Creek Nation. Tullahassee was built north of the Arkansas River opposite the Creek Agency in 1850. Near well-worn trails, these missions became landmarks for many persons who passed through the Indian country on their way to Texas or California. Farther from the roads of national importance, but connected with them, were Goodwater Choctaw Mission, established near the Red River southwest of Doaksville in 1837; Spencer Academy, northwest of Fort Towson in 1841; and Armstrong Academy, near the site of Bokchito in 1845. The Manual Training School for Chickasaw Boys, opened near Tisho-

[31] Angie Debo, *The Rise and Fall of the Choctaw Republic*, 61, 64, 239.

75

mingo in 1851 by Reverend J. C. Robinson; Wapanucka Academy, northwest of Boggy Depot, opened in 1852; and Bloomfield Academy for Chickasaw Girls, built in 1852 near the Red River south of present-day Durant and administered for fifteen years by Reverend John H. Carr, were all religious and educational centers of importance. Douglas H. Johnston served as superintendent at Bloomfield from 1882 until 1898, when he resigned to accept the governorship of the Chickasaw Nation.

## Scientists, Writers, and Painters in the Exploration of Oklahoma

Some of the best accounts of early travels in Oklahoma were by botanists and other men of science whose primary interest was in the observation of natural phenomena. Dr. Edwin James and Thomas Say, as noted above, were the principal authorities for accounts of the Stephen H. Long expedition, with its divided routes of exploration. Another scientist who left a record of his travels was Thomas Nuttall.

Born in Yorkshire, England, in 1786, Nuttall came to the United States at the age of twenty-two. In spite of poverty during his youth, he had gained some knowledge of the classics and had read with keen interest the available works on natural science. In Philadelphia he met Dr. Benjamin Smith Barton and began to specialize in the study of botany. Nuttall made a number of scientific expeditions south along the Atlantic coast and, with John Bradbury, west into the Missouri territory.[32] From 1811 until 1818 he made annual summer excursions for the purpose of collecting specimens, and spent the rest of the year at Philadelphia in study and scientific writing.

In October, 1818, he began his journey to Oklahoma. His route was from Philadelphia to Pittsburgh, thence down the Ohio River. "Today I left Pittsburgh in a skiff, which I purchased for six dollars, in order to proceed down the Ohio," Nuttall wrote in his journal.

[32] John Bradbury, *In the Interior of America, 1809–1811* (vol. V of Thwaites, *Early Western Travels*).

He took along a young man "who had been accustomed to the management of a boat," and who paid for his passage and food by helping on the labor involved in the rugged river travel. The youthful companion of the scientist proved to be insufferably "insolent," however; and at Augusta, Kentucky, he was dropped. Traveling by various conveyances and with a considerable variety of companions, Nuttall moved down the Ohio, into the Mississippi, and along that stream to Arkansas Post, which he reached on January 22, 1819.

He set out for Fort Smith about a month later and arrived there on April 24. The Nuttall *Journal* contains a brief, clear description of the two sandstone blockhouses, the rows of barracks, and the view of the hills and the Arkansas River at its junction with the Poteau. The elevation called Point de Sucre (Sugar Loaf) by the French hunters could be seen at a distance of thirty-five miles to the south.[33]

Several weeks after he arrived at the fort, Nuttall started out with Major William Bradford, the commandant, on an expedition to the Red River. The officer's purpose was to remove squatters from the Kiamichi Valley, and he was therefore accompanied by a company of soldiers. Nuttall studied the topography of the Poteau, the Kiamichi, and the surrounding hills. Later, he had an opportunity to examine the level region west of the lower Kiamichi River in present-day Choctaw County, and to tramp over the woods and prairies west of the site of Hugo.[34] The naturalist was strongly impressed by the beauty of the hills, the prairies covered with flowers, "serene and charming as the blissful regions of fancy," the picturesque Point de Sucre, and the mystic shadows of the Winding Stair Mountains. He was delighted by the discovery of new plants, amused by the efforts of the soldiers to capture a buffalo, and keenly interested in every phase of the crude but varied experiences of life in the camps of frontier soldiers.[35]

The region at the headwaters of the Kiamichi River suggested

[33] Thomas Nuttall, *Nuttall's Journal of Travels into the Arkansa Territory, October 2, 1818–February 18, 1820* (Vol. XIII of Thwaites, *Early Western Travels*), 198.

[34] *Ibid.*, XIII, 206–27.

[35] *Ibid.*, XIII, 209, 210. Editor Thwaites, in a footnote, confuses the San Bois with the Winding Stair Mountains.

to the scientist, at several points, a comparison with the Appalachian highlands. In one passage he wrote: "The wooded hills . . . on either hand . . . strongly resemble the mountains of the Blue Ridge, at Harper's Ferry, in Virginia."

Along with his story of the expedition and description of the country, Nuttall gives some interesting views on the character of the white settlers and their relations with the Indians. Two horse thieves, brothers named Gibbs, who had waylaid and killed a Cherokee because he was about to give information to federal officers concerning their crimes, fled to Texas upon the approach of Major Bradford's party. Returning later to the Kiamichi country, one of the Gibbs brothers was shot and killed by a hunter who had been sent out to apprehend him. The Cherokees were satisfied with the death of one guilty man, probably on the ground of their old custom of personal retaliation, not entirely discarded by the Indians.

Nuttall walked long distances in his search for specimens, and one day he became separated from his companions. Unable to follow Major Bradford's party without a guide, he was forced to spend several weeks in the region near the mouth of the Kiamichi River, where he occupied his time to good purpose by collecting plants. He lived at the house of a white squatter named Styles, a poor, hospitable man from whom Nuttall parted with real regret. Traveling with a party of Red River men he returned to Fort Smith, arriving there on June 21, 1819.[36]

From July 6 until the latter part of September, Nuttall explored the Arkansas, Grand, Verdigris, South Canadian, North Fork, Deep Fork, and Cimarron rivers. His observations in regard to the Osages are particularly interesting, and the story of his personal struggle against serious illness and the threat of hostile Indians reveals in colorful detail the conditions of early travel in Oklahoma. The account of Nuttall's relations with Mr. Bougie, in whose trading boat he traveled to the Verdigris trading post, and with Mr. Lee, the trapper with whom he journeyed to the Cimarron, throws additional light upon the crude life of men who lived in the Indian country during the year of the Spanish treaty.[37]

[36] *Ibid.*, 227.
[37] *Ibid.*, 228–79.

Washington Irving and Charles J. Latrobe left memorable accounts of their expedition through Oklahoma in 1832[38] Even more valuable for the historian are the published journals of Washington Irving's travels in the West.[39] Although Irving, in his introduction to *A Tour on the Prairies,* admits that he is much embarrassed by the demands made upon him for an account of his western journey and disclaims any ability to write of stirring adventures and wonders, he yet presents in his "simple narrative of everyday occurrences, such as happens to every one who travels the prairies," a fascinating story and an unforgettable picture.

Traveling from St. Louis with the party of Henry L. Ellsworth, a member of the Stokes Commission recently appointed by President Jackson to investigate and supervise Indian affairs in the Southwest, Irving arrived at Fort Gibson in October, 1832. Charles Joseph Latrobe, the English scientist who accompanied the expedition, had stopped at the Osage Agency with Colonel "A. P." Chouteau, the agent and proprietor of the post. Commissioner Ellsworth is presented by Irving as "a man in whom a course in legal practice and political life had not been able to vitiate an innate simplicity and benevolence of heart." Charles J. Latrobe is called by Irving, "a man of a thousand occupations; a botanist, a geologist, a hunter of beetles and butterflies, a musical amateur, a sketcher of no mean pretensions, in short, a complete virtuoso; added to which, he was a very indefatigable, if not always a very successful, sportsman."

Perhaps it is Tonish, "the squire, the groom, the cook, the tent man, in a word, the factotum," who inspires Irving's best efforts in sketching a character. The little French creole, "a kind of Gil Blas of the frontier, who had passed a scrambling life, sometimes among white men, sometimes among Indians," was a person to challenge the writer's skill in painting a colorful subject.

"We picked him up in St. Louis, near which he had a small farm, an Indian wife, and a brood of half-blood children," the story runs. "According to his own account, however, he had a wife in every tribe; in fact, if all this little vagabond said of himself were

---

[38] Washington Irving, *A Tour on the Prairies;* Charles Joseph Latrobe, *The Rambler in North America.*

[39] Irving, *Western Journals.*

to be believed, he was without morals, without caste, without creed, without country, and even without language; for he spoke a jargon of mingled French, English, and Osage. He was, withal, a notorious braggart, and a liar of the first water. It was amusing to hear him vapor and gasconade about his terrible exploits and hairbreadth escapes in war and in hunting. In the midst of his volubility, he was prone to be seized by a spasmodic gasping, as if the springs of his jaws were suddenly unhinged; but I am apt to think it was caused by some falsehood that stuck in his throat, for I generally remarked that immediately afterward there bolted forth a lie of the first magnitude."

At Fort Gibson, Irving received news that he and Latrobe would be permitted to join a party of mounted riflemen who had started northwest a few days earlier for an extensive tour along the Arkansas and Cimarron valleys, with a wide swing toward the southwest. Irving welcomed the opportunity to join the ranger expedition. With a lieutenant for a guide and an escort of fourteen horsemen, he and Commissioner Ellsworth started out on October 10 to overtake the rangers. Two Creek Indians had been sent off to carry a message from the commander at Fort Gibson to the captain of the rangers, ordering a halt until the visitors could catch up. At the Osage Agency, Latrobe rejoined the party and they proceeded up the Arkansas Valley.

Every page of Irving's *A Tour on the Prairies* contains vital information on the condition of the Indian Territory and its people. The description of Chouteau's Verdigris trading post, for example, opens many windows for glimpses of the frontier. "The little hamlet of the Agency was in a complete bustle; the blacksmith's shed, in particular, was a scene of preparation; a strapping negro was shoeing a horse; two half-breeds were fabricating iron spoons in which to melt lead for bullets. An old trapper, in leathern hunting frock and moccasins, had placed his rifle against a workbench, while he superintended the operation, and gossiped about his hunting exploits; several large dogs were lounging in and out of the shop, or sleeping in the sunshine, while a little cur, with head cocked on one side, and one ear erect, was watching, with that curiosity common to little dogs, the process of shoeing the horse, as if studying the art, or waiting for his turn to be shod."[40]

The Irving party overhauled Captain Bean and his rangers near the site of present-day Bixby, but on the opposite side of the Arkansas. On the following day, October 15, the mouth of Red Fork (Cimarron) was passed, and the entire party crossed the Arkansas, to travel westward through the region that now lies in Creek, Pawnee, and Payne counties. In this area where game was plentiful the rangers hunted buffaloes, tried their skill at catching wild horses, and supplied fresh meat by shooting deer and turkeys. At all times they kept a sharp watch for hostile Pawnees, whom the commander of the company considered the principal threat to peace on the north bank of the Cimarron.

Captain Jesse Bean of Independence County, Arkansas, had been commissioned recently to raise this company of mounted men consisting of one hundred privates, fourteen noncommissioned officers, and three lieutenants, in addition to the captain. The *Arkansas Gazette*, on July 18, 1832, gave the following opinion: "In the selection of a commander of the Arkansas Corps, we think the President has been quite fortunate. A more experienced woods-man, or one better acquainted with the Indian mode of fighting, can hardly be found in any country than Capt. Bean. He took a gallant part in most of the principal engagements at New Orleans, while that city was invested by the British Army, in 1814–15, and was with Gen. Jackson in some of the subsequent Indian wars in Florida, where he commanded a company of Spies, and rendered important services for which he was highly complimented by the Commanding General."[41]

Pierre Beatte, whom Washington Irving supposed to be the son of an Osage mother and a French father, was employed personally by Commissioner Ellsworth and the noted writer to serve as their guide, interpreter, and man of all work. He was the first of the party to capture one of the wild horses. The camp had been pitched several miles north of the Cimarron, probably on the prairie northwest of the site of Perkins. Late in the evening after a hunt that lasted all day and a hard chase that covered many miles, Beatte had succeeded in throwing his lariat around the neck of a handsome colt, about two years old. Several of the rangers tried

40 Irving, *A Tour on the Prairies*, 14.
41 Irving, *Western Journals*, 28, 45 n., 46 n.

to buy the animal from the successful hunter, tempting him with extravagant offers; but he refused to consider any of the offers. To one of the generous proposals of purchase he answered, "You give great price now; but tomorrow you be sorry, and take back, and say d——d Indian."[42]

On the morning of October 22, the party turned south across the Cimarron. Next day, on an open tract of rolling ground, the rangers sighted buffaloes; and after an exciting chase, Tonish succeeded in killing an old bull. Later, he served the men with highly seasoned soup and extremely tough beef. The party traveled southwest through a region heavily timbered with postoak and blackjack, which Irving identified as the Cross Timber. A fine black mare was captured by one of the rangers, and a colt about seven months old was taken by Tonish. At one camp an alarm arose over the danger of attack by a large band of Pawnee Indians, but the night passed without incident. At the end of the next day, October 23, Captain Bean decided that the expedition had gone far enough west and that the return march should begin the next morning. Washington Irving seemed to believe that he had traveled almost to the border of Texas; but from his description of the country, the elapsed time, and the route followed by the party since their crossing of the Arkansas, it is more likely that the expedition was ready to turn back at a point near the site of Okarche, on the northern border of Canadian County.[43] Actually, after fourteen days of exploring, Irving and his companions were about as far from the Texas border as they were from Fort Gibson.

Washington Irving had supplied Tonish with a mount on which the bragging little "factotum" performed all his feats of horsemanship, his buffalo hunting, and his runs after wild horses. Irving, galloping recklessly over rough ground during a chase, seriously lamed his own mount, however, and considered for a time depriving Tonish of his status as a horseman; but in the end, because of the fellow's obvious pride in his skill as a mounted hunter, Irving purchased another horse. Practically all of the rangers were addicted to "swapping" horses, and for a few days the touring author kept the market busy. Finally, he obtained the horse

42 Irving, *A Tour on the Prairies*, 74, 75.
43 Compare with map, Irving, *Western Journals*, 178.

that he regarded the best in the entire company, "a full-blooded sorrel of excellent bottom, beautiful form, and most generous qualities."[44]

The rangers killed turkeys, chased buffaloes, occasionally bringing one down, and hunted wild horses. In his *A Tour on the Prairies,* Irving confuses the North Canadian River with the "north fork of Red River," which may account for his notion that the party had almost reached the Texas border.[45] Traveling south, the rangers forded the North Canadian on October 24, probably some miles east of the 98th meridian; and as the party turned southeastward, roughly parallel to the course of the South Canadian, they encountered six Osage Indians. The leader of the band stated that he and his companions had separated from a great Osage hunting party, and that on their way home they hoped to take a few scalps and horses from some unprotected Pawnee camp. Commissioner Ellsworth made a speech, urging the six hunters to keep the peace and to co-operate with the government at Washington in establishing permanent harmony among the Plains Indians. The Osages listened quietly and, after a short conversation among themselves, departed. At his first opportunity to speak privately with Beatte, Irving asked him what the Osages had said to each other after the Commissioner's speech. According to Beatte, their leader had suggested to the others that since the great father intended to bring peace to the land, there was no time to lose and they would have to get on with their business at the Pawnee camps.

At one place where the party of rangers camped for the night, Beatte went out alone to hunt. He came upon a bear and fired a shot, wounding the big animal. As it tried to make off, limping through the waters of a brook, the hunter followed and attacked it with his knife, trying to disable it completely by cutting its hamstrings. After an exhausting struggle, however, the bear escaped, and Beatte returned to camp empty-handed. Completely worn out

[44] Irving, *A Tour on the Prairies,* 90.

[45] *Ibid.,* 92, 95. Compare with Irving, *Western Journals,* 139. No journal has been found in Irving's notes for the period between October 18 and October 30. McDermott, the editor, has reconstructed this part of the expedition, largely from Henry L. Ellsworth, *Washington Irving on the Prairie, or a Narrative of a Tour of the Southwest in the Year 1832,* edited by Stanley T. Williams and Barbara D. Simison.

and dejected by his failure, the hunter said: "I am all broke to pieces and good for nothing; I no care what happen to me any more." After a moment, he added, "For all that, it would take a pretty good man to put me down, anyhow."

On October 28 the party's three guides went on a buffalo hunt and killed four buffaloes. On the following day, Irving and Latrobe each succeeded in bringing down one of the big animals. On November 1 the rangers camped on a tributary of Little River; and next day came in sight of a stream which Irving called the North Fork of the Arkansas, but which was, obviously, the North Canadian, probably in the vicinity of the site on which Wetumka now stands. After a few more days the explorers came to a frontier farmhouse where Washington Irving, along with Captain Bean, ate boiled beef and turnips with slices of bread and butter, served by a "fat, good-humored negress." On the next day the expedition came to an end at Fort Gibson, "much tattered, travel-stained, and weather-beaten, but in high health and spirits."

*The Rambler in North America* gives another author's view of the same journey.[46] The writer, Charles J. Latrobe, devoted nine chapters to his trip down the Ohio, up to St. Louis, along the Missouri, into the Indian country, and the circuit through the valleys of the Arkansas, Cimarron, and North Canadian. Two later military expeditions—that of the Leavenworth party in 1834 and the journey of Randolph B. Marcy in 1852—will be described in a later chapter.

[46] Latrobe, *The Rambler in North America*, I, 99–242.

# CHAPTER FIVE

# The American Indian in Oklahoma History

## THE INHABITANTS OF OKLAHOMA
## BEFORE THE COMING OF THE EUROPEANS

At every stage in the development of Oklahoma, the American Indian has taken a leading part. In the time of Coronado the Caddoan Indians had an important place in plans of the Spanish conquerors. The slow advance of the Spaniards on the Southwestern Plains was directly related to the attitude and the activities of Comanches and Apaches; and the trading interests of the French were obviously connected with these tribes and other natives of the Plains, the Osages, Kiowas, and Pawnees. When the young republic, the United States of America, adopted policies which resulted in the establishment of an Indian Territory west of Arkansas, a new epoch of native influence in the region began. Even in more recent times the Indian, although numerically but a small fraction of the population, still played vital parts in the state's affairs, in such widely separated fields as politics, education, and the fine arts—to mention only a few modern interests of the native peoples.

The Bureau of American Ethnology has contributed notable studies on the society of the North American Indians. In these studies, classification is attempted on the basis of linguistic groups of tribes. Some of the tribes with related languages, such as the separate groups of the Algonquian family, are widely dispersed over North America. Perhaps the linguistic families which have most affected Oklahoma since the coming of Europeans to the Southwestern Plains are the following:

1) *Algonquian*, including the Algonkin, Arapaho, Blackfeet,

85

Cheyenne, Delaware, Fox, Illinois, Kickapoo, Miami, Mohegan, Pamlico, Pequot, Potawatomi, Powhatan, Sac, and Shawnee tribes.

2) *Iroquoian,* including the Cayuga, Cherokee, Conestoga, Erie, Huron, Mohawk, Oneida, Onondaga, Seneca, and Wyandotte tribes.

3) *Muskhogean,* including the Alabami, Apalachi, Chickasaw, Choctaw, Creek, and Seminole tribes.

4) *Siouan,* including the Biloxi, Catawba, Crow, Dakota, Iowa, Kansas, Missouri, Omaha, Osage, Ponca, and Winnebago tribes.

5) *Caddoan,* including the Caddo, Pawnee, and Wichita tribes.

6) *Shoshonean,* including the Comanche, Paiute, Shoshone, and Ute tribes.

7) *Shahaptian,* including the Nez Percé, Umatilla, and Walla Walla tribes.

8) *Athapascan,* including the Apache and Navajo tribes.

9) *Kiowan,* with one tribe, the Kiowa.

10) *Tonkawan,* with one tribe, the Tonkawa.[1]

The excavations made by archaeologists at Spiro, Fort Coffee, Muskogee, Eufaula, Tahlequah, and elsewhere in Oklahoma disclose patterns of material civilization in at least three distinct periods of development. Pottery, projectile points of many types, stone axes, beads, buttons, smoking pipes, matting, and textiles are among the thousands of items that have been brought to light and studied in the Spiro area. Rectangular and square dwellings and larger ceremonial houses were features of the villages studied. Burial ceremonies, similar in every respect to the rites described by Le Page Du Pratz, in his *Histoire de La Louisiane,* are traceable in the skeletal remains and other materials of the burial mounds.[2] Round grass houses, similar to Wichita dwellings of the seventeenth, eighteenth and nineteenth centuries, have been discovered by A. D. Krieger in his studies of ancient "Caddoan" culture in northeastern Texas.[3]

[1] Frederick Webb Hodge, *Handbook of American Indians North of Mexico,* Bureau of American Ethnology *Bulletin No. 30,* Parts I and II.

[2] Kenneth G. Orr, "The Archaeological Situation at Spiro," *American Antiquity,* Vol. XI, No. 4 (April, 1926); Le Page du Pratz, *History of Louisiana;* French, *Historical Collections of Louisiana,* I.

The ancestors of modern Caddoes, Pawnees, and Wichitas probably lived in Oklahoma for many centuries before Europeans came to America. As noted above, seminomadic tribes followed the migrations of buffaloes across the Southwestern Plains; and other tribes, more dependent upon agriculture, established permanent homes in the valleys of the Arkansas, Canadian, and Red rivers. From the upper waters of the Grand River to the Texas border, there is much evidence of ancient culture developed by "pre-Caddoan" Indians through centuries of residence in communities where substantial buildings and other items of permanence existed. Studies in the civilization of these older civilizations are closely related to research in the records of the later Indians.

## THE FIVE CIVILIZED TRIBES

Five of the Indian tribes that lived in the states south of Virginia after the American Revolution came to be known as the Five Civilized Tribes. Perhaps all of them excepting the Seminoles were sufficiently advanced in the civilization of the European invaders of their continent to justify the title. The Choctaws, Chickasaws, Creeks, and Seminoles belonged to the Muskhogean language group, while the Cherokees were a part of the great Iroquoian family.

The Choctaws lived in the central and southern portions of present-day Mississippi. They also occupied the land west of the lower Pearl and spread out to the west beyond the Mississippi River over a considerable part of southern Louisiana. Eastward, their settlements extended into the Tombigbee country of present-day Alabama. They were the largest of the Five Civilized Tribes, numbering perhaps twenty-five thousand at the beginning of the nineteenth century. Closely related to them by ties of blood and language were their neighbors on the north, the Chickasaws. Their population was about one fourth that of the Choctaws.

To the east of these two tribes lived the Creeks. They were

[3] Orr, "The Archaeological Situation at Spiro," *American Antiquity*, Vol. XI, No. 4 (April, 1926), 248n.

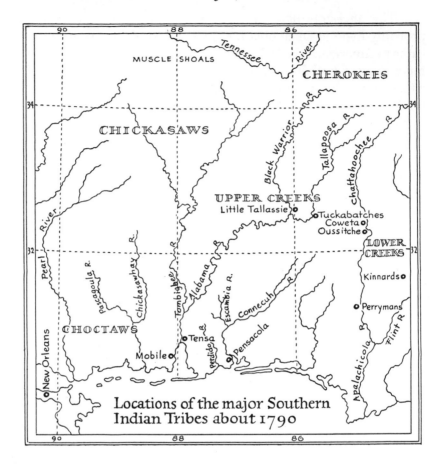

Locations of the major Southern
Indian Tribes about 1790

a powerful Indian nation and their lands extended over eastern Alabama and southwestern Georgia. On their north lived the Cherokees with wide possessions in northern Georgia, the western part of both Carolinas, and southeastern Tennessee. The Seminoles, a small and backward tribe, lived for the most part in the remote lands of Florida. Cut off from contact with white population by the difficult terrain of swamp land and dense woods, the Seminoles long remained the least civilized of the Five Civilized Tribes.

James Adair, who lived among the native inhabitants of the Southeast for several years about the middle of the eighteenth century, regarded them as kindly and hospitable people, inclined to share any provisions they possessed with visitors. In Adair's account, traveling Indians carried only a gun and "shot-pouch or a bow and quiver full of barbed arrows." Sometimes, he added, they carried both bow and gun. For food they depended upon their fellow tribesmen, who received them without question.[4]

It is enlightening to observe the relative speed with which Indians of the Five Civilized Tribes adopted the various traits of European culture. Weapons and improved transportation were eagerly embraced, as means of immediate and easily understood advantage. New plants and domestic animals, useful in stabilizing the food supply, were accepted readily enough. Basic concepts of right and wrong conduct, governmental institutions, and social traditions with highly complex ceremonials were practically unchanged through several centuries of Indian contact with the invaders. In some phases of cultural change, intermarriage of the two races appeared as the main factor of gradual Indian adaptation.

THE BASES OF CULTURE IN THE
FIVE CIVILIZED TRIBES: CHOCTAWS

Before their removal west during the first half of the nineteenth century, the Choctaws probably were more advanced in

[4] James Adair, *The History of the American Indians*, 17. A recent edition of Adair's work was published at Johnson City, Tenn., in 1930.

89

their economic life than any other of the Five Civilized Tribes.[5]
The bases of their food supply were the products of their fields—
corn, beans, melons, pumpkins, and squash, in particular. The most
important of these was corn, which the Choctaws raised in abundance. In fact, there was often a surplus of grain, which they sold
or bartered.[6] Like the other Indians of southeastern United States,
they obtained a part of their living by fishing and hunting. Nuts,
berries, and other edible products of the woods added variety to
their food supply. After the introduction of hogs and cattle, these
animals, ranging at large, furnished a considerable part of their
meat. The Choctaws raised many ponies, and there is evidence
that they, along with other southeastern Indians, slaughtered their
horses for food during war or other periods of emergency.[7]

Fields were made ready for cultivation by girdling the larger
trees, cutting out the saplings, and clearing away underbrush.
Frontiersmen followed the same process of cutting and burning
brush and girdling trees, all the way across the wooded portions of
North America. The essential difference in the Choctaw method
was the use of flint instead of metal axes, until acquaintance with
white men brought about, gradually, adoption of the more effective tool. The primitive hoe of the Choctaw farmer was also made
of flint or fashioned from the shoulder bone of a buffalo. Fields and
gardens were fenced against cattle, hogs, ponies, and deer.

At the end of the eighteenth century, forest buffalo were no
longer found in the land of the Five Civilized Tribes, but bears and
deer were plentiful. Indian hunters also found wild turkeys,
pigeons, and numerous kinds of small animals—beaver, otter, rabbit, squirrel, raccoon, and opossum. Before firearms came into
common use, the bow and arrow was the principal hunting weapon, and Indian youths became expert marksmen at an early age.
Selecting, fashioning, and feathering arrows played a part in the
education of every boy. The younger Choctaw hunters also used
a blowgun made from the hollow cane stalk and loaded with small
arrows for killing or stunning birds and rabbits.

[5] John R. Swanton, *Source Material for the Social and Ceremonial Life of the
Choctaw Indians*, Bureau of American Ethnology Bulletin No. *103*, pp. 1, 2.

[6] John R. Swanton, "Aboriginal Culture of the Southeast," Bureau of American Ethnology *Forty-second Annual Report*.

[7] Adair, *American Indians*, 230, 231.

The Choctaws made use of a light spear, as well as the bow and arrow, in killing fish. Barbed hooks were introduced by Europeans and quickly adopted by the southeastern Indians. A crude net made of brush and creeping vines was sometimes employed to drag fish from quiet pools, and buckeye or winterberries were put into the water to stun fish so that they might be easily picked up.[8]

European influence upon the Choctaws began in the first half of the sixteenth century with De Soto's expedition. The Spanish military party moved westward from Florida to the valley of the Tombigbee, where they met the district chief of the Choctaws, Tuscaloosa.[9] Spanish accounts of the incident describe him as a tall, handsome Indian, dressed in ceremonial garb with distinctive feather adornments, and attended by a companion who held a sunshade over his head.

The Spanish commander required that Tuscaloosa furnish him with carriers and women. The chief complied with the first demand and suggested that women for the invaders might be obtained at Mabila, the site of modern Mobile. Meantime, he sent messengers to the west; and when the Spaniards advanced, with Tuscaloosa practically a prisoner, they found the Choctaws assembled in force. It was here that the first battle of De Soto's expedition took place, with heavy losses for the Spaniards and much heavier losses for the Indians. Mabila was forced to permit Spanish occupation while the wounded soldiers recovered their health. Then De Soto moved northward into the territory of the Chickasaws.

James Adair assumed that the Choctaw ponies of the eighteenth century sprang from Spanish horses of the De Soto expedition, and the characteristics of the Indian ponies would seem to support his theory.[10] Spanish influence upon the Choctaws from the struggling Florida settlements was probably not strong; but the indirect acquaintance of Mississippi Indians with European plants, domestic animals, building devices, and other material culture traits over a long period of time, undoubtedly prepared them for the more obvious changes that resulted from French occupation of Louisiana.

[8] Swanton, *Choctaw Social and Ceremonial Life*, 49–54.
[9] Bourne, *Narratives of the Career of Hernando de Soto*, 87–128.
[10] Adair, *American Indians*, 340, 341.

Garden products, such as cabbage, melons, pumpkins, leeks, and garlic; domestic animals—hogs, cattle, and horses; poultry of various kinds; and implements for farming and building increased rapidly among the Choctaws after La Salle's voyage of 1682 and the later settlements and trading posts of French adventurers.

Occupation of the lower Mississippi by France placed the Choctaws in a position of strategic importance with respect to the struggle of European powers for empire. The English were pushing their settlements southward along the Atlantic coast and claiming all the territory to the west. Spain was well established in Mexico and less firmly planted in Florida. The Choctaws had little direct contact with British colonists, but were definitely under the influence of the French and Spanish. The French policy of making friends among the native peoples by means of trade and diplomacy was much in evidence in their dealings with the Choctaws. Some of the leading Choctaw families of a later period were the descendants of intermarried French traders and government officials. British influence upon Choctaw diplomacy, less evident in the tribe's early contacts with Europeans, became important before the end of the colonial wars.

Between the Treaty of Utrecht in 1713 and outbreak of the War of the Austrian Succession in 1740, the Choctaws were engaged in a struggle against the Natchez Indians. The Chickasaws fought against their kinsmen and nearest neighbors, the powerful Choctaw tribe, and on the side of the Natchez. England supported the Chickasaws and Natchez, France aided the Choctaws, and in 1736 a fierce battle was fought in which the Chickasaws, Natchez, and their English allies were beaten. In fact, the Natchez Indians were almost exterminated; and as a by-product of the war the Choctaws were divided internally so sharply as to result in a destructive civil conflict. Shulush Homa, or Red Shoes, hostile toward the French because one of their officers seduced his wife, took the British side of the contest. Soon the *Okla falaya* Choctaws were aligned with the British, the *Okla tannaps* with the French, and the *Okla hannali* were divided among themselves. Eventually, Shulush Homa was executed, in a move by the Choctaw Council to end the civil strife; but his brother continued the war until the

French party, aided by Governor Vaudreuil, crushed the Choctaw friends of the British.[11]

After the successful revolt of the British colonies in America, the United States became a strong factor in Choctaw diplomacy. Three trails crossed the Choctaw Nation from north to south, and one main road from east to west. The one-horse roads to the north gave easy access to the land of the Chickasaws and the east-west route, the Camino Real from St. Augustine to Mexico City, furnished means of communication with the French and Spanish.[12] In the efforts of the British, Spanish, French, and American governments to control Choctaw resources and to gain support from the tribe's armies, the Indians found an opportunity to develop their skill as crafty political traders. Later Choctaw generations displayed such skill in diplomatic relations as to suggest that cleverness in the conduct of foreign affairs is cumulative, the result of long experience in dealing with powerful neighbors.

In the Tallahaga Valley of east-central Mississippi stood an elevation which marked the heart of Choctaw ceremonial life. This sacred mound, less than a day's walk from the border of the Chickasaw hunting grounds to the north, was called Nanih Wayia. Rising forty or fifty feet above the surrounding level ground, the elevation sloped rather abruptly from a base one hundred yards in length and about half as wide. The mound was surrounded by a wall of solid earth some ten feet high with ample space on top for a defending army, enclosing six hundred or seven hundred acres. A trail extended northward into Chickasaw territory and another deep trail led away to the southeast.[13]

In Choctaw myths, the tribe's origin is explained in a variety of stories, some of which say that they migrated toward the north into Mississippi after emerging from a cavern under the Gulf. In one of these stories the starting place was beyond the Mississippi River—perhaps along the coast of southwestern Louisiana. Two

[11] H. B. Cushman, *History of the Choctaw, Chickasaw, and Natchez Indians*, 86; Charles E. A. Gayarre, *The Early History of Louisiana*, 20–22; James Adair, *American Indians*, 354–56; Nuttall, *Travels into the Arkansa Territory*.

[12] William E. Myer, "Indian Trails of the Southeast," in Bureau of American Ethnology *Forty-second Annual Report*, map, p. 748.

[13] Adair, *American Indians*; Swanton, *Choctaw Social and Ceremonial Life*; Nuttall, *Travels into the Arkansa Territory*.

brothers, Chahtah and Chickasah, were leaders, and their separation brought the founding of the two related tribes, the Choctaws and the Chickasaws. The story of a great flood was borrowed, probably from Christian missionaries but combined with Choctaw experience with high water in the lower valley of the Mississippi. In this myth the tribe was saved from extinction by the great raft-builder, Oklatabashih.[14]

The burial customs of the Choctaws were obviously connected with belief in future life beyond earthly existence.[15] Placing food and drink and the body of a favorite dog or pony near the corpse of a Choctaw was closely akin to the burial customs of many other Indian tribes, both in the East and on the Great Plains. In some respects, however, the Choctaw rites were unique. The body of the deceased was placed on a platform erected near his house, at sufficient height to prevent molestation by wild animals. The body was carefully covered with deerskin, or buffalo skin, and bark. In addition to one or more animals, the dead person's favorite utensils or weapons, and perhaps ornaments, might be placed on the platform. During the first few days a fire was kept burning, to afford the comfort of light and warmth for the departed. The body might remain on the platform for a period of five or even six months; and the stench became so great that mourners, appearing at frequent intervals to show respect for the deceased, sometimes fainted.

A class of Choctaw officials known as bone-pickers performed a final rite that was, to many observers of European descent, quite revolting. When the corpse was sufficiently decomposed, these men, with no other instruments than long, sharpened fingernails, mounted the platform and picked the flesh from the bones. The skull was painted with vermilion, and the skeleton was passed down to waiting relatives, who laid it in a well-constructed coffin. The platform and decayed flesh were then burned. The coffin was placed with others in the village bone-house and the mourners gathered for a ceremonial banquet, the bone-pickers presiding as honored officials. At intervals, all the coffins were carried to the burial mound, where several communities might find space for the bones of their dead.

Choctaw primitive religion was a strange mixture of weird

[14] Swanton, *Choctaw Social and Ceremonial Life*, 202–208.

94

mysticism and good, common sense. There were good spirits and bad spirits, and an important function of the medicine man, *alikchi,* was to perform the magic ceremonies that would render the bad spirits powerless and gain the support of the good spirits. Witch-craft was accepted as one of the evil influences, and occasionally the execution of a witch was advocated by the medicine men to justify their failure in a given case. The healers combined with their magic some knowledge of physiology and the properties of medi-cinal plants.[16] Occasionally they resorted to sweating the patient and then plunging him into cold water—a procedure which in some kinds of sickness probably guaranteed his demise.

Every warrior carried a medicine bag, a small deerskin pouch filled with secret, magic ingredients, such as ashes derived from the bones of a ferocious beast, particles of red clay or colored sand, and the bones or feathers of a brightly colored bird, carefully boiled together. The sacred medicine of the tribe was held in cus-tody by the chief and protected at any cost against capture by enemies.[17] Rainmakers were highly regarded by the Choctaws.

Probably the Christian missionaries introduced the idea of a Great Spirit to this tribe. Many observers have noted that the Choctaws were inclined to be casual in regard to supplication. The sun and fire came in for some attention as objects of worship, the medicine men preparing for their functions in the ceremonies by long periods of fasting, living apart, and mystic incantations. The people depended greatly upon tribal songs and dances, supple-mented by the magic of men entrusted with that art. The green-corn dance, the dance of the young people, dances in honor of the dove and other birds, the war dance, and the scalp dance were among the most popular of the festivals.

Games and a great variety of outdoor sports were strongly supported by the Choctaws.[18] *Ishtaboli,* the Indian ball game,

[15] *Ibid.,* 12–20; Nuttall, *Travels into the Arkansa Territory,* 304, 305; Adair, *American Indians,* 192, 193.

[16] Swanton, *Choctaw Social and Ceremonial Life.*

[17] Adair, *American Indians;* Cushman, *Choctaw, Chickasaw, and Natchez Indians.*

[18] Stewart Culin, *Games of the North American Indians,* Bureau of American Ethnology *Twenty-fourth Annual Report,* 29–809. See especially "Racket: Chero-kee," 574–88; and "Racket: Muskhogean," 597–608.

aroused the greatest competitive spirit and commanded the largest following. The deerskin ball was handled by players equipped with two *kapucha,* hickory sticks nearly four feet long, fitted at one end with a coonskin net in the form of a cup. Goals were set up at each end of a level field, which might be two or three hundred yards in length. The goal posts, made of split logs, were set firmly in the ground some six feet apart and joined by a cross bar. A point was scored when a player succeeded in tossing the ball against his own goal; and since the game ordinarily ran to one hundred points, it was likely to become a test of endurance. The players, dressed in breechclouts and decorated sometimes by the addition of a mane and tail, were noted for their agility, speed, and resourcefulness in obtaining a score. They dodged, used teammates for interference, and frequently resorted to hurdling an opposing player.

The rugged character of *ishtaboli* may be inferred from the fact that the players, equipped with stout hickory clubs, were allowed to stop an opponent by any means at their disposal. The old men who served as referees had the function of ruling on scores and keeping a record of points made by opposing teams. Any number of players could be matched in a game, which sometimes resulted from a challenge of one village by another, and sometimes by champions selecting their players alternately from the men present. When a point was scored, the players of the successful team would gobble like turkeys, perhaps to disconcert their opponents, or simply to deride them.

The Indian women were enthusiastic spectators at the games, and occasionally when the men finished their contest, the ladies would take the field and begin a new match. Many of the women played the game with great skill. There was also a less rigorous form of *ishtaboli,* which men and women played together.

Another popular game among the Choctaws was *alhchahpi,* in which a round stone was rolled along a smooth clay lane. The object was not the same as in modern bowling, to knock down pins; rather, it was to reach the end of the alley with the rolling disc. The opponents, back of a restraining line, hurled poles at the rolling disc to stop its progress. Many other North American tribes played games similar to *alhchahpi* and *ishtaboli.*

*Baskatanje* was a game of chance played with dice made from kernels of white corn, blackened on one side. Gambling on the results of their games was very common among the Choctaws, not only in connection with dice but on the outcome of any sporting event. Both men and women frequently risked all of their earthly possessions, including weapons, tools, domestic animals, and even their houses, on games of *ishtaboli.*

The strong tendency of the Choctaws to engage in active sports was reflected in their ability to give and take. Good sportsmanship among them was the general rule. In spite of the intense interest developed in communities over matched games of *ishtaboli,* players seldom lost their poise during the contests. Serious, even fatal injuries were not uncommon in the hard-fought games, but apparently the players maintained a good-natured spirit of friendly rivalry, announcing their scores with the derisive turkeygobble and taking the hard knocks as incidents of their recreation.

## CREEK SOCIETY AT THE TIME OF REMOVAL, 1820–1842

At the beginning of the nineteenth century, Indian administration was growing into a major domestic problem for the United States; and every Indian tribe was faced with the complex problem of dealing with foreign conquerors in their territory. Degree of advancement in civilization, as measured by standards of the European-Americans, became vitally important to all the Indians. Attempts to estimate relative progress of the tribes, especially when the differences between them were not wide and sharply defined, must necessarily remain matters of opinion. As indicated above, the Choctaws were outstanding in economic progress. In some other phases of civilized life, they were backward by comparison with the Cherokees and not in advance of the Creeks and Chickasaws.

Roman Catholic missions did not succeed in making the deep impression upon the Choctaws of Mississippi or the Creeks of Alabama that they made upon the Indians of the St. Lawrence Valley. A mission was built in the Choctaw Six Town District in 1726, and another was established on the Yazoo River in 1727.

97

These early contacts with Christian teachers did not create the powerful trend toward tribal education that the Cherokees found in their mission schools, and there was no Sequoyah among the Creeks or the Choctaws to interpret the white man's culture, to stand as a beacon guiding his people into the mysteries of an unknown future. The inevitable adjustments to an alien civilization were, in some phases, more difficult for the Creeks and Choctaws than for the Cherokees, and most difficult for the Seminoles.

The Creeks, or Muskogees, had a distinctive culture, which requires brief attention in our survey. The towns, with their public buildings, official classes, councils and assemblies, festivals and games, constituted the heart of Creek society. Two major divisions were clearly marked in the Creek Confederacy: the Upper Towns of the Tallapoosa and Coosa rivers, and the Lower Towns of the Flint and Chattahoochee.

During the first two and one-half centuries of their contact with Europeans, that is, from the time of De Soto to the years of George Washington's presidency, the Creeks incorporated many peoples into their loose confederacy. Some of these tribes and fragments of linguistic stocks were refugees from regions settled by whites; some were remnants of groups shattered by bitter intertribal warfare. Most of them belonged to the great Muskhogean family, such as the Alabamis, Arabekas, Hitchitees, Koasatas, Natchez, and Tuskeegees; but a few were of alien language groups, such as the remnant of a Shawnee tribe, another of the Euchees, and a small band of refugee Catawbas.[19]

Creek incorporation of tribes in Spanish territory, groups that were shattered by warfare, resulted in large movements of their own warriors from the Lower Towns to Florida. At first these Creek outposts retained their connection with the councils of the Confederacy; but gradually the distance between the Lower Town Creeks and the Florida settlements brought separation of governmental functions, and the Florida Indians developed their own tribal organization. The word *Seminole* meant to Muskhogean Indians, "people who camp at a distance," or "wild." The two meanings were equally applicable to the Seminoles of Florida.

[19] John R. Swanton, *Early History of the Creek Indians and Their Neighbors,* Bureau of American Ethnology *Bulletin No. 73.*

Visitors to the Creek towns found a well-established pattern of public and private buildings. In the center of the community were the three principal meeting places: the square, the *chokafa*, and the *chunkey yard*. The square was a court enclosed by four long sheds. Each building had three walls, built strongly with posts and plastered with clay. The open sides faced the court, and each shed was divided into compartments suitable for its functions. One building was devoted to council meetings, and each of the others had special uses connected with public business, ceremony, or recreation. Nearly all summer meetings of citizens and officials were held in the square.[20]

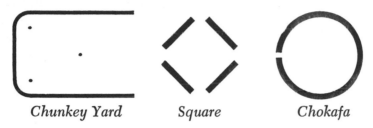

| Chunkey Yard | Square | Chokafa |

The *Chokafa* was a round structure with a tall, cone-shaped roof. Posts firmly planted in a circle some forty feet across, standing about as high as a tall man, constituted the outer wall. These posts stood so close together that there was no space between them except small cracks caused by irregularities, and the entire wall was well plastered with clay. An inner circle of posts, somewhat higher, helped to support the pointed roof. The *chokafa* was a lofty structure, looming high above other buildings, public and private. A fire burned in the center, making the enclosure a suitable meeting place for cold weather. Some compartments were built between the inner and outer circle of posts.

The *chunkey yard* was a long clay alley, in the shape of a croquet arch with nearly square corners. Here the young Creeks played a game with rolling discs, fashioned from stone, similar in every respect to the Choctaw game *alhchahpi*.

The Creek clans were named for various animals. The clan organization added some complexity to Creek society, and the

[20] William Bartram, *Travels through North and South Carolina, East and West Florida, the Cherokee Country . . . and the Country of the Choctaws.*

manner in which the clan allegiance affected family relations is not entirely clear to modern students of ethnology. Among the clans were the *Aktayatco* (moccasin), Alligator, Beaver, Bear, Bird, Deer, Panther, and Raccoon. James Adair remarked, in his account of the southeastern Indians, that "no tribe was called after the opossum, a creature that hath a head like a hog and a tail like a rat."[21] The Wind Clan of the Creeks was apparently an aristocratic group, with inherited distinction.

Marriage customs among the Creeks were similar to those of the other Muskhogean tribes. Young men and women exercised some degree of choice, although the advice of the woman's female relatives was usually sought and permission of her maternal uncles might be required. A Creek youth, seeking a wife, sent suitable presents to her mother, aunts, and grandmother after consultation with the girl's maternal uncles. If the presents were accepted, the simple marriage ceremony was quickly arranged. Afterward the man came to the bride's home to live, took the necessary steps for raising a garden and a crop of field corn, and began to conduct his affairs in a manner suitable to his new responsibilities. The marriage was regarded as being in a trial stage until he had built a house and harvested a crop.

Divorces were few; in families with children they were almost unknown. Probably our own society in the twentieth century has a divorce rate considerably higher. Polygamy was a common practice among the Creeks. Usually a husband obtained his first wife's consent before marrying a second time, and in many cases the later wife was a sister of the first.

Each Creek home had a garden plot, fenced against hogs, cattle, ponies, and the deer that were still quite plentiful in the woods. The town carried on its principal farming operations in a common field, in which each citizen worked his own land, separated from the rest by a strip of turf similar to the divisions among the holdings of medieval peasants in Europe. Families stored their produce in granaries specially constructed, or in their own dwellings. The town maintained a common storehouse to meet the needs of visitors, of families belonging to men who were engaged in war, and of relief cases in general.[22] Like most American Indians, the

[21] Adair, *American Indians*, 16.

Creeks made their greater hunting and fishing expeditions in common, with large parties and frequently with long journeys.

Creek games were similar to those of the other southeastern Indians. A ball game that was almost a duplicate of Choctaw *ishtaboli; chunkey,* a game played with rolling discs in a clay alley; and many variations of games of chance were perhaps the most characteristic games of Creek town life.

Young men who had reached maturity and had established their standing in Creek society by deeds of valor were entitled to receive a war-title. The new name was publicly bestowed, with appropriate ceremonial. Yohola, Emarthla, Fixico, and Harjo are examples of such titles.[23] The English equivalent of Harjo is "mad," with the same meaning as that of the whites in their reference to the brave general, "Mad Anthony Wayne."

The story of Creek diplomatic relations with English, French, and Spanish settlers in America cannot be presented here. Each of the three contestants for American empire used the Creeks, when it was possible, to further the selfish aims of white men. Eventually the tribe found among its own people a leader who was clever, adroit, and unscrupulous, who matched the white men in their efforts to gain advantages by cunning.

Alexander McGillivray, son of a Scottish father and a half-blooded Creek mother, was a man of unique ability. From Lachlan McGillivray, his father, he inherited the shrewdness that made him a successful trader. His mother, Sehoy, was the daughter of General Marchand of the French Army and a Creek woman who belonged to a distinguished family of the Wind Clan. From his mother he inherited the facility for making friends that marked him for a diplomatic career. The elder McGillivray was a loyalist during the American Revolution and, along with other supporters of the Crown in America, he lost his property by confiscation at the end of the war. This circumstance shaped the later years of Alexander McGillivray's life, since it caused him to go into the Creek Nation to live with his mother's people. Through the last dozen years of

[22] Angie Debo, *The Road to Disappearance,* 19.

[23] John R. Swanton, *Social Organization and Social Usages of the Indians of the Creek Confederacy,* Bureau of American Ethnology *Forty-second Annual Report,* 97–107.

his career, 1781 to 1793, he was the trusted agent of the Creeks. During that time he had the confidence of the British government and the eager attention of French ministers. He was the employee of a Spanish trading firm that had important governmental support, and he held a commission as brigadier general in the United States Army. His policies, in less able hands after his death, did not result in his people's escape from war against overwhelming odds; but he did, perhaps, save for the Creeks a share of their natural inheritance.

## THE CULTURE OF THE CHEROKEES

The settlement of the Cherokees in southeastern Tennessee, the western part of the Carolinas, and northern Georgia was an event so far back in time as to defy investigation. The tribe, clearly an offshoot of the Iroquoian family of New York, was in the Southeast when De Soto visited the area. Their hunting grounds covered the southern portions of the Appalachian Highlands and extended as far north as the site of Harlan, Kentucky, and Big Stone Gap, Virginia. The modern city of Chattanooga lies in territory that once belonged to the Cherokees, and the Great Smoky Mountains was within their range. In 1654 a band of Cherokees attacked their enemies, the Paumunkeys, at the falls of the James River in Virginia.[24] On the southwest, the Cherokees ranged over the Cumberland Plateau into northern Alabama, where they sometimes came into contact with Creek and Chickasaw hunting parties.

Cherokee mythology is difficult to separate from the Indian versions of stories learned from early Christian ministers. John Priber, a Jesuit who doubled as agent for the French Crown among the Cherokee Indians, visited them in 1736, and was the first known missionary to the tribe. The Moravian Brethren opened a school for Cherokee children in 1801, in return for the privilege of establishing religious services for adults. Baptists and Methodists soon made their appearance among the Cherokees, and the American Board of Foreign Missions sent out from Boston both Congrega-

24 Marion L. Starkey, *The Cherokee Nation*, 4, 5.

tional and Presbyterian ministers to the Cherokee Nation.[25] Baptism as practiced by the Baptist missionaries had a strong appeal to the Cherokees, whose own primitive religious practices included the rite of "going to the river." The Indians also responded to the lively Methodist services, in which each person present was permitted, even urged, to add his voice to the din of noisy supplication. The American Board of Foreign Missions reached many Indians, and had a deep influence upon Cherokee society by the steady pressure of its varied services. Boxes of clothing, prepared in New England and the middle states, were sent to the missions at frequent intervals. Educated men who devoted their lives to missionary effort were assigned to the Cherokees, in many cases bringing to the Indians a new concept of medical practice, along with introduction of the Christian religion.

The Methodist and Baptist missions were established chiefly in the Cherokee Valley Towns. The one Moravian mission, at Spring Place in northwestern Georgia, had a deeper influence than the limited number of its Indian members would suggest. Marion L. Starkey's estimate, in her book on the Cherokee Nation, is that the Moravians "served as a kind of ambassador of the more idealistic aspects of white man's civilization."[26]

First of the missions established by the American Board of Foreign Missions was Brainerd, at the site of present-day Chattanooga, near the northwestern border of the Cherokee Nation. The place had the advantage of being near the Tennessee River and in touch with both of the main transportation routes of the Cherokees—the river and the Federal Pike from Augusta to Nashville. The Indians were disappointed in the site selected for Brainerd, however, since they had expected it to be built nearer the center of the nation.

"Father" Ard Hoyt was put in charge of Brainerd during the first two years, 1817–19, and remained with the Cherokees after he was replaced as head of the mission. Other missionaries sent by the American Board of Foreign Missions included Cyrus Kingsbury, who was soon transferred to the Choctaw tribe; William Chamberlain, who quickly mastered the Cherokee language and

[25] *Ibid.,* 30.
[26] *Ibid.,* 30.

became influential through his ability to talk with fullblood Indians without an interpreter; Elizur Butler, who was lacking in general scholarship, but had the advantage of some knowledge of medicine; and Daniel S. Butrick, a young man recently ordained in Boston, whose greatest asset was his enthusiasm for the work of ministry among the Cherokees. Dr. Samuel Austin Worcester, who came to the Cherokee Nation late in 1825, was perhaps the greatest of all the missionaries to this tribe and one of the most influential men in the entire history of Indian relations.[27]

In addition to Brainerd and the Moravian school at Spring Place, several missions were established by the Baptists and Methodists in the Valley Towns. Carmel Mission, established by the American Board of Foreign Missions, was under the direction of Moody Hall, who fled from his station and took refuge at Brainerd when he was threatened by a drunken Cherokee. Miss Sophia Sawyer taught at Brainerd, New Echota, and Haweis. Unlike many of the maiden ladies who came to teach in the Indian schools, Miss Sophia did not find a husband among the young missionaries—perhaps for the simple reason that she was middle-aged when she arrived in the Cherokee Nation.[28] Like Samuel A. Worcester, Miss Sawyer played a significant part in the conflict between the state of Georgia and the United States over removal of the Cherokee Indians. On one occasion an officer of the Georgia Guard visited her schoolroom at New Echota to warn her against giving instructions to Negroes. Under Cherokee law, the children of slaves could attend school but under Georgia law it was a crime to teach Negroes. Since Miss Sawyer gave instruction, regularly, to a pair of little slave boys, she was subject to a fine of $1,000 to $5,000. The matter was solved by the owner of the slaves, who removed them from school to keep Miss Sophia from getting arrested.[29]

One of the factors in the progress of the Cherokees as a "civil-

[27] *Ibid.*, 89, 92, 134, 137.

[28] Lucy Ames married Dr. Elizur Butler; Elizabeth Proctor married Daniel S. Butrick. When his horse ran away from the Carmel Mission and left Reverend Butrick stranded there, a question of propriety arose, and Miss Proctor welcomed solution of the problem by her marriage to Butrick so that he might not be denied the hospitality of the mission. Delight Sargent married Elias Boudinot after the death of his first wife, Harriet Ruggles Gold. See *Dictionary of American Biography*, II, 478, 479; Starkey, *The Cherokee Nation*, 172, 173.

[29] Starkey, *The Cherokee Nation*, 75–78.

ized tribe" was the work of Sequoyah, or George Guess.[30] Sequoyah was the son of a Cherokee mother and a white father. Many persons have attempted to establish the identity of his father, but no records have been found which afford proof. It was the opinion of Grant Foreman that Nicholas Gist, an officer of the American Revolution and a friend of General George Washington, was Sequoyah's father.[31] People who knew Sequoyah well, in Georgia and in Arkansas, said that he looked like a fullblood Indian. He never attended white men's schools, never learned to read or write in English, could not even speak English. His name, appearing on some of the Cherokee treaties, was signed only by means of a cross-mark. Yet he was the inventor of an alphabet, or syllabary, of eighty-six characters, which became the basis of the printed Cherokee language.

Sequoyah was forced into sedentary occupation by a hunting accident. He worked for many years trying to perfect a system of symbols by which Cherokee basic sounds could be represented. In the early years he could not remember the multitude of symbols that he had used, and after the lapse of several months could not read the messages he had written. His neighbors, regarding the work he was doing unsuitable for a Cherokee, even though he had been crippled by an accident and rendered incapable of outdoor work or hunting, decided to relieve him of his obsession. Aided by his wife, who got him out of the house by trickery, his fellow citizens burned the cabin and all that was in it.[32] Sequoyah merely remarked, "Now I must do it again."

In 1817 he joined a party of Cherokees who were migrating to Arkansas Territory. The journey west gave him a new environment, new neighbors, and perhaps an inspiration to new effort. Within three years he was back in Georgia with his completed work. Not only was he able to remember the simple characters to which he had assigned certain sounds and to read his own messages after laying them aside for many months, but other Cherokees could

[30] Ibid., 77–99; Wardell, A Political History of the Cherokee Nation, 4, 22, 28, 30; George E. Foster, Se-quo-yah, the American Cadmus and Modern Moses; Grant Foreman, Sequoyah; Bureau of American Ethnology Nineteenth Annual Report.

[31] Foreman, Sequoyah, 75; Bureau of American Ethnology Nineteenth Annual Report.

[32] Starkey, The Cherokee Nation, 82, 83.

master the use of his syllabary within a few days. With much difficulty he persuaded the Cherokee Council to accept his work. He read messages from his friends in Arkansas and other passages written in his symbols, but the chiefs remained skeptical. He even recorded the testimony of a case in court and had his six-year-old daughter, who had not been present at the trial, read his record for the chiefs. Even the enlightened John Ross seemed to think that the result had been obtained by trickery.[33]

But after repeated demonstrations his people accepted his invention and made it their own gift to Indian civilization. The *Cherokee Phoenix*, edited by Elias Boudinot, printed material in English and in Cherokee, side by side in such manner that the sentences of one column could be compared readily with those of the other column. Over half of the Cherokees learned to use the Sequoyah alphabet. The illiterate half-blood, George Guess, had become the principal figure in the introduction of his tribe to the possibilities of written language and the printing press.

The principal chief of the Cherokees in 1817, when the tribe divided and a large fraction of it moved west to Arkansas, was Pathkiller. He was the last of the illiterate fullblood chiefs. By the time the missions were established at Brainerd, Carmel, Haweis, and elsewhere in the Cherokee Nation, Pathkiller was a very old man. In spite of his own lack of education, he was strongly in sympathy with the work of the mission schools. Thus, the last of the old fullblood chiefs was a link in the development of a new culture for his people. He visited classes, encouraged the pupils, and supported the work of instruction. Marion L. Starkey gives her estimate of the man in these words: "There was something simple and good, something touching greatness like the virgin timber in the Great Smokies, in the character of Pathkiller."[34]

The second chief, Charles Hicks, was well trained in white schools, was a devout Christian, and was a strong support for the work of mission educators. He regarded the establishment of missions as proof of the good will and intentions of white people. By comparison with Pathkiller, the second chief was optimistic and confident in regard to the future of the Cherokees. John Ross, who

[33] *Ibid.*, 84.
[34] *Ibid.*, 47–51.

was to follow Pathkiller and Charles Hicks as principal chief, was probably the ablest of the three. He was thoroughly trained in the fundamentals of English composition at the school in Kingston, Tennessee, and during his entire life he was a persistent reader. His father owned many books, and John Ross was familiar with a large number of the volumes in this home library. He lived near Brainerd, operated a store and a Tennessee River ferry, lived in a large, well-furnished house, and enjoyed the comforts of a substantial income. When Daniel Butrick first came to Brainerd, Ross was still under thirty but was already president of the National Council, a position of high rank. He was destined to be the most influential man in the Cherokee Nation almost continuously for a period of more than forty years.

Major Ridge was a leader among the Cherokees not so much from official position as from the force of his personality. He was well-to-do, progressive, and determined that his son should receive the advantages of education. The son, John Ridge, attended school at Brainerd and afterward at Cornwall, Connecticut. At Cornwall he married Sarah Northrup, daughter of the school's steward. The prim New England community was shocked at the marriage of an Indian boy to one of their white girls; but the aristocrat, "The Ridge," received his daughter-in-law with a warm Christian spirit of love and toleration. Cornwall was more severely shocked when John Ridge's cousin, Elias Boudinot, married another New England girl, Harriet Gold. As in the case of John Ridge, the marriage was a happy one.

The standing of each of the principal missionaries in the Cherokee Nation, if it could be understood thoroughly, would reveal a great deal concerning the character of Cherokee society. On the basis of well-known facts in the lives of missionary leaders, it is possible to reconstruct some phases of the tribe's progress. The Indians distrusted Moody Hall, because he fled from his post at Carmel in the face of danger from a rough, drunken citizen who threatened him with a knife. The Cherokees asked themselves two questions: Are Christian leaders afraid of ordinary dangers? Shouldn't a minister trust in God and fear no earthly danger?[35] Daniel Butrick, one of the most ardent supporters of Cherokee

[35] *Ibid.*, 68.

rights, in normal times, suffered great loss of prestige when he became conservative, after his marriage to Elizabeth Proctor, and advised the Cherokees to submit to the violence of white intruders supported by the state of Georgia. Obedience to the state, for a missionary, was the only way to avoid taking part in politics; and certainly political activity was not included in the duties of a pastor.

Samuel Austin Worcester gained in stature with the Cherokees when he went to jail for a principle, remaining loyal to his friends the Cherokees and firm in his insistence upon their treaty rights. In their judgment of a man's stature, the Cherokees did not differ greatly from current society in the United States.

# CHAPTER SIX

# The Indian Removal Treaties before 1834

## THE INDIAN QUESTION, 1789–1812

The steady growth of white population in the United States created difficult problems of Indian relations for the early presidents. Conflict between alien races, common the world over in all ages of history, was a major difficulty for Washington, Adams, Jefferson, and Madison, in turn. Cultural differences between North American Indians on one side and people of European descent on the other were many and hard to reconcile.

The white invaders and their descendants settled on individually owned farms and cultivated the soil. With a surplus of food such as the Indians had never seen, the European settlers established a flourishing domestic trade and exported goods to England, the Mediterranean, and the West Indies. Towns sprang up, highways were constructed, the population grew rapidly, and new settlers expanded into regions remote from coasts and rivers. The effect was disastrous from the Indian point of view. Strongly attached to their own manner of living, the natives witnessed the rapid disappearance of game, the clearing of vast acreages of land, the depletion of the plentiful supply of fish in the streams, the complete overthrow of the structure of Indian economy. The native population had no comprehension of the white man's laws concerning private property, particularly real estate.

The potent alcoholic beverages of the invaders, including corn whiskey made in large quantities by frontier settlers, furnished an item of discord. Not only did the Indian brave turn quarrelsome under the influence of alcohol; tribal councils, solemnly deliberating the problems of domestic order, found in the white man's whiskey a grievance and a permanent motive for distrust. Even the mission schools, set up by unselfish Christian ministers for the advancement of the red men, came in for Indian suspicion. Old fashioned Indians, even down to the present century, have sometimes persisted in their lack of confidence in the schooling furnished by white men.

Three possible plans for dealing with the Indian problem were laid before officials of the United States. The three solutions were tried, one after the other but with a large degree of overlapping. Weaknesses of Indian relations usually arose from failure to understand the problem, inability of the many agents, teachers, and minor administrators to see the purposes of broad, general plans, and lack of courage on the part of elected officers to brave public disapproval by giving this minority group adequate protection in their rights.

First of the plans to be tried was the establishment of an extensive separate domain for each tribe, with a treaty providing that the Indians should not be disturbed within the confines of their nation and that their own government should be in effect there. The plan involved many difficulties. Not all of the Indians understood the idea of segregated lands, and many times young warriors returned to hunting grounds assigned by treaties to other tribes or to the public domain of the United States. But the most serious trouble arose from the refusal of white citizens to accept the solemn stipulations of treaties entered into by the government. White farmers in the cotton-producing territories and states crowded around the borders of the Indian nations, looked with envy upon the fertile land within, found excuses to drift across the border, and exerted such pressure as they could to obtain revision of treaty restrictions. In this process of creeping default, the frontier settlers were abetted by states that claimed sovereignty and in effect nullified treaty agreements of the federal government. Georgia, Alabama, and Mississippi, in particular, took a hostile stand against the presence of Indian tribes within their borders. The plantation owners of the fertile lowlands in these states were struggling toward payment of their debts or for the building of great fortunes in land and slaves, and they were not inclined to view with scrupulous concern the treaty rights of backward natives. Small landowners on the frontier and landless citizens had about the same attitude as the plantation owners, unsoftened by educational advantages or intelligent grasp of minority rights.

A second plan for dealing with the Indian problem, and one which found ready acceptance among those who were intent upon expediency, was to remove the Indians west. The advocates of this plan were inclined to ignore the fact that white settlers were filling up the West at an increasing rate and that moving a tribe was at best only gaining time for permanent solution of the Indian's status. Even the humane and tolerant Thomas Jefferson seemed to be thoroughly convinced that moving the Indians into Louisiana Territory would abate their grievances and relieve white citizens from the presence of troublesome neighbors.[1] The weakness in this entire program lay in the bitterness inherent in the uprooting of a people from their homeland, the enormous suffering involved in the process of removal, and the fact that the new homes for the tribes could not, in the nature of things, be a permanent refuge for native culture. The process of crowding the Indians from their homes was to be repeated until the irony of making formal treaties with them finally became apparent to both peoples.

The third possible method of solving the broad problem of Indian relations was to educate the natives for citizenship in the United States. Like the other two, this plan involved great difficulties; but in view of the hope it offered for permanent results, it is regrettable that more attention was not given to it. There was greater immediate profit to be made by white men in moving the Indians out of their eastern lands than there was in furnishing tribesmen a costly schooling, which, as they clearly indicated, they did not want. Many of the Indians, comprehending even less than their white contemporaries the relentless surge of westward settlement, wanted to move beyond the Mississippi to escape the crowding of people who plowed the ground and hauled their goods in great wagons and boats. Except for a few thoughtful leaders, the Indians did not desire education and citizenship.

So the plan of moving the Indians west provided quick profits for influential citizens of the United States, and appealed strongly to Indians who were obsessed with ideas of preserving their own

[1] Jefferson, *Writings of Jefferson*, VIII, 241–49.

way of living. For government officials, this method of dealing with the native population postponed the difficult task of absorbing them into the national citizenship, and met the approval of white men who wanted their land or wanted to sell goods to farmers on the Indian land.

One of the fundamental injustices of Indian removal was denial to the Indians of the unearned increment of their property. Permitted to remain on the land originally assigned to them in treaties with the United States, the red men would have had the advantage of a powerful incentive for accepting the ways of their white brothers; denied the boon of steadily increasing property values, Indian leaders were prone to accept the view that justice was not the aim of United States officials. It is not remarkable that nearly all chief men of the Five Civilized Tribes considered, at one time or another, the possibility of escape from the strong arm of the government by removal into the wilds of the distant West or by crossing the international border into Mexico.

In 1802, Jefferson's secretary of war, General Henry Dearborn, sent James Wilkinson, Benjamin Hawkins, and Andrew Pickens to negotiate with Chief Efa Harjo of the Creeks.[2] Dearborn's immediate object was to obtain cession of the land between the Oconee and the Ocmulgee rivers and an additional tract on the Altamaha. In exchange for their land the Creek chiefs asked for items which seem to show some grasp of cultural values; they wanted weavers, blacksmiths, and goods instead of cash. The agreement was made on that basis, the Creeks receiving $10,000 for payment of their debts to white traders, $5,000 to settle property damages by members of the tribe, two blacksmith shops for a period of three years, distribution of $10,000 worth of goods, and a permanent annuity of $3,000.[3] In 1805 a Creek commission in Washington ceded more land in the Oconee Valley and gave the United States right of way for a narrow road from the Ocmulgee River to the Alabama.

The Choctaws during Jefferson's administration were also yielding to the requests of Secretary Dearborn's agents. A tract of land north of the site of Mobile, another along the Mississippi

[2] *A Compilation of all the Treaties between the United States and the Indian Tribes,* 100.

[3] *Ibid.,* 100, 113.

River near the site of Vicksburg, and a third across the southern part of the nation were ceded to the United States during this period. The Treaty of Fort Adams in 1801 made provision for the beginning of a narrow trail from Natchez to Nashville. This became a much-traveled road known as the Natchez Trace, following generally the route of the fine modern highway of that name.

President Jefferson talked to Cherokee commissioners who visited Washington in 1808 with the proposal that the Lower Town Cherokees should remove to the West, leaving the Upper Town Cherokees in Georgia. To the Upper Town Cherokee chiefs the President said:

"You propose, my children, that your nation shall be divided into two, and that your part, the upper Cherokees, shall be separated from the lower by a fixed boundary, shall be placed under the government of the United States, become citizens thereof, and be ruled by our laws; in fine, to be our brothers instead of our children. My children, I shall rejoice to see the day when the red men, our neighbors, become truly one people with us, enjoying all the rights and privileges we do, and living in peace and plenty as we do, without anyone to make them afraid, to injure their persons or take their property without being punished for it according to fixed laws. But are you prepared for this? Have you the resolution to leave off hunting for your living, to lay off a farm for each family to itself, to live by industry, the men working that farm with their hands, raising stock or learning trades as we do, and the women spinning and weaving clothes for their husbands and children? All that is necessary before our laws can suit you or be of any use to you.

"However, let your people take this matter into consideration. ... On our part I will ask the assistance of our Great Council, the Congress, whose authority is necessary to give validity to these arrangements."[4]

## EFFECTS OF THE WAR OF 1812

Progressive plans concerning the Indians, based on humane considerations and aimed at permanent settlement, were

[4] Dale and Rader, *Readings in Oklahoma History*, 141, 142, 143.

more or less dormant from 1811 to 1816. An agent of President Madison's administration, negotiating with the Creeks in regard to passage of the Coosa River in 1811, found the Indians stubbornly fixed in their purpose of keeping out white influence. Apothle Micco, speaking for the tribe, gave an emphatic negative to the request for the right to use the river as an artery of commerce between Tennessee and the town of Mobile.

"When friends ask for property we must tell him straight words," Apothle Micco declared. "If he asks for the waters of the Coosa or by land my chiefs and warriors will never say yes—I hope it will never be mentioned to us again."[5]

The southern Indians, particularly the Creeks and Seminoles, lost favor with the officials and citizens of the United States because a part of the Indians fought as allies of the British. Tecumseh had become a man of some influence among the Creeks, as well as among the tribes north of the Ohio River. Born in the Tallapoosa country of Alabama, Tecumseh frequently visited the land of his Creek mother, though he lived with his father's kinsmen, the Shawnees, in the upper valley of the Wabash. From 1808 to 1811, Tecumseh was engaged in planning, with his brother, the Prophet, the checking of United States expansion westward. The factors which made Tecumseh's scheme a real threat were his unusual ability as an organizer and the sympathy of the British with his plans. The war waged by Governor William Henry Harrison upon the Miamis, Shawnees, and confederated tribes in 1811 was an introduction to the War of 1812 against the British.[6]

Among the Creeks of Alabama, Tecumseh was regarded a miracle man who could stamp his foot on the ground of the upper Wabash and cause tremors of the earth on the Tallapoosa. He carried with him a quality of dramatic appeal which made him effective as a public speaker and gave him a great advantage in his purpose of organizing an Indian confederacy. According to tradition, the Creek audience which greeted his visit to the Tallapoosa in 1811 numbered five thousand. Among the Choctaws he was not so effective, perhaps because he was not related to the tribe by the

[5] Debo, *The Road to Disappearance*, 75.
[6] Dorothy Burne Goebel and Julius Goebel, Jr., *Generals in the White House*, 101–13.

114

ties of blood and in part because Chief Pushmataha, eloquent and popular, was strongly opposed to the British plans in America. The Choctaw Council heard the visitor, listened to the words of their own chief, and declared against joining the alliance against the United States.

Tecumseh's Creek followers, called Red Sticks because of their belief in the mystic powers of the small red wand which each warrior carried, opened their offensive in Alabama by an attack upon Fort Mims on August 30, 1813. Soldiers and civilians killed in the battle at the fort and the slaughter which followed its fall numbered 367; those who escaped, 18. The people in outlying settlements of the southwest fled to Mobile, and the neighboring states, Tennessee and Georgia, sent military forces against the Red Sticks.

At Talladega Town, Andrew Jackson's army defeated the Creeks, and General Floyd, invading from Georgia, destroyed Artussee and Tallasi. The Red Sticks, under Chief Menawa and William Weatherford, made their final stand at Horseshoe Bend of the Tallapoosa River on March 27, 1814. At that place Jackson's combined force of three thousand white soldiers and Indians attacked the Red Stick army, and when the battle was over the power of the Creek hostiles was broken.[7] Chief Menawa escaped, wounded, and William Weatherford surrendered to General Jackson. According to reports that were commonly believed at the time, Jackson sheltered Weatherford for some weeks at the Hermitage and later permitted him to go back to his people in Alabama. Weatherford was a nephew of Alexander McGillivray, and, like his Scotch forebears, was quite skillful in the conduct of his business affairs. His later years as a planter were prosperous.

William McIntosh, Creek chief, and the great Choctaw leader, Pushmataha, gave their support to the United States and placed their Indian troops under the command of General Jackson. Sequoyah of the Cherokees also served in the American Army, along with many other Indians of the Five Civilized Tribes.

The treaty dictated by General Jackson, after the surrender of the Red Sticks, is an example of loss by the Indians of the un-

[7] A lively account of the Jackson Indian campaigns in Alabama is given in Frederick Austin Ogg, *The Reign of Andrew Jackson*, chap. II.

earned increment of their property.[8] The tribe gave up a tract of land bordered by the Coosa and Tallapoosa rivers, and the western boundary of Georgia. Their compensation, paid only to Creeks who remained loyal to the United States during the war, amounted to $197,417 in goods and land, reserved for those who elected to settle there. Within four decades the land ceded to the United States was sold to white settlers for an aggregate sum of $11,-250,000. Although the treaty began with the words, "Whereas an unprovoked, inhuman, and sanguinary war, waged by the hostile Creeks against the United States, hath been repelled," it should be remembered that the larger part of the tribe fought on the side of the United States. The fact that the tribes have sometimes received adjusted compensation, though it gives evidence of a dawning sense of justice, does not alter the original loss to the Indians, in depriving them of a great incentive to individual ownership and a general acceptance of the white man's culture.

## CHEROKEE AND CHOCTAW REMOVAL TREATIES

The Cherokee Nation in the first decade of the nineteenth century had no formal constitution, but depended upon long established tribal customs and upon the wisdom of elders who sat in their council for preservation of internal order. In 1810 the leaders began to record and preserve the laws and these early statutes contain many examples of sound regulation. The Cherokee population, before the large-scale migrations to the West began, was probably above twenty thousand. The southeastern Indians had long been acquainted with the land that was known as Arkansas Territory and probably a considerable number of Cherokees lived there before the first removal treaty.[9]

Andrew Jackson, with Governor Joseph McMinn of Tennessee and General David Meriwether, negotiated an important treaty

[8] Charles J. Kappler, *Indian Affairs: Laws and Treaties,* II, 107–110. See also Debo, *The Road to Disappearance,* 81, 82.

[9] Marion L. Starkey estimates the population of the Cherokees in the time of De Soto at twenty-five thousand. Starkey, *The Cherokee Nation,* 4.

with the Cherokees in 1817.[10] This agreement was in effect a practical application of the Cherokee proposal to President Jefferson in 1808, and the preamble to the treaty quoted Jefferson as follows:

"The United States, my children, are the friends of both parties, and, as far as can be reasonably asked, they are willing to satisfy the wishes of both. Those who remain may be assured of our patronage, our aid, and good neighborhood. Those who wish to remove, are permitted to send an exploring party to reconnoitre the country on the waters of the Arkansas and White rivers, and the higher up the better, as they will be the longer unapproached by our settlements, which will begin at the mouths of those rivers. The regular districts of the government of St. Louis are already laid off to the St. Francis."

By the terms of the agreement in 1817 the Cherokees ceded approximately one third of their land east of the Mississippi River to the United States, and in return obtained an equal acreage in the White and Arkansas valleys. Cherokee citizens might move to their new home on a voluntary basis and the tribe's annuities were to be divided according to number of emigrants and number who remained in the East, as determined by United States census. White citizens were to be removed from the Arkansas lands of the Cherokees, with the exception of Mrs. P. Lovely, "who is to remain where she is during life." This was an affectionate reference to the wife of the old Cherokee agent, Peter Lovely.

The Cherokee "poor warrior," moving west, was to receive a blanket and a kettle or a beaver trap. He was to be paid for his real property improvements or to receive equal value in the Arkansas land. The United States was to furnish boats, vehicles, and provisions for the journey; and it was further agreed that intruders should be kept out of the Cherokee lands ceded by the treaty "until the same shall be ratified by the President and Senate of the United States, and duly promulgated."[11] This was a clause often repeated and often violated in removal treaties with the Indian tribes.

The treaty of 1817 was signed by Chief John Jolly, Charles Hicks, Katchee of Cowee, John D. Chisholm, Roman Nose, White

[10] Kappler, *Indian Affairs: Laws and Treaties*, II, 140–44.
[11] *Ibid.*, 144, Article 12.

Man Killer, Going Snake, Sleeping Rabbit, Sour Mash, Big Half Breed, Young Davis, Beaver Carrier, and thirty-four other Cherokees of the party that intended to go west. A large part of the signers made a simple cross-mark to indicate their signatures. Besides the three United States commissioners—Jackson, McMinn, and Meriwether—the treaty was signed by several other officials and interpreters as witnesses: Walter Adair, John Spiers, A. McCoy, Captain Isham Randolph, and Return J. Meigs, agent of the Cherokee Nation.

The Choctaws, in a treaty negotiated by John Coffee, John Rhea, and John McKee, for the United States in 1816, ceded their lands east of the Tombigbee River. Chief Moshulatubbee and twelve other Choctaws signed, all but David Folsom indicating their signatures by means of a cross-mark.[12] Four years later, "near Doak's Stand on the Natchez Road," the Choctaws made another cession treaty, General Andrew Jackson and Thomas Hinds representing the United States, and Puckshenubbee (or Apukshunubbee), Pooshawattaha (Pushmataha), and Moshulatubbee, heading a long list of Choctaw chiefs and warriors.[13] Among the witnesses was Andrew J. Donelson, brevet second lieutenant and aid-de-camp to General Jackson. A large area in the southwestern part of the Choctaw Nation was ceded to the United States in exchange for a tract north of the Red River and extending up to the Canadian and Arkansas rivers—the entire southern part of the region that is now Oklahoma, and a considerable area in the southwestern part of present-day Arkansas. As described in the treaty, the land thus assigned to the Choctaws was west of a line running northward from the mouth of the Little River, and it was supposed the area was beyond the western line of settlement in Arkansas Territory. In fact, however, a large number of white settlers had built cabins and were living in the region. The government of the United States agreed to furnish Choctaw emigrants with supplies as they moved west and for one year thereafter and, also, to send them a blacksmith and an agent.

At Washington in 1825 a new treaty was negotiated with the Choctaws to avoid the difficulty that had been encountered with

12 *Ibid.*, 137.
13 *Ibid.*, 191–95.

white settlers in southwestern Arkansas. Some of the leading Choctaw chiefs made the trip to Washington and two lost their lives: Apukshunubbee as the result of an overturned vehicle in Maysville, Kentucky, and Pushmataha after the party reached Washington. John C. Calhoun, secretary of war, signed for the United States. For the Choctaws, Chief Moshulatubbee, Daniel McCurtain, David Folsom, Robert Cole, Talking Warrior, Red Fort, Nitakechi, and J. S. McDonald signed the document. John Pitchlynn was present as interpreter.[14]

The terms of this new agreement provided an eastern limit for the Choctaw lands along the line of the present boundary between Oklahoma and Arkansas; or, as it was described in the treaty, "a line beginning on the Arkansas, one hundred paces east of Fort Smith and running thence due south to the Red River." In consideration of this cession of land by the Choctaws, which in effect was simply pushing them forty miles farther west, the United States agreed to pay them a perpetual annuity of $6,000 and for sixteen years an additional annuity of $6,000.

The diplomacy of United States officials, in dealing with American Indians, almost invariably verged upon bribery. For entertainment of the chiefs on this mission, the bill for lodging amounted to $2,029, for oysters and liquors, $349.75, a suit of clothes for each, $1,134.74, and bar bill, $2,149.50.[15] It is not remarkable that old Pushmataha, accustomed to the simple diet of *pashofa* and *to falla* in Mississippi, was unable to survive the negotiation of the treaty.[16]

The headmen of the tribe received advantages in other items which must have been important financial considerations to them —such as a free hand in the settlement of Choctaw claims amounting to $2,000 and the award of a small income to Robert Cole as the successor of Apukshunubbee.[17] Following the Treaty of Washington, the Choctaws moved west in small bands, as they had been doing for some years. By 1832 only 541 of them were living in the vicinity of Skullyville, fifteen miles above Fort Smith near the

[14] *Ibid.*, 211–14.
[15] Debo, *The Rise and Fall of the Choctaw Republic*, 50.
[16] For a brief treatment of Choctaw foods, see *ibid.*, 12, 13, 112, 114.
[17] Kappler, *Indian Affairs: Laws and Treaties*, II, 213, Articles 8, 10.

Arkansas River, where Captain William McClellan had established the agency.[18] There were several thousand Choctaws scattered through the larger area of their western domain, however, in Arkansas Territory and the Red River Valley farther west, before the principal migration which began in the spring of 1832.[19]

## INDIAN SPRINGS AND ITS AFTERMATH

The Creek chief William McIntosh was the recognized leader of his tribesmen who were allies of the United States during the War of 1812. After the Treaty of Ghent, he commanded a party of Creeks who aided United States troops in their attack on Negro Fort, built for fugitive slaves on the lower Apalachicola River in Spanish territory. William McIntosh also helped to negotiate the first Treaty of Indian Springs in 1821, by which the Creeks ceded approximately 5,000,000 acres of land between the Flint and Chattahoochee rivers for settlement of claims of the state of Georgia against the tribe and for other considerations in the form of annuities to be paid by the United States.[20]

Alarmed by the steady encroachment of United States officials and citizens upon their territory, the Creeks passed a law which made the ceding of land by any chief or group of chiefs without the consent of the full Creek Council a crime punishable by death. William McIntosh was one of the leaders who gave his approval to this severe measure. However, he became convinced, along with many thoughtful Creeks and leading men of other southern tribes, that it was for the best interest of the Indians to move west, where they might have an extension of time, at least, for adjusting themselves to the culture of the alien Europeans.

Near the end of President James Monroe's second term of office, Duncan G. Campbell and James Meriwether were sent to the Creek Nation to try again for a removal treaty. Governor George

---

[18] Grant Foreman, *Indian Removal,* 69.

[19] *Ibid.,* chaps. I–VII give in some detail the story of Choctaw removal.

[20] Kappler, *Indian Affairs: Laws and Treaties,* II, 195–97. Two agreements were made, one with commissioners of the United States and one with commissioners appointed by the governor of Georgia.

M. Troup of Georgia was especially eager to have the Creeks give up their remaining land in that state, including Indian Springs, where General McIntosh had erected substantial buildings, and the Creek village of Buzzard Roost, which had been specifically excluded from the land ceded in 1821. Monroe's commissioners met with the Creeks in council, and after due deliberation the tribal leaders voted to cede no more territory. Then, as head chief of the Cowetans, William McIntosh and a group of his followers met again with Campbell and Meriwether at Indian Springs for the purpose of reconsidering the question of removal. Principal Chief Menawa, aware of the second meeting which convened in February, 1825, sent Opothle Yahola to keep watch on events at Indian Springs and to warn McIntosh and his friends against violation of Creek law.

In spite of the warning, the Cowetan chief accepted terms offered by the officials from Washington and signed a removal treaty on February 12.[21] The terms included the following provision, which had been the principal object of Governor Troup's attention for several years: "The Creek Nation cede to the United States all the lands lying within the boundaries of the State of Georgia." Certain other Creek lands, lying in Alabama, were also included in the area ceded, and the usual stipulations were made concerning division of annuties between the Creeks who elected to remove and those who remained in the East. Also provision was made to exchange land in the Arkansas Valley westward from the mouth of the Canadian, acre for acre, and to pay the emigrant Creeks $400,000 for their real improvements and for the expense and inconvenience of moving. Signing the treaty for the Creeks, in addition to William McIntosh, were Etommee Tustennuggee, Cowetan Tustennuggee, Holahtau (or, Colonel Blue), Artus Micco (or, Roley McIntosh), Chilly McIntosh, Joseph Marshall, Benjamin Marshall, and forty-three other Creeks.[22]

On February 14 an additional agreement with William McIntosh provided that the United States should pay to the Cowetan chief the sum of $25,000 for his establishment at Indian Springs.[23]

21 Ibid., 214.
22 Ibid., 215, 216.
23 Ibid., 216, 217.

This sum, out of proportion to the tribal compensation for improvements, may be the key to McIntosh's readiness to sign the treaty, contrary to Creek law and at great personal risk. Certain it is that Creek resentment against the Cowetan chief flamed high when it became known that his personal advantages in the agreement were attractive. Undoubtedly he received substantial gifts and generous pay for his services, in addition to the high price for Indian Springs, as that was the customary manner of dealing with an Indian leader; and McIntosh had shown himself agreeable to such an approach. Letters between General McIntosh and John Ross of the Cherokees indicate a sharp difference between the two men in regard to the ethics of accepting gifts from government officials. John Ross had a more rigid sense of honesty which prevented his easy acceptance of money or property in exchange for his official influence.

In the Creek Council there was no doubt concerning the guilt of William McIntosh and his associates. The tribal council debated his case and decided upon the death sentence, which, in fact, was the only penalty provided by law. Because of the offender's prominence, Principal Chief Menawa in person led the party of one hundred warriors delegated to carry out the council's decree. William McIntosh, Etommee Tustennuggee, and Sam Hawkins, the son-in-law of McIntosh, were killed. Ben Hawkins, another son-in-law, escaped after being wounded. Chilly McIntosh, the chief's son, and Roley McIntosh, his half brother, escaped and became leaders of the party which was in favor of immediate removal west.

On March 4, 1825, John Quincy Adams became president of the United States. Three days later he proclaimed the Treaty of Indian Springs; but by the time he was ready to send his first message to Congress, in December, he had decided against the legality of the McIntosh agreement.[24] The Creeks were invited to send a commission to Washington, and on April 22, 1826, a new treaty was proclaimed.

James Barbour, secretary of war, signed for the United States, and among the Creek signers were Menawa, Opothle Yahola, John Stidham, Charles Cornell, and Mad Wolf. Two Cherokees who had enjoyed the advantages of schooling, John Ridge and David Vann, served as secretaries for the Creeks, all of whom indicated their

[24] Richardson, ed., *Messages and Papers of the Presidents*, II, 306.

signatures by means of the cross-mark. The agreement at Indian Springs was declared to be null and void and was replaced by new terms more favorable to the Indians, in many respects, than the McIntosh treaty. The Creeks ceded their land in Georgia, but not all of it. For this limited cession the tribe received $217,600 in cash and a perpetual annuity of $20,000.[25] In a supplementary article so worded, it was thought, as to provide for cession of all the remaining Creek lands in Georgia, the United States agreed to pay $30,000 cash in addition to the amount provided in Article 3 of the original treaty.[26] Payment for property improvements given up by the Creek tribe was also provided, and the sum of $100,000 was set aside for the payment of those followers of General McIntosh who desired to remove west of the Mississippi.

The boundary specified by the new treaty proved to be a complicated problem, however, and there was still Creek land in Georgia after the new lines were run. Thomas L. McKenny for the United States made a further agreement with the tribe in 1827, providing the cession of "all the remaining lands now owned or claimed by the Creek Nation, not heretofore ceded, and which, on actual survey, may be found to lie within the chartered limits of the State of Georgia."[27] As compensation for this final cession of lands covered by the false Treaty of Indian Springs, the Creeks were to receive $27,491 in cash and additional specified sums for educational and other immediate needs, as follows: $5,000 to send Creek children to R. M. Johnson's Choctaw Academy in Kentucky; $1,000 for Withington Academy and $1,000 for Asbury Mission; $2,000 for the erection of mills, $1,000 for cards and wheels (for spinning); and $5,000 for blankets and other goods.

In February, 1828, the first party of the McIntosh immigrants, 780 in number, arrived at Three Forks on the Arkansas River in the steamboat *Fidelity*.[28] Before the end of the year five hundred more came, and by 1830 over two thousand Creeks had settled on the Verdigris. A large percentage of the McIntosh Creeks were of mixed blood, and a considerable number brought slaves with them

[25] Kappler, *Indian Affairs: Laws and Treaties,* II, 264, 265.
[26] *Ibid.,* 267, 268.
[27] *Ibid.,* 284, 285.
[28] Debo, *The Road to Disappearance,* 95.

to the new land. However, the majority of these immigrants were classed by the government agents as "poor warriors."

## THE CHEROKEE TREATY OF 1828

In the White River Valley, as in southwestern Arkansas, the white settlers on Indian land proved hard to remove. Pressure of white farmers for the recovery of Cherokee land began almost with the removal of the first band of Indians to Arkansas Territory and continued until a new treaty was negotiated. The Cherokees in the West had also the difficulty of dealing with the Osages, bands of young hunters who were accustomed to ranging over the Arkansas and White River area, and could see no necessity of changing their habits. The young men of the Osages regarded the Cherokees as intruders.

In 1828, President John Quincy Adams sought to relieve the difficulties of the "Cherokee Nation of Indians, West of the Mississippi," by removing them to an area farther west of that river. The chiefs and head men were invited to come to the national capital and discuss with Secretary James Barbour the terms by which a more suitable region might be occupied. The resulting treaty was one of the less reprehensible steps in the history of Indian relations.[29]

The words of the preamble had in them a note of sympathetic interest for the native Americans. "Whereas, it being the anxious desire of the Government of the United States to secure to the Cherokee Nation of Indians, as well those now living within the limits of the Territory of Arkansas, as those of their friends and brothers who reside in States East of the Mississippi, and who may wish to join their brothers of the West, a permanent home, and which shall, under the most solemn guarantee of the United States, be and remain theirs forever–a home that shall never, in all future time, be embarrassed by having extended around it the lines, or placed over it the jurisdiction of a Territory or State, nor be pressed upon by the extension, in any way, of any of the limits of any exist-

[29] Kappler, *Indian Affairs: Laws and Treaties*, II, 288–92.

ing Territory or State; and Whereas, the present location of the Cherokees in Arkansas being unfavorable to their present repose, and tending, as the past demonstrates, to their future degradation and misery; and the Cherokees being anxious to avoid such consequences, and yet not questioning their right to their lands in Arkansas, as secured to them by Treaty, and resting also upon the pledges given them by the President of the United States and the Secretary of War, . . . in regard to the outlet to the West, . . . still being anxious to secure a permanent home, and to free themselves and their posterity, from an embarrassing connection with the Territory of Arkansas, and guard themselves from such connections in the future; and, Whereas, it being important, not to the Cherokees only, but also to the Choctaws, and in regard also to the question which may be agitated in the future respecting the location of the latter, as well as the former, within the limits of the Territory or State of Arkansas, as the case may be, and their removal therefrom; and to avoid the cost which may attend negotiations to rid the Territory or State of Arkansas . . . of either, or both of those tribes, the parties hereto do hereby conclude the following Articles: . . ."

Here was an obvious bid to the eastern Cherokees to join their western relatives and a repetition of the assurance, in the face of much contradictory evidence, that the Cherokees should have a tribal home of their own, forever.

The western boundary of Arkansas Territory was defined, based upon the Choctaw line of 1825. It will be recalled that the boundary between the Choctaw Nation and the Territory of Arkansas began at a point on the Arkansas River one hundred paces east of Fort Smith, and extended due south to the Red River. From the northern limit of this line, the boundary of Arkansas was to be surveyed in a "direct line to the South West corner of Missouri." The eastern line of the new Cherokee Nation followed the boundary of Arkansas Territory to the southwest corner of Missouri; thence along the western boundary of Missouri to the point where it crossed the Neosho River. West of this line, the Cherokee lands were to embrace seven million acres. In addition to the area thus described, the tribe was guaranteed a perpetual westward outlet to the limits of the United States sovereignty "and a free and unmolested use of all the Country lying West of the Western boundary of the above described limits."

The United States agreed to run the lines of the land ceded to the Cherokees without delay, and to remove all white persons living west of the Arkansas boundary. It was further agreed that all improvements on the Cherokee lands in Arkansas should be appraised and paid for by the United States, and that the property connected with the agency should be sold and the proceeds applied to erection of a grist mill and a saw mill in the new Cherokee Nation.

For loss in reduced value of land farther west, and for the inconvenience of moving, the United States agreed to pay the Cherokee Nation of the West the sum of $50,000. This was a start toward recognition of the important principle that the Indians, in moving away from settled territory, were giving up more than the value of their buildings, fences, and other improvements. For loss and inconvenience in moving livestock, the Cherokees were to receive an annuity of $2,000 for three years; for spoliations committed upon them, $8,760; for imprisonment of Thomas Graves on a false criminal charge, $1,200; and for the use of George Guess, $500, for the "great benefits he has conferred on the Cherokee people, in the beneficial results they are now experiencing from the use of the Alphabet discovered by him." The United States agreed further to spend $1,000 for a printing press and types to be assigned to the Cherokees, and to grant aid for the education of Cherokee children in the sum of $2,000 per year for a period of ten years.[30]

For laying off lands, when the Cherokees "may wish to own them individually," the United States offered the services of a surveyor. Also, the government was ready to furnish the tribe with "a set of plain laws, suited to their condition," at any time.

On their part, the Cherokees agreed to cede their Arkansas lands to the United States and to remove within a period of fourteen months to their new home. The United States offered definite inducements to Cherokees in the eastern states who would migrate to the western territory. To each head of a family at the time of his enrollment for emigration, the government would give a good rifle, a blanket, a kettle, and five pounds of tobacco. For each member of his family, a blanket. Real improvements on property in the

[30] *Ibid.*, II, 289, 290.

126

East would be appraised and compensation made to the owner. Cost of migration and subsistence for one year after arrival in the new Cherokee Nation were guaranteed. Families of five, emigrating from the state of Georgia, were guaranteed an additional gift of fifty dollars, payments for larger or smaller families to be made in proportion to this sum. James Barbour, secretary of war, signed the treaty for the United States; for the Cherokees, Chief Black Fox. Also signing for the tribe, in characters invented by Sequoyah, were the inventor himself and three other Cherokees.

## Conditions in the Region West of Arkansas, 1800–1830

The region between the Red River and the 37th parallel, west of the settled area in Arkansas Territory, gradually became recognized as the Indian lands. The uncertainty concerning national limits of the United States on the southwest was removed by the Adams-Onís Treaty in 1819. By the terms of that agreement, Florida was purchased from Spain and the international boundary was fixed, in part along lines that later were to become boundaries of Oklahoma. The eastern limits of the Indian Territory were established by the Choctaw Treaty at Washington in 1825, and the Cherokee Treaty, also at Washington in 1828, as noted above.

During President Monroe's term of office, from 1817 to 1825, the annual appropriation of $10,000 by Congress for Indian schools was turned over to the missions that had been established in the Indian nations. Dwight Mission began work among the Cherokees of Arkansas in 1820 and was removed to the new Cherokee Nation in 1829. At the settlement of Nicksville on Sallisaw Creek the missionaries purchased some log buildings from Colonel Walter Webber, and by the spring of 1830 were ready to hold classes. A two-storied dining room and kitchen, 24 by 54 feet, was built of hewn logs. As years passed, other buildings were added: a two-storied dormitory for boys, log residences—two rooms with connecting passageway—and outbuildings.[31] The school had enough room for

[31] Grant Foreman, *The Five Civilized Tribes*, 356, 357.

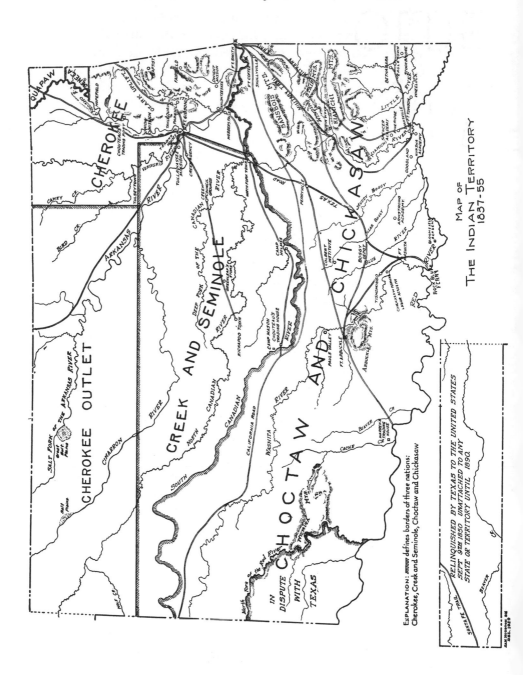

MAP OF
THE INDIAN TERRITORY
1837-55

EXPLANATION: ⁓⁓⁓ defines borders of three nations:
Cherokee, Creek and Seminole, Choctaw and Chickasaw

RELINQUISHED BY TEXAS TO THE UNITED STATES
SEPT 9TH 1850. UNATTACHED TO ANY
STATE OR TERRITORY UNTIL 1890.

65 pupils, and it quickly became a powerful influence in the lives of the Cherokees.

The Choctaws were gradually forming settlements in the land assigned to them and in the neighboring states—Arkansas, Louisiana, and Texas. They were widely scattered, and their exact number is not known; but probably there were fifteen hundred living west of the Mississippi.

Creek immigrants, settling more compactly in the vicinity of Three Forks and spreading out along the valleys of the Arkansas and Verdigris, were more numerous; and some of the families owned large numbers of Negro slaves. Benjamin Marshall, Roley McIntosh, Jane Hawkins—daughter of William McIntosh and widow of Sam Hawkins—Benjamin Perryman, and many other mixed-blooded Creeks conducted large farming operations almost from the first. They sold corn to the garrison at Fort Gibson and to the contractors who furnished grain for Indian immigrants. Some of the large-plantation owners built comfortable houses of hewn logs, two-storied structures with wide verandas and rooms fitted with solid pieces of good furniture. Actually, these great holdings of land were not owned individually by the men who farmed them, with slave labor; they were tribal holdings, and their occupation for use as cultivated, fenced fields reduced the range for the tribe at large. There was poverty among the followers of McIntosh, perhaps worse than the simple absence of wealth in other bands of the Creek people, where most of the fullblood Indians made no effort to accumulate goods. Drunkenness was a common source of disorder, degradation, and crime in the Verdigris and Arkansas River communities.[32]

Formal education made little progress among the Creeks in the new land during the first years. The Indians were suspicious of white men, and missionary teachers were handicapped by the inability of most Creeks to understand English. Some of the teachers were able to read Latin and Greek, but seldom were they trained well enough in any one of the Indian languages to make themselves understood. The preachers ordinarily depended upon an interpreter to convey their meanings to an Indian audience. John Davis, a Creek youth who became interested in missionary work, came to

[32] Debo, *The Road to Disappearance*, 96, 97, 110, 111.

the McIntosh settlement on the Verdigris in 1829. He entered Union Mission in 1830 and became a well-known interpreter for ministers who preached to Creek congregations. His example was followed by other students at Union and at Asbury Mission, which was built for the Creeks near North Fork Town.[33]

The Cherokees of Arkansas were the most numerous of the Indian bands transplanted in the West before 1830. Estimates of their number vary widely. Grant Foreman referred to the Arkansas migration as a movement of "more than two thousand" Cherokees.[34] This estimate may be low. At the time of their removal to the Indian Territory, they numbered more than 5,000, and in 1834 were reported at 5,800.[35] The Treaty of 1828, in which the United States offered new inducements to removal, had resulted in some additional migration.

Like their eastern kinsmen, the Cherokees in the West made rapid progress in government. While the tribe was in Arkansas, in 1820, a light-horse police force was provided in a written law instead of a verbal enactment, according to their older custom. Four years before the tribe migrated from Arkansas, their land there was divided into four districts and a general council was established. John Jolly, principal chief, approved laws concerning the organization of the government, regulation of matrimony, relations between white persons and Cherokee citizens, crimes, and various other subjects.[36]

The region west of Arkansas which became the recognized land of the Indian was crossed by many travelers after Texas was thrown open to settlement by citizens of the United States. Liberal land grants by the Mexican government, after 1821, brought about a steady movement of American farmers of Anglo-Saxon and other northern European extraction. The route followed through the Indian Territory came to be known as the Texas Road. This deeply marked trail, from the upper waters of the Neosho River, crossing the Arkansas at Three Forks near the site of present-day Muskogee and extending in a southwestern direction to the forks of the Cana-

[33] *Ibid.*, 116.

[34] Foreman, *The Five Civilized Tribes*, 281.

[35] Wardell, *A Political History of the Cherokee Nation*, 6 (from Commissioner of Indian Affairs, *Annual Report*, 1836, p. 402).

[36] *Ibid.*, 7.

dian, and on to the Red River just east of the Washita, saw a stream of travel that steadily increased with the years. Sometimes white settlers, bound for Spanish Texas, stopped to rest in a favorable location or paused during the illness of some member of their party, perhaps to bury the person after his illness. Some of these people built cabins and remained. Thomas Nuttall found many such settlers on the Kiamichi and the Red River in 1819, and other early explorers in the Indian Territory had the same experience. The number of immigrants to Texas steadily increased, and the problem of white settlers on Indian lands was a permanent difficulty in the removal of the Five Civilized Tribes. Every migration of an Indian tribe was accompanied by the necessity of removing squatters from the land assigned to the tribe. Often the settlers returned after they were driven out, and in some instances they found means of making themselves permanent inhabitants, by intermarriage with the Indians or otherwise.

In 1828 the Choctaws and Chickasaws were interested in exploring the West for the purpose of finding a suitable tribal home. On numerous occasions the southeastern Indians sent out parties for a similar purpose, but the exploration of 1828 was significant because of the persons who made up the expedition and the influence of their findings. The party of forty-two met at St. Louis and proceeded through Missouri and southeastern Kansas into the Indian Territory. Leader of the Choctaws was Peter Pitchlynn, who served his tribe in many important posts during his long and active career, becoming principal chief in 1864. The head man of the Chickasaw delegation was Levi Colbert. Four Creeks joined the party, and in addition there were guides, a surgeon, several army officers, and an interpreter. Isaac McCoy, famous for his work in the Baptist missions, accompanied the party.

In November, the Pitchlynn-Colbert party reached Three Forks on the Arkansas. They were well received by the McIntosh Creeks, who sent back a message to the Alabama members of the tribe, inviting them to come west. The explorers left Three Forks and moved southward along the Texas Road to the site of North Fork Town, where they added the meat of two buffaloes to their food supply. The general impression conveyed by the commissioners in their reports was that the Indian Territory would not be a suitable place for tribal settlement. Their negative comments were used in many a debate over the subject of western removal, and no doubt the attitude of these well-known tribal leaders delayed the westward migration of the Indians, in some instances. Perhaps the effects of the reports would have been greater if the pressure for Indian removal had not been so intense.

## ANDREW JACKSON AND THE NEW INDIAN POLICY

From the earliest days of the Republic until 1829, the policy of the United States in regard to its native inhabitants was a mixture of leniency and firmness and, it must be added, of wisdom and folly. The forces which made Indian affairs difficult were present from the start: two stages of human culture, vastly different and in many particulars in conflict with each other, were placed side by side in the same land. Humane impulses led to treaties with the Indians which were inspired by statesmen's concept of justice; the greed of men struggling for material advancement brought violations of the treaties. But on the higher levels of governmental decisions, at least, there were many examples of moderation, recognition of human rights, deference to the Indian's desire for independence, sympathy toward the Indian's yearning for liberty. It cannot be doubted that Thomas Jefferson thought of Indian problems chiefly as questions of welfare for the red man. The purpose of John Quincy Adams to see that full justice was done with respect to the Creeks is clear in his reopening of the Indian Springs affair, and his sincere interest in the western Cherokees is to be found in the treaty provisions of 1828.

After the War of 1812, the westward movement of white settlers increased. One state with most of its territory west of the Mississippi River, the state of Louisiana, was admitted to the Union in 1812. After the Treaty of Ghent at the end of 1814, western states were admitted in a steady procession: Indiana in 1816, Mississippi the following year, Illinois in 1818, and Alabama before the end of 1819. By that time, Missouri, west of the Mississippi, was ready for statehood and was admitted with Maine in 1821,

132

after acrimonious debate over the question of slaves in the West. Fifteen years were to pass before another pair of states, one in the South and one in the North, were ready for admission. Arkansas became a state in 1836; Michigan, in 1837.

The pressure of white population against the native tribes increased with the volume of western settlement until it was impossible for men elected to public office to take an unprejudiced view of the Indian problem. The election of Andrew Jackson to the presidency in 1828 brought a man into the chief executive office who grew to maturity in an atmosphere of hostility to the Indian. Isolated western settlers were sometimes in a position to fear for their lives because of savage native warriors, and Jackson himself had been among groups of white persons who were in danger of extermination. He had also commanded troops in the Indian wars when the natives had counterbalanced their weakness in numbers by alliance with a powerful, wealthy nation, Great Britain.

The attitude of President Jackson (1829–37) toward the Indian may be summed up briefly. The tribes, organized as governmental units, would have to move west beyond the Mississippi where advancing settlements would not, for a time, be disturbed by their activities and where white men would not interfere with them. The individual Indian had a choice: he could conform to the ways of the white men and remain in the vicinity of his homeland; or, he could go west with his tribe and live as he pleased. Jackson had no broad understanding of the Indian's difficult position, no scruples in regard to the letter of old Indian treaties, no concern for the ethical factors involved in making new ones. He was not so much concerned with the present education or future happiness and development of the Indian as he was with the immediate political contests of Democrats and Whigs. He was not lacking in humane sympathy with any Indian whom he could understand. As a hard, determined fighter, he understood William Weatherford and liked him. Wounded Red Stick prisoners found General Jackson a generous victor. But the influence of Jackson as president retarded the establishment of satisfactory relations with the native tribes of North America by many years. He placed the emphasis upon political expediency rather than permanent solution of the difficult problem.

Events that brought the problem of Indian relations to a climax moved rapidly after Jackson became President. The Cherokee Nation had elected a convention in 1827 for the purpose of making a national constitution. The instrument was written, and in a popular referendum the voters accepted it. The state of Georgia retaliated against this so-called assumption of authority in 1829 by extending her laws over the Cherokee lands and declaring all Indian regulations null and void. In effect, the new government of the Cherokee Nation was abolished by action of the state of Georgia. The president of the United States was in full accord with the action of the state which was a thorough repudiation of federal authority as provided in the Constitution.[37] The United States had been making treaties with the Indian tribes since the period of the American Revolution and the Confederation which followed. Washington, John Adams, and all succeeding presidents had made treaties with the Indian tribes under authority of the Constitution. The contention of Georgia, that the Cherokees had attempted to erect a state within a state, contrary to the federal Constitution, was a mere excuse for exercising a selfish, unjust, and unlawful power—the seizure of the Cherokee property.

The Confederation Congress of the United States entered into a treaty with the Cherokees in November, 1785, by which the Indians acknowledged themselves to be under the protection of the United States and the Congress agreed to punish crimes against the Indians.[38] In 1791, President Washington made a treaty with the Cherokee Nation in which the Cherokee boundary was defined and the following provision was included: "If any citizen of the United States or other person not being an Indian, shall settle on any part of the Cherokees' lands, such person shall forfeit the protection of the United States, and the Cherokees may punish him or not, as they please."[39] Other treaties made with the Cherokees in the administrations of John Adams, Thomas Jefferson,

[37] Article I, Sec. 8, "Congress shall have power . . . to regulate commerce . . . among the several states and with the Indian Tribes." Article II, Sec. 2, "The President shall have power, by and with the consent of the Senate, to make Treaties." Article IV, Sec. 3, "The Congress shall have power to . . . make all needful rules and regulations respecting the territory or other property belonging to the United States."

[38] Kappler, *Indian Affairs: Laws and Treaties*, II, 8–11.

[39] *Ibid.*, 30, Article VIII.

James Madison, James Monroe, and John Quincy Adams, with the approval of the Senate and the co-operation of Congress, indicate that the policy of the United States was recognition of tribal autonomy, under the protection of the federal government. President Jackson denied to the Cherokees the protection which he was bound by all legal and moral considerations to give them.

Mississippi and Alabama also abolished the Indian governments within their borders, and state officers neglected to protect the Indians against violence and all forms of fraud. In 1830, Congress passed the Indian Removal Act, which was effective support for President Jackson's position. The region for settlement of the tribes was not designated, but for the five great tribes of the Southeast, the region beyond the Territory of Arkansas was generally understood to be the future home. Indian hunters were already acquainted with the area, the climate was similar to their homeland, crops of Georgia and Mississippi could readily be raised in the land directly west of them, even the topography of the western area was similar to the tribal lands of the Five Civilized Tribes.

In 1830, Secretary of War John Eaton, a Tennessee man who was much interested in removal of the Indians from his own state, sent James Carroll and John Coffee into the Choctaw Nation with instructions to hurry the process of removal. Chief Greenwood LeFlore of the Choctaws had become convinced that the westward migration of his people was necessary. His influence was strong in the tribe, and he had the support of some well-known missionaries who also thought that removal was inevitable. In a council at Dancing Rabbit Creek, September 18 to 28, 1830, terms of the most important Choctaw removal treaty were agreed upon by Secretary John Eaton and John Coffee, for the United States, and by Greenwood LeFlore, Moshulatubbee, and Nitakechi, for their tribe.[40]

All the Choctaw land east of the Mississippi River was ceded to the United States. It was agreed that the Choctaws should have exclusive jurisdiction over their western lands, forever. The territory granted to the tribe extended west from the Arkansas boundary to the western limits of the United States—at that time the 100th meridian. The southern limit was the Red River and the

[40] Ibid., 310–17.

northern, the Arkansas and Canadian rivers. A grant of $10,000 for a council house and school houses, $50,000 to use for the employment of three teachers over a period of twenty years, three blacksmiths, and the customary individual gifts of blankets, axes, hoes, and plows, were made by the United States. For Choctaws who removed to their new home, expenses of transportation were guaranteed and subsistence for one year after arrival. For those who elected to stay in Mississippi, individual allotments of land and United States citizenship would be given to replace their tribal citizenship.

The Choctaws were allowed three years for disposing of personal belongings that could not be readily carried along and for arranging other personal affairs before migration. The treaty was ratified by the United States Senate and proclaimed by President Jackson on February 24, 1831.[41] Months before that date, however, anarchy had broken out in the Choctaw country, brought about by general confusion among the Indians in regard to removal, conflict among the Choctaw leaders, and invasion of white settlers.[42] A party of Indians consisting of two district chiefs and other leading men of the tribe journeyed out to Indian Territory to explore the new country. Other independent parties explored the area, one of them under the leadership of George W. Harkins and Robert Folsom. Their report was favorable and enthusiastic. Little River, Clear Creek, Gates Creek, and the Kiamichi were all praised for their natural beauty, fine springs, fertile valleys, and stock range. In regard to the Kiamichi the report declared: "This stream will afford fine navigation for boats; it is something like 80 yards wide. There is excellent prairies to be found on the Kiamissa, and salt springs in abundance; the timber is very good, and excellent stock range and plenty of game. The Kiamissa will afford fine settlement. The game is plenty on this stream, such as bear, deer, and turkeys, and on the west side . . . 15 or 20 miles there is buffaloe to be seen in great numbers."[43]

The official Choctaw exploring party, about twenty in number, conducted by George S. Gaines and accompanied by Nitakechi

41 *Ibid.*, 310.
42 Foreman, *Indian Removal*, 29, 30, 31.
43 *Ibid.*, 32.

and Moshulatubbee, district chiefs, met Harkins and Folsom returning, near Fort Smith on the Arkansas. At that point on November 28, Gaines issued winter clothing, a blanket, a rifle, and ammunition to each member of his party. General Arbuckle sent Lieutenant J. L. Dawson from Fort Gibson with an escort of twelve horsemen and an army surgeon, J. W. Baylor, to ride with the explorers. The party followed the Arkansas and Canadian rivers. South of Fort Gibson they were joined by a Chickasaw exploring group, led by Agent Benjamin Reynolds and by Levi Colbert.

This combined party of explorers and their escort numbered about sixty men. At one point on the Blue River, a larger band of western Indians seemed to be threatening attack, and the camp was in a state of watchfulness during one night. But no attack was made, and the party moved on next morning toward Red River. This party's report, like that of Harkins and Folsom, was quite favorable to this land of clear streams, wooded hills, and valleys as a future home for the Choctaws. Levi Colbert, a Chickasaw, apparently felt some reluctance about entering into any union with Greenwood LeFlore, and hesitated also to accept an assignment of territory where there would be danger from the wild tribes of the Plains. A region with abundant game, including buffaloes, bears, deer, turkeys, and many kinds of small game, besides large droves of wild horses, could not fail to please the Indians. There is no little contrast between the optimistic reports after the Treaty of Dancing Rabbit Creek, by which the Indians were committed to removal, and the Colbert-Pitchlynn report, two years before the treaty. Moshulatubbee, Nitakechi, Harkins, and other Indian leaders had nothing but praise for the clear streams, fertile valleys, excellent timber, and plentiful pasturage of the Kiamichi country.[44]

Many of the Choctaws, harassed by the crowding of white settlers into their country, hastily organized emigrant trains and started for the West. One of these early expeditions was accompanied by Reverend Alexander Talley, who left a vivid account of Choctaw suffering on the journey that was undertaken in the winter of 1830–31. The people who made up the party were poorly prepared for the journey, and Talley himself, from his meager missionary funds, helped to finance the migration.

[44] *Ibid.*, 36, 37.

State officers in Mississippi neglected to keep order in the Choctaw country, the Indian government had been abolished, and conditions grew steadily worse. Sale of whiskey to the Indians was a brisk and profitable business, and a large part of the Choctaw population became completely demoralized. Migration continued through 1831, 1832, and 1833. In the winter of 1831–32 there was a blizzard, and the suffering of those who attempted the journey during the cold weather, scantily clad and without sufficient shelter in their camps, was indescribable. During the following summer, cholera broke out among the bands moving west, and again the mortality was high.

Large numbers of the Choctaws gathered at Vicksburg and traveled by steamer up to the Arkansas, thence up that stream to Little Rock, where they landed. The journey was overland from Little Rock to the southeastern section of the Choctaw Nation. Some of the steamers that departed from Vicksburg with Choctaw passengers traveled down to the mouth of Red River, up to the Ouachita, and thence to Ecore à Fabri on the banks of that stream. The Great Raft in the Red River prevented steamboat travel directly up to the mouth of the Kiamichi, which was the goal of many Choctaw Indians. From their point of landing on the Ouachita the route was overland, 160 miles to Fort Towson.

Peter P. Pitchlynn, selected by Chief Moshulatubbe to be his successor, conducted the Indians of his district to the new country. Their route was by way of Memphis; but when they had marched to that town, they found the roads of Arkansas impassable because of heavy rains. The steamer *Brandywine* was engaged to take a party of them down the Mississippi to the White River, and up that stream to Arkansas Post. From that point, after another march and a long wait in camp, the band was crowded on board the steamer *Reindeer* and on February 20, 1832, arrived at Fort Smith. Thus, the routes and methods of travel for the Choctaws were numerous but the expeditions had one feature in common. The Indian families, many of them having all ages represented from infancy to senility, suffered incredible hardships.

Stations for issuing rations were established in various parts of the new Choctaw Nation: at Old Miller Court House, on the Red River thirty miles southeast of Fort Towson; at a point on

Mountain Fork near Eagletown; and at another point near Fort Towson. Supplies were issued also at Fort Smith. Unfortunately, most of the merchants there sold whiskey to the Indians, and many of the agents were engaged in the illegal trade.[45]

By February, 1832, six thousand of the Mississippi Choctaws had enrolled for emigration and actually removed, on authority of the government at Washington. An undetermined number had started the journey west on their own initiative. On November 23, 1833, the three years allowed for removal had expired; so the agents and other people employed especially for Choctaw removal were discharged. At that time about 7,000 of the original Choctaws were still in Mississippi.[46] Many of the Indians who remained and attempted to adjust themselves to conditions of United States citizeship in their old homes were quickly reduced to poverty and abject misery. There were many later Choctaw removals—1,280 in the year 1845, over 1,600 in 1847, and other bands at later dates. After allotment in severalty was begun in the Indian Territory by the Dawes Commission in 1893, 1,445 more Choctaws came west.[47] A considerable number of the tribe are still residents of Mississippi.

Two years after the Treaty of Dancing Rabbit Creek was signed, the neighbors of the Choctaws on the east, the Creeks of Alabama, yielded to official pressure and ceded the remaining part of their eastern lands to the United States. The Creek Treaty was made at Washington with Lewis Cass, secretary of war, representing the United States and Opothle Yahola the Creeks. The treaty was signed on March 24, 1832.[48] The individuals of the tribe who did not desire to move were given allotments in severalty: 320 acres for each head of a family, 640 acres each for ninety chiefs, and special allotments for Ben Marshall on the Chatahoochee River, for Joseph Bruner, a colored interpreter, and a few other persons who had valuable improvements on their land. Twenty sections were reserved in Alabama for Creek orphans, a grant of $100,000 was made for the payment of inflated claims against the Creeks by their creditors, with any surplus to be devoted to relief of the in-

45 *Ibid.*, 69.
46 23 Cong., 1 sess., *Sen. Doc. 512*, Vol. III, 149, 581; Foreman, *Indian Removal*, 102.
47 Foreman, *Indian Removal*, 104.
48 Kappler, *Indian Affairs: Laws and Treaties*, II, 341–43.

139

digent, an annuity of $12,000 for five years and $10,000 for a term of fifteen years, and $16,000 to pay the expenses of the Creek delegation in Washington.

Creek warriors who elected to remove with their tribe to the West were to receive expenses on the journey, subsistence for one year after arrival, a rifle, moulds, wiper, and ammunition. Each family was given a blanket. Also, the emigrants were to receive an educational grant of $3,000 per year for twenty years and support for one blacksmith (or two, if two thirds of the tribe should emigrate) for a period of twenty years. The land "solemnly guaranteed to the Creek Indians" by this treaty was in the same general area as that granted to the McIntosh Creeks. The boundaries of the new nation in the West were not defined accurately until February 14, 1833, when another treaty was signed at Fort Gibson, the members of the Montfort Stokes Commission signing for the United States and Roley McIntosh for the Creeks.[49] The region therein described was between the Choctaw Nation on the south and the Cherokee Outlet on the north, extending westward to the limits of the United States.

The eastern Creeks in 1832 numbered 22,694, of whom 902 were Negro slaves. The first band of emigrants after the treaty started west in December, 1834, and their suffering from exposure and hunger on the overland journey across Arkansas was a sad and terrible chapter in the history of Indian relations.[50] The ordeal of removal was complicated by an uprising against white invasion of Creek lands in Alabama, which was put down by United States troops supported by Creek regiments under Opothle Yahola. Afterward, 2,495 of the hostiles were brought west by the use of military force. Some of the Creeks found refuge in Texas, a few settled permanently among the Cherokees, a few among the Chickasaws, and some were reduced to slavery in Alabama. No tribe suffered more in removal than the Creeks. The decline of population, 1830 to 1860, was over 40 per cent.[51]

[49] Debo, *The Road to Disappearance,* 99, 103.

[50] Foreman, *Indian Removal,* 107–90.

[51] The best general treatment of the Creek Indians is *The Road to Disappearance,* by Angie Debo. *Tulsa: From Creek Town to Oil Capital,* by the same author, has additional material on the Creeks.

# CHAPTER SEVEN

# The Stokes Commission and the Later Removals

## THE MONTFORT STOKES COMMISSION

During his fourth year in office, President Andrew Jackson made a constructive move in the direction of improving United States relations with the Indians. On July 14, 1832, he appointed a special commission to report on conditions in the region that is now the state of Oklahoma. Chairman of the commission of three was Governor Montfort Stokes of North Carolina.[1] The other members were Henry L. Ellsworth, of Connecticut, and Reverend John F. Schermerhorn, of New York. Stokes was seventy years of age and had long been interested in the complex problem of Indian affairs. His work as a government representative in the Indian service was to occupy the last ten years of his life—perhaps the most important period of his busy career.

As related above in Chapter IV, Commissioner Ellsworth and Washington Irving arrived at Fort Gibson on October 8, 1832, and proceeded with Charles J. Latrobe, Pierre Beatte, Tonish, and others, to join Captain Bean's rangers for a tour through the Arkansas, Cimarron, and Canadian valleys. In many respects the plains of central Oklahoma were as they had been in 1541, when Castañeda and Jaramillo described the wanderings of Francisco Vásquez de Coronado. Possibly the buffaloes were not so plentiful at the later date, and certainly the herds of wild horses sighted by Commissioner Ellsworth and his party were not present on the Plains in the days of Coronado. Perhaps the Indians were somewhat less wary in meeting Coronado's men than they were in dealing with Henry Ellsworth nearly three hundred years later.

[1] *Dictionary of American Biography*, XVIII (article on Montfort Stokes by William H. Ghent).

In February, 1833, Montfort Stokes reached Fort Gibson, and the commission immediately began work on the boundary dispute that was threatening general conflict between the Creeks and Cherokees. The line along the eastern border of the Creek Nation, north of the Arkansas River, was the boundary in question. The disputed area, lying between the lower Verdigris and the Grand River, was rich soil, and part of it had been improved by Indian settlers. It was necessary to establish a compromise boundary line, and the Stokes Commission succeeded in reaching an agreement with both tribes.

The next problem concerned the Osage tribe. By the terms of treaties extending back to the administration of President Jefferson, this division of the Siouan Indians had been restricted, gradually, to a strip of land in Kansas; but many of the young men did not accept the limits set upon their residence as provided in the treaties. They roamed about in search of game as Osages had done for many generations. The region embraced in present-day Missouri, Arkansas, and Oklahoma had formed a part of their hunting ground, and they were reluctant to give up their established practices. Some of them still lived in Oklahoma on land assigned to the Cherokees in 1828; and some were prone to carry out raids against tribes with which they had been at war in times past.

The Stokes Commission met with Osage leaders by agreement at Chouteau's Post on February 25, 1833. The weather was cold, the Osages were poorly clothed, and the commissioners needed more time to study the conditions of settlement; so the meeting was adjourned with the understanding that conferences would be resumed on March 11 at Fort Gibson. By that time eight hundred Osages were in camp on the Grand River near the fort. Montfort Stokes and his associates held daily conferences with the tribal leaders, trying to make them understand the necessity of adjusting their way of life to the new order. On March 25 the chiefs suddenly announced that they would sign no treaty; and a short time later the news arrived at Fort Gibson that a war party of Osages had attacked a Kiowa camp on Cache Creek two hundred miles southwest of the scene of the conference on Grand River. The attacking party had caught the camp entirely unprepared, the Kiowa warriors being away on a raid across the Red River; and the Osages had brought back one hundred scalps. This triumph over their traditional enemies was a sufficient importance to justify a grand celebration, and the gruesome trophies became the occasion of an Osage scalp dance at Clermont's Village on the Verdigris.

Bitter hostility between the Osages and each of the neighboring tribes was a condition which complicated the work of the Stokes Commission. After conferences with the Choctaw agent at Skullyville, Major Francis W. Armstrong, and with General Matthew Arbuckle at Fort Gibson, Montfort Stokes determined to arrange a meeting with the chiefs of the principal southwestern tribes—Pawnee Picts, Comanche, Kiowa, Waco, Caddo, and others. Commissioner Ellsworth had attempted something of the sort on his expedition with Irving and Latrobe in the fall of 1832; and Colonel James B. Many had sought a conference with the plains chiefs during a similar tour through their territory in 1833. Both attempts had failed; but with the experience gained, the commissioners and army officers still hoped to meet in friendly conference with the wild tribes.

On June 15, 1834, General Henry Leavenworth and Colonel Henry Dodge started from Fort Gibson on an expedition into the southwest.[2] Their force consisted of Colonel Dodge's regiment of dragoons, about five hundred men, together with four parties of Indian scouts and interpreters—Cherokees, Osages, Senecas, and Delawares. Two Indian girls, a Pawnee of about eighteen and a Kiowa of fifteen, were taken along for the purpose of restoring them to their relatives as a gesture of friendship.[3] George Catlin, the distinguished painter of Indian life, was permitted to ride with the soldiers as a means of gaining closer contact with the wild tribesmen. The regiment contained some men who later attained prominence: Jefferson Davis, who was to become secretary of war,

[2] There are several firsthand accounts of this important military expedition. *American State Papers, Military Affairs*, V, 373–82, contains the journal of Lieutenant Thomas B. Wheelock; George Catlin, *North American Indians*, II, 40–86, gives the painter's account, together with numerous likenesses of Indians and Catlin's landscapes, reproduced in color. Louis Pelzer's *Marches of the Dragoons in the Mississippi Valley* was compiled by the author from the sources. The official report of the secretary of war is in *American State Papers, Military Affairs*, V, 169–72.

[3] Catlin, *North American Indians*, II, 72, 76. Catlin states that there were two Pawnee girls and one Kiowa. His book contains likenesses of the two Pawnee girls (Plates 176, 177). Pelzer, *Marches of the Dragoons*, 35.

143

United States senator, and president of the Southern Confederacy, served as lieutenant under Colonel Dodge; Stephen W. Kearny, distinguished later for his service in two wars, was lieutenant colonel of the dragoons.

The summer of 1834 was a period of severe heat and prolonged drought. The men traveled without adequate protection against mosquitoes and other insects, drank impure water, and on some parts of their journey marched on short rations. A large part of the band suffered from sickness during the expedition; and, according to the estimate of George Catlin, about one third of the men lost their lives.[4]

The party followed a road recently marked out at General Leavenworth's orders, approximately ninety miles in length, from Fort Gibson to Edwards' Trading Post, near the spot where Little River empties into the South Canadian. Turning due south at the crossing of the river, the dragoons proceeded to a point on the Texas emigrant road near the mouth of the Washita, where they were joined by two infantry companies from Fort Towson. By July 4, when the combined party was ready to cross the Washita, the daily additions to the sick list were appalling. Some of the stricken men were sent back to Fort Gibson, from time to time; and after the party had proceeded westward a few miles from the crossing of the river, a hospital camp was set up for the care of those who were not in fit condition to travel. The place was called Camp Leavenworth, and the commander himself was one of the patients.

George Catlin has given an account of the circumstances that led to General Leavenworth's serious illness. Apparently he was suffering from a fever for several days before the crossing of the Washita, but was still able to ride. After a herd of buffaloes had been put to flight by some of the officers and men riding at a little distance from the marching dragoons, a buffalo calf dashed across the General's path and he put his horse after the frightened animal. "I'll have that calf before I quit," Leavenworth shouted to the painter, as the chase began.

"I rode to the top of a little hill to witness the success of the General's second effort," Catlin wrote. But the officer's horse, dodg-

4 Catlin, *North American Indians*, II, 82.

ing about in pursuit of the elusive buffalo, fell into a hole and threw the general heavily to the earth. "I ran my horse with all possible speed to the spot, and found him on his hands and knees, endeavouring to get up. I dismounted and raised him to his feet, when I asked him if he was hurt, to which he replied, 'No, but I might have been,' when he instantly fainted."

A few days later, after the crossing of the Washita, in General Leavenworth's tent Catlin wrote: "At the time I am writing, the General lies pallid and emaciated before me, on his couch with a dragoon fanning him, whilst he breathes forty or fifty breaths a minute and writhes under a burning fever, although he is yet unwilling even to admit that he is sick."[5]

From Camp Leavenworth, Colonel Dodge pushed on westward, with a reorganized regiment of dragoons. Six companies of forty-two men each made up the new command. Eighty-six men including General Leavenworth and Lieutenant George W. McClure, were left in the hospital tents unable to rise from their beds. One hundred and nine soldiers under the command of Lieutenant Colonel Stephen W. Kearny were left for duty at the camp.[6] Dodge marched to the site of Lawton, and for several weeks explored the vicinity of the Wichita Mountains before continuing westward to the territory of the Pawnee Picts on the North Fork of the Red River. The leader of the dragoons had a problem of particular importance to settle with the tribe on the North Fork. Reference has been made to the presence of a Kiowa girl and a Pawnee girl with the Dodge expedition. Return of these former prisoners of the Osages was intended as a friendly move, proof in itself of the good will of United States agents. However, on the lower Washita, Colonel Dodge had learned that Judge Martin, a resident of Louisiana, had been murdered along with his Negro slave while on a buffalo hunt north of the Red River. The Comanches accused the Pawnee Picts of the deed.

The march from the "Great Comanche Village" at the foot of the Wichitas to Pawnee Village, about ninety miles farther west, required four days. After reaching his destination, Colonel Dodge held conferences with the Pawnee chiefs, assured them of the

[5] *Ibid.,* 50, 51.
[6] Pelzer, *Marches of the Dragoons*, 36.

friendly intentions of his party, and demanded an account of the murder of Judge Martin and his Negro servant. A rumor had been heard among the Comanches that a son of the murdered man, nine years of age, was still alive and a prisoner of the Pawnees.[7] The old chief, We-ta-ra-sha-ro, and all the other Indian leaders at first denied any knowledge of the murder and assured Colonel Dodge that they knew nothing of Judge Martin's little son. But a Negro who lived among the Pawnee Picts at last revealed that the little boy was, in fact, concealed near the camp, and the Indians eventually agreed to give him up. The exchange of prisoners was made, the relatives of the Indian girls were overjoyed at the evidence of the white men's good intentions, the attitude of the chiefs became more cordial, and the whole camp suddenly appeared more friendly. One immediate result of the camp's new attitude was the delivery of a plentiful supply of food to the dragoons.

Colonel Dodge distributed presents among the chiefs and warriors of all the southwestern tribes and cultivated harmonious relations to such good effect that some of the Indians agreed to make the trip back to Fort Gibson with the dragoons. Among those who joined the party on its return were We-ta-ra-sha-ro, the old chief of the Pawnee Picts who was reputed to be past ninety years of age; two other Pawnee chiefs, one Comanche chief, and one Waco chief; the head man of the Kiowas, Teh-toot-sah; and fifteen Kiowa warriors.[8]

His Indian hosts suggested to Colonel Dodge that the region of the upper Canadian River would be a suitable place for obtaining buffalo meat and also for the recovery of the sick men of his command. After the march back to the "Great Comanche Village," the dragoons turned northeast and traveled six days, crossing the Canadian River near the site of present-day Union City, south of El Reno. There a camp was established for the men who were unable to travel, and the entire command stopped for a few days to shoot buffaloes and to rest their jaded horses. A messenger arrived from the hospital camp near the lower Washita, bringing the sad news of the death of General Leavenworth, Lieutenant George W. McClure, and some others who were left in the sick camp.[9]

[7] Catlin, *Indians of North America*, II, 47, 71.
[8] *Ibid.*, 82.

Catlin, who was ill but able to sit up at the time when the message was received, wrote further evidence on Leavenworth's death:

"It seems that the General had moved on our trail a few days after we left the Washita, . . . a distance of fifty or sixty miles, where his disease at last terminated his existence; and I am inclined to think . . . in consequence of the injury he sustained in a fall from his horse when running a buffalo calf. My reason for believing this is, that I rode and ate with him every day after the hour of his fall; and from that moment I was quite sure that I saw a different expression in his face, from that which he naturally wore; and . . . two or three days after his fall, I observed to him, 'General, you have a very bad cough'—'Yes,' he replied, 'I have killed myself running after that devilish calf; and it is a very lucky thing, Catlin, that you painted the portrait of me before we started, for it is all my dear wife will ever see of me.'"

From the camp on the Canadian, Dodge's party required fifteen days to reach Fort Gibson. Some of the sick men were left in camp, some were taken forward on litters, some were buried along the way. Less than two hundred dragoons returned with the party on August 15, and nine days later Colonel Kearny arrived from Camp Leavenworth with fagged, worn-out horses, fever-ridden troops, and emaciated, delirious patients on litters.[10] Other men were brought in from time to time, but the expedition had been extremely costly in lives.

Perhaps some valuable lessons had been learned by the Army in regard to troop movements through such regions as the lower Washita, Boggy, and Canadian bottoms during hot weather. Certainly a great deal had been added to existing knowledge of Oklahoma geography. A most remarkable record was left by George Catlin, in words and paintings, of the people and scenes encountered by the dragoons. The painter required help to get on and off his horse during the first day out of Camp Canadian; later, he could not sit on his horse and was carried in an empty baggage wagon. At Fort Gibson he was under the care of the post surgeon, Dr. Wright, for several weeks before he was able to write his impressions of the last stages of the expedition.

[9] *Ibid.*, 79.
[10] *American State Papers, Military Affairs*, V, 382.

Pierre Beatte, the colorful guide of the Irving-Latrobe expedition in 1832, served in the same capacity for the Leavenworth-Dodge party. George Catlin, like Washington Irving, rated Beatte highly among the hunters of the southwestern frontier. Irving called him a half-blood, supposing him to be half French and half Osage Indian; but Catlin, apparently with good evidence, stated positively that both of Beatte's parents were French, that he had lived much among the Osages and "had acquired all the skill and tact of his Indian teachers, and probably a little more." The painter added, "he is reputed, without exception, the best hunter in these Western regions."[11] Catlin lodged with Beatte's parents one night as he was traveling from Fort Gibson to St. Louis, and it was on their evidence that he based his statement as to the hunter's racial origin.

"This was the most extraordinary hunter, I think, that I have ever met in all my travels," Catlin wrote. "He never told how many animals he had seen—how many he had wounded, &c.—but his horse was always loaded with meat."[12]

Colonel Dodge and Major F. W. Armstrong opened their conference at Fort Gibson on September 2, 1834. Chiefs of the Choctaw, Creek, Cherokee, Osage, and Seneca tribes met with delegates from the Comanche, Waco, and Wichita Indians. After Dodge and Armstrong had spoken, Chief Clermont made a long address in which he declared the friendship of the Osage tribe for all within sound of his voice. Wichita and Comanche chiefs accepted the offer of friendship, and the army officers felt that they had taken an important step toward permanent harmony in the Indian country. Dodge and Armstrong had not been authorized by the Stokes Commission nor the War Department to negotiate a treaty, but they did make plans with their Indian visitors for a great conference to be held during the following summer.

The spot selected for the general conference of the tribes was in the buffalo country, north of the site of Lexington near the Canadian River. Major R. B. Mason was assigned the task of cutting a road from Fort Gibson to the conference ground, and of preparing in advance such conveniences as brush shelters, benches, and a speaker's platform.

[11] Catlin, *North American Indians*, II, 59.     [12] *Ibid.*, 92, 93.

By July, 1835, over six thousand Indians had encamped near the place selected to wait for the meeting to begin. At Major Mason's request, General Arbuckle sent two additional companies of infantry from Fort Gibson to give added security against sudden disorder on the part of the wild tribes. Montfort Stokes, General Arbuckle, and Major F. W. Armstrong were to represent the United States at the meeting. Major Armstrong, the superintendent of the western tribes, died at Skullyville before the party set out; but the other commissioners, with delegates from the Cherokee, Choctaw, Creek, Delaware, Osage, Quapaw, and Seneca tribes, made the journey over Mason's road to the meeting place. At seventy-three, Stokes was a vigorous and determined official. Many of his associates expressed their astonishment at his rugged health, ability to work long hours, and apparent indifference to the discomforts of frontier travel. The Indians, even the chiefs from the Plains tribes, seemed to have confidence in the doughty old commissioner.

On August 24, 1835, a treaty of peace and friendship was signed by Montfort Stokes, General Matthew Arbuckle, and representatives of the various Indian tribes.[13] This was the first United States treaty with Indians of the Southwestern Plains. All of the major groups west of the land selected for the Five Civilized Tribes took part in the treaty making, with the exception of the Kiowas. The agreement gave the eastern Indians the right to trap and hunt westward to the limits of the United States. Citizens of the United States were to have free and safe passage through the lands of the Plains tribes. At a later date, the Kiowas and some smaller groups of the Southwest signed a similar agreement with Commissioner Stokes and Colonel A. P. Chouteau.

The active work of Montfort Stokes in the Indian service continued until his death at the age of eighty, in 1842. He was agent for the Cherokees and also acted as subagent for the Senecas, Shawnees, and Quapaws. The story of his small part in the fight for majority government in the Cherokee Nation, in which he was aligned with John Ross against General Matthew Arbuckle and Secretary of War Joel Poinsett, will be told later.[14]

[13] Kappler, *Indian Affairs: Laws and Treaties*, II, 435–39.
[14] Wardell, *A Political History of the Cherokee Nation*, 37–42; 29 Cong., 1 sess., *House Exec. Doc. 185*, 43; 28 Cong., 2 sess., *Sen. Doc. 140*.

## THE TREATY OF NEW ECHOTA

The invitation by the Western Cherokees for their eastern kinsmen to join them, contained in the eighth article of the Treaty of 1828, brought some results.[15] In 1829, about 1,500 Indians with over 100 slaves came west by way of the Tennessee, Mississippi, and Arkansas rivers. Through the following years other smaller parties came, by boat and on foot, and by 1834 the Western Cherokees had reached a total population of 5,800.[16]

In Georgia the years between the treaties of 1828 and 1835 found the relations of United States citizens with the Indians at their lowest stage. The Cherokee Nation was brought under the jurisdiction of the state, Cherokee tribal government was outlawed by state authority, and white persons who lived in the Cherokee lands were required to obtain a state permit. The state disposed of Cherokee homes by means of lottery sales, and the competition for choice property was keen. Chief John Ross's home was taken by lottery in 1834, and the beautiful estate of Joseph Vann was confiscated in the same fashion.

The Cherokee constitution of 1827 marked a stage of progress in Indian self-government, definitely in advance of the other tribes of southeastern United States. The basic tribal law was written by a convention elected for the specific purpose of framing a constitution. Clearly influenced by their acquaintance with the federal Constitution and with various state constitutions, the Indians established a two-house legislature, an executive branch with policy-making powers, and a judicial system with a supreme court at the top. The work of the convention was ratified by popular vote, which in itself was evidence of some progress in democracy. The state constitutions of that time, in the main, and the federal Constitution itself, had not been passed upon by a vote of the people.

The Cherokee chiefs of greatest influence were strongly attached to their homeland. Pathkiller, last of the illiterate fullblood

---

[15] Kappler, *Indian Affairs: Laws and Treaties,* II, 288ff.; Dale and Rader, *Readings in Oklahoma History,* 149–54.
[16] Commissioner of Indian Affairs, *Annual Report,* 1836, 391.

Cherokee chiefs, expressed his views in terms which bear the mark of sincerity, even in the language of the interpreter. "I love my country where I was raised," he said. "I never can find so good country and water to what I am used to. I hope you will have conscience to let me raise my children in my own country."[17]

Charles Hicks, the second chief before Pathkiller's death, was also an advocate of holding the Cherokee lands in Georgia and the other eastern states. These men relied strongly upon the words of President Monroe, who wrote in a special message of March 30, 1824: "I have no hesitation . . . to declare it as my opinion that the Indian title was not affected . . . by the compact with Georgia, and that there is no obligation . . . to remove the Indians by force."[18] Both Hicks and Pathkiller died in 1827.

Gold was discovered on Cherokee land in northeastern Georgia in 1829, and by June of the next year three thousand intruders were actively engaged in digging, with as many more swarming about the spot where gold had been reported, trampling Cherokee crops and in numerous cases stealing livestock and committing other depredations.[19] Most of these gold seekers were in the Cherokee Nation without authority of the license required by United States law. Nine were arrested and taken before Judge Clayton of the state superior court, who discharged them and reported to the governor that he felt a deep sense of shame in finding citizens marched through the streets guarded by soldiers of a government other than Georgia.

The Cherokees sought the legal advice of William Wirt, who had served the United States as attorney general under two administrations for a period of twelve years. Wirt assured them that in his opinion the Georgia statute abolishing their government and extending state jurisdiction over their lands was unconstitutional. A criminal case that arose in the Cherokee Nation was closely connected with the issues in controversy. Corn Tassel killed another Cherokee Indian, was arrested by Georgia police officers, and tried in the superior court of Hall County. The trial resulted in his con-

[17] Starkey, *The Cherokee Nation*, 48, 49, 100, 102.

[18] Richardson, ed., *Messages and Papers of the Presidents*, II, 235.

[19] John B. McMaster, *A History of the People of the United States from the Revolution to the Civil War*, VI, 46–48.

viction, and he was given the death sentence. On a writ of error his case was taken to the United States Supreme Court.

The Court ordered that the state of Georgia should appear and show cause why the sentence against Corn Tassel should not be reviewed. Governor Gilmer laid the writ before the legislature, declaring that he would resist it with all the force at his command. He was instructed, along with all other state officers, to ignore the action of the federal court. On the day set for the execution, Corn Tassel was hanged. Georgia's independence had been asserted and maintained by defiance of federal authority.

William Wirt and John Sergeant represented the Indians in the case, *Cherokee Nation* v. *Georgia*.[20] The attorneys for the Cherokee Nation declared in their complaint that Georgia had executed Corn Tassel, in defiance of the United States Supreme Court, had passed laws providing for the disposal of Cherokee lands by lottery, and had taken steps to get possession of gold and silver mines of the Cherokee Nation. The Indian state was declared by its attorneys to be a sovereign "foreign nation," competent to bring suit in the United States Supreme Court.

In an opinion written by Chief Justice John Marshall, the Court denied that the Cherokee Nation was an independent foreign state. The relation of such Indian tribes to the United States, declared the opinion, "resembles that of a ward to his guardian." The tribal organizations did not constitute foreign states, but "domestic, dependent nations." Thus the Indians lost their suit on a technicality concerning their exact status.

The Georgia law requiring white persons living in the Cherokee Nation, on and after March 1, 1831, to obtain a license and to take an oath of allegiance to the state of Georgia, provided a minimum penalty of four years' imprisonment for its violation. Under this law, six persons were arrested and tried on a writ of *habeas corpus* before a Georgia court. The attorneys for the accused men argued that the law was *ex post facto*, hence a violation of the Constitution of the United States. The judge held this contention and all others made by the defendants to be untenable. Four of the men were held, but two missionaries were released, as authorized agents of the United States. One of them, Reverend Samuel A.

[20] *Cherokee Nation* v. *Georgia*, 5 Peters, 1.

Worcester, was also postmaster at New Echota; but when he was removed from office and Governor Gilmer was informed that the missionaries were not agents of the United States, the two men were again taken into custody along with nine other violators of the Georgia license law. Four of the victims in addition to Reverend Worcester were ministers—James I. Trott, Martin Wells, Mr. Thompson, and Dr. Elizur Butler. All of them were chained to a baggage wagon and driven to jail, walking behind the clumsy vehicle under guard.[21] A jury convicted the eleven men, and each was sentenced to four years in the state penitentiary. The governor offered to pardon all who would promise that they would never again disobey the Georgia law concerning license to enter the Cherokee Nation. Nine of the prisoners gave the required promise, but Worcester stubbornly refused to consider this easy way out of their trouble, and he was sent, with his companion, to begin his term in the Georgia penitentiary.

Attorneys for the two missionaries appealed their case to the United States Supreme Court. Again the state was not represented at the hearing; but in this case the Court's decision was against Georgia. The state law extending the jurisdiction of Georgia over the Cherokee Nation was declared "repugnant to the Constitution, laws, and treaties of the United States." All of Georgia's acts with respect to control of Cherokee citizens and officials were held to be in violation of treaty rights under the United States, in direct "hostility with acts of Congress," and a violation of the president's authority.[22] Judge Clayton of the Gwinnett Superior Court of Georgia refused to obey the decree handed down by the United States Supreme Court, Governor Gilmer ignored it, and President Andrew Jackson seemed undisturbed by the fact that the federal decree was powerless.

Gradually, Cherokee leaders became convinced that removal westward was their only hope. Long-range adjustment to the dominant civilization that had been brought from Europe to North America was not their pressing problem; they had to look out for the immediate necessities of their people. The attitude of the state officials in Georgia and the white population pressing against the

[21] *Niles' Weekly Register*, August 27, 1831.
[22] *Worcester* v. *Georgia*, 6 Peters, 515.

Indian frontier made life almost intolerable for many citizens of the Cherokee Nation. Even William Hicks, interim chief after the death of Pathkiller and Charles Hicks in 1827, failed to be elected because he was suspected of softening toward removal.[23]

One prominent family that accepted the necessity of removal was that of Major Ridge, his son John Ridge and his two nephews Buck Watie and Stand Watie. Among the followers of the Ridge party for removal were a considerable number of mixed-blooded Cherokees. As a general rule the fullblood Indians opposed removal. The leader who proved to be most determined in his fight against removal was John Ross, principal chief after the death of Pathkiller and Charles Hicks. Ross was the descendant of a Scotch trader and was one-eighth Cherokee. Like Alexander McGillivray of the Creeks, his lot was cast with the Indians and his life devoted to their interests. John Ross was well educated, an eloquent speaker, a man of great dignity, and one who impressed nearly all who met him with his integrity and honorable purposes.

By the year 1835, the Ridge party was definitely committed to removal; and the only problem remaining, from their point of view, was that of the price to be determined for their sacrifice. There was some evidence that Ross himself was willing to leave Georgia if a sufficient amount of cash could be obtained for making a new start in Spanish territory. He seems to have had in mind the sum of $20,000,000; and it is possible that he might have gotten that sum, had he been free to negotiate without the handicap of powerful minority leadership in the Cherokee Nation. Major Ridge's followers, including not only the leading Indians of mixed blood but also the majority of those who had attended schools outside the Cherokee domain, regarded themselves the progressive members of the tribe.

In a tribal meeting at Red Clay in 1835, John Ross submitted a definite proposal of the United States to pay the Cherokee Nation $5,000,000 for their holdings in Georgia. By an overwhelming majority, the voters decided in the negative.

In spite of strong evidence that the Cherokees were not ready to leave their homes and migrate to the West, federal officials persisted in their efforts to arrange a treaty. General William Carroll,

[23] Starkey, *The Cherokee Nation,* 102.

Reverend John F. Schermerhorn, and B. F. Curry met with the leaders of the Ridge party before the end of 1835 and came to an agreement concerning removal of the tribe. The meeting was held at New Echota. Partisans of John Ross, opposed to removal, simply refused to attend; their position was that they had voted down the proposal of the federal government at Red Clay and could not reasonably be expected to reopen the question. Without tribal authority, the leaders of the Ridge-Boudinot faction signed for the Cherokee Nation, the agents of the government at Washington signed, and the "treaty" was rushed through the United States Senate in December, 1835.[24]

By its terms, the Cherokee Nation ceded to the United States all of its land east of the Mississippi River for the consideration of $5,000,000. For the "neutral lands," a strip of territory twenty-five by fifty miles in extent lying along the western border of Missouri and separating the state from the lands of the Osages in Kansas, the Cherokee Nation was to pay the United States the sum of $500,000. It was further agreed that the Cherokee Nation should be entitled to send a delegate to the House of Representatives in Washington, "whenever Congress shall make provision for the same." The Cherokees were to remove from their eastern lands within two years after promulgation of the treaty, and the United States agreed to pay the cost of migration.

On May 23, 1838, the limit set for their removal, only a small fraction, probably about one eighth, had started on the westward journey.[25] General Winfield Scott, under orders from the War Department to remove all Indians who were still in the old Cherokee Nation, began the difficult task of evicting them. Stockade camps were established, and the Cherokees were herded into them, with scant regard for precautions regarding sanitation and little concern for the food and clothing of the Indians. Their hardships, in camp and on the trail westward, were of such magnitude as to constitute a national disgrace for the great country of which the Cherokees were a "domestic, dependent" part. The infant

[24] Kappler, *Indian Affairs: Laws and Treaties,* II, 439. The text of the treaty and the names of the signers are in Dale and Rader, *Readings in Oklahoma History,* 159–170.

[25] Grant Foreman, *A History of Oklahoma,* 26. Foreman's figures are: two thousand removed, seventeen thousand in the East on May 23, 1838.

death rate was particularly high, very few aged Cherokees were able to survive the journey, and the suffering among other age groups was intense, the losses appalling. The Cherokees call their compulsory removal to the West, "The Trail of Tears," which seems to characterize the disasters of the event.

After a time, John Ross obtained from General Scott permission to organize the work of removal. The first bands had started in June, by boat and on foot, with military escort. By October, Ross had other parties ready to move under gradually improving conditions—better managed wagon trains, more attention to food supply and drinking water, better selection of sites for trail camps. Epidemic sickness declined, and with the leadership of their own chief, the Cherokees became more willing to accept the inevitable. Some of the bands went by way of Nashville, thence into Kentucky, across the Ohio River at the little town of Golconda, Illinois, thence to the crossing of the Mississippi at Cape Girardeau, Missouri, and southwestward across Missouri and Arkansas into Indian Territory. The party conducted by the Baptist missionary Evan Jones contained about one thousand emigrants, which was average for the fourteen bands that made the journey by wagon train. Many of the Cherokees followed a trail that passed through Memphis, across central Arkansas, and into the Cherokee Nation at Van Buren, or north of that Arkansas town.[26]

As the wagon trains and flatboats moved westward, some of the Cherokees slipped away and went into the new Republic of

[26] Foreman, *Indian Removal*, 294–312. The northern route varied somewhat in detail, particularly after the crossing of the Mississippi. Generally the wagon trains passed through Nashville, then into Kentucky and through Hopkinsville. Crossing the Ohio at Golconda, Illinois, the emigrants usually proceeded to the ferry across the Mississippi at Cape Girardeau, though a few went into Missouri above that town. One route ran almost due west from the river crossing to Springfield, Missouri, thence southwest across the corner of Arkansas and into the Cherokee Nation near the site of Fort Wayne. Another route passed through Jackson, Missouri, thence southward to Smithville, Arkansas Territory, thence westward to the Illinois River in the Cherokee Nation.

The second band to travel west under military escort, making the journey largely by flatboats, was conducted by Lieutenant R. H. K. Whiteley and contained 875 emigrants; three of the bands observed by Nat Smith contained a total of 3,000. Of that number, according to his estimate, 2,000 reached the Cherokee Nation. John Benge conducted a band of 1,103; Elijah Hicks, a party of 748—which was smaller by nearly 1,000 than the most numerous of the emigration bands.

Texas, or beyond the Río Grande into Mexico. A few escaped from the caravans and returned to the rougher, more remote sections of their old homeland. But the majority of those who started the journey and did not reach the valley of the Arkansas were buried along the way.

By 1839 the newcomers in the Cherokee Nation of the West outnumbered the "Old Settlers" and the "Treaty party" combined. Before the end of removal, recent immigrants were a two-to-one majority. John Ross enjoyed the confidence of this larger group, and it is not surprising that he was still in demand as principal chief. Perhaps it was natural, too, that the minority who had lived in Arkansas or joined the Western Cherokees after 1828 were not inclined to yield control to the Ross party. The United States War Department apparently gave substantial support to the Indians who had moved west voluntarily. General Matthew Arbuckle hindered the majority of the Cherokees in their efforts to set up a new united government, with the result that a strong movement for separation developed and several years of disorder followed. Not until the amnesty treaty of 1846 were the Cherokees able to devote the main energy of their government to civil affairs; and even in the decade just before the opening of the Civil War, violence was all too common, bitter animosity too close to the surface.[27]

The statesmanship of John Ross stood out above all other Cherokees of the time. A lesser man would have been defeated by the opposition of Secretary of War Joel Poinsett, General Matthew Arbuckle, and Superintendent William Armstrong, added to the difficulties inherent in the feuds of the Cherokee Nation. Major George Lowrey and Sequoyah worked for harmony and union. The aged Montfort Stokes, Cherokee agent, apparently had little weight with the War Department and with his superior officers in the West; but his strong belief in majority rule undoubtedly made him a valuable ally of the Ross party.

During the period of greatest disorder, on June 22, 1839,

---

[27] Wardell, *A Political History of the Cherokee Nation.* Appendix A gives a "Summary of the Memorial of John Ross to the House of Representatives"; Appendix B, a description of the signing of the treaty, quoted from the Washington *Daily Union,* August 16, 1846.

157

Major Ridge, his son John, and his nephew Elias Boudinot were killed for their part in signing the "false treaty" of New Echota. The action was similar in many respects to the execution of William McIntosh, Tustennuggee, and Sam Hawkins by the Creeks after those chiefs signed the Treaty of Indian Springs. In both cases, the death penalty was provided by law for the offense of making an unauthorized land cession; but in the execution of McIntosh and his associates, a formal verdict and sentence had been voted by the Creek Council, and the men who performed the act of execution were simply carrying out their function under Creek law. The Cherokee killers of the Removal Party leaders were unknown and no judicial decree had been passed. It is probable that John Ross had no part in the killing of the Ridges and no knowledge of the persons who committed the act.[28]

After two unsuccessful meetings, the first at Takatokah and the second at Illinois Camp Ground, the united Cherokees in a third assembly at Tahlequah agreed on a new constitution and elected John Ross as the first principal chief. Although the Secretary of War refused at first to receive him as the representative of his tribe and General Arbuckle persisted in his efforts to deal with the minority group, John Ross held the Cherokees together and gradually restored order. The principal chief proved himself a man of broad vision, capable of making effective compromise agreements, aloof from narrow, personal ambition, and sincerely attached to sound and long-range policies for the Cherokee people.

## REMOVAL OF THE SEMINOLES

The Seminoles, as indicated in a previous chapter, were small in number by comparison with the Creeks or the Choctaws and backward in civilization, measured by white men's standards. They were a comparatively recent off-shoot of the Creeks and undoubtedly contained some admixture of Negro blood through long contact with the territory of white planters, whose black fugitive slaves found the Seminole country a convenient hiding place. Soil

[28] Wardell, *A Political History of the Cherokee Nation,* 17.

cultivation among the Florida Indians was limited, although some of their tribal lands were rich and potentially valuable for the production of cotton, rice, and other crops. The Seminoles of Florida lived principally by hunting and fishing, in which they were highly skilled. They had, in the first half of the nineteenth century, very able leaders, such as Osceola, Wild Cat, Chief Philip, Cloud, Micanopy, and Toskogee.[29]

After the United States acquired title to Florida Territory in 1819, land that was not occupied by the Seminoles filled up rapidly with white settlers. The familiar pattern of agricultural, industrial, and commercial pressure against people who were dependent upon more primitive occupations was repeated in Florida.

In 1832, James Gadsden prevailed upon the Seminole chiefs at Payne's Landing to sign an agreement by which they were to send a party of explorers west for the purpose of finding a new home with their relatives, the Creeks. If the Creeks were willing to receive them and the Seminoles were satisfied with the conditions of removal and the territory offered them, they were to remove to the West. A party of Seminole delegates conducted by John Phagan, an Indian agent in whom they had great confidence, came west to New Orleans, up the Mississippi River and the Arkansas by steamboat, and finally, when low water impeded their progress, traveled the last two hundred miles to Fort Gibson on horseback.

At Fort Gibson the explorers met with the Stokes Commission and on March 28, 1833, signed a treaty by which it was agreed that the Seminole tribe would move in with the Creeks of the Indian Territory. For the United States the document was signed by Montfort Stokes, Henry Ellsworth, and John F. Schermerhorn; for the Seminoles, by means of the cross-mark, it was signed by Holata Emartta, John Jumper, Charlie Cmartta, Ya-ya-hadge, Ne-hath-clo, Fuch-a-lusti-hadgo, and Coi-hadgo.[30] Although the chiefs in Florida denied that the delegates who were exploring in the West had authority to sign a removal treaty, and there was reason for

[29] McMaster, *A History of the People of the United States*, VI, 463 ff.

[30] Kappler, *Indian Affairs: Laws and Treaties*, II, 394. The text of the treaty and names of the signers are in Dale and Rader, *Readings in Oklahoma History*, 213, 214.

doubting that these tribal representatives understood the full significance of the document, the United States Senate quickly ratified the agreement, and the Seminoles were informed that they would be expected to start preparations for removal immediately.

The tribesmen in Florida went back into remote hiding places in the swamps, and the war of removal began. General Thomas Jesup, in charge of United States military forces in Florida, adopted the policy of seizing Seminole women and children as a means of compelling the surrender of warriors. Concentration camps were established, and captives were held until a party was made up for compulsory removal.

The wife of Osceola had been captured early in the war. When General Jesup took the field with a powerful, well-armed force, he made an attack on the Withlacoochee settlement and captured about fifty women and children. The Seminoles countered with an attack on Fort Mellon but were beaten off. A few headmen surrendered from time to time, agreeing to go west and take up life there among the Creeks. Diplomatic handling of the situation would have reduced the war to a minimum, with great saving of lives on both sides; apparently many of the Seminoles were turning over in their minds the problem of surrendering, which of course involved acceptance of westward removal. But the United States commander made two serious blunders: he handed over a considerable number of Seminole Negroes to slave hunters, in some cases to men who had but flimsy claims to the fugitives; and he violated the truce at Fort Dayton under which Osceola, Wild Cat, and Cloud sought a conference. The Seminole leaders became prisoners; Chief Cloud and Wild Cat escaped, but Jesup later captured Cloud a second time, along with Micanopy and Toskogee, by suddenly seizing him during a peace talk at Fort Mellon. A delegation from Chief John Ross of the Cherokees, which had been instrumental in arranging the Fort Mellon conference, protested the captures, but General Jesup did not give up his prisoners. Chief Osceola died in prison at Fort Moultrie in Charleston Harbor.[31]

The Seminole War was a shameful episode in the relations of the United States with the Indian tribes. In addition to the broad injustice of the removal treaty, conduct of the war in its early stages

[31] McMaster, *A History of the People of the United States*, VI, 465.

was entrusted to the vigorous but untrained hands of General Thomas S. Jesup, who gave the Indians ample reason for regarding the white man's pledge a worthless thing.[32]

Zachary Taylor, placed in command of the campaign against the Seminoles, brought a new spirit of vigor and honorable conduct into the war. He marched into Florida with 1,100 soldiers, well-armed and equipped, and beat the Seminoles under Wild Cat near Okeechobee Swamp. The United States force lost 26 killed and 112 wounded; the Indian losses were much heavier. Seminole organized resistance was broken, and many of the Indians who did not surrender were searched out later and sent west as late as 1842. It was impossible to find all of them, and a considerable remnant remained in the vicinity of their old homes where some of their descendants are still to be found.

Camps were set up for the Seminole immigrants near Fort Gibson. The Creek land assigned to them, with consent of the Creek Council, lay between the Canadian River and its north branch. Many Creeks already lived in the area designated as the home of the Seminoles, and from the first the Florida tribe found the arrangement unsatisfactory.

## CHICKASAW REMOVAL

The Chickasaws of northern Mississippi, less than half as numerous as their Choctaw kinsmen, had made similar progress

[32] *Niles' Weekly Register*, Vol. LI, September, 1836–March, 1837, 74 ff., contains a part of the correspondence between General Jesup and his commander, General Winfield Scott, and between Jesup and some of the leading politicians of the period. If there were no other evidence than Jesup's own letters, there would be enough to brand him a "political general." In regard to his controversy with General Scott, Jesup wrote to F. P. Blair, editor of the *Globe* and a powerful figure in politics: "Occupied with my public duties, I have no time for defence; and as I do not meddle with the politics of the country, I would not consent to be defended on party grounds."

On June 17, 1836, General Scott wrote to Jesup: "I am infinitely astonished and distressed to hear of your near approach, and in starving condition, to Fort Mitchell. You knew that your forces were not wanted there. . . . Imagine my astonishment to hear that you have come through the heart of the Indian country, seeking private adventures."

in the production of goods and were advanced in their acquaintance with the civilization of white men. They were noted for their fine horses and cattle. A considerable part of the Chickasaws were of mixed blood, the result of intermarriage with Scotch, English, and other European stock, and a large number of them were able to speak English.

Like other Indians of the Southeast, the Chickasaws were strongly attached to their home country. Like the neighboring tribes, too, they knew something of the Red and Arkansas river valleys as a result of their hunting trips on the "buffalo plains." In 1832, President Jackson's agents were able to get from them a reluctant agreement that they would move west if suitable territory could be found for them. The Chickasaw land in Mississippi was ceded to the United States, with the stipulation that each Indian family was to select a farm to be retained until a satisfactory home could be found for the tribe in the region west of Arkansas Territory.

After two years their explorers had not found a satisfactory location, and the Chickasaw Council agreed that the search should be continued. There was strong pressure by government agents to induce them to move into the region that had been set apart for the Choctaws. In January, 1837, delegates from the Chickasaw Nation came west and met with the Choctaws at Doaksville, a short distance north of Fort Towson. In the presence of William Armstrong, acting superintendent of the western territory, the Chickasaw commissioners signed a new treaty with the United States and with representatives of the Choctaw Council. Among the Choctaw signers were Chief Peter P. Pitchlynn, George W. Harkins, and Israel Folsom; the Chickasaw commissioners were James McLish, Pitman Colbert, James Brown, and James Perry.[33] Choctaw district chiefs and others signed as witnesses: Joseph Kincaid, chief of Moshulatubbee District; Thomas LeFlore, Chief of Okla Falaya District; Nitakechi, chief of Pushmataha District; Henry R. Carter, who conducted the Chickasaw party west, Joseph S. Doak, and Daniel McCurtain. Doaksville was the largest town in the Indian Territory, and had enjoyed the services of a United States post office since 1832.[34]

[33] Kappler, *Indian Affairs: Laws and Treaties*, II, 486; Dale and Rader, *Read-*

Under the Treaty of Doaksville, the Chickasaws were assigned to a district with carefully defined boundaries in the western part of the Choctaw territory. Members of both tribes were to have the right to settle in any part of the original Choctaw Nation, and the governments were to be combined. It was agreed that any dispute over the terms of union should be submitted to the United States agent for the Choctaws; or, on appeal, to the president of the United States. Separate control of annuities was provided, but in all tribal privileges there was to be equality.

Some of the Chickasaws came west by steamer up the Arkansas River to Fort Gibson, then overland by way of Boggy Depot. Others came by wagon train, large numbers of the immigrants walking the entire distance; some rode horseback, and some of the aged members of the tribe, along with infants, found places in the wagons. A few parties left the Arkansas River at Little Rock, striking across the hills to the Red River in the vicinity of Miller Court House. The journey was a hard one, though not so long as the trail of the Alabama and Georgia Indians. Many Chickasaw children were buried along the road through the Arkansas swamps, victims of cholera or fever, exposure, undernourishment, or simply of exhaustion.

Dealers who were under contract to deliver food to the emigrants were sometimes guilty of negligence or fraud. Meat, grain, and other goods brought up the Arkansas River by steamboat were in some instances piled along the river bank to lie in the sun until it was entirely unfit for use. Medical aid for the migrating Indians was deplorably inadequate, and epidemic sickness struck with terrible speed, killing large numbers and leaving the survivors weak and unfit for travel or work.[35]

Most of the Chickasaws who elected to move west had reached their new home before the end of the year 1840. The district assigned to them was an area of unique charm. The fertile valley of the Washita ran through the heart of it from northwest to southeast; tree-covered hills, clear streams, and cool springs were in nearly every part; and the interesting Arbuckle Mountains added

ings in Oklahoma History, 215–17.
34 Debo, Rise and Fall of the Choctaw Republic, 58, 59, 71.
35 Foreman, Indian Removal, 193–226.

a touch of variety to the new tribal lands of the Chickasaws. The region was marked for stockraising by the large acreage of excellent native grass and the abundance of running water. In time, the Chickasaws were able to develop, on the rich soil of the Washita and other valleys, an extensive farming industry.

One factor of the new situation was not to their liking. Accustomed to a large degree of self-government, the Chickasaws were not satisfied with the tribal regulations passed by a council in which their own representatives were always in minority. Their movement for separate government was similar to that of the Seminoles in withdrawing from union with the Creeks. In its broader aspects, it was like the Belgian separatist movement of 1830, and like the American Revolution of 1776, except that the Indian tribes were not, as Chief Justice Marshall pointed out in 1831, "independent, foreign" states, but "domestic, dependent" nations. After several years of preparation, an agreement was reached in 1855 for permanent separation of the Chickasaw and Choctaw governments. The citizens of each tribe were still permitted to settle on the lands of the other and to enjoy tribal rights at the place of their residence. Tribal annuities were separate and each nation elected officers under its own separate basic law.

The Choctaws lived in widely scattered communities, while most of the Chickasaws had built their homes in the eastern half of their lands where protection against raiding parties from the plains was effective. Between the Canadian and Red Rivers, on land originally assigned to the Choctaws, some bands of Wichita, Caddo, and Kiowa Indians occupied permanent homes. Probably the Caddoan tribes, as they claimed, were descendants of people who had tilled the soil there for several centuries.

The Kiowas had come from the North more recently. During most of the eighteenth century this tribe had lived in the vicinity of the Black Hills and the plains northwest to the Yellowstone River.[36] About the time of the Lewis and Clark expedition (1804–1806), the Kiowas moved south to the Arkansas River and occupied a large area from the upper Cimarron to the Red River and southeast to the Wichita Mountains. The Southern Cheyennes had also moved into the Great Plains south of the Arkansas River, and for a

[36] Muriel H. Wright, *A Guide to the Indian Tribes of Oklahoma*, 170.

time there was warfare between that branch of the great Algonquian family and the Kiowas. After 1840, however, the Cheyennes and Arapahoes were at peace with the Kiowas.

In order to give the Plains tribes a place to call their own, Secretary of the Interior Robert McClelland made a perpetual lease of the land from the Choctaws, its owners, and assigned it to the Indians who lived there. The treaty of 1855 by which the Chickasaws separated from the Choctaws contained a provision that the United States should pay the two tribes $800,000 for a perpetual lease on their land west of the 98th meridian. The lease money was to be divided, three fourths to the Choctaws, one fourth to the Chickasaws.[37]

[37] *Oklahoma Red Book*, I, 211ff. The Constitution of the Choctaw Nation and the Constitution of the Chickasaw Nation contain definitions of the boundaries of the two nations. For the Choctaw Constitution, see Dale and Rader, *Readings in Oklahoma History*, 243–58; "Chickasaw Constitution," *ibid.*, 258–70.

# CHAPTER EIGHT

# The Indian Frontier
# from Removal to the Civil War

## FOUR DECADES OF TRANSITION

Indians of the Five Civilized Tribes who moved west from Georgia, Alabama, Mississippi, Tennessee, or Florida came, for the most part, during the years from 1817 to 1842. In that period most of the Indians were under severe pressure. State governments in the Southeast were unfriendly, the rapidly increasing white population was often aggressive and unscrupulous, officers of the United States too often were indifferent to Indian grievances. After 1829 the government at Washington adopted a general policy supporting the states that were most interested in removal. Bitter partisanship developed among the Indians themselves on the problem of dealing with the rising tide of white invasion. Factions in every tribe were to continue their internal strife for many years.

Leaders of the tribes and members of all the Indian families as well had to make difficult adjustments, such as learning to live in large temporary camps and to travel long distances on foot, without customary sources of food supply. Thousands of graves along the trails into the West afford grim evidence as to the cost of uprooting tribes and moving them into distant new homes.

For those who lived through the hardships of the overland journey on short rations or resisted the pestilence of steamboat passage, there remained the ordeal of pioneer settlement in a raw land. For several thousand Cherokees and smaller numbers of Creeks and Choctaws, there were four full decades of adjustment in the West before the disaster of large-scale civil war struck the Indian Territory. The majority of the Indians, however, had lived in their new homes less than thirty years when the great sectional conflict of the white men engulfed them.

Shelter for their families was an early necessity of all the new settlers. The first houses were crude structures, hastily thrown together without the use of any tools other than light tomahawks, knives, and stone axes, and nearly always without the use of nails. While building makeshift houses with their crude implements, settlers had to give thought to the clearing and fencing of fields and to planting crops. During the first years pioneer farmers simply "girdled" the trees and cleared out the underbrush. Removing dead tree trunks and pulling out stumps came gradually, in later years. All of these operations involved a great deal of heavy toil which must be included in the total cost of removal.

Another cost which was usually overlooked at the time of removal and has not been sufficiently emphasized in studies of the event was loss to the Indians of the unearned increment of their land. At the very time when missionaries and physicians were trying to acquaint the natives with virtues of an advanced culture, a government run by white men was trading them, acre for acre, land that was valued on the market far less than the ground they were giving up. Some fertile soil in the recently cleared cotton belt was selling presently for prices as high as $100 per acre, while lands in the new Indian Territory exchanged for prices below $1.00 per acre for a long time after removal of the Indians.[1]

The western homes of the Five Civilized Tribes were far removed from their old markets. Since the trading firms at Augusta, Pensacola, and Mobile were no longer easily accessible to them, Indian farmers quickly developed an intense interest in the problem of an outlet for their surplus goods. The Red River and Arkansas River were utilized for transportation of cotton, corn, meat, livestock, and pecans, to add to the peltries which earlier trading posts of the area had already been sending to eastern markets.

[1] Turner, *The Rise of the New West*, 90, 91; Samuel Eliot Morison and Henry Steele Commager, *The Growth of the American Republic*, I, 441; Daniel Clark, *The West in American History*, 250, 251; Lewis C. Gray, *History of Agriculture in the Southern States to 1860*, II, 642. In regard to the period about 1850, Gray notes the wide variety of land prices: $12 to $20, uncleared; $40, cleared; "well-improved cotton plantations, as high as $100 per acre." The Fortier plantation (La.) sold at $169 per arpent (approximately, an acre).

Commercial contacts were made with Mississippi River towns, particularly the port of New Orleans.[2]

Keeping order was a difficult matter in all the Indian nations. On occasions when money payments were due the Indians, white traders and also members of the tribes brought in whiskey to sell, and at such times drunkenness became a major problem, recognized as a great evil by all responsible agents of the United States and by officials of the tribal governments.

Disputes that arose among the Indians in the East over the question of removal continued as family and partisan quarrels, sometimes flaming into violence and ending in deadly feuds, with younger Indians carrying on the strife of their ancestors. Another disturbing factor in the West was the presence of small Algonquian tribes which claimed prior rights to the lands west of Arkansas Territory. These conflicting claims were settled satisfactorily, but only after some delay. Neglect by Congress to vote appropriations for sums due the Indians often caused misunderstandings and real want among the tribes. It was not always an easy task to get prompt and exact enforcement of terms embodied in treaties with the United States.

Perhaps the most elusive and difficult problem of all, for the tribes and for individual Indians, was to obtain honest values in their purchases of goods.[3] Swindling the Indian was all too common in the subsistence contracts, and many members of all the tribes were found to be in destitute circumstances upon their arrival in the West.[4] There was not enough concern for the rights of the Indian against the selfish interests of unscrupulous men whose highest principle was, "let the buyer beware."

## THE NEW CHOCTAW NATION

In 1831 a Choctaw census recorded a population of 19,554 east of the Mississippi, including 248 Negro slaves and 97 white

[2] Foreman, *The Five Civilized Tribes*, 34; Joseph B. Thoburn and Muriel H. Wright, *Oklahoma: A History of the State and Its People*, II, 786, 787.

[3] 27 Cong., 3 sess., *Hitchcock Report, House Exec. Doc. 219.*

[4] Office of Indian Affairs, Chickasaw Immigration, Agent William Armstrong to Commissioner Crawford, February 22, 1839.

citizens.[5] During the twelve years following this official count about 18,000 of the tribe moved west. There is no accurate record of those who died on the journey to the new Choctaw Nation, of the few who were diverted to other regions, or of the considerable number who returned to Mississippi; but it is known that the Choctaw population in Oklahoma in 1843 was less than 13,000.[6]

The Choctaw Council established three districts in the West for the settled portion of their land: Moshulatubbee, across the northern part of the nation, along the Arkansas and South Canadian rivers; Okla Falaya in the southeastern part, sometimes called the Red River District; and Pushmataha, west of the Kiamichi River. Chief Moshulatubbee died shortly after the large-scale migration began, and his place in the northern district was taken by his nephew, Joseph Kincaid. The Choctaw settlers were most numerous along the Arkansas River, especially in the vicinity of Skullyville and Fort Coffee. In Okla Falaya District, the principal centers of population were Miller Court House and Doaksville. Greenwood Le Flore had remained in Mississippi, and his position as district chief was filled by his nephew George Harkins. Pushmataha District, with settlements spread along the Texas Road from Perryville to the Red River, established its principal town at Boggy Depot. Nitakechi, nephew of Pushmataha, was district chief.[7]

The Choctaw Nation had in it a considerable variety of soil with a strip of flat, low land along the Red River and another similar belt of fertile land along the lower Canadian and Arkansas rivers in the north. The valleys of the Clear Boggy, Muddy Boggy, Poteau, Kiamichi, and other streams contained deep, tillable soil where good crops could be raised. The hilly ground, extensive in all three districts, with its thin topsoil and generally rough surface was less suited to farming, but had some advantages for raising livestock. There were many clear, spring-fed streams in the moun-

[5] *Sen. Exec. Doc. 512*, Vol. III, 149.

[6] Josiah Gregg, *Commerce of the Prairies* (in vols. XIX and XX of Thwaites, *Early Western Travels*), XX, 317n. Gregg observes that the Commissioner's Report for 1843 gives the Choctaw population as 15,177, whereas the *Choctaw Almanac* places it at 12,690. Many of the Indian Department figures, Gregg thought, were too high.

[7] Foreman, *The Five Civilized Tribes*, 25, 26.

tainous area. A dense growth of timber—pine, oak, walnut, pecan, hickory, elm, cedar, and other trees—covered a large part of the Choctaw lands, but there were prairies with excellent native grass for the grazing of Indian herds.

The principal crops in the early years of settlement were corn and cotton. Cattle, hogs, and horses were important from the start; and along with shipments of livestock and farm products, pecans were among the early exports. Economic progress was notable in the new Choctaw Nation, as it had been in the old region of the lower Mississippi.

A post office was established at Miller Court House in 1824, about one year before the permanent boundary was determined between Arkansas Territory and the Choctaw Nation. The little settlement was about twenty miles west of the boundary line, near Red River. Later post offices in the Choctaw Nation were provided as the population spread into widely separated areas. Postal service began at Doaksville in 1832, Skullyville in 1833, Eagletown in 1834, Perryville in 1841, and Boggy Depot in 1849.[8] Perhaps the most active trading centers were Doaksville, Skullyville, and Boggy Depot. Doaksville, the metropolis of southeastern Indian Territory during the eighteen forties, contained five busy stores, a blacksmith shop, and a hotel. Doak & Tims Mercantile Company was one of the stores; Berthelet, Heald and Company, in which the Choctaw planter, Captain Robert Jones, had a large interest, was another. Colonel Israel Folsom ran the hotel and forbade the use of liquor on the premises.[9] Barter of farm produce at the trading houses played a leading part in the business transactions of Doaksville and other Choctaw towns. Furs and a variety of hides were exported to New Orleans, where purchases for the Indian country included calico and other textiles, clothing, hardware, harness, and saddles. Some prices, as quoted in Choctaw newspapers of 1850, ran as follows: eggs, twelve and one-half cents a dozen; butter, twelve and one-half cents a pound; potatoes, fifty cents a bushel; and corn, one dollar a bushel.[10]

[8] Debo, *The Rise and Fall of the Choctaw Republic*, 58.

[9] Foreman, *The Five Civilized Tribes*, 53.

[10] Thoburn and Wright, *Oklahoma*, II, Appendix, 786, 787, quoting from the *Choctaw Intelligencer*. The blacksmith shop at Doaksville was run by Captain Caudle. There were also several flour mills in the area by 1850.

As indicated above, the Choctaws held relatively few slaves before they moved west. After removal the majority still had no direct interest in slave labor; but in a few instances the larger property owners sold their holdings in Mississippi, brought their slaves to the new Choctaw Nation, and expanded their farming activities. The most extensive plantations were established in Red River Valley, particularly in the vicinity of Doaksville. Before the Civil War began, Robert M. Jones had built his home at Rose Hill, on the site of the Old Providence Mission west of Fort Towson. He managed five separate plantations, in addition to his interest in the store at Doaksville, steamboats that he ran on navigable parts of the Red River, and extensive marketing of Negro slaves. At one time he owned five hundred slaves, which was double the entire number of Negroes in the Choctaw Nation before removal from Mississippi. There were other slaveholders in the tribe, but none of them approached the extensive interests of Captain Jones in slave property.

Tribal attention to schooling was a Choctaw characteristic even before the main body of the tribe removed from the East. Choctaw Academy, established by Richard M. Johnson in Scott County, Kentucky, was operated under provisions of the Treaty of 1825. The first pupils entered the school in that year, when twenty-one Choctaw boys arrived at Great Crossing in charge of young Peter P. Pitchlynn. This school was to play a prominent part in the education of Choctaw leaders.[11] By 1833 the tribe was engaged in building log schoolhouses for elementary pupils in all districts of the new Choctaw Nation, and were discussing in the council plans for providing advanced training in the manual arts for boys and in domestic arts for girls.[12]

An attempt was made to wipe out illiteracy by means of "sunday schools," week-end camps, for adults as well as children, with instruction in elementary reading, writing, and arithmetic. Agent Francis W. Armstrong was a powerful supporter of schooling as a means of adjusting Choctaws to the alien culture of white men. About two hundred children attended mission schools in 1836,

[11] Carolyn T. Foreman, "The Choctaw Academy," *Chronicles of Oklahoma,* Vol. VI, No. 4 (December, 1928), 453.
[12] Foreman, *The Five Civilized Tribes,* 36.

an additional hundred were enrolled in the five tribal public schools, and a movement had been started for opening one or more academies.

After passage of the Education Act of 1842, several academies began giving instruction: Spencer Academy for boys, ten miles from Fort Towson on the road to Fort Smith; Armstrong, fifty miles west of Fort Towson in Pushmataha District; Fort Coffee Academy for boys, on the Arkansas River in buildings formerly occupied by the garrison; New Hope School for girls, five miles southeast of Fort Coffee; and Chuahla Female Seminary at Pine Ridge, one mile from Doaksville. Reverend Alfred Wright had been conducting a school at Wheelock Mission, which was reopened on May 1, 1843, on an enlarged scale.[13]

Spencer Academy, built to accommodate one hundred boys, provided manual training and instruction in agriculture. The Fort Coffee school emphasized manual arts, also, and occupied sixty acres of land for the use of student farmers. This academy was placed under the charge of Methodist missionaries and was supported, like the other academies, in part by church funds and in part by money voted by the Choctaw Council. Among other schools that received support from the council were Goodwater, near the site of Hugo and Stockbridge Choctaw Mission, near Eagletown.[14]

Closely associated with the work of primary and secondary education, usually combined with it, were the religious services of Protestant missions. Cyrus Kingsbury, Alfred Wright, and Cyrus Byington, Presbyterians; Alexander Talley, Methodist; and Isaac McCoy, Baptist, were the best known of the missionaries. Chief Moshulatubbee, in his later years, became leader of an anti-Christian movement that affected the entire northern district, but did not continue long after the old chief's death. During the period when sentiment against missionaries was strong, the Indian Bureau received a request to expel Alexander Talley and to keep out all other ministers. A common agreement between missionaries and the Choctaw tribe was that elementary education should be

13 *Ibid.*, 58–64.
14 *Niles' Weekly Register*, LXVII (1844), 19, 178; Foreman, *The Five Civilized Tribes*, 19, 58, 59, 60.

provided as a condition for permission to preach the gospel. Before the outbreak of the Civil War about one fourth of all the Choctaws were listed as members of the Methodist, Baptist, or Presbyterian churches.[15]

Missionaries were well aware of the demoralizing effects of whiskey-drinking among the Choctaws. Under the influence of religious leaders, particularly native preachers who had been educated outside of the Choctaw Nation, the council passed various acts to restrict the sale of intoxicants. A traveler in the Choctaw Nation relates the story of a council which had to consider the problem of strong drink. After many speakers had been heard a resolution was passed to inflict the penalty of whipping—one hundred lashes on the bare back—of any person who should bring whiskey into the nation. Liquor illegally brought in was to be seized and destroyed; but to avoid the injustice of an *ex post facto* measure, the order for pouring out whiskey did not apply to goods previously brought in. After long and careful consideration, the council finally decided to drink up the available supply as a means of protecting the nation against its evil influence. The traveler added, "Bacchus never mustered a drunker troop than were these same temperance legislators . . . . The law, with some slight improvements, has ever since been rigorously enforced."[16]

The state legislature of Texas co-operated with the Choctaw Council to the extent of forbidding sales of whiskey to visitors from the nation. But the law was hard to enforce, and drunkenness was a common occurrence when the Indians traveled south of the Red River, or went on a journey to Arkansas.

Prosperity among the Choctaws was considerably increased by the success of their delegates in obtaining financial settlements with the United States. The Treaty of Doaksville, as given above, provided that the Chickasaws should pay $530,000 for the privilege of moving into Choctaw lands, "thirty thousand of which shall be paid at the time and in the manner that the Choctaw annuity of 1837 is paid," and the balance as an investment in "safe and secure stocks" under direction of the United States government.[17] The

[15] B. F. McCurtain, "The Indians of Oklahoma," *Sturm's Oklahoma Magazine*, Vol. XI No. 3 (1910), 23.

[16] Gregg, *Commerce of the Prairies*, 312, 313.

[17] Dale and Rader, *Readings in Oklahoma History*, 216.

Treaty of 1855, also with the Chickasaws and the United States, brought $600,000 into the invested funds of the Choctaws, 75 per cent of the total sum received from the "Leased District."

In 1853, Peter Pitchlynn went to Washington with a delegation to obtain revision of the terms in Choctaw land cessions. After two years of negotiation without reaching a definite settlement, the Indians agreed to arbitration and accepted the United States Senate as the court for determining the amount due them. In 1859 the Senate handed down its decision in this "net proceeds" case, awarding the Choctaw Tribe the sum of $2,981,247.30.[18] In effect, this was recognition of the fact that the original price paid to the Choctaw Nation for its property was terribly inadequate. It also gave point to Chief Justice John Marshall's distinction between "foreign nations" and "domestic, dependent nations."[19] It is possible that the settlement did not give the Indians complete justice in their position as a domestic nation under the protection of the United States, but it did show a disposition on the part of federal officers to grapple with the problem of Indian rights.

During early years of the Choctaws in the new land, many customs were drastically altered. The older practices of corpse disposal, already in process of change at the time of removal, rapidly disappeared. The dress of frontier whites became the common garb of Choctaws, although among the older Indians the blanket, beaded moccasin, and bright-colored turban persisted long after the majority had adopted new customs of dress. In some instances wealthy families imported fine cloth for women's dresses, while Choctaw planters dressed very much as white planters did in the eastern states. Family names, in imitation of mixed-blooded and white families, had become the general rule by 1860. Sometimes a schoolboy took the name of a white patron of the mission or the name of a famous early American statesman, such as John Adams or George Clinton.

The Choctaw Council took action to regulate the residence of white men in the nation. One statute provided that noncitizens living with Choctaw women should marry them, while another

[18] Kappler, *Indian Affairs: Laws and Treaties,* II, 706–14; *United States Statutes at Large,* XI, 611.
[19] *Cherokee Nation* v. *Georgia,* 5 Peters, 1 (1831).

174

prohibited the intermarriage of white men who were of bad character.[20] Because the number of white residents among the Choctaws was small and cases of intermarriage were relatively few, no rigid tests of character were set up until after the Civil War when it became necessary to adopt new restrictions.[21]

Cyrus Byington and other scholars who were associated with Indians of the Muskhogean family discovered that their language could be adjusted to use of the English alphabet. The Choctaws made some progress in printing before the Civil War. In addition to a considerable volume of printed matter in the form of religious pamphlets, hymnbooks, and treatises on doctrinal topics, Byington and Alfred Wright were responsible for publication of the New Testament and portions of the Old Testament in the Choctaw language.[22] Two newspapers were printed before the Civil War: the *Choctaw Telegraph* in 1848 and the *Choctaw Intelligencer* in 1850. All of these were published in the Choctaw language without use of a special Indian alphabet. Some of the material was sent to eastern presses, some to Park Hill in the Cherokee Nation or to Union Mission, and some was printed on small presses in the Choctaw Nation.[23]

## CREEK PIONEERS IN THE WEST

Creek population in the East at the time of Opothle Yahola's removal treaty in 1832 was nearly 23,000. The McIntosh Creeks, who had moved west at that time and were living along the lower Verdigris River and in the adjoining bottom land of the Arkansas, totaled about 2,000. The number who lost their lives during the period of removal cannot be determined with accuracy. Undoubtedly there were some who left the main body of the Creeks, and were not to be found either in Alabama or in the new Creek Nation after removal was over. The census of 1859 re-

[20] Joseph P. Folsom, *Constitution and Laws of the Choctaw Nation*, 499.
[21] *Acts of the Choctaw Nation*, 1875 (Phillips Collection).
[22] Debo, *The Rise and Fall of the Choctaw Republic*, 59–62.
[23] *Ibid.*

corded for the Creek Nation in Oklahoma a population of 13,357.[24]

The Creeks found early years in the frontier settlements very difficult. At first they built flimsy houses, using peeled saplings set up between corner posts for the outside walls. A roof of bark shingles and a covering of clay on the side walls completed the structure. The houses were built without nails and almost without the use of tools other than the light tomahawk which every Creek possessed. In the main cooking was done on open fires outside the houses. During early years in the West, food was generally roasted in the coals or ashes; but as earthen vessels were added to household utensils, more variety appeared in the form of boiled meats, broth thickened with corn meal, and numerous other combinations. In winter the houses were heated by means of round clay stoves, placed in the middle of the room, with an opening in the roof above to allow smoke to escape. In some houses, clay chimneys were attached to the stoves.[25]

Although there was a large expanse of fertile land in the Creek Nation, the food supply was short until fields were cleared and the first crops harvested. Subsistence from the government during the first year was not altogether satisfactory. The needs of the tribe were hard to anticipate, and goods furnished under contract were not always of the best quality. Sometimes contractors were dishonest in regard to the amount of merchandise delivered.[26] Guns, ammunition, and tools, as well as food, were definitely lacking as the Creeks tried to gain a foothold in their new territory. In 1833 the Stokes Commission made a boundary settlement between the Creeks and Cherokees which awarded some improved farms grist mills, twenty-four crosscut saws, and an annuity of $1,000 for educational purposes. In a measure this increase in goods and claimed by the McIntosh settlers to the Cherokee Nation. Perhaps as compensation for the Creeks, Stokes and his associates allotted to them an additional blacksmith, a wheelwright, four services relieved the distress of the Creeks.[27]

[24] Debo, *The Road to Disappearance*, 103.

[25] *Ibid.*, 109.

[26] 27 Cong., 3 sess., *House Exec. Doc. 219.* Major Ethan Allen Hitchcock, who investigated charges of fraud in 1841, made a complete report.

[27] Debo, *The Road to Disappearance*, 110.

North Fork Town, situated a few miles above the forks of the Canadian River, became the center of a thriving Creek population. The settlements extended westward along the South Canadian and along both banks of the north branch and of Deep Fork. The area contains a large acreage of deep, fertile soil, and the crops on recently cleared land were good.

The McIntosh Creeks, living in the lower Verdigris Valley and westward along the Arkansas, were a distinct community. Roley McIntosh, half brother of Chief William McIntosh who was executed in 1825, farmed extensively by means of slave labor. He was a prominent member of the mixed-blooded planters of this area and exercised great influence among the Creeks as a whole. He was elected principal chief and held the office for many years.[28] Other wealthy planters of the lower Verdigris were Benjamin Perryman, Sanford W. Perryman, D. N. McIntosh, Chilly McIntosh, and Benjamin Marshall, who owned one hundred slaves and large herds of cattle and horses. In the same region where the largest planters of the Creek Nation lived were also the poorest members of the tribe—families that struggled along on the barest necessities.

A change in Creek society that was probably in part a result of removal to the Indian Territory was their tendency away from town life. As trading centers and for certain political activities the towns were still important; but a large number of Creek farmers built their houses in the middle of cultivated fields, and many of them were too far removed from the town for active participation in its politics. With decline of town life, the common field was less in evidence, although the use of hoes, axes, and other tools as tribal property retarded the tendency toward individual farming. Community fencing was still the general rule, and the Creeks practiced the old custom of planting gardens and even field crops for the sick and aged.

Finances of the Creek Nation gradually improved. In 1838 the Treaty of Fort Gibson yielded $50,000 from the federal government to be paid in livestock as compensation for losses sustained in removal. The McIntosh Creeks were not included in this agreement, but they obtained $21,103.33, also payable in livestock, to

[28] Foreman, *The Five Civilized Tribes*, 184.

cover their removal losses; and the band that revolted over removal in 1836 received $10,000. Losses on real property ceded by the Creeks were at least recognized by deposit of $350,000 in the United States Treasury to the credit of the tribe. The excellent natural pasturage of Creek lands made livestock payments especially valuable, and prosperity in the form of surplus horses, cattle, and hogs had arisen in this tribe before 1860.

Along the eastern border of the Creek Nation ran the Texas Road, crossed by the California Trail at North Fork Town. Thus the tribe had overland connections with the outside world, while emigrants passing through on well-marked roads furnished one of the best outlets for salable products—meat, fowls, corn, pecans, fruit, and other things. Land for cultivation was plentiful, herds grew rapidly on the open range, and the Creeks supplemented their food supply by gathering wild products of the woods, by hunting within their own territory, and by extensive hunting expeditions to the "buffalo plains." Real want for necessities had been reduced—in most communities had practically disappeared—before the period of the Civil War. Nearly every family possessed one or two cows, a few hogs, and a few ponies.

The first Creek agency was established at Three Forks and a post office opened there in 1843.[29] Ten years later another was started at Micco, near North Fork Town. Here in the fertile triangle formed by the forks of the Canadian River was the most populous Creek community, with a brisk exchange in pelts, flourishing emigrant trade, and some importation of goods from trade centers of the East. Edwards' Store, on the California Trail at the mouth of Little River, Shieldsville, on Deep Fork near the site of present-day Okmulgee, and Honey Springs, on the Texas Road midway between Three Forks and Micco, were other busy trading points in the Creek Nation.

[29] Debo, *The Road to Disappearance,* 113; Grant Foreman, "Early Post-Offices in Oklahoma," *Chronicles of Oklahoma,* Vol. VI, No. 1 (March, 1928); No. 2 (June, 1928); No. 3 (September, 1928); and No. 4 (December, 1928).

## THE NEW CHICKASAW NATION

In Mississippi the Chickasaws had long been in touch with Europeans and had made a great deal of progress in learning the English language, together with other phases of adjustment to the alien white culture. Like the Choctaws, they had found markets for their surplus goods in Spanish Florida and in the growing settlements of Tennessee. By 1830 they were selling beef, livestock, pork, corn, and cotton, and importing dry goods, sugar, coffee, and slaves. Their agent, John L. Allen, reported Chickasaw sales of cotton at one thousand bales.[30]

The tribe had felt the influence of Christian missionaries, both in religious services and in the beginning of an educational system. Elementary schools had been established in the Chickasaw Nation of Mississippi under the supervision of missions, and the tribal council had provided an annual fund of $3,000 for sending boys to outside schools.

After removal to the Indian Territory there were two principal causes of discontent among the Chickasaws. As noted above in the story of their removal, Chickasaw leaders and citizens resented dominance by the Choctaws and were not satisfied until they had made arrangements for separation, so that they could make their own laws and elect all of their own officers. The other serious grievance was the menace of intruders within Chickasaw lands. Indian tribes of the Southwest—Caddo, Comanche, and Kiowa—together with roving bands of Yuchi, Cherokee, Kickapoo, Delaware, Shawnee, and Koasati Indians, made life miserable for many Chickasaw families for a decade after their removal.[31]

Most Chickasaws came to the Indian Territory by way of Memphis, Little Rock, and Fort Smith. From Skullyville a large part of them traveled by wagon train on a new road to Boggy Depot, where their supplies were issued. The largest of their early settlements were on Blue and Clear Boggy rivers. For some of the immigrant trains, the route followed after reaching Little Rock

30 Foreman, *The Five Civilized Tribes*, 97 ff.
31 *Ibid.*, 104.

was across southwestern Arkansas to the Choctaw Nation border and from there to the vicinity of Fort Towson and Doaksville. Those who settled in Choctaw communities near the Red River were not much disturbed by the wild tribes; but the Chickasaws who built their cabins on Blue River or pushed farther west were in constant danger. In 1841 the intruders became so numerous and bold that the Chickasaws asked for federal protection. Three companies of soldiers were sent from Fort Gibson, and the raiding bands from the west were temporarily pushed out, but after a few months the troops were withdrawn and disorder broke out again.

Frequently the raiders were fleeing from results of their depradations in Texas, and sometimes they were followed by armed bands from across the Red River. Chickasaw settlers suffered from the white pursuers as well as marauding Indian bands. Livestock was stolen, crops destroyed, and more than one Chickasaw slave was carried away to Texas. In 1842, General Zachary Taylor established Fort Washita near the southeastern corner of Chickasaw District to give added protection against the wild tribes.

Education of Chickasaw children had been seriously retarded by the upheaval of migration. Gradually elementary schools were established in the new Chickasaw Nation, and in 1848 work was begun on the first building for Chickasaw Academy. A road was cut to the site selected for the school, twelve miles northwest of Fort Washita, and a sawmill was set up there to provide lumber. The work was entrusted to Superintendent Wesley Browning, and building proceeded slowly under great difficulties. In July, 1849, the Chickasaw Council appropriated $5,000 to complete the building, and two years later the first classes were held in it. The academy opened with 60 boys and girls, but was soon filled to capacity, which was 120. In later years the school was conducted for boys and was called the Chickasaw Manual Labor Academy.

In 1852 a school was provided for Chickasaw girls at Bloomfield under the supervision of John Harpole Carr, a Methodist missionary. He was a frontier preacher who had traveled the circuits of the Southwest for eighteen years. Born in Tennessee in 1812, he came west with his parents to Arkansas Territory in 1819, settling in Lafayette County on the north bank of Red River. The area was raw and sparsely settled. Pioneers made their own cloth-

REVEREND SAMUEL A. WORCESTER
*superintendent, Park Hill Mission, 1836–59*

REVEREND ISAAC McCOY
*early Baptist missionary*

**GENERAL STAND WATIE**
*Confederate Indian leader*

GENERAL JAMES G. BLUNT
*commander of the Kansas District*

ELIAS CORNELIUS BOUDINOT
*Cherokee politician*

GENERAL PHILIP HENRY SHERIDAN
*sent to Indian Territory because of
unrest of Plains Indians*

*Courtesy Colorado Historical Museum*

MAJOR GRIERSON
*and party at Medicine Bluff, about 1870, selecting site
later to be known as Fort Sill*

*Photograph by Soule*

BLACK KETTLE
*Cheyenne chief, victim of Custer's Washita massacre*
*Drawing by John Metcalf*

ing, hats, and moccasins, lived in rough log cabins without glass in the windows, and attended churches of similar construction. The school houses, too, were crudely built, with log walls, clapboard roofs, and dirt floors. Usually their only furniture was split-log benches.

As a young man John H. Carr worked at the carpenter's trade; but falling under the spell of a frontier orator at a camp meeting, he determined to become a preacher.[32] After receiving his license to preach in 1834, he began work among white settlers near the Choctaw Nation, and eventually was sent to the Doaksville circuit, where he labored for six years. In the Choctaw country he was entertained at boarding schools, where he held religious services, and occasionally at the house of a friendly Christian Indian.

After the Indian Conference of his church selected him to take charge of Bloomfield, he supervised construction of the first building and opened school with twenty-five pupils in the fall of 1853. The second Mrs. Carr, formerly Miss Angelina Hosmer of Mt. Holyoke Seminary, acted as matron and Miss Susan J. Johnson served as teacher. Subjects taught to Chickasaw girls included reading and writing the English language, arithmetic, grammar, botany, and United States history. Superintendent Carr directed all construction on the campus during his fifteen years of service at Bloomfield and made practically all the coffins used by Indians of the community.

Bloomfield Academy became known among Indians of the Five Civilized Tribes as an institution of high standards and unique courses of instruction. During the difficult years after the Civil War, Captain Frederick Young held classes at the academy buildings for both boys and girls. Among the boys who attended was Douglas H. Johnston, who later was to serve as superintendent of Bloomfield and finally as governor of the Chickasaw Nation.[33] Resuming its original character as a boarding school for girls, Bloomfield became noted for its training in the fine arts, receiving high awards at the St. Louis Exposition in 1904 and in various other ways gaining national recognition.

[32] Susan Carr, "Bloomfield Academy and Its Founder," *Chronicles of Oklahoma,* Vol. II, No. 4 (December, 1924), 366 ff.
[33] *Ibid.*

Wapanucka Female Institute was opened in October, 1852, near the eastern border of the Chickasaw Nation. Colbert Institute was established at Perryville in 1854, but two years later was removed to a site in the upper valley of Clear Boggy, about eighteen miles north of Wapanucka. Chickasaw schools, beginning in the West slightly later than Choctaw, Creek, and Cherokee institutions of similar rank, were among the best Indian academies when the Civil War began.

The Chickasaws had able leaders, and after their greatest difficulties of adjustment were ended, the tribe made remarkable progress in government, economic stability, and other phases of development, as well as in their school system. General George Colbert, who came with an early band of Chickasaw immigrants to Fort Towson, was one of their best-known members. In the American Revolution he had served under General Anthony Wayne, and in the War of 1812, under Andrew Jackson. Elevated to the rank of major by George Washington, he had received from that president's hands a sword in recognition of his distinguished services as a soldier. In spite of his advanced age—he was ninety-three when the Chickasaws came west—he planned to engage in farming on a large scale and brought along tools and livestock for that purpose. He also brought 150 slaves to work the fields of his new plantation. Colbert died at the age of ninety-five.[34]

William R. Guy, an intermarried citizen of the Chickasaw Nation, served as an enrolling agent during removal, and later settled on Clear Boggy where he built a water wheel for a gristmill and sawmill. A Chickasaw woman set up a gristmill that was operated by means of a team of horses pulling a pole in a circle. Three gins were required to handle Chickasaw cotton production by 1843, and four years later the agent, A. M. M. Upshaw, reported that farmers of the tribe sold seven thousand bushels of corn to the Fort Washita garrison, at a price of 43 cents a bushel.[35] In addition, the Chickasaws furnished eggs, chickens, butter, and potatoes for the use of troops.

Removal of Indians from Mississippi continued from time to time, partly through the influence of relatives who had become

[34] Foreman, *The Five Civilized Tribes*, 102.
[35] Commissioner of Indian Affairs, *Annual Report*, 1847.

established in the new Chickasaw Nation and partly because pressure of white population continued in the eastern state. Benjamin Love was a prominent member of the tribe who had decided against removal when the first great wave of emigrants moved west. In the summer of 1840, largely because he was urged to do so by friends and relatives who desired to try their fortunes in the new land, he decided to make up a party for a wagon train. He sent to the commissioner of Indian affairs a roll of the 92 Chickasaws who proposed to move, with their 340 slaves, requesting in advance the necessary funds for the journey. He then made a preliminary trip to the Indian Territory to seek out a favorable place for settlement. Love's emigrants traveled with less hardship than earlier bands, and other small parties followed during the succeeding years: 288 in 1842; 64 in 1846; 44 in 1847.[36]

## THE CHEROKEE NATION, 1840–1860

Partisan hostility was at its worst in the Cherokee Nation after the murders of removal party leaders in 1839. Not even among the Creeks did conflict over removal take so firm a hold upon the entire tribe as a permanent obstacle to harmony. The threat of civil war and separation of the Cherokee tribe, as indicated above, was averted by the cool statesmanship of John Ross, who was opposed not only by a powerful minority within the tribe, but also by United States officials who worked with that minority. Undoubtedly the fact that the Ridge party and Old Settlers had been less reluctant to move west than the followers of John Ross made a deep impression at Washington. The official attitude was shown in President Polk's message to Congress on April 13, 1846, including a report of the Secretary of War and recommending separation of the tribe.

"It will be perceived that internal feuds still exist which call for prompt intervention of the Government of the United States," wrote the President. "Since the meeting of Congress several unprovoked murders have been committed by the stronger upon the

[36] Foreman, *Indian Removal*, 225, 226.

weaker party of that tribe, which will probably remain unpunished by the Indian authorities; and there is reason to apprehend that similar outrages will continue to be perpetrated unless restrained by the authorities of the United States.

"From the examination which I have made into the actual state of things in the Cherokee Nation I am satisfied that there is no probability that the different bands or parties into which it is divided can ever again live together in peace and harmony, and that the well-being of the whole requires that they should be separated and live under separate governments as separate tribes."[37]

The President included another suggestion in this message which pointed toward absorption of the Cherokees into the citizenship of the United States. He proposed that Indians who were guilty of felonies, even when no citizen of the United States was involved, should be subject to the jurisdiction of federal courts.

Jacob Thompson of Mississippi, a member of the House Committee on Indian Affairs, attempted to carry out the Chief Executive's proposal of Cherokee separation into two tribes by introducing a bill providing such a division in June, 1846.[38] The bill, had it been enacted into law, would have authorized the President to appoint a commission to divide the Cherokee Nation and to remove to the Indian Territory all Cherokees who were still in North Carolina.

Before decisive action could be taken upon this program of separation, John Ross and his fellow delegates in Washington had prevailed upon President Polk to study conditions among the Cherokees and make an effort to preserve their unity. The President appointed Albion K. Parris, Edmund Burke, and Superintendent William Armstrong, all of whom were in Washington, to serve on a commission for obtaining an amnesty treaty.

After five months of negotiation with chiefs of three factions—Old Settlers, Treaty party, and Ross party—Albion Parris arranged a meeting of Indian leaders with the Commissioner of Indian Affairs. President Polk attended the conference. Terms of an amnesty agreement were presented and the Indian leaders agreed. John

---

[37] Richardson, *Messages and Papers of the Presidents*, IV, 429–31.
[38] Wardell, *A Political History of the Cherokee Nation*, 71.

Ross and Stand Watie shook hands. The treaty had already been debated and approved by the United States Senate.[39]

The Treaty of 1846 recognized the right of the United Cherokee Nation, John Ross's followers included, to occupy the 7,000,000 acres of land west of Arkansas, granted in the agreement of 1828. All past crimes committed by Cherokee citizens were pardoned; animosities were buried. Cherokee laws were to provide equal protection for all citizens; the right of peaceable assembly and petition were guaranteed. Old Settlers were to receive *per caput* payments along with other Cherokees, and a special indemnity of $115,000 was to be paid by the United States to the Treaty party. Of this, the heirs of Major Ridge were to receive $5,000; the heirs of John Ridge, $5,000; and the heirs of Elias Boudinot, $5,000. The United States government also agreed to pay certain damage claims resulting from invasion of the Cherokee Nation in the East by white intruders.[40]

A strange combination of partisanship and banditry added to the difficulty of keeping order in the Cherokee Nation, even after the Treaty of 1846 was duly ratified. Tom Starr, son of a Treaty party member and one of a large family of turbulent boys, became leader of a band of outlaws who carried on their activities far beyond the borders of the Cherokee Nation. Organized soon after the killing of their party leaders in 1839, the "Starr gang" held together for about nine years through the period of greatest Cherokee disorder. Eventually they were wiped out by a posse of citizens led by John A. Bell and C. S. Bean in 1848, apparently with the approval of Acting Chief George Lowrey and the Cherokee Council.[41]

Collection of funds due the Cherokees under provisions of the Treaty of 1846 was a tedious and difficult process. Attorneys who represented the various groups were, of course, entitled to fees for their services; but in some cases the Cherokees believed that the charges were exorbitant. For example in 1852, Colonel John Drennen, superintendent of the Western District, paid claims

[39] *Ibid.*, 73, citing an account in the Washington *Daily Union*, August 18, 1846.
[40] Kappler, *Indian Affairs: Laws and Treaties*, II, 561–65.
[41] *Cherokee Advocate*, June 12, 1848; H. F. and E. S. O'Beirne, *The Indian Territory*, 92–96.

amounting to $70,369.50 to S. C. Stambaugh, Amos Kendall, John Kendall, and other attorneys. In view of the niggardly sums paid to Indians for their land and other property, the attorney fees were generous, to say the least.

Public education had not taken root among the Western Cherokees; but after the Ross immigrants arrived and the new constitution was adopted in 1839, the council established a system of elementary schools. In 1846, John Ross proposed that two academies should be built, one for boys and one for girls. Four years later the Male Seminary near Tahlequah and the Female Seminary near Park Hill were opened for Cherokee pupils. Like many other Indian boarding schools, the Cherokee seminaries held classes for day pupils who lived in the vicinity, as well as those who came from a distance and lived in the dormitories. In tribal schools, as in other factors of cultural progress, the influence of John Ross was indispensable.

## THE SEMINOLES IN THE WEST, 1840–1860

Between 1836 and 1842 the majority of the Seminole Indians were hunted down in the Florida swamps and transplanted in the Indian Territory. Their war against removal and the cruelties of their enforced emigration have been summarized above. The first two decades of Seminole life in the West will now be traced in brief.

Several factors of the tribe's new situation deserve attention. More than any other Indians of the Five Civilized Tribes, the Seminoles resisted efforts to place them upon their own resources as an agricultural people, to make them self-supporting under conditions imposed by men of an alien culture. Most of them reached Indian Territory on river boats, and when they landed near Webbers Falls or Fort Gibson, their tendency was to settle down in camp on land of the Cherokees under federal protection and to live on issued rations, without attempting to occupy land assigned to them by the Stokes Commission. They had to effect a more drastic change in their way of living than any other tribe was called upon to make. Forced to move westward, they were of necessity under military control on subsistence furnished by the War Department for a period of several months. Beyond Fort Gibson they hesitated to venture. The Creek Nation, in which they were expected to settle down, had little resemblance to the land in Florida which they had left behind. It was a changed, new world in which they found themselves, and they were appalled by it. They lingered among the friendly Cherokees, farmed a little on land which their hosts permitted them to use, and received rations doled out to them at an expense of three and one-half cents per day for each Indian.[42]

There were other reasons for their hesitation to leave Fort Gibson and its vicinity. Creek farmers already held the best land in the area where the Seminoles were expected to settle; the Creeks had an established government and were far more numerous than their kinsmen from Florida; and perhaps of greater importance, the Creeks claimed a large number of Seminole slaves which had been promised to them by United States officials as the price of their helping to remove the Florida Indians. Negroes of the Seminole tribe had a great deal of influence with their owners, many of them serving as interpreters and helping in all business transactions with white persons. Generally, their condition of servitude was not accurately described as slavery. In Florida they had lived in separate villages, free to go and come as they pleased, but bound to furnish a small annual tribute of grain or other produce to their masters. The Seminoles very rarely sold their slaves, and the Negroes were strongly opposed to exchanging their masters for new Creek owners.[43]

In Florida, General Zachary Taylor had personally guaranteed the Seminole slave owners that they should retain their chattels—slaves, livestock, and other movable goods—upon removal to Indian Territory. General Jesup had promised the Negroes that they should enjoy the same freedom in the new land that they had been accustomed to in Florida, with light tribute in the form of produce and separate villages to live in. The Creek chief, Tustennuggee Emarthla (Jim Boy), had aided General Jesup in the war

[42] Foreman, *The Five Civilized Tribes*, 224.
[43] *American State Papers: Military Affairs*, VI, 534.

by sending him 776 warriors, many of whom were well acquainted with the Florida battleground.[44] These Creek soldiers had been promised that they should keep possession of captured Seminole slaves, and they were ready to claim what they regarded as their rightful share of the booty. Seminole Negroes who ventured to establish separate towns in the Creek Nation would be in immediate danger of capture and enslavement.

The Seminole slave issue was further complicated by the claims of William J. Du Val, brother of the tribal agent. This attorney who helped at Fort Gibson in the recovery of slaves for the Seminole tribe claimed that he was entitled to about one third of them on the basis of an agreement with Chief Jim Jumper.

Many of the Seminole bands lingered for several years on land belonging to the Cherokees in Grand River Valley. They made themselves obnoxious in various ways, including theft of Cherokee livestock to supplement their pitifully short rations. By March, 1842, only two large parties of Seminoles had moved to their own territory in the Creek Nation: Micanopy's band on Deep Fork and Black Dirt's band farther west on Little River.[45]

As a general rule, army officers at Fort Gibson turned over Negro slaves who were brought from Florida to their Seminole owners rather than to other claimants. One of the slaves who attained some distinction was John Coheia, or Gopher John, who loaned Lieutenant E. R. S. Canby $1,500 on the way to Indian Territory, to help provision the party of Seminoles with which he traveled. For this and other public services, the Seminole Council declared Gopher John a free man, which placed him in immediate danger of capture or assassination by the Creeks. One attempt to shoot him from ambush resulted in the killing of his horse. He conducted a party of Seminole Negroes westward to the Little River country, however, and founded a town which they called Wewoka.[46]

Gradually the Seminoles moved away from the Cherokee lands on which they had been permitted to make temporary settlements. General Zachary Taylor, in command of United States

[44] Debo, *The Road to Disappearance*, 102.
[45] Commissioner of Indian Affairs, *Annual Report*, 1841 and 1842.
[46] Foreman, *The Five Civilized Tribes*, 258.

troops at Fort Smith, had considered the expedient of forcible removal but decided against it, since John Ross and Acting Chief George Lowrey would not press for military action against the Seminoles. By April, 1845, all but 417 had moved west; and, under continued peaceful pressure by their Cherokee hosts, most of this remnant eventually joined their kinsmen on Little River.

Agent Thomas L. Judge was in a large measure responsible for Seminole recovery from their apathy. He urged them to move upon their land, pressed for the delivery of hoes, axes, and other needed tools, and gave them instruction in the planting of crops, care of livestock, and building of houses. His reports show a marked growth of confidence and prosperity among the Seminoles.[47]

In the meantime, efforts of the United States government to remove the last Seminoles from Florida continued. A band of 302 refugees under Captain T. L. Alexander landed at Webbers Falls on June 1, 1842. Lieutenant E. R. S. Canby's band, including Gopher John, reached Little Rock in August of the same year and obtained wagons to complete the journey. In February, 1843, a band of Seminole prisoners left Florida for New Orleans, and the survivors reached Webbers Falls on April 26. They, also, had with them a Negro interpreter, but his status was not enviable, since the Indians held him responsible for their capture. In camp near Webbers Falls they killed him and buried him before the Agent Thomas Judge discovered there was trouble.

In April, 1843, Halleck Tustennuggee made his last stand in the Great Wahoo Swamp of Florida. With 70 warriors he surrendered to General William J. Worth, who sent him and his followers to New Orleans and on to Fort Gibson. Perhaps 360 Seminoles and allied Indian remnants still remained in Florida. Their principal chief was Billy Bowlegs, or Bolek. General Worth agreed that this remnant of swamp dwellers might remain where they were.

In 1849, however, the murder of a white man by four Seminoles on Indian River opened again the question of complete removal, and General D. E. Twiggs was sent with a force of 1735 soldiers to deal with Billy Bowlegs and his little band. The Semi-

[47] Commissioner of Indian Affairs, *Annual Report*, 1843; Office of Indian Affairs, "Miscellaneous Seminole Affairs."

nole chief delivered three of the murderers to General Twiggs and brought a hand of the fourth, who had been killed resisting arrest; but Bowlegs refused to go to Indian Territory or to permit removal of his people.

The government made attractive cash offers: $800 to each warrior, $450 for each woman, an equal amount for each child, subsistence en route and for a year thereafter, together with other substantial presents. John Jumper, brother of the west Seminole chief, and other men of influence came to Florida on a mission to persuade their relatives to make Seminole migration complete by moving out to Indian Territory. In 1854, Billy Bowlegs visited Washington. In 1859, his band of 165 Seminoles, accompanied by Superintendent Elias Rector of the Western District, Samuel M. Rutherford, Seminole agent, and William H. Garrett, Creek agent, started on the long journey to Indian Territory. A small remnant of the "Boatmen Indians" still remained in the Everglades.[48] Thomas Judge reported 3,400 Seminoles in the western territory by 1843, not including Negro slaves. Subsequent reports indicate that their number decreased after that time.[49]

In 1856, Seminole dissatisfaction was reduced by a new treaty with the Creeks and the United States, whereby the Florida tribe was given separate land and tribal government. The tract was west of the region where most of them had settled, lying between the two Canadian rivers and extending westward to the 100th meridian. There was ample room for development of agriculture and for cattle range, since the region as defined contained 2,169,000 acres. The United States agreed to erect an agency building and council house, to pay the Seminoles for all real improvements made on land previously occupied, and to pay all costs of removal. The treaty gave other substantial advantages to the Seminoles: $3,000, to provide better facilities for farming; $2,200, "for the support of smiths and smith-shops among them"; $250,000, to be invested for supplying an annuity; and $3,000 a year for ten years, to be devoted to tribal education.[50]

[48] Commissioner of Indian Affairs, *Annual Report*, 1859.

[49] Foreman, *The Five Civilized Tribes*, 331. By the time of the Dawes Commission, 1893–1905, the number had decreased to 2,133, not including 986 freedmen.

[50] Kappler, *Indian Affairs: Laws and Treaties*, II, 756–63.

The Seminoles had made little progress in education, but had found a leader in the field who is now a legendary figure among them. John Douglas Bemo was the son of a Seminole chief and the nephew of Osceola. As a small boy he was abducted by Jean Bemeau and sent on sea voyages for a period of about eight years. In Philadelphia he came under the observation of Reverend Orson Douglas, who sent him to school and prepared him for missionary work among his people.[51]

John Bemo opened his first school for Seminoles near the Creek Agency in 1844. He married a Creek woman, Harriet Lewis, and together they became a powerful influence for cultural advancement among the Indians. In 1848 the Presbyterian Board set up a mission school for Seminoles at Oak Ridge, putting it in charge of Reverend John Lilley and his wife. John and Harriet Bemo taught for about ten years in the Oak Ridge School.

## The Constitutions of the Five Civilized Tribes

All the major tribes of Indian Territory except the Seminole adopted written constitutions. Least advanced at the time of their removal, the Seminoles followed a pattern of government similar in most respects to that of the other tribes, but did not find it necessary to put their basic law into written form. Between 1845 and 1856 the tribe was practically autonomous, but its government was not separate from that of the Creeks. Each of the twenty-five Seminole towns was under the control of a headman. The council, composed of these town executives, had authority to pass laws with approval of the principal chief. In the agreement of 1845 it was provided that no law of the Seminole Council should be in conflict with Creek law. After the treaty of 1856, when separation of the two tribes was provided, the Seminoles simply turned their autonomous district government into a national organization.

All the tribal constitutions, including the unwritten code of

[51] Office of Indian Affairs, File D 816.

the Seminoles, had common features.[52] Each provided a mixture of Indian and Anglo-Saxon usages. The United States Constitution and state constitutions that had come under the observation of educated Indians clearly had their effect upon the constituent assemblies. Also, Indian customs of long standing were incorporated in the basic laws. For example, there was general acceptance of eighteen years as the minimum age for voting, corresponding with fair accuracy to the age when Indian boys were admitted to war parties.[53] There is evidence that acceptance in war and suffrage alike was more dependent upon maturity and self-confidence than upon strict regard for date of birth.

All the basic laws were democratic in their provisions for manhood suffrage and liberal rules of eligibility for office. All recognized, in some manner, the fundamental right of people to change their laws and the equality of free citizens. On the other hand, the existence of slave labor among the Indians placed a definite limit upon the popular character of their institutions.

Separation of governmental powers had made a tremendous impression upon the Indian lawmakers. Not only did their constitutions describe in some detail the separate functions of civil officers; but they also provided specifically that no officer should exercise powers belonging properly to a branch of government other than his own.

The Choctaw Constitution contained an elaborate bill of rights.[54] It provided traditional safeguards of human liberties: freedom of conscience, guarantees against an established church, second jeopardy, confiscation of property, unreasonable search, imprisonment for debt, excessive bail or fines, and bills of attainder. The rights of trial by jury, petition and assembly, free speech and a free press, counsel for defense, and the right to compulsory process for obtaining defense witnesses were stated. There was to be

[52] *The Oklahoma Red Book,* I, 201–40, contains the constitutions of the Cherokee, Choctaw, Chickasaw, and Creek tribes. Dale and Rader's *Readings in Oklahoma History* contains the texts of the four constitutions and other pertinent material, such as lists of the delegates, amendments, and introductory comments, pp. 227–70.

[53] *Ibid.*

[54] *Oklahoma Red Book,* I, 211; Dale and Rader, *Readings in Oklahoma History,* 243–58.

no life tenure in office and no property qualification for voting or holding office. "All political power is inherent in the people, and all free governments are founded on their authority . . . and they have at all times an inalienable and indefeasible right to alter, reform, or abolish their form of government in such manner as they may think proper or expedient," the document declared.

The Choctaw legislature was composed of a senate of twelve members elected by the voters for a two-year term, and a house of representatives chosen annually by the voters of the several counties at the ratio of one member for one thousand inhabitants. The age limit for senators was thirty, for representatives, twenty-one. To become law it was necessary that a bill pass both houses and be approved by the Choctaw principal chief; but both houses, by two-thirds majorities, might pass a measure over the chief's veto.

The supreme court was composed of three justices chosen by joint vote of the two houses. The judges were to be at least thirty years old, their terms were for four years, and the court had jurisdiction over errors and appeals. Original jurisdiction might be extended to the supreme court by an act of the legislature. For each district a court was provided with an elected judge and jurisdiction over a wide variety of civil and criminal cases. County courts with elected judges had duties connected with disbursement of county funds and many other local functions.

The principal chief was elected by a plurality vote of the entire nation for a term of two years. It was his duty to execute the laws, fill vacancies by appointment, and recommend measures to the legislature. Three subordinate chiefs were head executive officers of their respective districts. The sheriff and ranger in each county were elected; the mounted police, called light-horsemen, were appointed by the district chiefs.

The Choctaw Constitution provided that any citizen who discovered a mine was entitled to work it for one mile in every direction from the point of discovery. There were clauses in the constitution dealing with use of Choctaw funds, including liberal provisions for public education. The process of impeachment was borrowed directly from the Constitution of the United States. The amending process was far more democratic than that of the United States or of separate states in the period before the Civil War. The legislature might propose amendments by majority vote; qualified voters passed upon the proposed measures, rendering a decision in each case by a majority of the ballots cast. By a two-thirds majority in both houses the legislature might propose calling a constitutional convention, and the voters decided by a simple majority the question thus raised.

The first amendment that was proposed and adopted provided for election of four national officers: secretary, treasurer, auditor, and attorney. It also provided that the permanent seat of the Choctaw government should be located at Armstrong Academy (Chahta Tamaha). Among the twenty delegates who signed the Choctaw Constitution were Forbis Le Flore, L. P. Pitchlynn, Ellis W. Folsom, Joseph W. Folsom, William McCoy, Pliny Fisk, and Adam Nail.

The constitution of the Chickasaw Nation, adopted twelve years after separation from the Choctaws, was quite similar to the basic law of the larger tribe.[55] It contained an extensive bill of rights which included, like the Choctaw Constitution, a clause forbidding imprisonment for debt. Along with guarantees of personal liberty, the Chickasaws included strict prohibition of polygamy and concubinage. The chief executive officer was designated "The Governor of the Chickasaw Nation." One of the officers provided by this constitution was the superintendent of public instruction, elected by joint vote of the senate and house of representatives. Suffrage was extended to "free male persons of the age of nineteen years and upwards, who are by birth or adoption members of the Chickasaw Tribe of Indians."

The Creek Constitution was relatively short, and it contained some unique features.[56] The foreword, echoing the Preamble of the United States Constitution, stated simply: "In order to form a more perfect union, establish justice, and secure to ourselves and our children the blessings of freedom, we, the people of the Muskogee Nation, do adopt the following Constitution."

The legislative body contained two houses: the house of

[55] *Oklahoma Red Book,* I, 228; Dale and Rader, *Readings in Oklahoma History,* 258–70.

[56] *Oklahoma Red Book,* I, 224; Dale and Rader, *Readings in Oklahoma History,* 239–42.

kings, composed of one member from each town, and the house of warriors, with one member from each town and an additional member "for every two hundred persons belonging to the town." Members of both houses were elected by the voters for four-year terms. Voting age was eighteen, and the minimum age for members was twenty-two.

The principal chief was elected by the voters for a term of four years. It was his duty to report annually to the legislature on the condition of the nation. He had the obligation of enforcing the laws and exercised powers of veto, pardon, and reprieve. The principal chief was allowed the services of a private secretary, to be "compensated out of the National Treasury as provided by law." The principal chief had extensive powers of appointment.

The Creek Nation was divided into six districts, each of which had the services of a judge chosen by the legislature for a term of two years; a prosecuting attorney appointed by the principal chief; and a light-horse company consisting of a captain and four privates, elected by the voters and under the orders of the district judge. The prosecuting attorney was paid the sum of twenty-five dollars for each conviction.

The national supreme court was composed of five justices, aged twenty-five years or more, selected for a four-year term by the legislature. The jurisdiction of this high court extended to civil cases in which the amount in dispute was more than one hundred dollars. Criminal cases were tried by jury in the district courts.

The Creek bill of rights was short and simple. "No laws impairing contracts shall be passed; no laws taking effect upon things that occured before the enactment of the law shall be passed; all cases shall be tried according to the provisions of the respective laws under which they originated; all persons shall be allowed the right of counsel." Other guarantees of rights are to be found only by implication, in the preamble and elsewhere. Treaty making was the function of the legislature, since delegates for making treaties were appointed by the principal chief only upon approval of the two houses, and all treaties were subject to approval of the lawmakers. All officers of the Creek government were subject to impeachment and removal from office for neglect of duty. It was required that all bills of impeachment should originate in the house of warriors.

195

As indicated above, the Cherokees were first among the Five Civilized Tribes to adopt a written constitution. The constitution of 1839, written for the "United Cherokee Nation in the Indian Territory," was modeled after the earlier basic law.[57] The legislature was authorized "to make all laws and regulations which they shall deem necessary and proper for the good of the Nation, which shall not be contrary to the Constitution." Specifically, the body was given authority to raise revenue. The principal chief, elected by the voters for a term of four years, was under no restriction as to re-election. His duty was to see that the laws were executed, and he was assisted by a second chief. An executive council of five members, appointed by the legislature, sat with the principal chief and his assistant for "ordering and directing the affairs of the Nation according to law."

The judicial power was in the hands of a supreme court and such circuit and inferior courts as the legislature might provide. The judges were appointed by the legislature for four-year terms and might be removed by a two-thirds vote in each branch of the legislature. Amendments might be proposed by a two-thirds majority in both houses and ratified by the same majority in the next legislature. Cherokee voters were male citizens who had reached the age of eighteen. The Cherokee Bill of Rights contained the customary guarantees of individual rights and liberties. In addition to George Lowrey, president of the national convention, the Cherokee constitution of 1839 was signed by forty-seven delegates.

## THE PLAINS TRIBES, 1840–1860

Peace was arranged between the Kiowa and Southern Cheyenne tribes in 1840 after a major clash near the present location of Supply on Wolf Creek, a tributary of the North Canadian.[58] This costly battle came as the climax of a long struggle for control of the High Plains, when Indian leaders were beginning

---

[57] *Oklahoma Red Book*, I, 201; Dale and Rader, *Readings in Oklahoma History*, 227–36.
[58] Wright, *Indian Tribes of Oklahoma*, 79.

to realize that the menace to their way of living was not from rival tribes, but from white men. Long wagon caravans, moving out to Santa Fé under the protection of hardy frontiersmen; units of mounted soldiers, pushing into the Indian country and withdrawing without understandable motives; and a steadily advancing frontier line of white settlers—these were the dangers to Indian tribal existence. The Southern Cheyennes were at peace with the Sioux, Kiowa, Kiowa-Apache, Arapaho, and Comanche tribes after 1840.

The Comanches had raided Mexican settlements in Texas, and on rare occasions Anglo-American settlements, from the beginning of white colonization there. They had held a council with Sam Houston, representing the United States, in 1832 and with representatives of other Plains tribes had met with members of the Stokes Commission at Camp Mason, north of present-day Lexington, in 1835.[59] After the meeting with Montfort Stokes, in which the Plains Indians agreed to peaceful passage of their territory by white men and by eastern Indians, the Comanche raiding parties concentrated upon Anglo-American settlements of Texas and wagon trains crossing the Texas plains. President David G. Burnet and his successor, Sam Houston, made determined efforts to establish satisfactory trade relations with the Comanches, but received little effective support from their congress. President Mirabeau Lamar adopted a policy of war against the Comanches and obtained an appropriation of $1,000,000 for the purpose.[60]

On March 19, 1840, twelve Comanche commissioners met with agents of the Texas Republic at Bexar, in an attempt to arrange terms of peace. The clash of interest between the Indians and the Texans was fundamental: the Comanches wanted to stop westward expansion of white settlers; the Texans wanted to obtain the return of all white prisoners, and desired further that the Indians should settle down to farming and ranching—that they should adopt the ways of white civilization.[61] When a unit of General

[59] Ernest Wallace and E. Adamson Hoebel, *The Comanches: Lords of the South Plains*, 291. The "Camp Holmes" mentioned in this account is not to be confused with Fort Holmes, farther down the Canadian at the mouth of Little River.

[60] *Ibid.*, 294.

[61] *Ibid.*, 292, 294. Cynthia Ann Parker, white mother of the Comanche chief, Quanah Parker, was captured by Indian raiders at Parker's Fort in 1836.

Hugh D. McLeod's soldiers were brought into the peace conference to overawe the twelve Comanche chiefs, a fight took place in which the Indian commissioners were killed. For this violation of the flag of truce, Comanche raiders took many lives of white immigrants south of the Red River over a period of years. While Lamar was president, the Texans defeated the Comanches at Plum Creek, destroyed Comanche Village on the Colorado, and placed a temporary check upon raids of the Plains Indians.

During Sam Houston's second term as president of Texas an attempt was made to establish friendly relations with the Comanches, on a trading program. Houston regarded trade, with mutual advantages for Indians and whites, the only basis for permanent harmony on the Southern Plains. When he sent a peace delegation to urge the Comanches to take part in a conference, his agents found Chief Paha-yuca encamped in the upper Canadian Valley. With three commissioners of the Texas Republic in their hands, most of the Comanches were in favor of taking revenge for the killing of their chiefs at Bexar; but Paha-yuca persuaded the council by a slim majority to allow the white men to return to Texas.

President Houston succeeded later in reaching an agreement with a part of the Comanches that they would cease their raids south of the Red River. But many bands of the tribe were not parties to the agreement, and it was impossible for Texas to enforce peace for any considerable period of time. Raiding and disorder were to continue for thirty years after the annexation of Texas by the United States.[62]

Effects of the Santa Fé trade in the Indian Territory are difficult to estimate. It is certain that some goods from Santa Fé were exchanged for products of the Arkansas Valley, but the large volume of manufactured articles passed through Independence or some other Missouri River town on the way to the New Mexico trading center. Probably the trade in livestock, destined for Arkansas, Tennessee, or the lower Mississippi Valley, frequently was routed through the Indian country. Van Buren was the starting point for some Santa Fé traders, and apparently some caravans came down the Texas Road from Springfield and Baxter Springs to North Fork Town, then turned west and followed the Canadian

[62] *Ibid.*, 215, 295.

198

River across the Texas Panhandle and into northeastern New Mexico.

Josiah Gregg, on the last of his trips to Santa Fé, proceeded by a well-known route along the north side of the Canadian River, on the outward journey. He returned by a trail which he believed to be a new one. "Although we will no doubt frequently be at some distance from our former trail," he wrote in his diary in February, 1840, as he was about to start back for Van Buren, "we will endeavor to straighten the route." Gregg returned along the south side of the Canadian, traveling about four hundred miles through new territory.[63] He brought back twenty-eight wagons, a large flock of sheep and goats, and more than two hundred mules. The party consisted of forty-seven men—teamsters, scouts, hunters, a Comanche interpreter, a shepherd named Vicento Ximener, cooks, outriders, and others. The journey was enlivened by a prairie fire, by buffalo hunting, and by a clash with hostile Pawnees. In the neighborhood of Rock Mary, in present-day Caddo County, Oklahoma the Comanche scout with Gregg's party killed four buffalo cows. The leader of the expedition thereupon gave the name Cow Creek to the little stream where the animals fell.[64] The caravan reached Van Buren on April 22, after spending about eight weeks on the trail.

[63] Gregg, *Diary & Letters,* I, 43 ff., 43 n.

[64] *Ibid.,* 63. Rock Mary is in present-day Caddo County. Dewey County lies farther northwest.

# CHAPTER NINE

# The Civil War and the Five Civilized Tribes

## SLAVERY AND THE PROBLEM OF SECESSION IN THE INDIAN TERRITORY

Indian slaveholders were relatively few, and by comparison with the cotton-producing areas of the Southeast the territory of the Five Civilized Tribes contained but a small per cent of slave population.[1] The tendency to drive for production of cotton or any other crop was rare in the Indian nations, where marketing was likely to be more difficult than raising a crop. Indian slave codes were milder than corresponding laws of the states, at least until 1860, when the contest over secession had begun and slave restrictions in the Indian nations were tightened.[2]

The southern secession movement of 1860 and 1861 was largely a matter of latitude. It was no coincidence that seven states of the deep south seceded before Fort Sumter fell, four slave states farther north withdrew reluctantly after that event, and four other slave states adjacent to the Mason and Dixon's line, the Ohio River, or free states of the West, failed to reach the stage of overt separation from the Union. There was a sharp difference between the attitude of South Carolina and that of Virginia during early stages of secession, and a sharper difference between the position taken by Louisiana and that taken by Missouri. Similarly, the Choctaws reacted more favorably than the Cherokees to the Confederate call for secession. Wedged in a corner between strong pro-slavery populations in southwestern Arkansas and northern Texas, the Choc-

---

[1] 23 Cong., 1 sess., *Sen. Doc.* 512, III, 149; Wardell, *A Political History of the Cherokee Nation*, 84; Debo, *The Road to Disappearance*, 48, 95, 99, 110.

[2] Debo, *The Road to Disappearance*, 143.

taws had little chance to assert any choice in the matter of secession. Although Chief George Hudson preferred a neutral stand, he was overawed by the threatening attitude of determined Texans and by pressure of influential Choctaws who thought as the Texans did. There was never a remote possibility that the tribe as a whole would take the Federal side in the terrible contest.

Creeks, Chickasaws, and Seminoles were in a similar position, but with less direct pressure from Confederate interests. The Creeks were almost equally divided on the subject of secession.[3] Federal authority was closer to the Creeks than to the Choctaws— in the form of army units stationed in Kansas. Some Creeks were ardent supporters of the Confederacy; some families threw themselves into the great struggle on the side of the Union; and some of the Creek warriors, trying in their simple fashion to identify themselves with the winner, fought first on one side and then on the other. The Cherokees, too, were divided.[4] Probably most of them with their great leader, John Ross, sincerely desired neither a Confederate nor Federal alliance, but neutrality and peace. Yet the tribe allied itself with the South and the young men fought for the Confederacy or the Union; or, like the Creeks, shifted their support from one side to the other, trying to anticipate final results from the evidence of the moment.

After the defeat of Union forces at Wilson's Creek near Springfield, Missouri, on August 10, 1861, the surge of Confederate sentiment was so powerful in the Cherokee Nation that John Ross was no longer able to maintain his neutral position. Surrounded by armed Cherokees who were eager to fight for the Confederacy, this chief who had taken a stand for peace felt obliged to sign a treaty of alliance with the South.[5] The Battle of Pea Ridge, Arkansas, fought between March 6 and March 8 in 1862, brought a sharp reversal of Cherokee opinion. Although Chief Ross would not repudiate the Confederate alliance, Cherokee recruitment into the Union service became very brisk. Many soldiers who enlisted were veterans of Confederate regiments.

[3] *Ibid.*, "The White Man's War," 142–76.
[4] Wardell, *A Political History of the Cherokee Nation*, chaps. VII and VIII, 118–76.
[5] Annie Heloise Abel, *The American Indian as Participant in the Civil War*, 49.

The relative value of Indian Territory to the warring sections was a matter of dispute among strategists. Certainly the Federal government neglected to take effective steps in 1860 for maintaining allegiance of the Five Civilized Tribes. The Confederacy courted the Indians for a time, signed alliances with tribal factions, and then failed to give them adequate support in the form of supplies for their soldiers and military protection for their civilians. Both powers regarded occupation of Indian Territory as subordinate to plans for taking and holding Arkansas and Missouri. Eventually, conquest of the lower Mississippi River by Federal forces and the dominant position of Federal fleets along the Gulf Coast made Confederate occupation of Indian Territory impracticable. By the time this stage of the war was reached, Indian manpower was divided between North and South, and surplus Indian goods was almost nonexistent. In fact, Indian families were in need of food supplies that had to be hauled in from Kansas and Arkansas.

Early in the war, the Choctaws were in close touch with secessionists of Arkansas and Texas. The influence of southern men was strong, especially with Choctaw slaveholders. On October 31, 1860, the Choctaw Council passed a resolution in favor of continuing Douglas H. Cooper as agent. Cooper was an earnest supporter of Southern rights and was to become an active Confederate military commander in the Southwest.

In a meeting of Choctaws and Chickasaws at Boggy Depot on March 11, 1861, for the purpose of considering measures of tribal safety, Texas men were present, urging the Indians to join with the South as a means of protecting their own interests. Chief George Hudson at one time prepared a message to the Choctaw Council proclaiming neutrality for his nation. Robert M. Jones, the tribe's largest slaveowner, gave the chief some food for thought by delivering a bitter denunciation of those Choctaws who were not willing to fight for Southern rights, and a Texas vigilance committee "won Chief Hudson over" by direct threats. The neutrality message was never delivered.[6]

The impulse toward union among the Five Civilized Tribes, strengthened by the Asbury Mission Compact of 1859, was an aid

[6] Annie Heloise Abel, *The American Indian as Slaveholder and Secessionist,* 75 ff.; Thoburn and Wright, *Oklahoma,* II, 823 ff.

to Confederate diplomacy.[7] At the Asbury meeting an intertribal code of laws had been adopted. Leadership in framing written regulations had been taken by educated Cherokees and Choctaws. Perhaps the impulse toward intertribal organization had been most pronounced among the Creeks, whose traditional policy had been based upon incorporation of small tribes and fragments left stranded by the uncertainties of European invasion and settlement. In their new western home the Creeks had continued their old custom by absorbing small bands of Delaware, Kickapoo, Piankashaw, and Shawnee Indians. Mexican children, bought from Comanche traders, were commonly adopted into the Creek tribe.

When the intertribal council met at the Creek Council Ground on February 17, 1861, to consider matters of common concern, imminence of a great sectional war in the United States was apparent to Indian leaders. Although John Ross came out strongly for a neutral position—"Do nothing, keep quiet, comply with treaties" —it must have been clear to Indian delegates that adherence to the Southern cause had immediate advantages.


## CONFEDERATE DIPLOMACY IN THE INDIAN TERRITORY

Most United States officials assigned to the Five Civilized Tribes were southern men. Elias Rector, southern superintendent, was the cousin of the governor of Arkansas, Henry M. Rector.[8] The influence of both men was strong among Arkansas people and among the Indians of all classes in each of the nations. Both of the Rector brothers were early advocates of secession in Arkansas. Douglas H. Cooper, Choctaw agent since 1853, was a powerful secessionist who was soon to become a Confederate general.[9] William H. Garrett of Alabama, Creek agent, and Samuel Rutherford, Seminole agent, were also strong believers in southern rights, thorough proslavery men and staunch upholders of the legality of

[7] Debo, *The Road to Disappearance*, 138, 142.
[8] *Ibid.*, 142; Wardell, *A Political History of the Cherokee Nation*, 125 ff.
[9] Debo, *Rise and Fall of the Choctaw Republic*, 80 ff.

secession. George Butler, Cherokee agent, was another Arkansas citizen who vigorously upheld both slavery and secession.[10]

Withdrawal of Federal troops from Indian Territory at the outbreak of war made a definite impression upon Indian leaders. Chiefs and council members felt that they were being abandoned in an emergency. To supplement this appearance of neglect, officials of the Indian Bureau hesitated to pay annuities when they were due, especially through agents who were southern men and avowed secessionists. The situation of these Indians is well defined by Professor Roy Gittinger: "The position of the Five Civilized Tribes on the border, not their sympathy for the Southern Confederacy, caused them to take part in the war between Union and secession. The abandonment of the Indian Territory by the United States and its occupation by the Confederacy made it necessary for the Indians to recognize the authority of the Confederate government or oppose it unaided."[11]

Like other population groups in the United States, Indians of the Five Civilized Tribes contained elements who opposed slavery and some who were warm supporters of that system of labor. It was natural for large owners of slave property, such as Robert M. Jones of the Choctaws and Benjamin Marshall of the Creeks, to identify their interests with the course of planters who controlled politics in the adjacent states, Arkansas and Texas. Perhaps it was natural, too, for fullblood Indians and others who had no direct interest in slavery to sense the fact that the system of plantation labor was not of advantage to them. Revival of the ancient Cherokee society, Keetoowah, in 1859 was definitely a movement against slavery. Its leaders were fullblood Cherokees, its sponsors were the Baptist missionaries, Evans Jones, and his son John, its opponents were mixed-blooded owners of slave property and agents of the Cherokee tribe who had strong political connections with planters of the neighboring southern states.[12]

Perhaps the most successful Civil War diplomat sent to Indian tribes of the Southwest was Albert Pike of Arkansas.[13] New

[10] Wardell, *A Political History of the Cherokee Nation*, 111, 119.
[11] Roy Gittinger, *Formation of the State of Oklahoma*, 68.
[12] Wardell, *A Political History of the Cherokee Nation*, 120 ff.
[13] *Dictionary of American Biography*, XIV, 593, 594 (article by Harris Ellwood Starr).

England born, Pike had identified himself for many years with the frontier, particularly the Indian country west of Arkansas. He had been active in politics since the admission of his state in 1836. Personally opposed to the institution of slavery, he had advocated recognition of slave property in the constitution of Arkansas, on the ground of its geographic position adjacent to Missouri, Tennessee, Mississippi, and Louisiana. Arkansas, he thought, would become a refuge for runaway slaves from other states if it did not maintain slave labor by its own laws.

With leaders such as Robert M. Jones of the Choctaws, Chilly McIntosh of the Creeks, and Stand Watie of the Cherokees taking a stand for Confederate alliance, Albert Pike worked diligently to settle terms with each tribe.[14] On July 10, 1861, the Creeks agreed to raise a regiment of soldiers for Confederate service, in return for protection and assumption of annuities which the Federal government had not paid. Creek chiefs who opposed such an agreement were absent on a mission to the Antelope Hills, where they were consulting with leaders of the Plains tribes. When Opothle Yahola and Oktarharsars Harjo (Sands) returned home and found that their names had been signed to the Confederate treaty without their consent, they denounced the alliance and took steps to organize Creek resistance to it.

Pike signed treaties with other tribes, including some of the Plains Indians. He reached an agreement with the Cherokees early in October, 1861, two months after the Confederate victory at Wilson's Creek, when many young Cherokees were joining the Confederate Army.

## The Beginning of Armed Conflict

Opothle Yahola had taken command of those Creeks who were determined not to fight with the Confederacy.[15] His original stand, like that of John Ross, had been in favor of neutrality. Unlike the Cherokee leader, Opothle Yahola did not permit himself to be

[14] Debo, *Road to Disappearance*, 144 ff.
[15] Wiley Britton, *The Civil War on the Border*, I, chap. XIII.

forced into Confederate ranks; but he found that he could not live in the Creek Nation as a neutral. With Sands, he appealed to the Federal government for aid, and received nothing but vague promises of future action.

Opothle Yahola and his followers went into camp on Deep Fork, a few miles north of Asbury Mission.[16] Indians of many tribes —Creeks, Comanches, Delawares, Kickapoos, Seminoles, Shawnees, and Wichitas—came to join the band. Against this "neutral" camp, Douglas H. Cooper led a force of Confederate Choctaws and Chickasaws supported by a regiment of Texas cavalry. With advice from his scout on the strength of Cooper's war party, Opothle Yahola broke camp and began a retreat northward. Of necessity his withdrawal was slow, since women and children accompanied the warriors and many Indians attempted to save their personal belongings, including horses and cattle, pigs, and even crates of poultry. The Civil War had come to the Creek Nation. "Loyal Creeks" elected Oktarharsars Harjo acting principal chief, and the Confederates posted a price of $5,000 on his head.

North of the Cimarron River at Round Mountain the slowly retreating followers of Opothle Yahola made a stand. On November 19, 1861, the first battle of the war on Indian Territory soil was fought, with "Loyal Creeks" and their allies putting up a surprising defense. They fought so well that their leader was able to withdraw them in good order and continue the retreat northward, under cover of the darkness.[17]

At Little High Shoals (Chusto Talasah) on Bird Creek, a second indecisive battle was fought about three weeks later. Colonel Douglas Cooper again attacked the Loyal Indians who had taken a strong position at a bend in the stream. After a battle that lasted about four hours, Cooper withdrew his army and fell back to Fort Gibson, where he hoped to get supplies of food and ammunition and substantial reinforcements. Colonel James McIntosh, in command of a Confederate force at Van Buren, Arkansas, agreed to join a new expedition against Opothle Yahola. Cooper, with better weapons and equipment than the Union Indians and with better-trained soldiers, had fought against superior numbers led

[16] Commissioner of Indian Affairs, *Annual Report*, 1861.
[17] Britton, *Civil War on the Border*, I, 166, 167.

by crafty, stubborn Indian leaders who took advantage of every natural feature of the landscape in selecting their battle ground. Cooper had lost far more heavily, in the first two battles, than his opponents.[18]

Colonel McIntosh marched 1,600 mounted soldiers to Fort Gibson and planned with Cooper the combined attack upon Opothle Yahola. Cooper was to proceed along the Arkansas River and attempt an approach from the rear. McIntosh was to follow the Verdigris and march directly against Yahola's camp on Bird Creek. Colonel McIntosh moved rapidly and made his first contact with Union Indians long before Cooper came up. The engagement took place at Chustenahlah on Shoal Creek. Again Opothle Yahola held a position that had many natural advantages and handled his troops with skill. He placed his infantry under the Seminole chief, Halleck Tustennuggee, an experienced fighter. The two Union leaders rallied their troops time after time; but in this third battle the Loyal Indians were overwhelmed. After four hours of stubborn resistance the pressure was too great and the defenders fell back. McIntosh led a furious charge; and when his men reached ground that was too rough for cavalry action, he ordered them to dismount and fight on foot.[19]

Opothle Yahola's surviving soldiers escaped into the rugged country north of Chustenahlah with the Creek families ahead of them. About 160 women and children had been captured, and nearly all the movable property of the Union Indians, including 20 Negroes, had been lost. Wagons, oxen, sheep, horses, and other goods were seized by the victorious Confederates or abandoned in the hasty flight from Chustenahlah. Opothle Yahola's flight across the frozen, snow-covered hills into southern Kansas was an example of civil war at its worst. Colonel McIntosh encamped on Chustenahlah battlefield and next morning pursued the defeated army, keeping almost in sight of their rear guard and occasionally engaging them in a skirmish. The greatest suffering was endured by Creek women and children, some of whom were

[18] *Ibid.,* 169–71.
[19] *Official Records: War of the Rebellion,* Series I, Vol. VIII, 23, 24; Britton, *Civil War on the Border,* 173; Wiley Britton, *The Union Indian Brigade in the Civil War,* 43, 44.

frozen to death. When survivors reached the protection of Federal troops in Kansas and went into camp, it was found that many of them had frozen their hands or feet so severely that the limbs had to be amputated.

## FEDERAL RECOVERY OF INDIAN TERRITORY

Yahola's Indians pitched their camp on the Verdigris River a few miles north of the Cherokee border, where they were joined by other Indians fleeing from the Confederates. Many tribes and peoples were represented in the refugee camp, including Creeks, Cherokees, Chickasaws, Seminoles, Kickapoos, Quapaws, free Negroes, and Creek slaves. By April the number in camp had grown to 7,600.

Some families belonging to minority groups of Indian Territory took the risk of remaining in their homes. It was impossible for any partisan faction in temporary control of a community to maintain even a semblance of order. The Choctaw Nation, committed to one side in the war and not threatened by invasion, was relatively quiet. The Chickasaws suffered less disorder than the tribes farther north, but some lawless men took advantage of relaxed police power and committed various crimes against property and persons. In the other three nations there was anarchy. Theft and crimes of violence went unpunished, women and children were in constant peril, families of Union soldiers suffered from raids on their livestock, destruction of crops, and burning of houses. When the opportunity came, the Federal Indians retaliated.

Probably no portion of the United States endured more hardships from civil war than the people of Indian Territory. The flight of refugees, first Union families to the north and then Confederate families to the south, was a regular feature of the Indian campaigns; and before the fighting ended, a class of lawless raiders sprang up whose interest in war was the opportunity it offered them to live by violence.

In general, Confederate Indians fared better than those who supported the Union. Partisans of the South were able to collect some annuities early in the war, and a little money was brought into the country by white Confederate soldiers and by tribal delegates sent to Richmond. Even in the later stages of war, when Union soldiers were driving the Confederates out of their homes to take refuge in Choctaw camps or across the Red River, their condition was not so miserable as that of the Loyal refugees in 1861 and 1862. All factions in each of the Five Civilized Tribes, however, suffered greater losses than other participants in the Civil War.

In March, 1862, the Federal authorities planned an invasion of Indian Territory by Union Indians supported by white regiments. On April 1, James G. Blunt was promoted to the rank of brigadier general and placed in command of southern Kansas and Indian Territory. He selected Colonel William Weer to lead the Indian expedition and ordered that units for the invasion be assembled at Baxter Springs.[20]

Colonel Weer's force consisted of the Second Ohio Cavalry, the Sixth Kansas Cavalry, three white infantry regiments, and two regiments of fugitive Indians. In addition there were two artillery units, the First Kansas Battery and Rabb's Second Indiana Battery. During the invasion a third Indian regiment was organized under the command of Colonel William A. Phillips, an able officer who was destined to win the complete confidence of Union Indian soldiers and their people. The total number of invading soldiers was about six thousand.[21]

Colonel Weer's regiments moved southward on June 23 and pursued a Cherokee force commanded by Colonel Stand Watie and a larger unit of white Confederate soldiers under Colonel J. J. Clarkson. Before daylight on July 3, Weer closed in upon the camp of Colonel Clarkson near Locust Grove, caught the Confederates off guard and routed them.[22] Clarkson's men were so completely demoralized that they were unable to form a battle line; and when their commander saw that their case was hopeless, he surrendered the soldiers who had not fled at the first volley or lost their lives in the surprise attack. Men who escaped went south to Tahlequah,

[20] Britton, *Civil War on the Border*, I, 297 ff.
[21] *Ibid.*, 297, 298, 304; James G. Blunt, "General Blunt's Account of His Civil War Experiences," *Kansas State Historical Quarterly*, Vol. I, No. 1 (1932), 223.
[22] Britton, *Union Indian Brigade*, 65, 66.

where their story of Clarkson's defeat gave a powerful impulse to Union recruiting of Cherokees.[23] Sixty ammunition wagons, sixty-four mule teams, and large quantities of provisions were captured, along with 110 men who surrendered.

Colonel Weer crossed Grand River and went into camp, where his force was considerably increased by new enlistments of Cherokees. He learned that the main Confederate military party of Indian Territory had taken a position just south of the Arkansas River at the newly constructed Fort Davis. Weer marched his troops to Tahlequah and at Park Hill arrested John Ross, placing him on parole. The Union forces had enjoyed unbroken success since beginning the invasion; but their position was not entirely secure, and after two weeks of comparative inaction, their officers began to consider withdrawal. Their real or imagined peril was the result of complex factors, involving the broad distribution of troops among western armies, uncertainty concerning the number and strength of Confederate units, and especially the personalities of Colonel Weer and his second officer, Colonel Frederick Salomon.

On July 17, Weer called a conference of his officers to consider their situation. A Confederate force which was reported to be approximately equal in number to the Union army was stationed across the Arkansas River a few miles to the south; supplies were short at Fort Gibson and Tahlequah, with no more food and ammunition immediately obtainable; and it was possible that a Confederate band, moving in from Arkansas, might cut off communications with the Union base of supplies in Kansas. The council of officers agreed that it would be prudent to withdraw northward. Apparently Colonel Weer accepted that view, but in a short time reversed his decision and ordered his officers to take up a permanent position at Fort Gibson.

Whereupon, Colonel Salomon ordered Weer's arrest and took upon himself the responsibility of withdrawing the force to Kansas.[24] In his report to General Bunt, Salomon suggested that Weer might be insane or disloyal and charged him specifically with habitual drunkenness, ignoring the advice of his subordinates, and various cases of neglect of duty. In a general court martial later,

[23] *Official Records: War of the Rebellion*, Series I, Vol. XIII, 137, 138.
[24] *Ibid.*, 484, 485.

General Bunt attempted to sift out the truth from a vast array of charges and countercharges; but since most officers who could serve as witnesses were partisan supporters of Salomon or of Weer, the general decided to dissolve the court and restore Weer to his rank as Colonel.[25]

John Ross was arrested a second time and removed to Fort Scott with the Federal troops. From there he was sent to Washington and was finally permitted to remain in Philadelphia for the duration of the war. His position was not clearly understood by civil officers of either section. Before hostilities began he was a slaveowner, but not an ardent supporter of the view that men had an unassailable right to own slave property. He was against secession and in favor of maintaining existing treaties with the Federal government. Most of all, however, he was in favor of any course that promised security for the Cherokee people, and it was this attitude that caused him to take a stand for neutrality. When it became clear that the Cherokees could not remain aloof from the war and pressure to join the Confederacy became irresistible, he signed Albert Pike's treaty. It is well understood now that he accepted Confederate alliance with great reluctance, and only in the hope that civil war for his people could be avoided.

When Frederick Salomon withdrew the Union regiments from Indian Territory, he left Indian troops on the Verdigris River to keep watch on developments there. Colonel William A. Phillips, in command of these soldiers, performed remarkable services for the Union Indians. Under conditions of extreme disorder with raids and counterraids sweeping the country, he gave much-needed protection to Indian families that elected to stay in their homes. He hauled grain from Arkansas and from little gristmills in the Cherokee Nation to fugitive Indians, and did all that he could to offset the demoralizing effects of Stand Watie's forays. William C. Quantrill brought his guerrillas down from Kansas into the Cherokee Nation in October, 1862, and added to the general disorder. The Indian Territory became a wasted, desolate region of terror and despair.

On October 20, 1862, General Blunt moved from the Federal

[25] Blunt, "General Blunt's Account of His Civil War Experiences," *Kansas State Historical Quarterly*, Vol. I, No. 1 (1923), 234.

camp on the Pea Ridge battleground against Douglas H. Cooper's Indian force, which was camped near Maysville, Arkansas. General Cooper had occupied Fort Wayne, and was preparing to move from this point, just inside the Cherokee Nation, into southern Kansas. Blunt's party consisted of two brigades under Colonel Weer and Colonel William Cloud.[26] On the night of October 21, Blunt marched from Bentonville to Maysville, hoping to catch the Confederates by surprise. Cooper was warned of his approach, however, and was ready to fall back when Blunt's first cavalry units arrived. The Union forces were not in a compact body, but their commander decided to attack with three companies of cavalry in order to hold Cooper until the rest of the Federal party came up.

General Cooper, noting the small number of men in the attacking force, attempted an enveloping movement on both flanks; but a Kansas regiment arrived and supported Blunt on the right, while Colonel Phillips came up on the left with his Third Indian Regiment, and the Confederates were forced back. Five cavalry companies charged the Confederate center and captured their four artillery pieces. General Cooper was forced to retreat, and the Union mounted troops pursued him to Spavinaw Creek.[27] His army continued southward to the Arkansas River, crossing near Skully- ville and ending for a time the danger of Confederate invasion of Kansas. The action at Fort Wayne gave evidence that the Union commander, though lacking in military training and experience, was a man of courage and vigor.

On December 7, 1862, a battle at Prairie Grove, Arkansas, had far-reaching results for the entire Southwest. General Hindman, preparing for a drive northward toward the Missouri River with a strong Confederate division, was met by General James G. Blunt in command of the principal Federal force of northwestern Arkansas. After a conflict which lasted through an entire day, the two armies were still locked in a desperate struggle when darkness ended the fighting. Both commanders claimed the victory, but after nightfall the Confederate infantry began a withdrawal toward Van Buren, leaving their fires burning along the woods

[26] *Official Records: War of the Rebellion,* Series I, Vol. XIII, 754, 325, 326.
[27] J. C. Hopkins, "James G. Blunt and the Civil War" (unpublished master's thesis, University of Oklahoma, 1952), 46–52.

where they were camped and muffling the wheels of artillery carriages with torn blankets. General Hindman asked for an interview, and the two generals agreed upon a period of six hours for burial of the dead. During that interval the Confederates moved out of danger of pursuit and later continued southward to the Arkansas River. Casualties were heavy on both sides. General Blunt reported 167 killed, 798 wounded, and 183 missing. Hindman's official report listed a total of 1,317 casualties—164 killed, 817 wounded, and 336 missing. Wide differences appeared in the reports on number of men engaged. It is probable that the Confederate force was larger than Blunt's army, and it is certain that the Union commander enjoyed an advantage in superior artillery.[28]

From the battle of Prairie Grove on the upper Illinois, Colonel Phillips marched 1,200 Federal Indian troops and two white companies, supported by artillery, to the Arkansas River near Three Forks. He crossed at Frozen Rock Ford and captured Fort Davis, which he burned.

During the campaigns of 1862 in the Creek and Cherokee nations, a Union Indian raid occurred in the Leased District. A band of seventy Delawares and twenty-six Shawnees led by the Delaware chief, Ben Simon, came down from Kansas and attacked the Wichita Agency on Sugar Creek north of the Washita. Matthew Leeper was the agent. He had taken charge of the Wichitas and neighboring groups in 1860 and had made some progress in teaching farming to Indians of the middle Washita—Delawares, Caddoes, Pawnees, Kichais, and others. Like Indian agents of the Five Civilized Tribes, Leeper was a supporter of the Confederacy. According to reports of the Delaware agent, F. Johnson, spies from the raiding party found a band of well-armed Confederate Indians at the agency; but before the main force could be brought up for an attack, these Indians escaped. When Ben Simon and his party reached the agency, Matthew Leeper demanded that he state his business; and the Delaware answered, "You are my prisoner." Whereupon, Ben and his followers attempted to rush into the

[28] Each of the opposing generals in the official reports overestimated the number of opponents engaged in the battle. Blunt placed Hindman's forces at about 25,000; his own at 8,000. Hindman estimated Blunt's army at 14,000 to 18,000 and gave his number as 10,000. *Official Records: War of the Rebellion,* Series I, Vol. XXII, Part I, 41–158; Britton, *Union Indian Brigade,* 118–52.

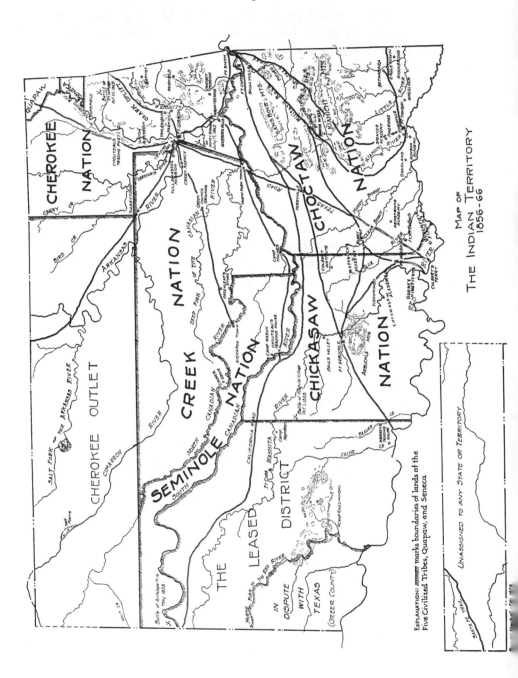

MAP OF
THE INDIAN TERRITORY
1856-66

EXPLANATION: ///////// marks boundaries of lands of the
Five Civilized Tribes, Quapaw, and Seneca

UNASSIGNED TO ANY STATE OR TERRITORY

agency building, and as they ran forward the white men inside fired, killing one Delaware and wounding one Shawnee. Leeper and the other three white men were killed by the raiders, who also burned agency buildings and carried off such livestock and other property as they could move. About one hundred ponies were captured, and Ben Simon brought back $1,200 in Confederate money, together with the Albert Pike treaty and Matthew Leeper's commission as Indian agent, signed by President James Buchanan on February 1, 1861.[29] On the way back to Kansas, Ben Simon's Indians overtook the party that escaped from the agency, numbering about one hundred and fifty men, women, and children, and killed one hundred of them. The Delawares and Shawnees were commended very highly by Agent Johnson, but their action was regarded as an Indian outrage by southern observers, who were inclined to regard the killing of Matthew Leeper and his assistants as murder.

Albert Pike was sent from Tishomingo with a military party to punish the raiders, but he reached the Wichita Agency after Ben Simon had gone back to Kansas. It was shortly after his return that General Pike was relieved of his command and his resignation accepted by the Richmond government.[30]

The year 1863 was a period of decisive action not only at Gettysburg and Vicksburg, but also in the Indian country. In February the Union Cherokees held a council at Camp Ross on Cowskin Prairie in which they repudiated the Confederate alliance and affirmed their loyalty to the United States. At the same tribal council all Cherokee slaves were freed. In April, Colonel Phillips drove Stand Watie out of Fort Gibson, which the Confederates had occupied while Union Indians were engaged elsewhere. Phillips built stronger fortifications, more commodious barracks, and storage space to enable a relatively small force of defenders to stand a long siege or repel a powerful attack. He renamed the place Fort Blunt, but the name was not much used except in official correspondence. Colonel Phillips, in command of the Third Indian Regiment, hauled grain to refugee Cherokees, tried to check Stand Watie's

---

[29] Abel, *The Indian as Slaveholder and Secessionist*, Appendix B (from the Leeper Papers), 329, 330.

[30] Wardell, *A Political History of the Cherokee Nation*, 147.

raids, and occasionally led forays south of the Arkansas River. On April 24, Phillips raided Webbers Falls, preventing a meeting of the Confederate Cherokee Council. Afterward, when Union Indian forces were depleted for a Missouri campaign, Stand Watie attacked Fort Gibson, but was beaten off. It was then that the work of Colonel Phillips in erecting fortifications was fully appreciated.

In June, 1863, General Blunt sent a long supply train guarded by 1,600 soldiers from Kansas into the Cherokee Nation. At Cabin Creek, during a period of flooded streams, this rich prize—218 mule wagons and 40 ox teams—was attacked by Stand Watie and D. N. McIntosh with a party of approximately 1,400 men. After a bloody battle which was somewhat complicated by swollen waters, the Confederates were defeated and fell back to Honey Springs, their supply depot south of Three Forks.[31] Stand Watie's personal retreat, when pursuit became too hot for comfort, was Briartown southeast of Honey Springs and near the great bend in the South Canadian River.

General Blunt followed his supply train south, accompanied by Colonel William R. Judson and about six hundred men with two twelve-pound howitzers.[32] Colonel Phillips and other officers at Fort Gibson arranged a reception for their commander when he arrived. Phillips introduced General Blunt and called attention to his record during the previous year: victories over Confederate armies at Newtonia, Missouri, Cane Hill and Prairie Grove, Arkansas, and Fort Wayne in the Cherokee Nation. He pointed out that Blunt's aggressive tactics had resulted in the capture of Van Buren and valuable Confederate steamers on the Arkansas, loaded with military supplies. Blunt delivered a brief address in which he announced news recently received which the people at Fort Gibson had not heard. During the first days of July, General George Meade had turned back the great army of Robert E. Lee at Gettysburg, Pennsylvania; and General Grant had, with the help of gunboats on the Mississippi, succeeded finally in capturing Vicksburg. Blunt believed that the turning point had been reached, that the opening of the Mississippi would release Union soldiers for service in the Southwest, and that conditions would steadily improve for the Union cause.[33]

[31] *Official Records: War of the Rebellion*, Series I, Vol. XXII, Part I, 378–82.

216

Little time was lost in ceremonies or social functions for the General. Blunt had learned of a Confederate plan to attack Fort Gibson with Cooper's Indian and Texas regiments combined with a force under General William L. Cabell, who was ready to march from Fort Smith to Honey Springs. It was Blunt's purpose to strike before the two Confederate units could join, and he moved rapidly after reaching Fort Gibson. When he stood on the Arkansas River bank he could see a Confederate advance guard across the stream. Late at night on July 15, Blunt crossed a small party with artillery at Hitchiti Ford and moved down the right bank toward the Confederate outpost. General Cooper's soldiers withdrew to Honey Springs, and the Union commander was free to transport his entire army across the Arkansas. On the morning of July 17 he marched against Cooper's force, which formed its lines for the defense of the principal Confederate supply depot.

The first contact of the opposing armies was at a point just north of Oktaha, a few miles from Honey Springs. Blunt's artillery quickly demonstrated its strength, and the Confederates fell back to take a position previously selected by General Cooper in the timber along Elk Creek. In the Confederate army, Colonel Stand Watie commanded two Cherokee regiments, Colonel D. N. McIntosh led two Creek regiments, Colonel Tandy Walker, a regiment composed of Choctaws and Chickasaws, and Colonel T. C. Bass led the Twentieth Texas Cavalry. Other units under General Cooper's command were the Fifth Texas Rangers, the Twenty-ninth Texas Cavalry, and an additional cavalry force stationed at Honey Springs as reserves. The Confederate artillery consisted of one battery of four guns.

General Blunt's army consisted of two cavalry regiments, the Second Colorado Infantry, the First Kansas Colored Infantry, and two Indian regiments. His two howitzers and two artillery batteries of four guns each gave him a marked advantage in that branch.[34]

The Union force advanced and after several hours of bitter fighting succeeded in driving the Confederates from their position and across Elk Creek. Their withdrawal became a rapid retreat

[32] Britton, *Union Indian Brigade*, 268.
[33] *Ibid.*, 269–71.
[34] *Official Records: War of the Rebellion*, Series I, Vol. XXII, Part I, 447–62.

and turned into a rout. Only the effective rear-guard action of Cooper's cavalry units prevented complete disaster as Blunt's mounted units pursued the retreating confederates for several miles.

As in many other battles of the Civil War, reports on the number of troops engaged were contradictory and misleading. Probably Cooper's army had more soldiers than the attacking force; but, as noted above, the Confederates were lacking in effective artillery, and they had an unusual amount of trouble with defective ammunition. General Blunt reported that his men buried 150 Confederate dead, took 77 prisoners, and estimated that there were about 400 of Cooper's men wounded.[35] He stated in the same report that his army lost 17 killed and 60 wounded.

Late in the afternoon General Cabell arrived from Fort Smith in command of two thousand mounted men and four pieces of artillery. He was in no condition to attack Blunt's victorious troops, however, since his men were tired and widely spaced in the line of march. He joined Cooper, and the combined forces went into camp south of the Canadian. In retiring, Confederate troops had hastily set fire to the buildings that housed their supplies at Honey Springs. However, Blunt's men arrived in time to save large quantities of bacon, flour, and beef, which they used in preparing supper on the battlefield.[36]

Late in August, Confederate troops numbering about nine thousand under General William Steele approached within fifteen miles of Fort Gibson. Blunt again went out to meet them, but Steele's army divided, General Cabell marching part of the force toward Fort Smith and General Steele moving southward along the Texas Road toward Perryville. Blunt's army pursued Steele, and on the evening of August 25 fought a skirmish with a part of the Confederates at Perryville. Again the defenders were beaten, and Blunt destroyed the Perryville supply depot. At North Fork Town another Confederate store of supplies was destroyed.

Turning from his campaign against Steele, General Blunt moved against Cabell in the eastern part of Indian Territory. As the Union army advanced, the Confederates fell back slowly be-

35 *Ibid.*, 448; Britton, *Union Indian Brigade*, 284, 285.
36 Britton, *Union Indian Brigade*, 282.

218

yond the Poteau; and General Cabell turned southeast toward Waldron, where the rough, mountainous land and lack of roads made pursuit more difficult. General Blunt sent Colonel William F. Cloud with a cavalry force to follow the retreating Confederates while he occupied Fort Smith with the main part of his army. Colonel Cloud fought a minor engagement at Backbone Mountain, sixteen miles southeast of Fort Smith. During the fighting three regiments of Confederate soldiers broke ranks and left the field, taking with them eighty men who were under sentence of death for desertion. These regiments and the deserters were hill people who had been conscripted into the Confederate military service and had no desire to fight for the Southern cause.

The major conflicts of 1863 were over for the Indian country when General Blunt marched into Fort Smith on September 1. His forces had pushed the war south of the Arkansas and Canadian, and for the remaining months of civil war, northern Indian Territory was in Union hands. Stand Watie raided north of the Arkansas many times, inflicting severe damage against Federal supply bases almost to the end of the war; but larger movements of Confederate armies were no longer a threat in the north.

## The End of Trial by Battle

There was still great disorder in the Cherokee Nation and in many other parts of Indian Territory through 1864 and for a long time afterward. Northern refugees were not safe in their homes, because partisan military groups in the western counties of Arkansas and Missouri kept up a constant reign of terror, and the danger from Stand Watie's raids did not end until his surrender in the summer of 1865. Some small bands were commanded by guerrilla leaders who had no clear military status. Before the outbreak of war, William C. Quantrill was identified with Kansas abolitionists taking part in a raid into the Cherokee Nation for the purpose of freeing Negro slaves. Later he received a commission as colonel in the Confederate Army, but remained primarily a bandit raider. His activities became a threat to civilians who sympathized with the Confederacy as well as those who supported the Union. In northern Texas and southern Indian Territory he made himself so obnoxious to all classes of decent citizens that his arrest was ordered by the Confederate government. His operations, like those of his principal guerrilla rival, Bill Anderson, were chiefly in Missouri, Kansas, Texas, and Kentucky; but on occasion he came to Indian Territory, and some of the men who rode with him were quite active in the Cherokee Nation.[37]

Colonel Stand Watie, who was commissioned brigadier general before the war ended, was a persistent and implacable enemy of Union Indians; but in spite of his partisan background as a figure in the Cherokee removal troubles, he did not stoop to raids that were unconnected with military objectives. He raided at Tahlequah and Park Hill after the Confederate defeat at Honey Springs. His band destroyed the house of John Ross at Park Hill and on June 12, 1864, captured the steamer *J. R. Williams* at the mouth of the Canadian River. In the following September he captured a Federal wagon train at Cabin Creek near the place where his forces had met defeat earlier in the war. The raiders captured seven hundred mules, one hundred wagons, and vast quantities of war materials.

From May to June, 1864, the new Federal superintendent of southern tribes, William G. Coffin, undertook the task of moving Union refugee Indians back to their homes. In one wagon train there were three hundred mule teams, which made a procession three miles long with three thousand Indians traveling on foot and many more, aged and small children, in baggage wagons. There were sixteen births and six deaths on the journey to Fort Gibson, where the agent was already trying to feed nine thousand refugees. The new party arrived on June 15, 1864.

In the issue of supplies to refugee Indians, a service which lasted for several years in varying amounts, serious abuses arose. McDonald and Company, an established firm at Fort Smith and Fort Gibson, furnished corn to the government at $7.00 per bushel and beef at 6 cents a pound. Superintendent Coffin bought the

[37] Abel, *The Indian as Slaveholder and Secessionist*, 48, 214n.; Britton, *Union Indian Brigade*, 301, 312ff., 375ff., 382–86; William E. Connelley, *Quantrill and the Border Wars*, 198.

corn from Indians and others at $2.50 per bushel, paying for it with drafts on McDonald and Company. Government supplies were stored in warehouses of the mercantile company, after being delivered by means of wagon trains furnished by the War Department, to be sold in a new transaction with agents of the United States. Many cattle stolen in the Cherokee Nation and Creek Nation, sometimes by army officers, were sold to the government for use in feeding refugee Indians. In commenting on the sad condition of six thousand Creeks who were encamped on the west bank of Grand River, almost within shouting distance of their homes but unable as yet to return to them, Angie Debo has written: "Here within sight of the familiar valley and stream and distant hills they were more homesick than ever. Worst of all they were forced to watch the systematic looting of their country by its supposed protectors."[38]

In February, 1864, Colonel Phillips led 1,500 Union soldiers into southern Indian Territory. He marched to Edwards' Post at the mouth of Little River, crossed the Canadian, and turned south. He met little opposition either in the Creek Nation or farther south among the Choctaws and Chickasaws. He sent copies of Lincoln's Amnesty Proclamation to Confederate leaders and distributed copies at Boggy Depot. His purpose was to obtain formal repudiation of Confederate treaties and to gain active support among the southern Indians. His efforts were along the line that might have been followed early in 1861 to secure support of the Five Civilized Tribes for the Union without unnecessary cost in men and goods. But his mission was not successful. The Choctaws refused to talk terms of amnesty with Phillips and gave every indication of remaining loyal to the Confederacy in its period of obvious decline. Confederate Choctaws, Chickasaws, Creeks, Seminoles, Caddoes, and Osages held a conference at Tishomingo to counteract the propaganda of the Phillips expedition. Later when a small group of "loyal" Choctaws tried to set up a government at Skullyville, Phillips refused to recognize them on the ground that they did not represent the Choctaw people.[39]

[38] Debo, *Road to Disappearance*, 163; Britton, *Union Indian Brigade*, 453 ff.
[39] *Official Records: War of the Rebellion*, Series I, Vol. XXX, Part IV, 694, 695; Vol. XXXIV, Part II, 190, 994 ff.; Annie Heloise Abel, *The American Indian under Reconstruction*, 17–21.

Confederate refugee camps were filled during the last year of the war. Federal Indians who were able to come back to their homes under Union military protection were full of hate because of their own hardships. When survivors of the Kansas refugee camps with bitter memories of the terrible northern flight, found themselves able to turn the tables on their Confederate neighbors, they were not inclined to be generous victors. Many southern refugees crossed the Red River into Texas while others established camps on the lower Washita or Kiamichi.[40]

While Confederate Indians showed little inclination to curry favor with the United States by repudiating their alliances, they did make strong efforts to unite with Plains tribes and Union Indians as a means of approaching the peace talks. To avoid the influence of Superintendent William Coffin, they changed the place of their meeting from Council Grove near the site of Yukon to Camp Napoleon on the Washita, forty miles farther southwest. The meeting took place in May, 1865, and by that time the Confederate cause was clearly lost. Leaders of the Five Civilized Tribes, meeting with Caddo, Comanche, Kiowa, Osage, and Cheyenne chiefs, resolved on permanent peace among themselves and renewed their pledges of union. In a sense the meeting at Camp Napoleon was a continuation of the movement toward federal union begun at Asbury in 1859 and carried on during the war at Chahta Tamaha and Tishomingo.

Gradually the Confederate Indians learned that their alliance was with the losing side. Robert E. Lee surrendered at Appomattox on April 9, 1865, less than a week before the murder of Abraham Lincoln; Joseph E. Johnston surrendered his army in Georgia on April 26; President Jefferson Davis was captured on May 10; Kirby Smith surrendered on May 24; and Chief Peter Pitchlynn yielded to a Federal commission on June 19. Four days later Stand Watie surrendered—last of the Confederate generals to lay down his arms.

During the war a political movement for relocation of Indian tribes had developed, largely upon the activities of Samuel C. Pomeroy and James H. Lane, United States senators from Kansas. The purpose of these men was to find a place for Kansas Indians—

[40] Angie Debo, "Southern Refugees of the Cherokee Nation," *Southwestern Historical Quarterly*, Vol. XXXV (April, 1932), 255-66.

the Osage, Pottawatomie, Kickapoo, Sac and Fox, Ottawa, Kansas, Iowa, and Shawnee tribes—in order that their lands might be thrown open to settlement.[41] It was a form of pressure, different only in detail from that which had driven the Indians out of Georgia, Alabama, Mississippi, and Florida. Representative Cyrus Aldrich of Minnesota was a supporter of the plan, as a means of removing Indians from valuable land coveted by white citizens of his state, and Secretary of the Interior Caleb Smith of Indiana gave his approval and aid.

By 1865 a large number of men in public life were interested in providing room in territory belonging to the Five Civilized Tribes for new Indian settlements. Originally given to southern tribes in exchange for their land in the East, which was vastly more valuable as marketable property than the western area, this final home of the Indians was now to be wrested from its owners on the theory that they had forfeited their treaty rights.

Secretary of the Interior James Harlan, who took office early in President Johnson's administration, determined to acquaint leaders of the Indian tribes with their new status by means of a council. Various places were considered for the conference. Confederate Indians were eager to meet with representatives of the Plains tribes and Union Indians, in order that common interests of the natives might soften the hatred developed by war. Perhaps it was fear of the setting where Indian unity was likely to take root that caused Harlan to decide against Chahta Tamaha, deep in the Choctaw Nation, and in favor of Fort Smith as the meeting place.[42]

[41] Gittinger, *Formation of the State of Oklahoma,* 81–85.
[42] *Ibid.,* 87.

# CHAPTER TEN

# Reconstruction in the Indian Territory

## CONDITIONS AT THE END OF THE WAR

The Civil War, like the War of 1812, was an occasion for transformation of United States relations with Indian tribes. The Red Sticks, co-operating with Great Britain in 1812, furnished many plausible arguments for annulment of treaties with the southern Indians, and for moving them west of Arkansas Territory. Alliances of the Five Civilized Tribes with the Confederacy in 1861 provided a new excuse for violating treaties, entered upon with the constitutional formality of a great nation. The fact that southern Indian tribes had no alternative but to sign agreements with Albert Pike, and that their helpless condition resulted from neglect by United States authorities, had no bearing upon the decisions of 1865 and 1866. Terms of the new treaties at Washington were dictated by the demands of politicians whose constituents wanted to possess Indian property in Kansas, Minnesota, and elsewhere.

In 1865 the Indian Territory was a region of desolation. No great armies had operated there, and no battles that were broadly decisive had been fought within the area; but the entire population had been involved, and the destruction of homes, public buildings, crops and fences, livestock, tools and implements had been almost complete. Streams of fugitives moving along trails and roads or slipping along rivers and through the woods toward neighboring states, first to the north and then to the south, tell the story of war conditions in the land of the Five Civilized Tribes.

About 2,220 Cherokees served in Union armies and about 1,400 with Confederate forces. Official records do not give with accuracy the number who lost their lives in battle, and only the roughest estimate can be made concerning the number of women and children and aged Cherokees who perished as an indirect result of the war, from neglect, exposure, starvation, or from epidemics that attacked the fugitives in their crowded quarters. After two years of battles, guerrilla warfare, and refugee camps, one third of the Union Cherokee women were widows and one fourth of the Cherokee children were orphans. A census taken just after the war set the total population at 13,566—a figure that does not take into account those who had not returned from exile in Texas or elsewhere.[1]

The Creek tribe supplied 1,675 men for the Union Army and 1,575 for the Confederate. Their losses were heavy, both from fighting in the field and from general disorder. Although Choctaw territories were not much invaded by enemy troops and Choctaw soldiers were generally close to their homes, the tribe was still in a pitiable condition at the end of the war. One third of the Choctaw people were then described as "entirely destitute."[2]

Livestock losses were heavy throughout the Indian Territory, but probably were not so great in the south as they were in the Creek, Seminole, and Cherokee nations. Cattle theft became a profitable occupation for border ranchmen north of the Cherokee Nation and even for army officers late in the war, when the United States government was purchasing large numbers of beeves for military contracts and for refugee supplies. It is estimated that 300,000 Cherokee cattle were stolen and sold to the contractors.[3] By comparison with the other tribes, Choctaws and Chickasaws wasted little effort on factional contests, and their losses were correspondingly less; but even in these southern nations, the neglect of land, burning of homes, and destruction of public buildings created a general atmosphere of ruin and desolation. Fear, suspicion, and hatred were among the heritages of internal strife, and in the regions of old partisan feuds, these dangerous tendencies were at their worst.

[1] John Ross Manuscripts, Census Report, Frank Phillips Collection, University of Oklahoma Library; Wardell, *A Political History of the Cherokee Nation*, 216.

[2] *Official Records: War of the Rebellion*, Series I, Vol. LIII, Supplement, 1034–5.

[3] Wardell, *A Political History of the Cherokee Nation*, 175. There is evidence of organized theft of cattle in the Choctaw Nation, however, especially in 1864 and 1865. Commissioner of Indian Affairs, *Annual Report*, 1864, 1865.

Public education was in a low state throughout the Indian Territory. Schools were suspended during the war, and the buildings had fallen into a condition of disrepair, even when not completely destroyed. Sometimes the schoolhouses had been used as barracks or hospitals, and in such cases retreating armies almost invariably burned them. Tribal finances were much restricted after the war, and the heavy expense of rebuilding schools was undertaken with painful slowness.

By 1868 the Cherokees were conducting such schools as their limited funds permitted, and the missions were recovering some lost ground. An act of the National Council on March 1, 1867, resulted in the opening of thirty-two public schools. By 1869 the appropriation for schools was $18,820, including support for Negro education and for the expense of educating orphan children. By 1877 the number of public day schools in the Cherokee Nation had grown to seventy-five.[4]

The Creek Council was authorized to spend $2,000 from funds received under terms of the treaty in 1866 for restoration of school buildings at Asbury and Tullahassee.[5] The council appropriated $6,000 additional funds, and by 1871 the buildings were repaired and the two schools were filled to capacity, each with eighty children. Under a contract with the Creek Council, Joseph M. Perryman opened a new boarding school for girls with a capacity of forty at Prairie Grove, ten miles west of Eufaula. Division of expenses in boarding schools of the Creek Nation was as follows: the mission boards paid salaries of teachers; the tribal government paid for food and other expenses of the pupils and furnished buildings, land, and equipment for operating the schools. The boarding school trustees selected one boy and one girl from each town to attend, under restrictions which forbade naming more than one person from the same family. When space was available this regulation was dropped. By 1871, elementary day schools had been established in many communities, six of which were operated for Negroes.[6]

[4] Wardell, *A Political History of the Cherokee Nation,* 216.

[5] *A Compilation of All the Treaties between the United States and the Indian Tribes,* 116 (5127, 5128).

[6] Debo, *Road to Disappearance,* 204.

The Chickasaw and Choctaw tribes also received additional sums of money from the United States under terms of their new treaty in 1866, and a general provision directed that the funds should be devoted to tribal interests, including educational needs.[7] Boarding schools gradually recovered from the disasters of war and resumed their work, but before the first of them reopened, the Choctaw Council had made provision for neighborhood elementary schools. In 1867 the first pupils were admitted, and within two years enrollment was 1,764 in eighty-four schools. The most difficult problem in Choctaw education, as in the other tribes, was to raise enough money to support schools with adequate standards of instruction. Many teachers were poorly prepared, and in some instances a term of school planned for nine or ten months would have to be cut to half length. When the first two academies were opened, some of the neighborhood schools were closed to meet the added tribal expense.[8] New Hope Seminary near Fort Coffee, was ready to receive pupils in 1871. The Methodist Episcopal Church South contracted to operate the school for fifty girls, paying all expenses of pupils, salaries of teachers and superintendent, and maintenance of the school plant, for the sum of $5,000 annually. Spencer Academy for boys was placed under the Presbyterian mission board with a contract for annual payment by the Choctaw Council similar to the New Hope agreement. By 1882 a new building for Spencer had been built several miles west of the original site, and each of the boarding schools had been enlarged to accommodate one hundred pupils.[9]

Like the United States as a whole, the Indian nations displayed a tendency toward low political standards after the Civil War. There had always been more than a trace of undue influence upon tribal chiefs when United States officials were intent upon driving a bargain with them. The distinction between paying Indian delegates a legitimate sum for their time and expenses, on the one hand, and giving them bribes to purchase their influence with the tribe, on the other was always a difficult line to draw. Offi-

[7] *A Compilation of Treaties between the United States and the Indian Tribes,* 301, 302 (13457–13474).

[8] Debo, *Rise and Fall of the Choctaw Republic,* 96, 97.

[9] *Ibid.,* 237, 238; Commissioner of Indian Affairs, *Annual Report,* 1870, 1871, 1882, 1897.

cials at Washington and commissioners in the field were constantly engaged in winning the support of tribal leaders by means of personal favors.

The Choctaw delegation at Washington in 1866, containing some of the ablest men in the nation, became involved in a financial transaction which was regrettable, to say the least. Robert M. Jones, appointed as one of the delegates, did not serve. Chief Peter Pitchlynn, John Page, James Riley, Alfred Wade, and Allen Wright, representing the Choctaw Nation, employed Douglas H. Cooper, John D. Cochrane, and John H. B. Latrobe as attorneys in a long and difficult negotiation with Federal officials. Cochrane had been attorney for the Choctaws in the Net Proceeds case of 1855, and as a result of arbitration the United States Senate in 1859 had awarded $2,981,247.30 to the Choctaws. Of that amount the government had paid $250,000 in 1861, and had appropriated an equal sum in bonds, which were withheld when the tribe made an alliance with the Confederacy. Since John D. Cochrane and Douglas H. Cooper had recently been associated with the Southern Confederacy, Latrobe took the lead in obtaining a financial settlement for the Choctaws in 1866. Latrobe's fee as presented to the Choctaw national treasurer was $100,000. By comparison with legitimate charges allowed for similar work in legal proceedings, the amount was excessive. Sampson Folsom, Choctaw national attorney, charged that Albert Pike had been displaced as net proceeds adviser in 1855 by John D. Cochrane, who obtained the post when he offered to divide his fee with the Choctaw commissioners. Cooper, Cochrane, and Latrobe, not unfamiliar with fraud, maneuvered in the settlement of 1866 to involve Indians whose records were clean.[10] Attorneys who sold their influence with Congress rather than their knowledge of the law were not new in American politics; but the large number of such cases during the period of reconstruction following the Civil War served to place the brand of corruption on the era.

Attorney fees collected in connection with the Creek tribe's claim in 1866 were also the subject of much criticism.[11] In view of the relatively small sums awarded Loyal Creeks for their losses in

[10] Debo, *Rise and Fall of the Choctaw Republic*, 90 (from *Court of Claims Reports*, LIX, 775–76, 799, 806).

the war, the fees of Colonel L. B. Luce and Perry Fuller were excessive. Each attorney received a cash payment provided by the treaty; but in addition, each obtained from the Creek delegates and tribal council a promissory note for $84,396. The payments provided in the treaty for "losses of soldiers enlisted in the United States Army, and to loyal refugees and freedmen," amounted to $100,000. The amount provided by the treaty for expenses incurred in the negotiation was $10,000, "if so much be necessary."[12]

## THE TREATIES OF 1866

The commissioner of Indian Affairs, Dennis N. Cooley, opened the council at Fort Smith on September 8, 1865, with Chief Clerk Charles E. Mix of the Indian Office acting as secretary. Other agents representing the United States were Elijah Sells, recently appointed southern superintendent; Thomas Wistar, of Pennsylvania, a Quaker who had deep interest in Indian affairs; General W. S. Harney, speaking for the Army; and Colonel Ely S. Parker, a Seneca Indian who had a great deal of influence both with men of his own race and with the Army.[13]

The southern Indians, attending the regular meeting of the Grand Council at Chahta Tamaha, arrived at Fort Smith more than a week after the conferences had begun. They took little part in the meetings, but received copies of proposed new treaties which they conveyed to the Choctaw and Chickasaw councils.

Commissioner Cooley explained to the Indian delegates at Fort Smith their new status in relation to the United States. They had forfeited their rights under old treaties, and new agreements must be reached. Loyal Indians would be protected in their just claims, but the nations had "lost all their rights to annuities and lands." Cooley informed the delegates that a part of their lands must be taken for the settlement of "such Indians, from Kansas or

11 Commissioner of Indian Affairs, *Annual Report*, 1866, 10, 11; Debo, *Road to Disappearance*, 175.

12 Commissioner of Indian Affairs, *Annual Report*, 1866, 10, 11.

13 Gittinger, *Formation of the State of Oklahoma*, 88–92.

elsewhere, as the government may desire to settle thereon"; that they must abolish slavery and provide homes for their freedmen; and that they must accept a territorial government of the consolidated Indian tribes under authority of the United States.[14]

Neither Indians who had fought with the Union nor former Confederate Indians were ready to accept all of the proposed terms. Only Elias C. Boudinot, son of Buck Watie, was agreeable to the general tenor of the government's proposals. He advocated consolidation of Indian tribes with a territorial government, and was not a determined opponent of Cooley's other terms. This made it possible for him to consult freely with government officials, and gave a considerable advantage to the Confederate Indians. John Ross, strongly opposed to giving up Indian lands, was the natural spokesman for Union Indians; but Boudinot denounced him bitterly, Cooley suggested that he had been more friendly to Confederate commissioners in 1861 than was generally supposed, and Union Cherokees were thrown on the defensive.[15] The council adjourned to meet in Washington early in 1866.

Oklahoma Indians used the intervening period to work for unity among themselves. Although D. N. McIntosh as leader of the southern Creeks had at first expressed a desire to divide the tribe, chiefs of the two factions quickly worked out a basis of harmony. In a council of both parties Samuel Checote, principal chief of the Confederate Creeks, laid down his office, and leaders recognized Sands as principal chief of the united Creek Nation.[16] In October, 1865, the Cherokee National Council took action toward obtaining recognition of John Ross as their principal chief, an office to which he had been re-elected while he was absent in Washington. Commissioner Cooley had shown a preference for dealing with E. C. Boudinot and the southern Cherokees, because that leader was obviously more friendly than Ross toward the new order proposed for Indian Territory.[17] The Cherokees did not attain as much unity as the Creeks, in this emergency, largely because of interference by United States officials.

[14] Commissioner of Indian Affairs, *Annual Report*, 1865, 32–42.

[15] *Ibid.*, 35. "The documents establishing the bad faith of John Ross had but recently come into possession of the department," declared the Cooley Report.

[16] Debo, *Road to Disappearance*, 169.

[17] Wardell, *A Political History of the Cherokee Nation*, 194.

Federal policy was fixed by the circumstances of politics. Secretary of the Interior James Harlan, who took office under President Johnson on May 15, 1865, was determined that Indians of the Five Civilized Tribes should surrender a part of their land. As a member of the United States Senate in 1864, he had supported James Lane's bill directed toward acquisition of land in the Indian Territory for all Indians who lived east of the Rocky Mountains. As a member of President Johnson's Cabinet, he used language in his report of 1865 that gave a clear indication of his attitude toward the Indians. He referred to the "unprovoked war" of the Five Civilized Tribes against the United States and of the Indians' "flagrant violation of treaties which had been observed by us with scrupulous good faith."[18] Harlan intended no irony in his reference to the "scrupulous good faith" of the United States in its treaty obligations with the Indians—which indicates ignorance of the subject or deficient sense of humor. In the case of Secretary Harlan perhaps both information and humor were lacking.

In the meetings at Washington the United States was represented by Commissioner D. N. Cooley, Elijah Sells, and Colonel Ely S. Parker, in addition to Secretary Harlan.

The Cherokees sent two delegations. John Ross, although he was too ill to attend conferences, directed the work of his colleagues and determined the stand taken by the Union Cherokees. He died shortly after the Cherokee treaty was completed. The Southern Cherokee delegation included Stand Watie, E. C. Boudinot, William Penn Adair, Saladin Watie, and John Rollin Ridge. This faction succeeded in discrediting Chief Ross and probably deprived the Cherokees of benefits that united bargaining would have gained for them.

The Choctaws were headed by Robert Jones, who had served as their commissioner to Richmond during the Civil War. After a time Jones withdrew, and his place was taken by Chief Peter Pitchlynn, whose colleagues were Allen Wright, John Page, Alfred Wade, and James Riley. The Seminoles were represented by John Chupco. The Southern Creeks, still with commissioners separate from the Union Creek delegates, were represented by D. N. McIntosh and J. M. C. Smith. The Northern Creeks sent Oktarharsars

[18] Gittinger, *Formation of the State of Oklahoma*, 92, 93.

Harjo (Sands), Coweta Micco, and Cotchoche (Little Tiger). The Negro Harry Island acted as interpreter for the Creeks who could not speak or understand English. Colonel J. B. Luce acted as attorney for the former Confederate Creeks and charged them an unreasonably high fee for his work, while Perry Fuller performed a similar disservice for the Union Creeks. The Creek Council later repudiated the obligations, and they became the subjects of endless litigation, the Fuller note finally being paid in part, probably because the holders of the paper were men who had influence with members of Congress. The amount paid was $42,198, one half of the original note.[19]

All the tribes were required to make concessions.[20] Slavery was abolished in the Indian nations, which everybody expected and practically all parties agreed upon. It was intended that freedmen should be admitted to tribal rights, or given compensation in the form of separate lands. Admission to citizenship in the Cherokee, Creek, and Seminole nations was unqualified; in the Choctaw-Chickasaw treaty, the tribes were given a choice between incorporation of the freedmen and their removal by the United States. For the expense of such removal and separate establishment, the Choctaws and Chickasaws agreed to give the sum held in trust for them by the United States as pay for their surrender of the Leased District. The Choctaws and Chickasaws also agreed that in case freedmen were admitted to citizenship, each of them should receive forty acres of land "on the same terms as the Choctaws and Chickasaws, to be selected on the survey of said land, after the

[19] Debo, *Road to Disappearance*, 348, 349.

[20] *A Compilation of Treaties between the United States and the Indian Tribes,* Cherokees, 85–97; Creeks, 114–22; Choctaws and Chickasaws, 285–303; Seminoles, 810–18. The Cherokees had already abolished slavery and their treaty provided: "The Cherokee Nation having, voluntarily, in February, eighteen hundred and sixty three, by an act of their national council, forever abolished slavery, hereby covenant and agree that never hereafter shall slavery or involuntary servitude exist in their nation otherwise than in the punishment of crime, whereof the party shall have been duly convicted, in accordance with laws applicable to all members of said tribe alike. They further agree that all freemen who have been liberated by voluntary act of their former owners or by law, as well as all free colored persons who were in the country at the commencement of the rebellion, are now residents therein, or who may return within six months, and their descendants, shall have the rights of native Cherokees: Provided, that owners of slaves so emancipated in the Cherokee Nation shall never receive any compensation for the slaves so emancipated." 89, Article 9, 3871–86.

Choctaws and Chickasaws and Kansas Indians have made their selections, as herein provided."

The Five Civilized Tribes agreed to send delegates to an inter-tribal council, apportioned on the basis of one representative for each tribe and an additional member for "each one thousand Indians, or each fraction of a thousand greater than five hundred." The superintendent of Indian Affairs was to be the proposed union's chief executive.

Right of way was granted by each nation for one railroad running north and south and one running east and west through its territory. Provision was made with each tribe, also, for "the better administration of justice and the protection of the rights of person and property within the Indian Territory." To secure this desirable end, a court or courts were to be established there "with such jurisdiction and organization as Congress may prescribe."

The Cherokees ceded their "neutral lands" in Kansas to the United States to be held in trust and sold to the highest bidder, but at a price not lower than an average of $1.25 an acre. The United States might settle any friendly tribes of American Indians in the Cherokee Outlet at a price to be agreed upon by the immigrant group and the Cherokees, subject to approval by the president; and, "if they should not agree, then the price to be fixed by the President."[21] The "Cherokee Strip," about two and one-half miles wide and lying along the 37th parallel within the state of Kansas, was also held in trust by the United States to be sold to settlers for the benefit of the Cherokee Nation.[22]

In a joint treaty the Choctaws and Chickasaws ceded the Leased District to the United States for the sum of $300,000. The Indian delegation that took part in this agreement, in addition to the Choctaw commissioners mentioned above, included four Chickasaws: Winchester Colbert, Holmes Colbert, Robert H. Love, and Colbert Carter.[23] The money due the tribes for cession of their western territory was to be invested for the Choctaws and Chickasaws "at an interest not less than five percent" and held in

[21] *Ibid.*, 93.

[22] Gittinger, *Formation of the State of Oklahoma*, 98n.; *A Compilation of Treaties between the United States and the Indian Tribes*, 93.

[23] *A Compilation of Treaties between the United States and the Indian Tribes*, 285.

trust until the former slaves had been given full citizenship rights, including use of land but not including the right to participate in annuities. The clause which provided for an intertribal council referred to the proposed union as the "Territory of Oklahoma," a name suggested by Allen Wright, a member of the Choctaw delegation. In the Muskhogean languages, the name means *Red People,* and this was its first use in any official document of the United States.

The Creek Treaty, proclaimed by President Andrew Johnson on August 11, 1866, provided that the tribe should cede the western half of its land—3,250,000 acres—for the sum of $975,168. Of this total, $200,000 was to be paid in cash, "to enable the Creeks to occupy, restore, and improve their farms," to repair public buildings, and to pay their delegates. The sum of $100,000 was to be divided among Union soldiers and refugees of the Creek Nation, and $400,000 was to be paid "in money and divided, per capita to said Creek Nation, unless otherwise directed by the President of the United States." The residue, $275,168, was held in trust in the Treasury of the United States at 5 per cent interest, to be paid annually to the Creek tribe. The Creeks also agreed to Federal military occupation "at any time," troops to be sent at the expense of the United States for the purpose of keeping or restoring order.[24]

The Seminoles, negotiating through Chief John Chupco, Chocote Harjo, Fos Harjo, and John F. Brown, agreed to cede all their land to the United States at a price of fifteen cents an acre—half the price obtained by the Creeks for their holdings. The government thus received 2,169,080 acres from the Seminoles, for use in settling other Indian tribes, at a cost of $325,362. It was further agreed that the Seminoles should purchase 200,000 acres recently acquired by the United States from the Creeks, between the Canadian and its North Fork, immediately west of the new Creek boundary. It will be recalled that the Creek lands had been sold to the United States at the rate of thirty cents an acre, the Seminole lands went at fifteen cents an acre, but the purchase by the Seminoles from the United States was at the rate of fifty cents an acre.[25]

[24] *Ibid.,* 114–22.
[25] *Ibid.,* 810–18.

## SETTLEMENT WITH THE PLAINS TRIBES

Relations between the United States and tribes of the buffalo plains had been growing steadily in importance. Westward travel had increased through the years under such impulses as that afforded by the great Mormon migration, settlement of the Oregon boundary, acquisition of vast southwestern territories from Mexico in 1848, and the California gold rush soon afterward. Indians who lived on the prairies were wild and free; they moved about easily because of their lack of attachment to real property, and rapidly because their chattels were few and consisted largely of ponies, on which they hunted buffaloes and raided western emigrants.

Attention has been directed to achievements of the Leavenworth expedition in 1834 and conferences with the Plains Indians that grew out of it. From time to time councils were held on the Plains for the specific purposes of acquainting Indians with aims of the Washington government, with its peaceful attitude toward Indian tribes, or with the military power of the United States. At Fort Laramie on the North Platte in 1851, the Cheyennes and Arapahoes of the Southwest met with government officials and with tribes of the Northern Plains—Sioux, Northern Cheyennes, and others. The Cheyennes and Arapahoes agreed to occupy the upper region of the Arkansas in Colorado and Kansas as their permanent home. At Fort Atkinson two years later Thomas Fitzpatrick signed a pact with the Kiowa, Kiowa-Apache, and Comanche tribes, in which the Indians agreed to establishment of posts, building of roads, and peaceful passage of emigrants through their hunting grounds. They promised not to raid the homes of unprotected settlers, emigrant bands, or the camps of other tribes, to give up all captives, and to cease their forays across the Río Grande. The United States agreed to deliver to them annually for ten years goods valued at $18,000.[26] The president of the United States was authorized to extend the payment of this "tribute" five years; but in 1861 when Albert Pike went among the Plains In-

[26] *Ibid.*, 310.

dians to obtain their support for the Confederacy, he found the Kiowas ready to consider a new alliance because their annuities from the United States had not been received for two years. At the Wichita Agency, Pike signed agreements with the Comanches of the Washita and with the Comanches of the prairies and Staked Plain.[27]

Agreements of peace and perpetual friendship entered into between tribal head men and the United States did not always mean that hostilities ceased. Opportunity for profit in a quick raid was a temptation for young Indian warriors, and danger from such attacks upon emigrant bands and frontier settlements was constant. Territorial troops retaliated upon Indian tribes, and sometimes blunders were made by militia officers in the form of attacks upon peaceable communities. Expeditions against the Cheyennes in Colorado in April and November, 1864, are examples of outrages against the Indians. The second of these raids, Colonel John M. Chivington's attack upon five hundred peaceable Cheyennes at Sand Creek on November 30, was especially bad. In commenting upon Chivington's massacre, in which five hundred sleeping Cheyennes—men, women, and children—were attacked by seven hundred mounted and well-armed troops, General Nelson A. Miles called the incident "the foulest and most unprofitable crime in the annals of America." Black Kettle (Moke-ta-ra-to) survived this raid only to perish in a later attack led by General Custer against the Cheyenne camp on the Washita.

In 1867 the Department of the Interior obtained an appropriation for a peace commission to go among the Plains Indians. Three main purposes were put forward to justify the expenditure: to take steps to prevent Indian attacks upon emigrant bands, frontier homes, and railroad construction; to abolish Indian wars by removing their causes; and, to encourage farming and stock raising among the Indians, instead of their restless wandering about in search of a precarious living by hunting buffaloes and other game. Thomas Murphy was sent west to make arrangements for conferences with Kiowas, Comanches, Cheyennes, Arapahoes, and Apaches. With the full co-operation of Black Kettle, Murphy arranged for a council at Medicine Lodge Creek, setting the date early in October.

Meantime, the commission was appointed and its functions explained in a series of meetings at Washington. Nathaniel G. Taylor, commissioner of Indian Affairs, was chairman. Senator John B. Henderson of Missouri, William S. Harney, Alfred H. Terry, C. C. Augur, J. B. Sanborn, and S. F. Tappan were the other members.[28] Five of the seven were officers of the United States Army; but it is worthy of note that General Sanborn, Colonel Tappan, and Commissioner Taylor were all convinced that the best policy to pursue in dealing with Plains Indians was to grant many concessions and strive for a constructive program of harmony. Furthermore, Senator Henderson was known to be friendly toward the Indians. General William T. Sherman, who accompanied the party to the North Platte, in the first stages of the tour, had an attitude definitely less conciliatory. He informed the Sioux and Northern Cheyennes that the visit was that of a peace commission which was also a war commission. Sherman was soon recalled to Washington, and was not with the party on its subsequent visits to Fort Laramie, Fort Larned, and Medicine Lodge Creek.

Between its conferences the peace commission traveled in two ambulances followed by thirty baggage wagons loaded with provisions for the party and presents for the Indians. They were guarded by three companies of United States cavalry and a battery of Gatling guns. Henry M. Stanley, a newspaperman who later was to become noted for finding Dr. David Livingstone in Africa, reported the tour of the peace commission and perhaps added a bit of color for his readers where color was lacking. When fully understood, the contacts of Indians and commissioners, representing two distinct cultures groping toward understanding and a common ground for future meetings, and trying to adjust terms of their agreements to the demands of their respective peoples, were dramatic enough to satisfy anyone.[29]

Among the United States commissioners were men of widely separate interests. Nathaniel G. Taylor was a Methodist minister, described by his friends as a man of sincerity and piety, working

[27] Wallace and Hoebel, *The Comanches*, 299, 300, 304.

[28] *A Compilation of Treaties between the United States and the Indian Tribes,* 319.

[29] Stanley Vestal, *Warpath and Council Fire,* chap. XI, Medicine Lodge Treaty.

for the advancement of the Indian. An unfriendly contemporary called him a "simpering White House courtier," and referred to the "florid speeches which he inflicts on the red infidels."[30]

John B. Henderson of Missouri, who had resigned as brigadier general in the Union Army to take a United States Senate seat in 1862, was at that time thirty-six years old, second youngest member. He held many important committee posts in the Senate, including chairmanship of the Committee on Indian Affairs. After his service with the peace commission, he was to prove a powerful support for Secretary William H. Seward in the purchase of Alaska. In spite of a strong tendency toward partisanship, he was to take his place among the "honorable seven" Republicans who voted to acquit President Andrew Johnson in 1868. Wavering between party loyalty and his sense of right, Henderson received an "insolent telegram of instructions" from his state and immediately decided for the President and against his instructions. On this occasion he wrote: "Say to my friends that I am sworn to do impartial justice according to law and conscience, and I will try to do it like an honest man."[31]

General William S. Harney was a towering giant with white hair and beard, a frontier hero with a wide reputation as an Indian fighter. Mrs. Adams, who accompanied the commission as an interpreter for the Arapaho Indians, was dressed in a striking manner with a crimson skirt, black coat, and a small hat with a large ostrich feather. The Indians were impressed. "She must be the daughter of a great chief," they said.

The Indians had notable warriors at the conference, too. The Comanche chief Ten Bears made a speech of welcome to the commissioners and began with words of warm friendship. "My heart is filled with joy when I see you here, as the brooks fill with water when the snows melt in the spring; and I feel glad as the ponies do when the fresh grass starts in the beginning of the year." As the address continued, however, Ten Bears expressed some of the burning grievances of his people:

"There has been trouble on the line between us," he said, "and

[30] Quoted in *ibid.*, 114.
[31] "John B. Henderson," *Dictionary of American Biography*, VIII (article by J. G. de R. Hamilton).

my young men have danced the war dance. But it was not begun by us. It was you who sent out the first soldier and we who sent out the second. . . . The blue-dressed soldiers and the Utes came from out of the night when it was dark and still, and for campfires they lit our lodges. . . .

"So it was in Texas. They made sorrow come in our camps and we went out like the buffalo bulls when the cows are attacked. When we found them we killed them, and their scalps hang in our lodges. The Comanches are not weak and blind, like the pups of a dog when seven sleeps old. They are strong and far-sighted like grown horses. We took their road and we went on it. The white women cried and our women laughed."[32]

Satanta of the Kiowas, the tall, powerful "orator of the Plains," was also induced to make a speech. "A long time ago this land belonged to our fathers," he told the men from Washington. "But when I go up to the river, I see a camp of soldiers, and they are cutting my wood down, or killing my buffalo. I don't like that and when I see it, my heart feels like bursting with sorrow."[33]

The chiefs of the Plains tribes signed agreements to settle on reservations. Probably they signed them without fully understanding their meaning, and certainly their marks on the documents did not mean that the young men of the tribes were ready to settle down to farming. The treaties of Medicine Lodge Creek were preludes to a series of wars on the Great Plains.

The Kiowas and Comanches signed a joint treaty on October 21, 1867, by which they agreed to live on a reservation in the Leased District, the region between the Canadian River and the Red, west of the 98th meridian, formerly leased from the Choctaws and Chickasaws. A band of Apaches, represented by Wolf's Sleeve (Mah-Vip-Pah) and Poor Bear (Kon-Zhon-Ta-Co), accepted a place on the same reservation and agreed to "confederate and become incorporated" with the Kiowas and Comanches. Sitting Bear (Santank) and White Bear (Satanta) were among the Kiowa chiefs; Ten Bears (Parry-Wah-Say-Men) and Painted Lips (Te-

[32] Wallace and Hoebel, *The Comanches*, 282–84 (Quoted from Recorded Copy of the Proceedings of the Indian Peace Commission, MS, National Archives, Office of Indian Affairs, I, 104).

[33] Vestal, *Warpath and Council Fire*, 123, 124.

Pe-Navon) spoke for the Comanches. The reservation described in the treaty with the Kiowas and Comanches and accepted by the Apaches in their agreement to become incorporated was east of the North Fork of Red River. The northern boundary began at a point where the 98th meridian crosses the Washita, and extended up that stream to a point thirty miles west of Fort Cobb, thence due west to North Fork. The boundary on the east was the 98th meridian, the western limit of the Chickasaw Nation.[34]

The Cheyennes and Arapahoes were assigned to a reservation between the Cimarron River, the Arkansas River, and the southern border of Kansas, largely within the Cherokee Outlet.[35] President Grant on August 10, 1869, changed the location of their reservation by executive order, to make an adjustment with the obvious preference of the Indians. Most of the Southern Cheyennes and Arapahoes had settled along the North Canadian River in what is now western Canadian County and Blaine County, Oklahoma. Eastern limits of the new Cheyenne and Arapaho reservation were the 98th meridian and Cimarron River; northern limit, the Cherokee Outlet; western, the 100th meridian; and southern, the Kiowa-Comanche Reservation.[36] The southeastern portion of the area, south of the Canadian River and east of 98 degrees and 40 minutes west longitude, was assigned to the Wichitas, Caddoes, and Delawares, also, by executive order, in 1872.[37]

In 1865 the Great and Little Osages represented by White Hair, Little Bear, and other chiefs had signed a treaty with D. N. Cooley and Elijah Sells, at Canville Trading Post in the Osage Nation, state of Kansas, by which the Indians agreed to cede to the United States their surplus land. The area thus surrendered for the sum of $300,000 was in the eastern portion of the Osage Nation. The tribe agreed, at the same time to sell a strip twenty miles wide across the north side of their remaining land, to be held in trust by the United States and sold to settlers at a price not less than $1.25 per acre. It was further agreed that in case the Indians should desire to remove from the state of Kansas, the remaining portion

[34] *A Compilation of Treaties between the United States and the Indian Tribes,* 312, 313, 314; 314–18; 318–24.

[35] *Ibid.,* 130, 131.

[36] Gittinger, *Formation of the State of Oklahoma,* 109.

[37] *Ibid.,* 110.

of their land in that state should be disposed of by the United States. Fifty per cent of the revenue obtained from such sale might be used to pay for their new reservation.[38]

By an act of Congress in 1872, that portion of the Cherokee Outlet lying between the Arkansas River and the 96th meridian was assigned to the Osage and Kansas Indians.[39] Other small groups were settled in the Cherokee Outlet and adjacent territory during the following decade. The Pawnee Reservation of 283,000 acres was established in 1876 south of the Arkansas River and extending beyond the limits of the Cherokee Outlet southward to the Cimarron, including a small area ceded by the Creeks in 1866. In 1878 the Ponca Reservation for a band of approximately six hundred Indians was established west of the Osages in the Cherokee Outlet. The Ponca Indians were removed from their reservation on the Niobrara and Ponca rivers in Nebraska and settled on a tract approximately 158 sections in extent. The Otoes and Missouris were placed directly south of them, and a band of Nez Percé were removed from Idaho and settled on 144 sections lying along Salt Fork northwest of the Poncas. In 1885 after eight years in the Southwest this group was moved back to Idaho, and their reservation was turned over to the Tonkawa remnant from Texas who were living in Indian Territory.

While settlements of these western tribes were being made in the Cherokee Outlet, other reservations were established on land ceded by the Creeks and Seminoles. Prior to the Civil War, bands of Senecas, Seneca-Shawnees, and Quapaws had been removed from Ohio to the northeast corner of Indian Territory between the Neosho River and the Missouri state line. In 1867 room was made in this area for several small bands of Indians from Kansas. Kaskaskias, Miamis, Peorias, Piankashaws, and Weas were placed on land vacated by readjustment of the Seneca-Shawnees. Also, Wyandottes occupied 20,000 acres ceded by the Senecas, the Ottawas moved to a small reservation along the Neosho River, and the Modocs were settled on the border of Missouri.[40]

[38] *A Compilation of Treaties between the United States and the Indian Tribes,* 584–89.

[39] Gittinger, *Formation of the State of Oklahoma,* 110, 111, and 111n.

[40] *Ibid.,* 106. For acreage of the reservations and population of the several tribes, see *ibid.,* Appendix C, 263; Appendix D, 264–66.

By a treaty signed in February, 1867, by Lewis V. Bogy for the United States and Chief Keokuk for the Sacs and Foxes of the Mississippi, this band of Indians sold their land in Kansas to the United States and removed to the Indian Territory.[41] The reservation assigned to them extended along the western Creek border between the Cimarron and North Canadian rivers and included 750 sections. The population of this reservation in 1879 was 873, of whom less than half were Indians.[42]

A band of "absentee Shawnees" had withdrawn before the Civil War from their tribal organization and settled west of the Creeks between the two Canadian rivers. In 1867, Pottawatomies of Kansas selected for their reservation the area occupied by these Shawnees. By an act of Congress in 1872, both Pottawatomies and Shawnees were allotted individual holdings of land in this reservation which was approximately nine hundred square miles in extent. In 1879 the two bands of Indians numbered just over 900.[43] The Shawnees took allotments in the northern part, extending from the borders of the Sac and Fox reservation across Little River. The Pottawatomies took individual allotments distributed over the southern half, extending to the South Canadian boundary.

The Kickapoo Indians, an Algonquian tribe, had moved often and traveled far in their efforts to escape the white man and maintain their own way of living. In Illinois they were restless and discontented, in Texas they clashed with western settlers and raided across the Río Grande, in Mexico they were poverty-stricken and prone to raid Texas ranches. After the Sacs and Foxes had been settled on Creek land, about four hundred Mexican Kickapoos were moved to a reservation just west of them. Some bands of Iowas, previously located in Kansas, had come into the same general area; and in 1883, President Chester A. Arthur established two new reservations, one for the Kickapoos and one for the Iowas. The Kickapoos were placed in the area south of Deep Fork, between the Sac and Fox Reservation on the east and the Indian Meridian on the west. The Iowas, numbering about ninety, were given the

---

[41] *A Compilation of Treaties between the United States and the Indian Tribes,* 767–75.

[42] Gittinger, *Formation of the State of Oklahoma,* 265.

[43] *Ibid.,* 265.

territory between the Cimarron and Deep Fork, also west of the Sacs and Foxes.[44]

There was wide variety among the tribes that were settled in the Indian Territory after the Civil War. Indians of the Five Civilized Tribes had many characteristics in common, including related languages of the Creeks, Seminoles, Choctaws, and Chickasaws, and similar economic background for all five tribes in the Southeast. The numerous Algonquian, Iroquoian, Siouan, and Caddoan bands that were settled on the western territories had no such heritage. Even the fragments of tribes that were placed northeast of the Cherokees represented a wide variety in culture and experience with white men. The Shawnees from the Ohio Valley are of Algonquian stock. The Quapaws, like the Osages, are Siouan. Hernando de Soto encountered this tribe in the lower Arkansas Valley, a region in which they appeared to be well established by 1540 and to which they returned from time to time for a period of more than two hundred years. Pressure of white settlement caused the Quapaws to move many times, and in the process of seeking a suitable home they suffered greatly from epidemics. About one third of their number moved to the reservation established for them in 1833 west of Missouri and south of 37th parallel. This remnant was joined later by other members of the tribe, and before the Civil War more than three hundred were enrolled as Quapaws. During the war their territory was overrun by partisan bands, and women and children of the tribe were forced to take refuge in Kansas with the Ottawas. The men were divided between Federal and Confederate forces.[45]

The Senecas, removed to Indian Territory from Sandusky, Ohio, in 1832, are of Iroquoian stock. Probably many neighboring bands joined with the Sandusky Senecas, including Eries, Conestogas, and other remnants of Iroquoian Indians from central New York.[46] The Peorias, Ottawas, Weas, Piankashaws, Kaskaskias, and Miamis are of the Alogonquian family. The Wyandotte tribe was another Iroquoian fragment brought to their reservation on the Neosho River in 1867. The Modocs are a small band from

44 *Ibid.*, 151.
45 Wright, *Indian Tribes of Oklahoma*, 9, 211, 218, 219.
46 *Ibid.*, 238.

Lutuamian linguistic stock indigenous to Oregon and northern California.[47]

In the Cherokee Outlet settlement of the Plains tribes created another great "Melting Pot." The Osage, Kaw, Ponca, Otoe, and Missouri tribes are of Siouan stock. The Pawnees are Caddoan, and the Tonkawas belong to a separate linguistic stock.

On the land ceded by Creeks and Seminoles were Iowas of the Siouan family and Kickapoos, Pottawatomies, Shawnees, Sacs, and Foxes of the Algonquian. Without the great diversity of linguistic stock found in some other parts of Indian Territory, these tribes differed sharply in many cultural traits. For example, the Kickapoos had avoided white settlements except for raiding, and as a result the tribe was definitely backward in the language and all phases of white men's civilization, in comparison with those tribes that had lived for many years under the influence of mission schools and religious establishments, sermons, printed materials, and related educational factors.

Kiowas, Comanches, and Apaches, placed together on a single reservation, are of three different linguistic families: the Kiowan, Shoshonean, and Athapascan. Cheyennes and Arapahoes are Algonquian. Wichitas and Caddoes, like the Pawnees, are of Caddoan stock. The Delaware tribe, of the Algonquian family, has two branches in Oklahoma. One settled in the northern part of the Cherokee Nation in 1867, the other with the Wichitas and Caddoes in 1859. Many Delawares of the Indian Territory became famous as scouts and guides.[48]

### RAIDS AND INDIAN WARFARE IN THE SOUTHWEST, 1867–1876.

Much disorder on the Western Plains in the decade following the Civil War arose from failure of tribal headmen to control their young braves, and from a lawless tendency among white settlers of the frontier. Neither the peace commission of 1867 nor

[47] *Ibid.*, 184, 208, 209, 254.
[48] *Ibid.*, 145–55.

ruthless attacks upon Indian bands by militia forces had settled frontier disorders and freed the lonely border dwellings, wagon trains, and railroad labor gangs from the dangers of Indian attack.

Among reservation Indians who continued restless and hostile were the Southern Cheyennes. Fort Cobb, built in 1859 near the Washita River in the Leased District, was repaired and occupied by troops after the Civil War was over. Fort Supply, near the mouth of Wolf Creek on the North Canadian, was built in 1868 by a cavalry unit under command of Colonel Alfred Sully and promptly occupied by General George A. Custer's forces. During the winter months when pasturage for their horses was lacking, Indians were reluctant to come out of camp. It was suspected by many army men that bands of raiders who were active in warm weather took refuge among more peaceable Indians in camp when winter came. General Philip Sheridan, commander of the Southwestern Department, determined to carry on a winter campaign in 1868–1869 and ordered George A. Custer to march against the Cheyennes. United States cavalry units, having supplies of grain for their horses, were at a considerable advantage over Indian horsemen.

After trying in vain to persuade General Hazen at Fort Cobb to promise safety for his band of Cheyennes, Chief Black Kettle had gone into winter camp on the Washita near the site of present-day Cheyenne. Custer rode south from Fort Supply with twelve troops of the Seventh Cavalry, a baggage train of supplies, and a corps of first-class guides. The weather was cold, and a heavy snow covered the plains. On the night of November 26 Custer approached the Cheyenne camp of 180 lodges. Baggage wagons had been left behind near Antelope Hills on the Canadian River. Each soldier carried only a small supply of hardtack and coffee, a bag of oats for his horse, and one hundred rounds of ammunition.

The attack was at daybreak on November 27. The Cheyenne camp was caught by surprise, and there was no time to raise a white flag in token of surrender. Perhaps after the Cheyenne experience at Sand Creek, there was no inclination among them to try for safety by means of surrender. Indian women and children fired upon the charging troops, and women and children were slaughtered along with Cheyenne warriors. Major Benteen afterward gave an account of a Cheyenne boy of twelve or fourteen who charged his squadron, singlehanded. The major raised his hand in a gesture of conciliation, but the lad fired three shots from his revolver and the third bullet struck Benteen's horse in the shoulder. Then the major shot the Indian boy.[49]

Major Joel H. Elliot, following the fleeing Cheyennes downstream, was cut off with eighteen men from the main body of Custer's force, and his party was wiped out. Another casualty in the pursuit was Captain Louis M. Hamilton, a grandson of Alexander Hamilton. When Custer learned that an Indian camp of perhaps one thousand lodges a few miles down the Washita had been aroused by the noise of battle, he called in his forces and ordered a retreat. His men carried away from the Cheyenne camp a large amount of supplies—saddles, rifles and ammunition, bows and arrows, buffalo robes, blankets, and other goods.

Kiowas, like Comanches and Cheyennes, found it difficult to give up raiding across Red River. In January, 1869, General Philip Sheridan began construction of a new fort southeast of the Wichita Mountains. For a time the place was called Camp Wichita, but soon received an official name, for a Union officer killed during the Civil War, General Joshua Sill. Fort Sill became the seat of the Kiowa-Comanche Indian Agency, and before the end of the year the Quaker agent Lawrie Tatum was sent to the office to administer affairs of the two tribes.[50]

In February, 1870, Little Raven (Hosa), an Arapaho chief who was a signer of the Medicine Lodge Creek Treaty, settled with his people in the vicinity of Fort Supply. Other bands came in later and settled near the Cheyenne and Arapaho Agency at Darlington. Before midsummer, a majority of the two tribes were in camp. However, some of the warriors continued to take part in the Indian uprisings until after the surrender of Quanah Parker and his Quahada Comanches on January 24, 1875.[51]

The Kiowa chiefs of the Reconstruction period were not the tribe's ablest men of all time. Little Mountain (Dohasan) of the previous generation, who was principal chief for more than three decades, and Wooden Lance (Ahpeatone) in the next generation,

---

[49] Vestal, *Warpath and Council Fire,* 157.
[50] Wright, *Indian Tribes of Oklahoma,* 174.
[51] *Ibid.,* 80, 126.

were leaders of far more ability than that shown by Big Tree, Kicking Bird, Lone Wolf, Satank, and Satanta.[52] There is ample evidence that Big Tree, Satank, and Satanta were all engaged in raids across Red River that finally brought disaster to a large number of the Kiowas. Lawrie Tatum tried hard to explain to Satank the laws of white men concerning ownership of livestock. Challenged in regard to his possession of a mule stolen in Texas, Satank offered to fight Tatum with knives for the animal. After a Kiowa attack on a wagon train near Fort Richardson, Texas, in May, 1871, Satanta boasted that he led the raiding party of one hundred men, including Satank, Big Bow, Big Tree, and Eagle Heart, and that the raiders had killed seven teamsters and captured forty-one mules. Arrested by order of General William T. Sherman, old Satank, the "meanest, fiercest, and bravest of the Kiowas," was killed on his way to trial and certain conviction. Satanta and Big Tree were convicted of murder in Texas, but their death sentence was commuted; and eventually they were freed to return to the reservation, where they became involved in more trouble. Satanta was sent for a second time to a Texas prison where he committed suicide. In 1875, seventy Indians from the Southwestern Plains were arrested, tried, and sentenced to long terms in a Florida military prison. Of the seventy, twenty-six were Kiowas.[53] Kicking Bird, a chief respected alike by his people and federal officials, died suddenly while engaged in the thankless task of helping to select the guilty Kiowas. Probably he was poisoned by one of his tribe.

The worst disorders were subsiding on the Southern Plains as the great conflict arose over possession of the Black Hills in the Northwest. In the broad view, war in the North was another phase of the struggle for control of the plains, not fully settled by the Battle of the Washita or by the arrest of Kiowa warriors. On the Little Big Horn in Montana, General George A. Custer was caught in a military blunder by Indian leaders who were shrewd and experienced: Crazy Horse of the Oglala Sioux and Sitting Bull of the Hunkpapa hostiles of the same tribe. Custer's army was all but annihilated. Later, the Plains chiefs were all worn down and beaten. Both Crazy Horse and Sitting Bull died by violence, and

52 *Ibid.*, 169–77.
53 *Ibid.*, 174.

the Indians of the Northwest, like their kinsmen on the Southern Plains, yielded to overwhelming numbers and resources.

Important changes took place in United States relations with the Indians during the decade following the Civil War. An act of Congress on March 3, 1871, declared all existing treaties with Indian tribes valid, but put an end to treaties as a method of dealing with tribal governments.[54] Reservations established after passage of that law were located and their boundaries defined either by act of Congress or by the president in an executive agreement with the Indians. The settlement of diverse tribes and remnants in the Indian Territory began a new era in Indian affairs; but the unoccupied areas soon became entering wedges for opening the entire region to settlement by white farmers.

In 1874, Union Agency was established for the Five Civilized Tribes at Muskogee. The commissioner of the Five Civilized Tribes with headquarters there had general supervision of relations with the Choctaws, Chickasaws, Creeks, Seminoles, and Cherokees. The Quapaw Agency at Wyandotte had charge of government business with Senecas, Seneca-Shawnees, Quapaws, Peorias, Ottawas, Miamis, and Wyandottes. The Sac and Fox Agency, situated near the site of Stroud, in present-day Lincoln County, was the seat of government for Sac and Fox, Iowa, Kickapoo, and Shawnee-Pottawatomie Indians. The agency for Osages and Kaws was at Pawhuska, that of the Ponca, Otoe-Missouri, Pawnee, and Tonkawa tribes near the site of Ponca City. The Cheyenne and Arapaho Agency was at Darlington, north of present-day El Reno; and the Kiowa-Comanche Agency was at Fort Sill until 1879, when it was consolidated with the Wichita-Caddo Agency at Anadarko.

With few changes, these seven offices were continued in charge of government business with the Indians until 1947, when further consolidation was put into effect. The small tribes in northeastern Oklahoma were placed under the administration of the Union Agency, and all the tribes of the west side, except the Osages and Kaws, were consolidated at Anadarko. The Osage-Kaw Agency continued at Pawhuska.

Political reconstruction of Indian Territory involved drastic

[54] Gittinger, *Formation of the State of Oklahoma*, 111 (from *Statutes at Large of the United States*, 1850–1907, XVI, 566).

changes in the lives of some thousands of Indians and definite revision of tribal relations with the government. On the economic side, Indians took up the slow and painful work of rebuilding very much as other people did. Indian Territory had suffered more than other areas, but there was ample land for the number of people concerned, and the Indians wasted little time on regrets. Also, the greatest bitterness of partisan strife was ended, and a new era of comparative good order was at hand. After 1875 even the western reservations were areas of peace and progress.

# CHAPTER ELEVEN

# Cattle, Coal, and the Iron Horse

## THE RANGE CATTLE INDUSTRY
## AND THE NEW FRONTIER, 1865–1885

The United States frontier line in 1865 was pushing toward the 98th meridian from southern Texas to North Dakota except in the Indian Territory. Between Red River on the south and Kansas on the north, there were forty thousand square miles of territory that lay east of that frontier line. Thus, land assigned to the Indians was in the nature of a peninsula stretching out from the unsettled West into the agricultural areas of the Mississippi Valley.

At every step in settlement of the American frontier, distinct stages of economic development can be traced. Americans from earliest colonial days have hunted, fished, and trapped at the beginning of their settlement in each belt of the frontier. A stage in which livestock grazing on the open range is the principal means of livelihood has been repeated many times as the population moved west. This pastoral phase has been followed regularly by tilling of the soil, production of greater surpluses, commercial development, and growth of industry in every section. Middle New York and Pennsylvania, the Virginia and Carolina Piedmont, the Appalachian Highlands, and successive belts through the Mississippi Valley, have witnessed these changes.[1] The speed with which any given area moved from one stage of development to another depended upon many factors. Railroad building into the West after 1830 was revolutionary in its effects, but the stages of change were still discernible in altered form. Machinery used in farming, local

[1] Turner, *The Rise of the New West*, 31; E. E. Dale, "History of the Range Cattle Industry in Oklahoma," The American Historical Association, *Annual Report*, 1920, p. 307.

deposits of lead, zinc, iron, or coal, discoveries of oil, and many other factors have given endless variety to actual development of the American frontier. But regardless of mineral resources, varieties of soil, and differences in climate—hunting, grazing, and farming have appeared successively in every major area.

The American frontier in 1865 was the region of one million unsettled square miles, extending roughly one thousand miles from the western fringe of settlement in the Mississippi Valley to the settled portions of California and Oregon. The area was due for rapid growth of population, in part because of peculiar economic effects of the American Civil War and in part because means of long-range transportation were available in the form of transcontinental railroads. Demobilization of 2,500,000 soldiers stimulated two related economic phenomena: extermination of the buffaloes on the Western Plains, and rapid substitution of range cattle for the buffaloes.

In Oklahoma the three stages of development—primitive hunting, pasturing on the open range, and cultivation of the soil—followed each other in quick succession with much overlapping, not because of mechanical inventions or mineral discoveries, but because of the sudden release of population that was pressing hard for entrance on three sides.[2] A vital factor in opening Indian lands to farming was the gradual development of large-scale cattle grazing.

In 1865 the state of Texas had enormous resources in livestock. Range cattle there had not been depleted during the war as they had been across the Red River by theft, partisan raids, or legal government purchases. Cattle herds developed almost undisturbed in an area of low altitude, excellent grass, and mild winters, as wide in extent as the entire Ohio Valley or as modern France. Cattle herds developed as the buffalo herds had grown in an earlier period. By 1870, the state of Texas contained about 13 per cent of the nation's cattle and only 2 per cent of its population.[3] The great need of Texas cattle growers was a market for their surplus. In

[2] *Ibid.*, 307–22.

[3] The population of Texas in 1870 was 818,579; of the United States, 38,558,371. The state contained about 4,550,000 head of cattle at that time. U. S. Bureau of the Census *Tenth Report.*

eastern centers of meat production a grown steer in good condition would sell for $80.00 or $90.00; in Texas at the same time, fine beef animals sold at a price of $5.00 and less desirable steers exchanged regularly at $2.00 or $3.00.[4] In October, 1866, one hundred and thirty Texas steers sold in Chicago at an average price of $65.00 each; in June of the same year, a small herd of longhorns brought $88.00 each in Kentucky.

The Texas cattle were descended from Spanish breeds introduced from Mexican ranches during the seventeenth century. The Texas longhorn was a hardy animal, well suited to range conditions that involved little in the way of feeding or artificial shelter. These cattle could live through the Southwestern Plains winters without grain or hay, subsisting only on the scant winter pasture. Improved breeds of the present day are a later development, dating from the period following the great northern cattle drives. Moving cattle along the trails from Texas to the Kansas cowtowns, as a large-scale means of transportation, was limited to the period 1865–85.

Railroad lines from the Mississippi Valley to the Pacific Coast began the solution of transportation needs in central Texas. The earliest of these railroads were along the lines of middle surveys, in the latitudes of Chicago, Omaha, Kansas City, and St. Louis. and did not enter the state of Texas; but as their rails pushed westward to points in Nebraska and Kansas that were due north of Texas trading centers, the idea of the northern cattle drive took root among Texans and others interested in the cattle business.

THE NORTHERN DRIVE

There was precedent for the cattle drive through Indian Territory even before the Civil War. The principal route of northern passage was along the Texas Road, where some thousands of cattle were driven annually between 1849 and 1860. In 1854, according to evidence of the *Texas State Gazette,* about fifty thou-

[4] Joseph G. McCoy, *Cattle Trade of the West and Southwest* (ed. by Ralph P. Bieber), 94.

sand cattle were driven across Red River bound for northern markets. Kansas City, Westport, and Independence, Missouri were among the principal markets.

Drives of varying length and in many directions had been attempted before the war. In a land of great distances the problem of transportation was never an easy one, and ranchmen had resorted to moving their cattle by means of drives to Texas Gulf ports, New Orleans, and even to California after the Mexican War. In 1854, steers purchased in Texas at $5.00, $10.00, or $15.00 a head, might be sold in California at a price that ranged from $60.00 to $150.00.[5] There were many obstacles to driving cattle through farming areas. There was generally opposition by farmers on the ground that the herds destroyed crops and spread disease among the local livestock. It was difficult, too, for large herds from the range country to find subsistence on a long drive through settled country. It is not correct, however, to assume that such drives were never successfully made.

The northern drives that began in 1866 after a period of almost complete lapse during the war, had three principal markets that were in contact with cowtowns of Kansas. Herders on the northern ranges of Nebraska, the Dakotas, Wyoming, and Montana, were willing to purchase Texas cattle, which they fattened in the bracing climate of the upper Missouri Valley. There were some cattlemen who maintained a ranch in Texas for breeding and grazing young stock, and another in the Northwest for "finishing" beef stock. Another important feeding area was the corn belt, through Iowa, northern Missouri, Illinois, and Indiana. Farmers in this region bought range cattle and fed them for the beef market. If the cattle were ready for the packing houses when they came up from Texas, they might be shipped directly to Cincinnati, East St. Louis, or Chicago.

The drives of 1866 through the Indian Territory were not completely successful. More than a quarter of a million cattle were driven up the Texas Road that year, following the route of the

[5] Professor Ralph P. Bieber, who edited McCoy's *Cattle Trade of the West and Southwest* in 1939, has pointed out that McCoy erred in his original estimates of the earlier drives. There is ample evidence that western military establishments and the towns of Missouri, eastern Kansas, and Illinois obtained large numbers of Texas cattle and horses by means of drives before the Civil War.

earlier drives and aiming for the railroad connections in southeastern Kansas; but only a small part of the animals reached the market. The trail, sometimes called the "East Shawnee Trail," was through timbered, hilly country, in which the Indians were attempting to gather up their own herds scattered during the war and to resume farming activities. Some of the streams are deep with steep banks and difficult to cross in periods of high water. Some of the drivers lost many cattle by drowning, and there were instances of men losing their own lives in swollen streams. Red River, Blue, Boggy, both branches of the Canadian, Deep Fork, and many other streams were at times quite dangerous to cross with cattle.

The diary of George Duffield, an Iowa man who attempted a drive through the Indian Territory with a herd of about one thousand in 1866, affords many examples of obstacles encountered on the Texas Road.[6] Under May 31 Duffield wrote:

"Swimming Cattle in the order We worked all day in the River & at dusk got the last Beefe over—& am now out of Texas—This day will long be remembered by me—There was one of our party Drowned today (Mr. Carr) & Several narrow escapes and I among the no."

The entry for June 1 reveals further hardships:

"Stampede last night among 6 droves & a general mix up and loss of Beeves. Hunt Cattle again Men all tired & want to leave. am in the Indian country am annoyed by them believe they scare the Cattle to get pay to collect them—Spent the day in separating Beeves and Hunting—Two men & Bunch Beeves lost—Many Men in trouble. Horses all give out & Men refused to do anything."

Later entries give a picture of the drive: "Hard rain & wind Storm Beeves ran & had to be on horseback all night Awful night. wet all night clear bright morning." On June 5, "We hauled cattle out of the Mud with oxen half the day"; and June 6, "50 Beeves lost." On June 12, "Last Night 5,000 Beeves stampeded at this place & a general mix up was the result." At the Arkansas River, "Longs Herd cross with a loss of 25 head." On June 23, "Worked all day hard in the River trying to make the Beeves swim & did

[6] Dale and Rader, *Readings in Oklahoma History*, 415–20 (from *Annals of Iowa*, Vol. 14, no. 4, pp. 243–62).

not get one over." The incurable optimism of the era and the country is shown in this entry: "Had to go back to Prairie Sick & discouraged. Have not got the Blues but am in a Hel of a fix. Indians held High Festival over stolen Beef all night."

It was too much to expect that the Indians should remain complacent when great herds trespassed upon their lands, eating the available supply of grass and perhaps knocking down fences and destroying crops. Even before the Civil War, the Creeks had sent commissioners to Washington to deal with the subject of emigrants passing through their land, grazing livestock on the Indian range.[7]

There were lawless men in the Indian country, and a cattle drive in which a dozen cowboys were attempting to control more than two thousand animals offered an opportunity for raiding. Often trail drivers were unacquainted with the country through which they were passing. A herd, stampeded and scattered through the rough, timbered hills adjacent to the Texas Road was lost to its owners, but often could be salvaged by riders who knew the country.

If any part of a cattle drive reached southern Kansas, a new difficulty arose. The farmers were much disturbed by the possibility of Texas fever invading their own herds, and they feared that Texas cattle would spread the ticks that carried the disease among Kansas cattle. Armed "Jayhawkers" sometimes met the trail herds and turned them back. After 1866, small drives of cattle were attempted from Texas to Muskogee and even farther north. The Indians regularly moved their cattle by means of drives to their own markets and outside of the Indian Territory. Some Creeks and Chickasaws bought Texas cattle on a large scale and fattened them for the market. After the possibility of improved beef stock began to be recognized in the Southwest, some Indian ranchmen prospered on this exchange and became quite wealthy. F. B. Severs of Okmulgee held extensive properties—farms, orchards, and a store in Muskogee. He raised horses on a large scale and every year

---

[7] Debo, *Road to Disappearance*, 141. After the war the Creek Council levied a small tax on the passage of cattle through their lands, usually twenty-five cents a head. *Ibid.*, 188.

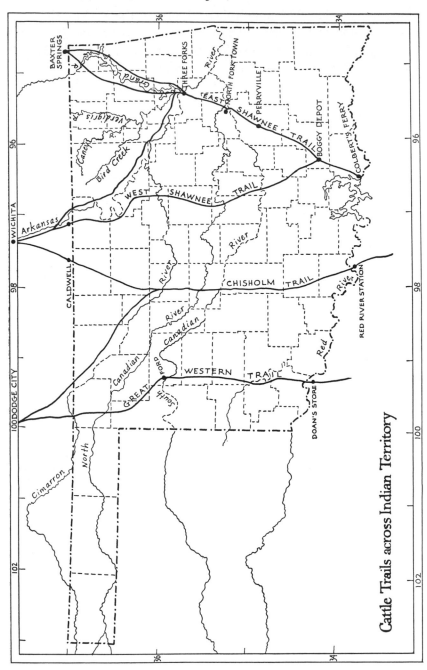

Cattle Trails across Indian Territory

bought from fifteen to twenty thousand cattle in Texas to feed on the Creek range.[8]

The West Shawnee Trail, leaving the Texas Road before the crossing of Blue River, struck northwest toward the site of Sulphur, across the North Canadian near Shawnee, north to the Arkansas River, and along the west bank of that stream into Kansas. The drive was not so difficult as the East Shawnee Trail, but was not without obstacles in the form of hostile Indians, lawless white men in the cattle business, difficult fords, and embattled farmers. The great trail herds for the Kansas cowtowns found a more satisfactory route farther west.

The Chisholm Trail, running roughly parallel to the 98th meridian, had many advantages. That famous trail was named for Jesse Chisholm, who was the son-in-law of the proprietor of Edwards' Store.[9] Chisholm drove his own cattle from his ranch on the Canadian River near modern Asher to the site of Kingfisher and there joined with herds of cattle that had come up the trail from Texas. The name Chisholm Trail was extended to the route from Red River crossing north of Ringold, Texas, along a line that runs parallel to the present-day Rock Island Railroad through Waurika, Duncan, Chickasha, El Reno, Kingfisher, Enid, Medford, and Caldwell, Kansas.

Still farther west, another great cattle trail joined the ranches of Texas with Dodge City, Kansas, and the more distant market of Ogallala, Nebraska. In Texas, the Great Western Trail drew together herds that came from long distances, east, west and south. It ran north from Vernon to Doan's Store on Red River, where it crossed into Greer County, claimed by Texas for many years under an erroneous interpretation of the Adams-Onís Treaty of 1819. Across Greer County to the crossing of North Fork, through the Kiowa-Comanche Reservation and into Cheyenne and Arapaho lands, north past the site of modern Elk City, Camargo on the South Canadian, and Woodward on the North Canadian, the trail bore to the northwest across the Cherokee Outlet and to Dodge City in Kansas.

[8] *Ibid.*, 286; H. F. and E. S. O'Beirne, *Indian Territory.*

[9] J. Evetts Haley, *Charles Goodnight: Cowman and Plainsman*, 232; Wright, *Indian Tribes of Oklahoma*, 68; Debo, *Oklahoma: Foot-loose and Fancy-free*, 24, 25; Foreman, *A History of Oklahoma*, 76.

For a decade, Dodge City handled more live cattle than any other market on earth, and has preserved more of the tradition of that turbulent, brawling era than any other cowtown of the region.[10] Eighty miles north of Wichita on the Kansas and Pacific Railroad was Abilene, promoted as a cattle market by Joseph G. McCoy, of Illinois, and a rival of Dodge City. The place was a new, raw village when McCoy built his first cattle pens there, but it grew rapidly and was the principal shipping point for Texas cattle from 1867 to 1871. McCoy also established a store and built the Drover's Cottage, a three-story frame hotel with forty or fifty rooms, at a cost of $15,000.[11]

Newton, between Wichita and Abilene, Ellsworth, northwest of Newton, and Ogallala, Nebraska, all had their era of giant cow pens, bawling cattle, sharp deals between buyers and herd bosses, and reckless spending of hard-earned money by cowhands released from the monotony of the long drive. All the towns witnessed some lawlessness, and all found it necessary to adopt harsh measures of law enforcement. All found it possible, too, in their entertainment of men who worked the trail herds, to offer recreation designed to relieve them of their wages.

The ordinary herd in the northern drive was made up of 2,500 cattle, more or less, depending upon circumstances of its formation. Frequently the herd represented a number of owners, and usually the person in charge was a trusted and experienced cattleman. In many instances, the drover gathered the herd by contracting with various ranches at a uniform price for each beef, taking only steers that were over four years old if the expected market was Kansas City packing houses.[12] Stock intended for further feeding might be younger and animals half starved on a drouth-stricken range might be purchased at a low rate, as an investment risk. George Duffield, mentioned above, was an example of the drover-owner. Many drovers gave only their notes or even oral promises to pay, for cattle delivered to them with a bill of sale at the time when they were collecting beeves for the long drive.

The crew for a trail herd generally consisted of about two

[10] Haley, *Charles Goodnight*, 433.
[11] McCoy, *Cattle Trade of the West and Southwest*, 58, 186, 187.
[12] *Ibid.*, 149, 150.

men for each drove of 300 cattle, or for a full herd of 2,400 beeves about sixteen men besides the cook. In addition to his culinary duties the cook drove the "chuck wagon," a clumsy, strongly constructed vehicle, ordinarily drawn by oxen. Each cowboy was supplied by the drover with at least two horses. The men who worked the trail herds developed great skill in riding, cutting out cattle, and other duties of the long trail. For the first few days, until the cattle had moved away from their home range, the herds generally were driven hard—perhaps twenty-five miles a day. Afterward the rate was ten or fifteen miles and in the lush grass of western Indian reservations might be much slower, with long rest periods.[13]

The total of the cattle driven north from Texas over a twenty-year period, 1866 to 1885, was probably well over 6,000,000 head. Not all of these animals reached market, but as the techniques of driving improved and the advantages of western trails became apparent, losses were reduced. Actually, many herds that crossed the Cheyenne and Arapaho Reservation and the Cherokee Outlet gained in weight on the northern drive. The greatest drives were in 1871, when about 600,000 cattle were moved north on the trails. In 1880 the drives totaled nearly 395,000.[14]

## FROM DRIVES TO GRAZING CONTRACTS

It was inevitable that Texas drovers, moving their cattle in leisurely fashion through Indian reservations and finding excellent grazing lands, should gradually utilize the grass. The reaction of the Indian leaders was a natural one: if the cattlemen wanted use of the pasturage, it had value. The Indians, kept at a low economic level by their slowness in adopting farming and livestock raising, by congressional economies in determining the amount of their income, and by fraud in providing their rations, were constantly in need of money.

There were regions in western Indian Territory where free grazing was almost unchallenged for many years. Before 1879

13 Edward Everett Dale, *The Cherokee Strip Live Stock Association*, 4.
14 *Ibid.*

there was little organized effort to collect for pasturage in the Kiowa-Comanche or Cheyenne-Arapaho reservations, or the Cherokee Outlet. Greer County, the Unassigned Lands (major portions of present-day Payne, Logan, Kingfisher, Canadian, Oklahoma, and Cleveland counties), and No Man's Land (the Oklahoma Panhandle) were practically open for use by any drovers or ranchmen who wanted to occupy them.[15] Indian tribal headmen and also Indian mounted police were in a position to make conditions relatively smooth, or rough, as trail herds moved through the reservations. Gifts to the Indians by cattlemen were commonly regarded as part of the cost in driving cattle north or holding them for protracted periods of grazing on Indian lands.

Contractors who furnished beef to the Indian agencies frequently held their stock on reservation grass while waiting to deliver it. Sometimes herds were carried through the winter on Indian range. Along the northern border of the Cherokee Outlet, Kansas ranchmen gradually encroached upon the Indians' grazing land; and in other parts of western Indian Territory fences were stretched, shacks for line-riders erected, and permanent ranching activities carried on without any official sanction.

In 1883, John D. Miles, Cheyenne and Arapaho agent, made a tentative agreement with seven cattlemen to lease 3,100,000 acres to them at an annual cost of $62,000, or two cents an acre. The lease was to run ten years. The Indians agreed to the terms, but President Arthur's Secretary of the Interior, Henry M. Teller of Colorado, threw the proposed contract into hopeless confusion by adopting a policy half in agreement, half negative. Teller thought he could not approve the lease under existing law; yet the department would "endeavor to see that parties having no agreement are not allowed to interfere with those who have."[16]

The situation created by this semirepudiation of the Miles lease was one which promised trouble—a promise that was soon fulfilled. Cattlemen who signed the agreement and sent their first installment, thirty thousand silver dollars carried by pack horses from Caldwell, Kansas, to the Darlington Agency, were not in a position to enforce their rights. Indian chiefs, mounted police, agency

---

[15] Dale and Rader, *Readings in Oklahoma History*, 407.

[16] *Ibid.*, 409, 427, 428. Quoted from Secretary Teller's "Fenlon Letter."

officers, and other persons who might be useful to cattlemen on the reservation were immediately the object of much attention by rival interests. The rivalry was not a normal, healthy condition of competition in which parties concerned were stimulated to hard effort and keen judgment, but rather a condition in which bribery and corruption were sure to flourish. Some ranchmen not parties to the Miles agreement had separate understandings with headmen in Indian communities by which they were permitted to graze their cattle on limited portions of the reservation. They paid the Indians, without going through official channels, for the right to graze and refused to remove their cattle on the strength of a lease which the Interior Department would not approve. Robert Todd Lincoln, secretary of war, declined to take military action in favor of the unapproved lease, a decision which resulted in a clash between the Interior and the War departments. There was internal friction on the reservation, with rival Indian groups cutting wire, raiding cattle herds, and threatening a violent uprising. A Kiowa-Cheyenne boundary dispute added to the general confusion. John D. Miles resigned and his successor, D. B. Dyer, found it impossible to keep order with his limited police force. At last in 1885, President Cleveland ordered troops to the Cheyenne and Arapaho Reservation and removed all cattle from the range as a means of settling the Indian disorder. The number of beeves removed was not accurately determined, but was probably more than the 210,000 reported in the military estimate. During the severe winter which followed, a large number of cattle died of starvation on the overgrazed ranges of Kansas and Texas. Thus, an incompetent secretary of the interior playing at politics for the benefit of large and small politicians lost the services of a capable Indian agent, brought on a minor range war, aroused internal bitterness between parties of Indians, contributed to the corruption of agency officers and Indian leaders, and probably contributed in a large measure to range cattle losses by the enforced reduction of their range.[17]

[17] *Ibid.*, 409, 423–27.

## THE CHEROKEE STRIP LIVE STOCK ASSOCIATION

The Cherokee Outlet was a belt of land nearly sixty miles wide extending from the 96th meridian on the east to the 100th meridian on the west. The length of the Outlet was approximately 220 miles and the region, as finally defined after many surveys and supplementary agreements, contained nearly 8,000,000 acres of land. After the Osages and other Plains tribes had been placed on the Cherokee Outlet and the strip north of the Kansas border had been ceded to the United States, Cherokee lands west of the 96th meridian still totaled 6,344,562 acres.[18] This region was a vast expanse of excellent grazing land which appealed strongly to cattlemen who crossed it, and contained a large acreage that was suitable for wheat, oats, and other farm crops. The potential wealth in minerals was not discovered for some years after the era of the cattle drives; but farming possibilities were apparent to many cowboys who came north with Texas cattle and to many casual visitors—hunters, emigrants en route to western Texas, and Kansas ranchmen who permitted their herds to drift across the 37th parallel into Cherokee territory.

Cattlemen on the Kansas border had enough grazing interest in the Cherokee Outlet by 1880 to justify a general meeting for determining a date for the spring roundup, division of grazing space, and other common problems. Trail herds—"pilgrim cattle" from Texas—had mingled with herds from the Kansas ranches—"drift cattle"—and because of numerous brands involved, the roundup promised to be rather complicated. The meeting at Caldwell provided for a permanent organization to set roundup dates, determine rules of procedure, means of settling disputes, and means of protection against theft, wolves, prairie fires, and other risks of grazing the Cherokee Outlet.[19]

The Cherokees sent agents to the Outlet to collect a fee from each cattleman who grazed his herds there. The first collections

[18] Gittinger, *Formation of the State of Oklahoma*, 263.
[19] Dale, *The Cherokee Strip Live Stock Association*, 5; Wardell, *A Political History of the Cherokee Nation*, 237, 304, 340.

were only a fraction of the actual grazing value involved, but payments into the Cherokee treasury grew from $1,100 in 1879 to $41,233.81 in 1882. By that time the cattlemen's organization was functioning so well that its leaders decided to bargain with the Cherokee Nation for a lease of the entire Outlet.

Early in the winter of 1882, Secretary of the Interior Henry M. Teller was called into a controversy involving an oil company and the Scott and Topliff Ranch. Disputes over range between competing cattlemen were ordinarily settled by arbitration; but the Pennsylvania Oil Company began fencing a tract claimed by the ranch and refused to negotiate over conflicting interests. Secretary Teller made another of his confusing decisions which resulted presently in an order for all cattle companies to remove their fences and other improvements within a period of twenty days. The time limit was so chosen as to fall about midwinter, and the cattle affected numbered about 250,000.[20]

Robert Todd Lincoln of the War Department held up the order to remove cattlemen and their property from the Outlet, indefinitely. The Cherokee agent, John Q. Tufts, was ordered to investigate the situation and to make a complete report to the commissioner of Indian Affairs. The Tufts Report recommended that the ranchmen be authorized to extend their fencing and other improvements on two conditions: first, that permission be obtained from the Cherokee Nation and second, that all fences be subject to removal upon notice from the secretary of the interior.[21]

While this controversy was going on, the cattlemen were engaged in obtaining a charter from the state of Kansas, with the purpose of making a long-term lease of the Outlet through an act of the Cherokee Council. The Cherokee Strip Live Stock Association, with no other capital than money derived from membership fees at ten dollars each, began a business which was to exercise a deep influence upon the affairs of Oklahoma Territory. Each member of the organization had one vote in determining its general policies.

[20] Dale, *The Cherokee Strip Live Stock Association*, 8, 9 (from J. Hubley Ashton, *Opinions of the Attorneys General*, XVI, 470; Robert Todd Lincoln to the Secretary of the Interior, December 30, 1883, 48 Cong., 1 sess. *Sen. Exec. Doc. 54*, Vol. IV, 148–49).

[21] Dale, *The Cherokee Strip Live Stock Association*, 9 (from Tufts' Report, 48 Cong., 1 sess., *Sen. Exec. Doc. 54*, Vol. IV, 148–49).

The member might be a ranchman or a corporation with many stockholders. Honorary members were admitted, although they might have no direct interest in grazing the Cherokee Outlet, in cases where their herds were likely to be involved in spring round-ups of the organization. The members elected nine directors who chose an arbitration board of three and named the following officers: Benjamin S. Miller, president; John A. Blair, secretary; and Milton H. Bennett, treasurer.

The association employed a Fort Gibson attorney, John F. Lyons, who was an intermarried citizen of the Cherokee Nation and a man who "practiced influence rather than law."[22] The Cherokee themselves were sharply divided over the question of granting a lease to the Cherokee Live Stock Association; but Principal Chief Dennis Bushyhead and a small majority of the council were found to support the agreement. On May 19, 1883, an act of the council authorized the contract. Andrew Drumm and Charles Eldred, representing the association, agreed to pay to the Cherokee Nation the sum of $100,000 annually for a term of five years, in exchange for the exclusive right to graze cattle on the Cherokee Outlet. The money was to be paid in semiannual installments, in advance.

On October 1, 1883, Milton H. Bennett delivered the first payment, $50,000 in silver, which he hauled from Caldwell to Tahlequah for that purpose. During its brief existence this cattlemen's association was quite active. It established the range boundaries for each of its members, who numbered about one hundred. Records of the organization were extensive, since each member paid a rental of two and one-half cents an acre for the privilege of grazing his range, and the association surveyed the separate ranges, trails, and quarantine grounds. Each member built his own corrals and fences, but the association hired men to hunt wolves and prevent cattle theft, and took steps to improve the breeds of beef cattle on the range.

In 1885 a congressional investigation of grazing in the Indian Territory led to charges against Eldred and Drumm of bribery in the Cherokee Council as a means of obtaining their five-year lease.[23] No prosecutions resulted.

[22] *Ibid.,* 11.
[23] 49 Cong., 1 sess., *Sen. Reports,* Vol. VIII, 1278.

In 1888 the association, after a hard fight in the Cherokee Council, obtained a new five-year lease at the rate of $200,000 per year. The United States Congress, however, passed an amendment to the Indian appropriation act of 1889 which was to have immediate bearing upon the status of the Cherokee Strip Live Stock Association. The act of March 2, 1889, approved by President Grover Cleveland two days before the end of his first term, provided for opening the Unassigned Lands in Oklahoma, the two million acres lying west of the Iowa, Kickapoo, and Potawatomie-Shawnee reservations, between the Cherokee Outlet and the Canadian River, by such means as the President might direct. The Springer Amendment to this bill authorized appointment of a commission to deal directly with the Indians concerning disposal of their unused lands. The act specified the amount to be offered the Cherokees, $1.25 an acre.[24] Since the Cherokee Strip Live Stock Association had offered $3.00 for the Outlet, Cherokee reluctance to deal with the federal commissioners is not hard to understand.[25] Undoubtedly cattlemen encouraged the Indians to hold out for more money than the United States was willing to pay them, but Secretary of the Interior John W. Noble had powerful arguments in favor of sale to the government. He stated that the Cherokee Strip Live Stock Association had used corrupt influence upon the Cherokee Council in obtaining its lease, that the Cherokee title to the Outlet was of doubtful value, that grazing contracts with the Indians were not valid, and that the United States had authority to remove cattlemen at any time and take over the land for the public interest.[26] President Benjamin Harrison gave strong support to Noble's position in a proclamation on February 17, 1890. The President gave notice that no more cattle should be brought on the Cherokee Outlet for grazing, and that all cattle on the Outlet should be removed by October 1, 1890. The proclamation stated further that the Cherokee Nation had no right to contract for grazing cattle on the Outlet and gave the opinion of two attorneys general, A. H. Garland, who served under Cleveland, and William H. H. Miller of his own cabinet, in support of his view that the

[24] *Statutes at Large of the United States*, XXV, 1004 ff.
[25] Gittinger, *Formation of the State of Oklahoma*, 199.
[26] Dale, *The Cherokee Strip Live Stock Association*, 15.

Cherokee Strip Live Stock Association lease was "wholly illegal and void."[27]

This positive stand against ranchmen and in favor of settlement by farmers was, perhaps, in accord with majority interests. But in settling the dispute between grazing the land and plowing it, rights of the Indians were ignored, as usual. In 1892, Cherokee leaders came to an agreement with commissioners sent by President Harrison, and next year the Outlet was ceded to the United States for the sum of $8,595,736.12, or approximately $1.40 per acre.[28]

Cattle ranches on Indian land and the great herds of Texas cattle that moved along the trails to northern markets introduced thousands of white men to the land that had been set aside for Indian tribes. Many other thousands were to enter Indian Territory as a result of two other great economic developments: coal mines and railroads.

## BEGINNING OF COAL MINING IN THE INDIAN TERRITORY

In recent times, mineral production has proved most important in Oklahoma's economic development. Petroleum and gas are comparatively recent and some other mineral products came into prominence slowly; but coal production began during the great cattle drives and coal was closely allied with another major development, railroad transportation. Before the Civil War coal found in the Choctaw Nation was used in local blacksmith shops, but no attention was given to production for a wider market.[29]

In 1865 young J. J. McAlester ended his service with the Confederate Army and went to Fort Smith, Arkansas, for the purpose of attending school. Captain Oliver Weldon placed in McAlester's hands the memorandum book of a geologist who recorded evidence that "Crossroads" was in the midst of extensive coal deposits. At that place in the Choctaw Nation, Colonel McAlester determined

[27] Richardson, *Messages and Papers of the Presidents*, IX, 97, 98.
[28] Gittinger, *Formation of the State of Oklahoma*, 200, n. 52.
[29] Thoburn and Wright, *Oklahoma*, I, 469.

to establish a retail business. He worked for Harlan and Rooks in a store at Stonewall, Chickasaw Nation, before starting on his own mercantile venture. With J. T. Hannaford of Fort Smith as his partner, he obtained a trader's license and opened a store at the "Crossroads" in 1870, where the firm made a net profit of $5,000 the first year. J. J. McAlester married a Chickasaw girl and bought out his partner's interest in the store.[30]

As an intermarried citizen of the Chickasaw Nation, McAlester had a citizen's rights under the Choctaw Constitution.[31] He discovered coal and organized the Oklahoma Mining Company, which leased the mine to an operating coal company. Trouble arose with the Choctaw Council over collection of royalties on this mine, and eventually McAlester compromised with Chief Coleman Cole, the Choctaw Nation receiving half the royalties and McAlester's company, half. Afterwards, McAlester sold his mining interests and devoted his attention to the store at the "Crossroads," where business was good.

Coal mining was closely associated with Choctaw politics for many years. Greenwood McCurtain was an advocate of national control of all mineral production and in his efforts to nationalize coal mines he was opposed by Chief B. F. Smallwood. In 1895 a bill to make the mines national property failed and in 1896 the law was re-enacted giving rights to those who discovered minerals. The McCurtain group charged that passage of the measure was obtained by bribery but could not stop operation of the law.

The Choctaw Nation prospered in many ways as a result of coal production. Royalty legislation under which rates were revised from time to time brought a steady income to the Choctaw treasury. Under provisions of the Atoka agreement and the Curtis Act of 1898, coal and asphalt land was reserved for the Choctaw and Chickasaw tribes and placed under trustees appointed by the influence of the respective tribal governments. Funds derived from coal and asphalt were devoted to education for the two tribes. The Indians sold timbers to mining companies and produced railroad ties for numerous branches that connected main-line tracks with the coal diggings. The new mining population created a market

---

[30] *Ibid.*, II, 879, 880.
[31] Debo, *Rise and Fall of the Choctaw Republic*, 128.

for various kinds of Choctaw produce, such as butter and eggs, grain, meat, and livestock. They also created an increased demand for the opening of Indian land to white settlement.

Besides the McAlester mines, production was begun at Krebs, Coalgate, Lehigh, Alderson, and elsewhere.[32] By 1889 the mining population was about two thousand and composed largely of Europeans—Czechs, Slovaks, Slovenes, Hungarians, Belgians, Germans, Frenchmen, Englishmen, Swedes, and Italians. Within five years the number had more than doubled and included, in addition to groups mentioned and some American miners from eastern coal fields, several hundred Negro miners from Texas.

Labor disputes were numerous in the Choctaw mines, in part because the rate of fatal accidents was high. Furthermore, these miners did not receive compensation in the form of wages and shortened hours for the dangers of their occupation. The Knights of Labor carried on a vigorous campaign of agitation, promoting demands for better wages and safer mining conditions. In labor disputes the Indian agents and tribal governments invariably took the side of operators against strikers. The council, principal chief, and other tribal officers had the responsibility of meeting necessary expenses and never looked with approval upon any move to cut off sources of support. Mining companies were in a good position to build or destroy the agent's reputation for effectiveness as a federal official; hence, his interest was bound strongly with theirs.

In 1884, the miners of McAlester, Savanna, and Krebs succeeded in obtaining an agreement with the operators on a nine and one-half hour day and a uniform wage of $2.50 a day, which was above the national level for similar work underground. In 1889 the average wage for miners below the surface was $2.41 in the Indian Territory, by comparison with $2.17 per day in the Iowa coal mines. Foremen's daily wages averaged $2.46 in the Iowa mines, for underground work; in the Indian Territory, $3.10.[33]

In 1894, Indian Territory coal companies announced that a reduction of 25 per cent on wages would be put into effect on April 1. The reasons given for the wage cut were depleted markets

[32] *Ibid.*, 129.

[33] Gene Aldrich, "A History of the Coal Industry in Oklahoma to 1907" (unpublished Ph.D. dissertation, University of Oklahoma, 1952), 73.

and reduced production, neither of which was confirmed by tonnage figures of the years immediately preceding. In 1891 production was 1,091,032 tons valued at $1,897,037; two years later 1,252,110 tons were produced, valued at $2,235,209.[34]

The miners struck. On May 10, 1894, about one thousand of the Lehigh and Coalgate mining population marched upon a strip pit operated by Williamson Brothers, where work had not stopped, and made a noisy demonstration. Fifty women marched in advance carrying banners; behind them marched more than one hundred miners, armed with shotguns and Winchester rifles; then came the Coalgate band, giving the occasion a festive atmosphere by their lively tunes; and at the end of the line were some hundreds of men and boys armed only with clubs and other makeshift weapons. Deputies surrounded the workers who were continuing their labor at the pit; but no clash occurred, and after a brief conference, the Williamsons agreed to suspend operations.[35] At Krebs, strikebreakers were driven off.

The miners on strike numbered about five thousand. They were not joined by men who worked for the Choctaw Coal and Railway Company, probably because the receivers in bankruptcy for that firm were protected by orders against strikers by the federal court. Choctaw Chief W. N. Jones and Indian Agent Dew N. Wisdom appealed to the federal government for troops. Secretary Hoke Smith of the Interior Department obtained an order from the secretary of war, and three companies of infantry were placed in the mining area. Soon afterward two cavalry companies from Fort Reno appeared on the scene, and plans were made to eject from the Choctaw Nation all strikers who were not willing to return to work. After conferences with strike leaders, some men were declared intruders by Choctaw authorities and were placed in cars belonging to the Choctaw Coal and Railway Company and sent to Jenson, Arkansas, by way of Wister Junction. In June about eighty-five were removed from Hartshorne and Alderson and in July a list of seventy-four "intruders" was made up by D. N. Wisdom. Not all of these men were apprehended; in fact, only

34 *Ibid.,* 74 (from Oklahoma Geological Survey, Bulletin No. 4, *Coal in Oklahoma*).
35 *Ibid.,* 77, 78.

fifteen of them were actually ejected. The strike ended on July 31, 1894, after about three and one-half months of interrupted work.[36]

Before statehood, Oklahoma mines were producing about 2,500,000 tons of coal per year, which was approximately 1 per cent of the national total at that time. In addition to the Choctaw fields, coal was produced in the areas of present-day Tulsa, Rogers, Wagoner, and Craig counties, then in the Cherokee Nation. The site of Henryetta in the Creek Nation was also the center of extensive coal mining.

## THE BEGINNING OF RAILROADS IN THE INDIAN TERRITORY

In early Oklahoma rivers were of great importance in the determination of trade routes. Indians and white traders moved their peltries and other goods along the Arkansas, Grand, Verdigris, Canadian, Washita, Kiamichi, Red, and other streams on the way to New Orleans or some closer market. Rivers marked the routes for early exploration and often determined trails for overland caravans, such as wagon trains that moved into Texas or struck off for the Pacific Coast. The California Trail, Texas Road, the great cattle drives, and military roads connecting frontier forts—all played their part in the beginning of Oklahoma commerce. In 1858 the John Butterfield stagecoaches began their mail service from Fort Smith to San Francisco, operating on a contract made with Postmaster General Aaron V. Brown. The mail coaches from Memphis and from St. Louis came by separate roads to Fort Smith, and from that point the route ran across Indian Territory, reaching the Texas Road at the site of McAlester. From that place the Butterfield line followed the old emigrant road to Boggy Depot, Fort Washita, and Preston on the Red River. From the ferry at Preston, the coaches turned west across Texas to El Paso and on to Gila Bend, Yuma, San Diego, Los Angeles, and San Francisco. For twice-a-week mail service from St. Louis and Memphis to San Francisco, the United States paid Butterfield $600,000 annually. Concord coaches made the journey over rough roads at fair speed with sta-

[36] *Ibid.*, 84, 88.

tions for changing teams at intervals of twelve or fifteen miles. Passengers paid $200 for the three-thousand-mile journey, purchased their own meals en route, and each might carry forty pounds of baggage without extra charge. In 1861, as Civil War began, the eastern terminal point of Butterfield service was moved northward to St. Joseph, Missouri.

Steam locomotives for transportation in America were in their first generation at the time of the Civil War. The second generation of railroads, from 1865 to 1900, was to witness vast changes in travel and a corresponding revolution in commerce and industry. It was no accident that each of the Indian tribes was required in 1866 to agree upon railroads through their lands. Three major plans for railroad building at the end of the war, involved connection of the Great Lakes with the Missouri River, joining the Missouri Valley with the Gulf Coast, and linking the Mississippi with California. The Indian Territory was in the path of the second and the third of these developments.

The Union Pacific and Central Pacific, built west from Omaha on the Missouri and east from Sacramento, California, and meeting near Ogden, Utah in 1869, first connected the Mississippi Valley with the Pacific. These roads were followed by Southern Pacific; Atchison, Topeka, and Santa Fe; Northern Pacific, completed in 1883; Atlantic and Pacific; Great Northern; and other lines that partially or completely spanned the vast distances of western plains and mountains.

The builders of the Union Pacific planned to connect northeastern Kansas and the Gulf of Mexico with lines running along the old Texas Road. The properties of this southern branch of Union Pacific were sold, along with all rights acquired from the government, to the Missouri, Kansas and Texas Railroad, chartered in 1869 by Kansas. In May, 1870, the Missouri, Kansas and Texas Railroad had been pushed south to Chetopa, Kansas, on the border of the Cherokee Nation. Among the rights acquired by Union Pacific and sold to the new railroad company was a charter to build its lines through Indian Territory and a conditional grant of public land along its right of way. The railroad which reached the border first was entitled to enter the Cherokee Nation and the Missouri, Kansas and Texas claimed the right. The secretary of the interior, after an investigation, approved the application to enter Indian Territory, and President Grant confirmed the approval on July 20; but by that time graders and track layers were already far across the border and building rapidly in a direct line toward the northeast corner of the Creek Nation. The M. K. & T. had not waited for official permission either from the United States or from the Cherokee Council.[37]

The railroad company posted bond for $500,000 against violation of property rights of the Indians, and looked forward eagerly to legal acquisition of a vast expanse of Indian land, as the charter for the road provided.[38] The conditional land grant of from ten to twenty square miles for each mile of track constructed was to become effective only after Indian title should be extinguished and the land should become a part of the public domain. Among the promoters and stockholders of the Missouri, Kansas and Texas Railroad were August Belmont, J. P. Morgan, John D. Rockefeller, George D. Dennison, Levi Morton, and Levi Parsons. These men fully expected to obtain three million acres of Indian land for the purpose of building their line from north to south, and an additional one million acres along a line which was planned from Fort Smith to Fort Gibson. Since the Indian title was extinguished only by allotments in severalty and Indian land did not become a part of the public domain, the railroad company was unable to gain possession of this valuable Indian property. Friction developed between the railroad and Cherokee tribal officials, and it was due to the clash over land grants, location of town sites, and sale of town lots that the company changed its original plans and built into the Creek Nation at the nearest point from the Kansas border, instead of crossing Grand River and building into Fort Gibson.[39]

By September, 1871, the M. K. & T. had reached Chouteau, a distance of forty-nine miles from the Cherokee border. In January, 1872, it had built to the Arkansas River, completed an 840-foot bridge across the stream, and established Muskogee as the terminal town. Beyond Muskogee, the road pushed on to a site near North Fork Town, which was named Eufaula. In October, 1872, the track

[37] Wardell, *A Political History of the Cherokee Nation*, 258.
[38] *Statutes at Large of the United States*, XIV, 238, 291, 294.
[39] Wardell, *A Political History of the Cherokee Nation*, 257–59.

had been extended to Atoka and by the following January to Colbert's Ferry on Red River. Cattle cars were being constructed in St. Louis for the expected shipments of Texas cattle in 1873.

As the M. K. & T. line was built through Indian Territory with teeming, brawling, terminal towns at Chouteau, Gibson Station, Muskogee, Eufaula, McAlester, and Atoka in turn, stagecoach companies and freighters along the Texas Road gradually withdrew their vehicles from portions of the route covered by rail. Sawyer and Ficklin, who ran the stage line from Baxter Springs, Kansas, to El Paso, Texas, the Southwestern Stage Company, and other common carriers, made contracts with the "Katy" for through rates from all points in Texas over the railroad to northern towns.[40] The business of transportation in the Southwest steadily increased, and Ben Colbert's Ferry at the crossing of Red River was busy night and day, transporting a great variety of vehicles. From the spring of 1870 to October, 1872, when Atoka was the terminal of the M. K. & T., stagecoaches running from Sherman, Texas, to El Paso doubled in number.

The Atlantic and Pacific Railroad constructed its line from St. Louis through Springfield, Neosho, and to Seneca, Missouri, by April 1, 1871, and was the first railroad to apply for entrance into the Indian Territory from the east. Four years earlier the road's president, John F. Tremont, had made an offer of $1,000,000 for the Cherokee Neutral Lands in Kansas, but a treaty with the Indians providing for the sale was defeated in the United States Senate.[41] Permission to enter the Shawnee and Cherokee lands was granted to the Atlantic and Pacific on terms similar to those in the M. K. & T. grant and by September 1, 1871, the second road had formed a junction with the north-south line at Vinita. This was the end of the line for the Atlantic and Pacific until 1882, when building was resumed. The company had been reorganized under the name, St. Louis and San Francisco Railroad Company. By 1886 it had bridged the Arkansas River, established an important cattle-shipping center at Red Fork on the west side of the stream, and pushed its track on to Sapulpa.

Between 1882 and 1887 the St. Louis and San Francisco Rail-

[40] V. V. Masterson, *The Katy Railroad*, 93.
[41] Wardell, *A Political History of the Cherokee Nation*, 213, 214.

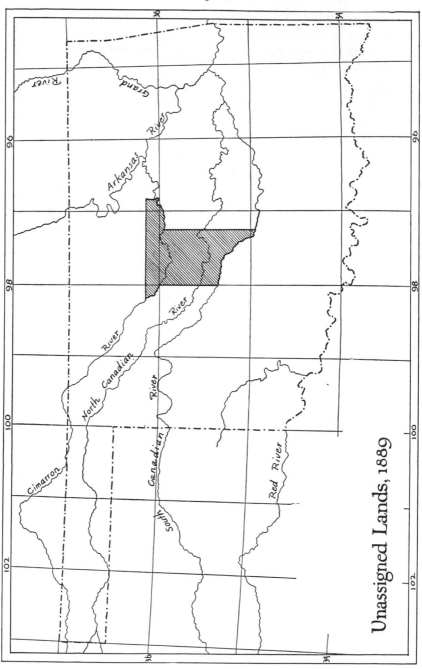

Unassigned Lands, 1889

road constructed a line through the Choctaw Nation from Fort Smith through Poteau, Wister, Tuskahoma, Antlers, Hugo, and across Red River to Paris, Texas. Jackson McCurtain, chief of the Choctaws, was an Indian leader who was in favor of building the road, and in spite of determined opposition by Governor B. F. Overton of the Chickasaws and B. F. Smallwood, Isham Walker, and Joseph P. Folsom of the Choctaws, Chief McCurtain obtained an act of Congress authorizing construction of the road.[42]

In 1888 the Choctaw Coal and Railway Company obtained a charter from Congress to build a railroad in the Choctaw Nation from Wister Junction to McAlester, with branches to the coal mines. The company built and operated a line eighty miles long but in 1891 was forced into bankruptcy. The Choctaw, Oklahoma and Gulf Railroad Company obtained possession of this property in 1896 by an act of Congress, and was able to run trains from El Reno through Oklahoma City to McAlester and east to Wister Junction. In 1890 the Chicago, Rock Island and Pacific Railroad had constructed a line south of Caldwell, Kansas, running approximately along the route of the Chisholm Trail, across Cherokee Outlet, Unassigned Lands, and to the South Canadian border of Chickasaw Nation. In 1902 the Rock Island obtained possession of the Choctaw, Oklahoma and Gulf, which provided a connection for El Reno with Oklahoma City, Shawnee, Seminole, McAlester, and Wister Junction.

The Atchison, Topeka, and Santa Fe Railroad started building a line from Kansas to the Gulf Coast in 1886 and in the spring of 1887 reached the Cherokee Outlet. The road was extended south from Arkansas City through the sites of present day Newkirk, Ponca City, Perry, Orlando, Guthrie, Edmond, Oklahoma City, Norman, Purcell, and Pauls Valley. This road became the key to opening the Unassigned Lands and played a large part in runs for homesteads and location of important townsites.

Like cattle grazing and coal production, the building of railroads was a major factor in opening the Indian country to white settlement. Before Oklahoma became a state nine railroads had built their lines through the Cherokee Nation and six through the Choctaw Nation. There were railroads in the other Indian nations

42 Debo, *Rise and Fall of the Choctaw Republic*, 121–25.

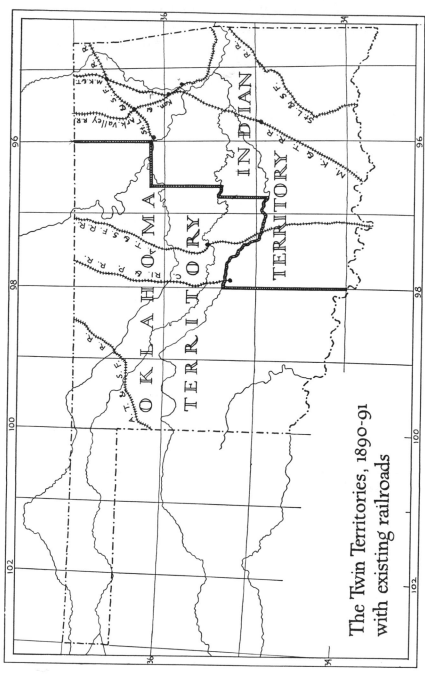

The Twin Territories, 1890-91 with existing railroads

COLONEL GEORGE ARMSTRONG CUSTER
*as he appeared during the Washita campaign*

SATANTA
*Kiowa*

**SATANK**
*Kiowa*

QUANAH PARKER
*half-blood leader of the Comanches*

GERONIMO
*and family, gardening, Fort Sill, 1896*

HUNTING HORSE
*describing Lost Valley fight, on site*

JAMES J. McALESTER
*promoter of coal-mining industry*

DAVID L. PAYNE
*leader of the Boomers*

too; and the Unassigned Lands on the west side, the Cherokee Outlet, and each of the large Indian reservations had been penetrated
by rapidly expanding lines of the western railroads.[43]

Each line brought large gangs of laborers for the actual work
of railroad building and for related occupations, such as tiemaking,
lumbering, and furnishing supplies for railroaders. Sight-seers
flocked to Indian Territory by the thousands and the number of
intruders who took up residence in various parts of Indian lands
grew rapidly. In 1885 Indian Agent Robert Owen reported 25,000
white persons, including more than 3,000 intruders, in territory of
the Five Civilized Tribes. Five years later Agent Leo E. Bennett
reported 140,000 whites in a total population of about 210,000. Of
these about 64,000 were intruders; 48,000, laborers; and 26,000,
other employees.[44]

[43] For a map showing Oklahoma railroads to 1889, see Gittinger, *Formation of
the State of Oklahoma*, 186; for the Creek Nation railroads in 1898, Debo, *The Road
to Disappearance*, 381; for the Choctaw Nation in 1887, Debo, *Rise and Fall of the
Choctaw Republic*, 224.

[44] Gittinger, *Formation of the State of Oklahoma*, 214.

# CHAPTER TWELVE

# Opening, Growth, and Government of Oklahoma Territory, 1889-1907

## THE PRESSURE FOR WHITE SETTLEMENT

Grazing contracts, discovery of coal in the Indian Territory, and admission of railroads into the five nations all had the effect of increasing pressure for opening the land to white settlement. Indian opposition to allotments in severalty was a formidable obstacle, because diplomats of the Five Civilized Tribes were skilled in their art and they were experienced in playing one political group against another. Their experience had given them many advantages in the form of powerful acquaintances. The view was gradually gaining ground with the American public that the Indians had been badly treated. Many people were ready to accept their position on almost any question that concerned their land or their lives, because it had become clear that in many instances justice had not been done.

The contacts of Indian leaders with cattlemen, mine operators, and railroad companies reduced the opposition of the tribes to white settlement. Many Indians found direct advantage in dealing with white men, and their point of view changed accordingly. Leaders were found in every tribe who argued that absorption of Indians into the citizenship of the United States was inevitable and that their people would be better off after the change. Cattlemen in the Cheyenne-Arapaho Reservation gave Quanah Parker a new view of the Indian's future. Coal operators in the Choctaw Nation produced tribal revenues which made them acceptable to many Indians. Railroads gave Indian merchants, ranchmen, attorneys, and many others a revised concept of relations between the tribes

278

and the United States. But most Indians were strongly attached to their own government and way of living.

Although cattlemen steadily opposed any measures which would convert their grazing districts into farm land, the process of driving cattle through the Indian country and covering the prairies with herds of beef stock led inevitably to tilling the soil. Many men who worked with range cattle were farmers. Many men who crossed the Indian country on business connected with cattle speculated upon the possibilities of cotton, corn, or wheat in the rich Washita bottoms and level prairies between the Cimarron and Salt Fork. Farmers who occupied land in states adjacent to tribal property had a natural interest in the virgin soil of Indian Territory.

The number of these people who were acquainted with the possibilities of Indian land increased rapidly. In two decades after the beginning of the Civil War, the national population increased by nearly 40 per cent, and in three decades it doubled.[1] The West, however, was growing at a much higher rate than the country as a whole. Kansas and Texas in particular, to the north and south of Indian Territory, were filling rapidly with farmers and with towns to serve the needs of rural population. Between 1870 and 1890 the population of Texas grew from 818,579 to 2,235,527, and in the same period the number of inhabitants in Kansas increased from 356,399 to 1,428,000. Pressure for white occupation of Indian lands kept pace with the growth of population in these two areas.

Well-defined groups took a stand against abolishing tribal governments, alloting a farm to each Indian, and selling surplus land or opening it to white settlement as a part of the public domain. It was a separate problem on the west side, where population was sparse and land was divided into reservations, quite distinct from that of the east side, where four of five great tribes had written constitutions and many years of experience in self-government. The entire Indian country, however, from Arkansas west to the 100th meridian, was an unused area much in the public mind; and it was only a question of time until the law protecting Indians in their tribal rights would yield to the pressure of public demand.

[1] U. S. Bureau of the Census, *Eleventh Census*. The total population in 1860 was approximately 31,400,000; in 1870 it had grown to 38,558,000; in 1880 to 50,000,000; and in 1890 to 63,000,000.

Indian leaders as a whole were opposed to the change. Elected officers of the Indian governments were usually men who possessed large property interests, based upon large exploitation of tribal property, and these men had a direct personal interest in maintaining existing Indian governments. Their people, often following the leadership of headmen with unquestioning loyalty, were not ambitious for obtaining wealth, wanted only their own simple means of gaining a livelihood, and were suspicious of white men's schemes for absorbing the tribal governments.

White ranchmen wanted no increase of farming in the Southwest. Grazing contracts were lucrative for big cattlemen, who were strong supporters of the Indian majority in their hostility to land settlement. Usually, Indian agents came to sympathize with the native point of view. These officials of the United States were quite often in disagreement with higher officers who appointed them; influences at Washington pressed for individual allotments, while the force of Indian opinion was in favor of continuing tribal government.

Churchmen, especially the missionaries who worked with Indian tribes, were opponents of white settlement. Impressed by the long series of injustices suffered by Indians, these devoted men had the point of view that was held by native leaders. Licensed traders, some of whom were permitted to make excessive gains, were opposed to a reorganization which would interfere with their profits. Whiskey peddlers wanted no change for the same reason. Beef contractors, most intermarried citizens, criminal fugitives from the states, and some men who leased Indian property for farming aligned themselves with the opponents of land opening.

Opposed to these supporters of tribal government were the railroad builders who wanted settlement as a means of increasing traffic on their lines. Backward Indian population, basing their economy upon self-sufficient production supplemented by simple exchange at trading posts, were not good customers for railroads. Business would flourish only when farms covered the country with towns and cities growing up at convenient distributing points. The Missouri, Kansas, and Texas Railroad Company was a powerful force working for a major change in the Indian Territory. The St. Louis and San Francisco Company, the Santa Fe, and all other railroads sought the opening of Indian lands to settlement. Whole-sale grocers in St. Louis and other middle western cities were allies of the railroad companies, and border-town merchants of Kansas, Texas, and Arkansas were generally advocates of the change. Caldwell, Arkansas City, Coffeyville, Wellington, Win-field, Baxter Springs, and Chetopa, in Kansas contained hundreds of active boosters for the opening of Oklahoma lands. All of these groups had powerful and persistent representation in both houses of Congress. Perhaps in the long view it was farmers, looking for-ward eagerly to opening new land for cultivation, who constituted the most powerful influence in favor of a changed status for Indian tribes. In the Garfield, Arthur, and Cleveland administrations, Kansas and Texas people pressed against Indian tribal control in very much the same way that Georgia, Alabama, and Mississippi citizens had done in the days of Monroe, John Quincy Adams, and Jackson.

## ORGANIZED DEMANDS FOR OPENING: THE BOOMERS

Among the men who helped to build a strong demand for opening the new territory was Elias C. Boudinot, member of a dis-tinguished Cherokee family. He broke with leading men of his tribe and threw himself into the struggle with great fervor. During the years of defeat for the Southern Confederacy, 1863 to 1865, Boudinot had served as Cherokee delegate to the government at Richmond. Afterward, he worked as an attorney in Washington and maintained his residence in Arkansas, with occasional business ventures in Vinita and other parts of the Cherokee Nation. He steadily lost favor with the majority of the Cherokees, and the in-tensity of feeling against him may be judged by the burning of his hotel on the M. K. and T. right of way at Vinita in 1872. Boudinot had a wide acquaintance with men in public life through his work as an attorney at Washington and his service as clerk of the House Committee on Private Land Claims. Like his father, who lost his life as leader of an unpopular movement, Boudinot braved Chero-kee public disapproval by joining with railroad officials to promote wide interest in the unoccupied Indian lands. With T. C. Sears, attorney for the M. K. and T. Railroad, Boudinot published messages in newspapers, compiled pamphlets, and wrote many personal letters in which he sent maps of Indian Territory and gave a great variety of information to prospective settlers.[2] It was the claim of Boudinot and Sears that citizens of the United States had the right to settle in the Unassigned Lands, under existing law. The region, containing nearly two million acres of land, the major portions of six present-day counties—Payne, Logan, Kingfisher, Canadian, Oklahoma, and Cleveland—was in the heart of the area ceded by Indian tribes after the Civil War. Boudinot's claim concerning the rights of homesteaders became the basis for a great deal of activity directed toward forcible entrance into Indian Territory. It was suggested that the Cherokee Outlet, Greer County, and No Man's Land—the region between Kansas and the Texas Panhandle, west of the 100th meridian and east of New Mexico—were also subject to settlement.

In 1879 the activities of Boomers along the Kansas border brought the agitation to a climax in which the United States government resorted to military sanction. C. C. Carpenter assembled a considerable number of families along the southern border of Kansas, principally in Labette and Montgomery counties. It was the avowed intention of many who camped near the Cherokee Outlet to cross and take up land in the region just south of it, the Unassigned Lands. The leader, Carpenter, had previously taken part in an attempt by white settlers to occupy Sioux territory in South Dakota, and he seemed to be confident of his right to settle on Oklahoma land.[3] G. W. Stidham and Pleasant Porter, Creek diplomats, William Penn Adair of the Cherokees, leading cattlemen, Indian agents, and many other persons protested the threatened invasion. Officers of the Indian Bureau conferred with Secretary of the Interior Carl Schurz, and President Rutherford B. Hayes ordered troops to the Kansas border. Major General John Pope stationed soldiers at Chetopa, Coffeyville, Sedan, Caldwell, and other Kansas towns, and Carpenter's courage declined. In the absence of resolute leadership the Boomers melted away.

2 Gittinger, *Formation of the State of Oklahoma,* 118–20.
3 *Ibid.,* 122.

David L. Payne was one of the men who followed Carpenter's experiment with great interest.[4] His career was a checkered pattern with many failures, a few periods of moderate success, and an enormous variety of enterprise. He fought with the Union Army in Arkansas during the Civil War. After the war he was a member of the Kansas legislature, a captain of the Nineteenth Kansas Volunteer Cavalry, postmaster at Leavenworth, a soldier again, and an officer in the peacetime army. He farmed in Kansas, operated a sawmill, and served as a guide for hunting parties in the Southwest. He dug waterwells for the town of Newton, Kansas, receiving two dollars and a pint of whiskey for each day's work. He borrowed money, mortgaged his property, failed to pay, and lost his home. Although he had a political connection which obtained introduction of a pension bill in the United States Senate for his service in the volunteer cavalry, the pension was not granted. At a later date the bill was introduced a second time with the same result.[5] He served for a time as assistant doorkeeper of the lower house at Washington.[6] Probably he was interested in the propaganda of E. C. Boudinot and T. C. Sears concerning the opening of Indian lands, and certainly he met and exchanged ideas with Boudinot in Washington.[7] After the failure of Carpenter's colonization project in 1879, Payne returned to Kansas and became recognized leader of the Boomers.

The colony for settlement of Oklahoma was organized on a membership basis, with a fee of two dollars for the right to a quarter section of land and twenty-five dollars for a town lot in Payne's proposed capital city. The two-dollar memberships were bought by men who expected to go in with Boomers and obtain a claim; the town-company memberships at twenty-five dollars each, mainly by business men in Wichita who did not march with Payne.[8]

On April 26, 1880, with a party of twenty-one, Payne eluded

[4] Thoburn and Wright, *Oklahoma*, II, 519; Dan W. Peery, "Captain David L. Payne," *Chronicles of Oklahoma*, Vol. XIII, No. 3 (December, 1935), 438–56; Gittinger, *Formation of the State of Oklahoma*, 127, 135.

[5] *Ibid.*, 127, 128.

[6] Carl Coke Rister, *Land Hunger: David L. Payne and the Oklahoma Boomers*, 34, 35.

[7] *Ibid.*, 50.

[8] *Ibid.*, 52.

the soldiers stationed on the border near Arkansas City and crossed into the Cherokee Outlet. With experienced scouts to warn them in regard to military units in the area, the invaders made their way south, avoiding fords occupied by troops, and on May 2 pitched their camp on the North Canadian in the Unassigned Lands at the site of present-day Oklahoma City.[9] Payne sent an account of his progress to Wichita, and presently the newspapers were carrying his message, which was more optimistic than accurate:

"Please say to any that may wish to know that the public lands in the Indian Territory are not only open to settlement, but settled. We are here to stay; are building houses and making homes. Brought with me 153 men, all of them with good teams. Will have one thousand people here in thirty days." (signed) D. L. Payne.

The Boomers constructed a stockade, brought in a supply of wood, and each man located a claim. They also surveyed and marked out a "capital city" of 720 blocks. On May 15, Lieutenant G. H. G. Gale came down from Fort Reno and arrested Payne and his men. They were escorted back to the Kansas border and set free.

By July 6, Payne and a score of followers were ready to try another invasion. Again they eluded the watchful soldiers and reached their former camp site on the North Canadian. Here they were arrested again and taken to Captain T. B. Robinson, who turned first offenders loose but held Payne and three other second offenders. Captain Robinson entertained the Boomer leader, and under the influence of liquor, Payne revealed his method of entering the Indian country, one wagon at a time. He also explained to his host that he had the backing of powerful friends and the best legal talent. Robinson guessed that the legal talent was attached to the staffs of railroad companies that had entered Indian Territory.[10]

Payne and his friends were taken to Fort Smith and into the court of Judge Isaac C. Parker. The judge postponed Payne's case until the November term of court and allowed him to go. As the Boomer leader returned to Kansas, he was met with great enthusiasm in St. Louis and elsewhere. Wichita greeted him as a returning hero.

[9] *Ibid.*, 57, 58.
[10] *Ibid.*, 71, 72.

In December, 1880, the Boomers were camped near Arkansas City. They had announced November 25 as the date for their entrance into Oklahoma lands, but Payne had become ill and was unable to start. In the meantime, Wichita, headquarters for the colony, was seething with excitement and enjoying a harvest of business activity. At that time the organization boasted a membership of five thousand. Merchants exchanged goods for Oklahoma Town Company shares, discounting the stock from 50 to 80 per cent, however.[11] On December 9, a party of two hundred Boomers with sixty-eight wagons left their camp near Arkansas City and moved west, parallel to the Cherokee Outlet boundary. A cavalry unit composed of Negro troops that had been stationed nearby took a position between Payne's Boomers and the border, marching west with them. At Chilocco Creek both parties went into camp.[12] For two more days the Boomers went slowly west, the soldiers keeping up with them. Near Hunnewell, Colonel J. J. Coppinger visited Payne's camp and tried to obtain a promise that his band would not cross into the Indian country. In the discussion which followed it became clear to Colonel Coppinger that the Boomers were not in agreement concerning their next move, and he warned them that his soldiers had orders to fire if they attempted to cross the line.

Payne's followers remained in camp while two of their number slipped around the soldiers and explored through Oklahoma. After two weeks of scouting these men reported that a party of fifty wagons had been in the region south of the Kansas line, but had become discouraged and gone home. These potential allies were from Texas, Arkansas, and the Chickasaw Nation. On December 14, the Boomers marched west again for Caldwell, where they were received with great enthusiasm. The soldiers went with them. On Christmas, people who supported the Boomer cause brought supplies of food and other presents, including a roll of money and two revolvers for Payne. After Christmas, however, men in camp gradually withdrew to their homes. A messenger sent to President Hayes returned with a noncommittal statement from the President, and most Boomers were ready to go home.

[11] *Ibid.*, 80.
[12] *Ibid.*, 81.

When, after some delay, Payne's case was finally heard before the federal court at Fort Smith, Judge Parker ruled that Payne was guilty and subject to a fine of $1,000. Since the defendant had no property, the fine could not be collected; and since the law provided no penalty other than the fine, he could not be imprisoned.

David L. Payne's biographers have sometimes tried to picture him as a rugged, dynamic, courageous fellow, of iron will and unchanging purpose. In fact, he had more iron than some of his followers, and more courage than the boastful C. C. Carpenter, who preceded him as a leader of the Boomers. But he was not a great pioneer of the Western Plains, to be compared with Kit Carson or David Crockett. His physical stamina was lacking, for one thing. Exposure and the hardship of long marches gave him rheumatism. He was more at home as the center of attention of big, heterogeneous, unthinking crowds in the towns, with plenty of liquid refreshment close at hand, than he was in the actual work of establishing a colony. Colonel Edward Hatch stated that Payne collected about $100,000 over a period of four years in promoting the Boomers, and that he did not want settlement of Oklahoma since that would shut off his harvest of bank notes.[13] He was in and out of the Indian country many times after his first failure to effect a permanent foothold. The federal authorities were unable to imprison him for trespass and unable to collect the fines imposed. Payne died suddenly on November 28, 1884, at the age of forty-eight.

His immediate successor was William L. Couch who headed an expedition into Oklahoma about ten days after the death of Payne. The invaders camped on Boomer Creek, in the northeastern part of the Unassigned Land, near present-day Stillwater. Two hundred men made up the original party, but they were joined by additional members, including a few women and children, until the number was about doubled. A small cavalry unit ordered Couch and his party to break camp and go back to Kansas, but the Boomers refused to move. On January 7, Colonel Edward Hatch came up to the Boomer camp with a larger body of troops. By January 24 he had gathered seven cavalry companies and one infantry company supported by two artillery pieces. Captain Carroll was sent to

[13] Gittinger, *Formation of the State of Oklahoma*, 134.

demand the surrender of the Boomer leader. Couch replied that his men were peaceable citizens, that they were there on the lawful business of obtaining claims, and that they were prepared to fight for their rights. Since Colonel Hatch was in command of approximately 350 men and was in a position to hold them out of the range of small arms while shelling the camp, the battle probably would not have lasted very long. W. L. Couch did show courage, however, to accompany his convictions. Far less spectacular than Payne, he had more of the nerve that distinguishes successful pioneers.

Colonel Hatch did not fire upon the Boomer camp. Instead, he posted his forces in such fashion as to cut off their supplies. Faced with shortage of food, Couch ordered his wagons loaded for travel; and on January 30 the Boomers drove back toward Kansas, escorted by federal cavalry.[14]

Meantime, from the political point of view, change in the status of Indian Territory had become imperative.[15] On January 30, 1885, as Couch and his disappointed Boomers were pulling out of the Stillwater Valley, the Secretary of the Interior at Washington, Henry M. Teller, was recommending the opening of Indian lands. President Chester A. Arthur, who had taken the chief executive office when Garfield was assassinated in 1881, was openly in favor of the change. On March 3, 1885, the day before his term was to end, Congress passed an act authorizing the president to negotiate for cession of the Creek, Seminole, and Cherokee surplus lands in western Indian Territory. There was not time for Arthur to act on this authority and the new president, Grover Cleveland, was not inclined to rush negotiations.

The Indians, in a sense, took the initiative. In January, 1889, Pleasant Porter of the Creeks came to Washington with a delegation of his tribesmen with a proposition to sell their western land.[16] William F. Vilas, secretary of the interior, reached an agreement with the Porter Commission. The United States contracted to pay the Creek Tribe at the rate of $1.25 per acre for 1,392,704 acres in the Unassigned District; and at the rate of $1.05 per acre

14 John Alley, *City Beginnings in Oklahoma Territory*, 88, 89; Rister, *Land Hunger*, 189–93; Gittinger, *Formation of the State of Oklahoma*, 137.

15 The definitive treatment of the final success of forces in favor of opening Indian lands is in Gittinger, *Formation of the State of Oklahoma*, 138–57.

16 *Ibid.*, 179.

for land in the Cheyenne and Arapaho Reservation. Thirty cents per acre of this price had been paid in 1866. The sum of $2,000,000 was to be held in trust by the United States with 5 per cent interest paid to the Creeks. The balance, $280,000, was to be paid by the United States in cash.

To the Seminoles, Secretary Vilas agreed to pay $1,912,942 for 1,669,080 acres in the Cheyenne-Arapaho Reservation and 500,000 acres in the Unassigned Lands. With this cession of land, the United States acquired title to the Unassigned District and on March 2, 1889, a bill was rushed through Congress and sent to President Cleveland, authorizing the chief executive to open the area to white settlement.[17] The measure was in the form of a rider to the Indian appropriation bill, which left Cleveland little choice. He could leave the Indian Bureau destitute of funds by executive veto, or he could sign the bill and admit white settlers to the Indian lands. He signed and the proposed measure became law.[18] The region thus designated for opening was 1,887,796 acres in extent, a little over 4 per cent of the total area that was eventually to be incorporated in the state of Oklahoma, the same rectangle in the center of the Indian country which for a generation had held the attention of land seekers from many states.[19]

On March 23, 1889, during President Harrison's third week in office, he issued a proclamation for settling the territory. At noon on April 22, eligible persons were authorized to enter for the purpose of occupying a quarter section. Laws governing homesteads were to be in effect, with the additional restriction that any person who entered before the time designated by the President's proclamation would not be permitted to take a homestead. Eligible persons included male citizens twenty-one years of age and unmarried women, twenty-one, who were citizens of the United States. Widows and women legally separated from their husbands were eligible for claims. Aliens who had declared their intention of becoming citizens were eligible. No person who owned more than 160 acres of land was allowed to stake a claim.

The customary reservation of sections sixteen and thirty-six

---

[17] *Ibid.*, 182.
[18] Alley, *City Beginnings*, 8, 9.
[19] Gittinger, *Formation of the State of Oklahoma*, 186, n. 4.

in each township, for the support of elementary education was provided. Persons who expected to make the run for a home were allowed to cross the Cherokee Outlet on the north and the Chickasaw Nation on the south three days before the date set by the President's proclamation, in order that they might be on the border of the Unassigned Land when the time came for the opening. People camped in large numbers along the southern border of the Outlet, and along the banks of the South Canadian, boundary of the Unassigned Land on the south. Some persons in their adventures as Boomers or otherwise had previously located desirable claims in the area, and naturally they took their position as near the prospective homestead as possible. From east to west the area measured about thirty miles and from north to south, about fifty. It was planned that Santa Fe trains carrying passengers should run south from Arkansas City, and north from Purcell, traveling slowly in order that the homesteaders might alight and stake a claim in a desirable spot.

## SETTLEMENT OF THE OKLAHOMA DISTRICT

At the signal for opening the territory, which was passed along the border by soldiers who fired their pistols, fifteen Santa Fe trains pulled slowly into Oklahoma Territory from the north and other trains from the southern limits. People traveled by many other means also—on horseback, in wagons, carriages, buggies, and on foot. The process of establishing a claim involved putting down a stake bearing the claimant's name and entry at one of the United States land offices, which had been established at Guthrie on the Santa Fe and at Kingfisher, thirty miles west on a stagecoach line. A small fee was charged for formal entry of a claim, and the settler was required to live on the land for a period of five years before obtaining title to the property. The period for obtaining title was shortened to fourteen months, provided payment of $1.25 per acre was made to cover the cost of purchase from the Indians. With the passage of the Free Homes Act in 1900 this charge, amounting to $200 for a quarter section of land, was abolished.

289

Townsites were restricted to 320 acres by the law of March 2, 1889, authorizing opening of Oklahoma lands.[20] Six of the townsites established in 1889 were to become county seats: Guthrie, Oklahoma City, Kingfisher, El Reno, Norman, and Stillwater. One of them, Guthrie, was to become capital of the territory and later capital of the state for a brief period; another, Oklahoma City, was to become the permanent capital of Oklahoma. Restriction of townsites to 320 acres was an unwise provision of the lawmakers which taxed the ingenuity of early settlers, led to evasion, and occasionally to fights in the courts. In Guthrie, where some ten or twelve thousand persons were encamped on the night of April 22, there was not room for all of them to obtain town lots on 320 acres of ground.[21] Five adjacent townsites were laid out with the names: East Guthrie, South Guthrie, West Guthrie, Capitol Hill, and "Dyer's Guthrie."[22] A similar expedient was used at Oklahoma City and Kingfisher. At Stillwater, the townsite company began with a core of eighty acres and obtained additions from the claims of three adjacent homesteaders.[23] At Norman, not more than 150 settlers appeared during the first days after the opening, and the townsite company had no trouble in providing lots on one legal townsite.[24]

Estimates on settlers who came during the first day vary greatly. Brigadier General Wesley Merritt, in command of troops stationed in the area during settlement, placed the number at ten or twelve thousand. This estimate was too low, as a glance at the numbers seeking town lots in various places would show. Probably, Guthrie and Oklahoma City each contained as many settlers as the

[20] *Ibid.*, 189, n. 16; Alley, *City Beginnings*, 13.

[21] Thoburn and Wright, *Oklahoma*, II, 546.

[22] Gittinger, *Formation of the State of Oklahoma*, 192.

[23] Alley, *City Beginnings*, 90. The settlers who contributed land for the townsite were Robert A. Lowry, eighty acres; David Husband, forty acres; and Sanford Duncan, forty acres.

[24] *Ibid.*, 74–78. Some of the men who composed the townsite company were D. L. Larsh, T. R. Waggoner, Tyler Blake, E. P. Ingle, and Andrew Kingkade. Larsh was station agent for the Santa Fe Railroad at Purcell, Kingkade was station agent at Norman, Blake was a druggist at Purcell, and Ingle founded the *Norman Transcript*. Later, as a member of the territorial legislature, T. R. Waggoner was an effective spokesman for Norman as the site of the University. Roy Gittinger, *The University of Oklahoma: A History of Fifty Years, 1892–1942*, 5.

General's estimate for the total. Kingfisher contained a smaller number, and the other townsites were even less crowded. Probably the number who made the run was not much over or under fifty thousand. Captain Stiles said that Oklahoma City on April 23 contained more than twelve thousand; Hamilton S. Wicks estimated Guthrie at ten thousand on April 23 and fifteen thousand three months afterward.[25] Within one hour after the signal for opening the lands, about twenty-five hundred "West Liners" waiting on the line of the Cheyenne-Arapaho Reservation had occupied choice lots at King Fisher's station, naming their town Lisbon, and two hours later the "North Liners" traveling from the Cherokee Outlet, took lots to the north of the earlier group.[26] For a time Kingfisher (or Lisbon) was the third town in population.

For nearly thirteen months there was no organized territorial government in Oklahoma. All the towns established provisional machinery for regulating the conduct of people, based upon consent of the governed and following traditional forms. There were many able and experienced men among the first settlers, and they set up effective units of government. Ordinarily they elected at once a mayor, city council, and city marshal. Authority of the United States in Oklahoma during these months was represented only by United States marshals and by the men of General Merritt's command who were stationed near the land offices at Kingfisher and Guthrie.

There were few crimes, particularly of the violent type, either in the race for homes or during the days of uncertainty which followed. This comparative orderliness in the absence of official authority was due to the character of the population. Conditions of settlement did not attract adventurers. People who came to Oklahoma seeking farm homes were not likely to resort to murder if some contestant appeared who laid claim to the same quarter section. Men who brought lumber into Guthrie or Stillwater and constructed shacks for sheltering a little stock of groceries bought with their savings were not given to shooting their way out of difficulties. There were no large payrolls in Oklahoma nor enough ready cash

25 Hamilton S. Wicks, "The Opening of Oklahoma," *Cosmopolitan*, Vol. VII (September, 1889), 460.
26 Alley, *City Beginnings*, 49, 50.

in any form to attract gamblers. At first, the population was in a large per cent men, most of them young. Later the men were joined by their families, and the total number grew rapidly by the simple process of migration. Within a few years, however, children born in Oklahoma occupied a large place in the population figures.[27]

## ORGANIZED GOVERNMENT FOR OKLAHOMA TERRITORY

On May 2, 1890, Congress passed an Organic Act for the Territory of Oklahoma. Seven counties, designated only by numbers, were provided by the act—six in Oklahoma District and one in the Panhandle, lying between Texas and Kansas west of the 100th meridian and extending all the way to the boundary of New Mexico Territory, with more than fifty miles bordering on the state of Colorado. This western arm of the new territory was still very sparsely settled, but its extent was approximately 5,681 square miles, nearly twice the area of the Unassigned Lands, and about five times as large as the State of Rhode Island. Eventually, in the August election of 1890, the voters of the several counties gave them these names: Kingfisher, Logan, Payne, Canadian, Oklahoma, and Cleveland in the Unassigned Lands, and Beaver County in the Panhandle.

The Organic Act followed the model of territorial government in the United States which was older, in most of its features, than the Constitution itself.[28] An appointed governor, a secretary, and three judges, together with an elected legislature of two houses, constituted the principal elements of the territorial government. The president, with approval of the United States Senate, appointed the executive and judicial officers. The judges, sitting together, constituted the territorial supreme court; separately, they were district judges. As the territory grew by successive additions

[27] In a population of 400,000 in 1900, Oklahoma Territory contained more than 125,000 persons of school age. See U. S. Census Bureau, *Twelfth Census: Population; Report of the Governor of Oklahoma*, 1891–1907.

[28] The Ordinances for governing the Northwest Territory, passed by the Confederation Congress in 1784, 1785, and especially in 1787, contained the essential principles of territorial government in the United States.

of Indian lands, the number of judges was increased to five and later to seven. Indian reservations in the Cherokee Outlet and reservations south of them—Iowa, Kickapoo, Pottawatomie and Shawnee, and Sac and Fox—were under the jurisdiction of Oklahoma courts. The statutes of Nebraska were adopted as a guide for the courts until Oklahoma had an opportunity to establish its own laws.

The upper house of the territorial legislature, the council, was composed of thirteen members elected by the voters for four-year terms. The usual provision was added for giving the upper house a continuing membership; that is, terms were staggered so that approximately half would be elected every two years. The House of Representatives had twenty-six elected members serving terms of two years.

George W. Steele of Indiana was appointed by President Harrison as Oklahoma's first governor. One of his first duties after he reached Guthrie, named by the Organic Act as territorial capital, was to take a census of Oklahoma as a basis for apportionment of the legislature. The population of the counties at the time of the first election was as follows: Logan, 14,254; Oklahoma, 12,794; Cleveland, 7,011; Canadian, 7,703; Kingfisher, 8,837; Payne, 6,836; and Beaver, 2,982. Total for the territory was 60,417.[29]

The governor called an election for August 5; and three weeks later, the first legislature met. The composition of the first legislature was as follows: senate, six Republicans, five Democrats, and two People's Party Alliance members; house of representatives, fourteen Republicans, eight Democrats, and four People's Party Alliance members.[30] The two major parties were not in a position to ignore the Alliance members, who held a balance in the Senate and were influential throughout the territory. George W. Gardenhire, Alliance member from Stillwater, was elected president of the council and Arthur N. Daniels, Alliance representative from Frisco, became speaker of the house. The "Element of Discontent" as a balance between major party groups was often to play an important part in Oklahoma politics.

President Harrison appointed as members of the territorial

[29] Gittinger, *Formation of the State of Oklahoma*, 195.
[30] Alley, *City Beginnings*, 102, 103.

supreme court, F. B. Green of Illinois, Abraham J. Seay of Missouri, and J. G. Clark of Wisconsin. Oklahoma Republicans who had hoped the major appointments would be made from residents of the territory were inclined to regard Harrison's selections as proof that he was a second-rate politician. The Democrats looked upon Steele, Green, Seay, and Clark as "Carpetbaggers."

In addition to officials previously mentioned, the territory was entitled to elect a delegate to Congress who would have no vote with the members of either chamber, but would serve to present the views of Oklahoma on the floors of both. First of the territorial delegates to be elected was David A. Harvey, a Republican, whose principal claim to distinction seems to be that he introduced a bill in the House of Representatives on January 25, 1892, to make Oklahoma a state.[31] He served from 1890 to 1893, and was succeeded by Dennis Flynn of Guthrie, also a Republican. Flynn was a Pennsylvania man who came to Guthrie in the run of April 22, 1889, served as chairman of the committee that wrote the first city charter in June, and was a member of the Republican territorial convention in January, 1890. He was delegate to Congress during eight of the years between 1893 and 1903 and was the foremost advocate of the Free Homes Act for Oklahoma. James Y. Callahan of Kingfisher was the only territorial delegate elected by the Democrats. He defeated Flynn in the election of 1896 by a combination of Populist voters with the Democrats. During the last four years of territorial government (1903–1907), Bird S. McGuire of Pawnee was the Oklahoma delegate to Congress.

The first legislature in Oklahoma was interested chiefly in location of the capital and territorial schools. Spoils in the form of institutions resulted in a struggle among towns and their representatives, bitter and prolonged in regard to location of the capital. Governor Steele sent a message to the legislature in which he recommended relief for destitute settlers whose crops had failed because of drouth, establishment of an elementary school system, attention to bridges and public roads, and restrictions on the sale of intoxicants. The lawmakers ignored his demands and proceeded with their fight over location of the capital.[32]

[31] 52 Cong., 1 sess., *Cong. Rec.*, 522.
[32] Alley, *City Beginnings*, 104, 105.

Three towns fought for the distinction and profit that would follow location of the permanent capital: Guthrie, Oklahoma City, and Kingfisher. A fourth town, Frisco, was an interested party and perhaps contained some citizens who hoped that the three main contestants would all fail and fall back on their town as a capital site. Guthrie had the advantage of being designated temporary capital by the Organic Act and was, at the time of the first legislature, more populous than either of its rivals.[33]

The town of Frisco was a phenomenon peculiar to Oklahoma's unique process of settlement. It was established on the left bank of the North Canadian about twelve miles east of Reno City, also on the north bank, and El Reno just south of the river. The three Canadian County towns were rivals for leadership in the county, and gradually El Reno outgrew the other two, becoming county seat and principal retailing point for that part of the territory. In the meantime, Frisco displayed a remarkable interest in politics, becoming the center of activity for organizing a provisional territorial government and rival of the two larger towns on the Santa Fe for choice as permanent capital. The Frisco Convention of July 15, with its plan for territorial government, has been called "the outstanding political incident in the first decade of Oklahoma . . . politics."[34] Sixty of the original settlers of Frisco were veterans of the Union Army. They and their families were keenly interested in politics, a fact which may account in part for the activity of the place in holding the convention and in all the early elections. Reno City and Frisco have entirely disappeared. In commenting upon the brief attempts of Reno City and Frisco to gain footholds as towns, Professor Alley wrote: "In the three-cornered battle for local and county honors waged by Reno City, Frisco, and El Reno, nature favored Reno City, the politicians favored Frisco, but the railroads favored El Reno. And the railroads won by a wide margin."[35] The Rock Island Railroad bypassed Reno City in favor of El Reno and the Choctaw Coal and Railway Company built along the south bank of the river, leaving Frisco to wither and making Yukon possible as a retailing center.

[33] The *Report of the Governor of Oklahoma,* 1891, gave Guthrie 5,884; Oklahoma City 5,086. The Federal Census Report of 1900 gave each city just over 10,000.

[34] Alley, *City Beginnings,* 66.

[35] *Ibid.,* 60.

The First Territorial Legislature, by an act of December 19, 1890, established the University of Oklahoma at Norman. A week later Governor Steele approved the bill establishing the Agricultural and Mechanical College in Payne County, and before the month ended provision had been made also for a normal school at Edmond. Each of the counties and towns chosen for the location of a territorial school was required to vote bonds to help defray original expenses and to furnish land for a campus. Cleveland County voted the required $10,000 in bonds and the city of Norman gave forty acres of land, purchasing it for approximately $1,500.[36] The bonds sold for $7,200, and the city of Norman made up the deficit. Payne County voters rejected the proposition to furnish bonds, but the city of Stillwater voted by an overwhelming majority to raise the necessary $10,000 besides furnishing two hundred acres of land for the campus and experiment station. Oklahoma County and the city of Edmond also met requirements of the act creating the normal school, and the institution was ready to begin its first term of instruction on November 9, 1891, earlier than either of the other territorial schools. Classes opened with nineteen students and the number grew to seventy-six within the first year.

The struggle over location of Oklahoma's permanent capital began with a bill introduced into the council by J. L. Brown of Oklahoma City on September 2, 1890, and continued for several years after statehood in 1907. Senator Brown's bill (Council Bill Number 7) provided that the capital should be established at Oklahoma City. After two weeks of debate, this passed the council by a majority of one. In the house of representatives the contest lasted three weeks and finally resulted in passage of the bill. Governor Steele promptly vetoed it, and the supporters of Oklahoma City for capital could not pass it over his veto.[37] Another bill was passed locating the capital at Kingfisher, which the governor also vetoed. Damaging charges were made against many officials at Guthrie during this bitter fight, including accusations of bribery and various kinds of unethical behavior. Governor Steele accused members of neglecting needed laws in favor of their contest over spoils;

[36] Gittinger, *The University of Oklahoma,* 6, 7.
[37] Alley, *City Beginnings,* 103, 104.

leaders of the legislature charged the governor with defeating the people's will. The term "carpetbagger," which had subsided while Governor Steele was making choices for temporary county officers, became popular again. Governor George W. Steele, like many other provincial executives of the United States, gave up the contest and left Oklahoma.[38]

His administration cannot be regarded as successful. Undoubtedly, some of the accusations he made against the legislature were correct; but Steele himself was narrow-minded, set in his opinions, unyielding on questions little connected with public interest, small in every respect. He had entered the Union Army as a private in 1861 and emerged as a colonel four years later. Ten additional years as an officer in the peacetime army had not strengthened his grasp of civilian affairs, and eight years in Congress had not erased the intolerant views and the bearing of a martinet, developed by fourteen years in the army.

### GROWTH AND GOVERNMENT OF OKLAHOMA TERRITORY

The brief term of Governor Steele was in many respects a pattern of politics, repeated in later administrations. The struggle for location of territorial institutions continued with Granite contesting Weatherford, Woodward and Alva maneuvering for advantage, Tonkawa and Langston winning legislative favors.

The Dawes Act of February 8, 1887, authorizing the president to allot lands in severalty to any tribe of Indians that he regarded sufficiently advanced to benefit by the change, had been implemented by the Springer Amendment to the Indian Appropriation Act of March 2, 1889. This clause gave the president specific authority to negotiate for the purchase of all surplus Indian land west of the Five Civilized Tribes. After several changes in personnel, the commission which actually made most of the agreements for sale of land by the Indians was composed of David H. Jerome, Alfred M. Wilson, and Warren G. Sayre. The Sac and Fox, Iowa,

[38] In the troubled era just before the Civil War, Kansas Territory had four different governors in a period of two years, 1855–57.

and Pottawatomie-Shawnee tribes agreed to cede their surplus lands and to accept allotments in severalty in July, 1890. In October of the same year the Jerome Commission signed an agreement with the Cheyennes and Arapahoes, and on December 19, 1891, finally came to an agreement with the Cherokees concerning sale of the surplus land in the Outlet. As indicated above, the government exerted a great deal of pressure upon Indians and cattlemen to obtain this agreement. Commissioners Jerome, Wilson, and Sayre represented the government; Elias C. Boudinot, Joseph A. Scales, George Downing, Roach Young, Thomas Smith, William Triplett, and Joseph Smallwood, the Cherokees.[39]

To replace Governor Steele, President Benjamin Harrison selected A. J. Seay, who left his office in the territorial supreme court and was inaugurated as governor on October 18, 1891. Like Steele, he had some constructive ideas for territorial government, and he was better able to adjust his program to the practical needs of politics.

The second run for homesteads in Oklahoma occurred on September 22, 1891, about a month before Governor Seay took office. The area opened, lying east of the original six counties, contained approximately 1,120,000 acres. The surplus lands of the Iowas north of Deep Fork and of the Sac and Fox on both sides of Deep Fork, along with ceded lands of the Shawnee-Pottawatomie Indians, were thrown open to settlers by means of a presidential proclamation. The great opening of April 22, 1889, was repeated on a somewhat smaller scale. Lying near the center of the great tract of land was the Kickapoo Reservation, which could not be opened because no agreement had been reached concerning allotment and sale of surplus land.[40]

About twenty thousand persons made this second race for homes—nearly three times the number of quarter sections available for settlement. After the initial rush was over, the experiment of opening townsites by run was made at Tecumseh and Chandler. A great deal of confusion and at least one death resulted from the close-packed scramble for town lots.

[39] Dale and Rader, *Readings in Oklahoma History*, 499–503 (from *Oklahoma Red Book, I*, 469–72).

[40] *Ibid.*, 531–35. The Kickapoo agreement was reached on March 3, 1893.

The third opening was that of the Cheyenne and Arapaho lands on April 19, 1892. The United States had agreed to pay the Indians of this reservation the sum of $1,500,000 for 4,300,000 acres. About twenty-five thousand persons took part in the run, and for the first time there were more claims available than the number of settlers. Many who made the run and were unable to get land in the eastern half of the vast tract declined to stake a claim farther west. About 2,000,000 acres, roughly the western half of the reservation, remained in use by ranchmen for several years. Before statehood, however, nearly all of it had been occupied by persons seeking farm homes.[41] Two new counties, Lincoln and Pottawatomie, were added to Oklahoma by the second run and six were added by the Cheyenne and Arapaho opening: Blaine, Dewey, Roger Mills, Custer, Washita, and Day.[42] Also, Canadian and Kingfisher counties, formed in the original Oklahoma lands, were almost doubled by land annexed from the Cheyenne-Arapaho cession.

In May, 1893, a short time after Grover Cleveland began his second term as president, he replaced Governor Seay by appointing a Democrat, William C. Renfrow, of Norman, to the office. The third governor was a North Carolina man. Born in 1845, he served as a Confederate soldier and was only twenty when the war ended. He came west and engaged in a variety of business enterprises in Arkansas. At the town of Norman he established a bank shortly after the opening of Oklahoma Territory. He was an able and popular business man and he made a good chief executive. He remained in office as governor during Cleveland's entire term but was replaced by a Republican shortly after the election of William McKinley as President.

Two races for homes were made in Oklahoma during Governor Renfrow's term of office: the Cherokee Outlet opening on September 16, 1893, and the Kickapoo opening in May, 1895. The Cherokee Outlet run was the largest and most spectacular of them all, with 100,000 persons taking part in the contest. In addition to unoccupied portions of the Outlet, surplus lands of the Tonkawas

[41] Dale and Rader, *Readings in Oklahoma History*, 495 (from *Oklahoma Red Book*, I, 473–75).

[42] Day County lost its separate organization as a county at the beginning of statehood.

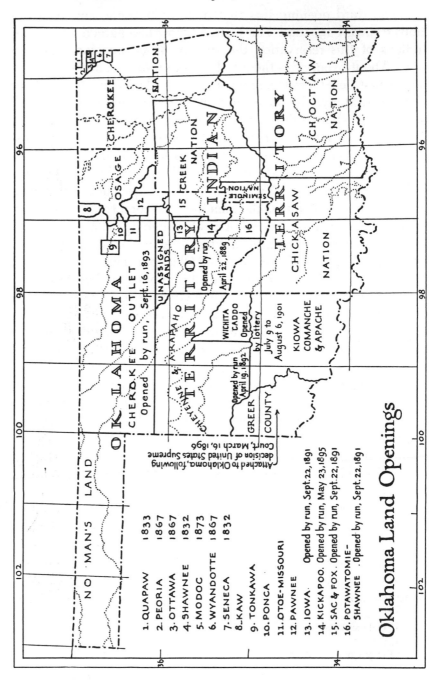

Oklahoma Land Openings

1. QUAPAW ............ 1833
2. PEORIA ............ 1867
3. OTTAWA ........... 1867
4. SHAWNEE ......... 1832
5. MODOC ............ 1873
6. WYANDOTTE ...... 1867
7. SENECA ........... 1832
8. KAW
9. TONKAWA
10. PONCA
11. OTOE-MISSOURI
12. PAWNEE
13. IOWA. ........ Opened by run, Sept. 22, 1891
14. KICKAPOO. Opened by run, May 23, 1895
15. SAC & FOX. Opened by run, Sept. 22, 1891
16. POTAWATOMIE-
      SHAWNEE. Opened by run, Sept. 22, 1891

and Pawnees were opened to settlement at the same time. The land available for white settlement totaled 6,361,000 acres after Indians had received their allotments and four sections in each township had been reserved for public purposes. Thus, there were approximately 40,000 claims for 100,000 prospective settlers.[43] Even with a large balance of homeseekers there were still unclaimed quarter sections after the run in western townships where rainfall was light and markets were distant. Again the land least in demand filled up slowly, with ranching gradually giving way to cultivation of the soil, and with many homesteaders solving their personal economic problems by a combination of livestock and grain production. Reservation of two sections in every township for support of elementary education was a well-established custom in the occupation of public lands. Two additional sections were reserved in the Cherokee Outlet, one for higher education and one for public buildings. Thus, sections thirteen and thirty-three, as well as sixteen and thirty-six were reserved for future use of the people; and since Indians had sometimes built their homes on these reserved areas, they were permitted to select them as their allotments. In such cases, "indemnity lands" for public purposes took the place of farms so allotted.[44]

The Kickapoo opening was for a tract of land about 200,000 acres in extent, before reservations for special purposes. But a large part of the land was thus reserved.[45] Allotments of the Kickapoo Indians required 22,640 acres, and a large acreage in addition was set aside for school lands to take the place of reservations in the Osage and Kaw tribal holdings for that purpose, since allotments were not to be made to those tribes immediately.

Greer County, extending west from North Fork of Red River to the 100th meridian, was awarded to Indian Territory by the United States Supreme Court in a suit which ended on March 16, 1896.[46] Texas had claimed the region, contending that North Fork of Red River was the boundary stream indicated in the Adams-Onís Treaty of 1819. Between eight thousand and nine thousand settlers

[43] Gittinger, *Formation of the State of Oklahoma*, 203, 207, 208.
[44] Dale and Rader, *Readings in Oklahoma History*, 507–26.
[45] *Ibid.*, 531–34. Each Kickapoo received an allotment of eighty acres.
[46] *United States* v. *Texas*, 162 U. S. 1.

had taken land in the area under Texas law, and Greer County, Texas, had been organized in 1886 with Mangum as the county seat. President Grover Cleveland proclaimed the disputed area a part of Indian Territory on December 30, 1887, and the Post Office Department listed Mangum as a station in the Indian Territory. The suit over this fertile region of 2,300 square miles began in the Supreme Court in 1890 and continued for six years. On the day of the court's decision, President Cleveland issued a proclamation warning settlers against occupying land in the area, until such time as the status of all claimants might be determined. The Choctaw Nation claimed the land, settlers who had occupied land in good faith under the jurisdiction of Texas had claim to their homes, and the United States had a claim on the whole area as a part of the public domain.[47] Eventually, Congress left to the Court of Claims the task of determining the amount of compensation due the Choctaws for their interest in Greer County.[48] An act of Congress on January 18, 1897, permitted old settlers to file upon 160 acres of land already occupied and to purchase an additional quarter section at one dollar per acre. Congress declared the region a county in the Territory of Oklahoma and made provision for opening the unoccupied land to settlement. Some four thousand old settlers in Greer County had preference rights on approximately half of the unoccupied land, leaving over four thousand homesteads to be settled.[49]

Two important territorial schools were established by acts of the legislature just before the end of Governor Renfrow's term of office. One was the Northwestern Normal School at Alva, the other was the Agricultural and Normal University for Negroes at Langston. Classes began in the Congregational Church at Alva in September, 1897, and moved to the first building on the forty-acre campus in 1899. By the end of territorial days the enrollment at Northwestern was over eight hundred. The school at Langston, beginning with an enrollment of forty, also grew steadily.

Cassius M. Barnes became the fourth governor of Oklahoma in 1897. He was born in New York in 1845, enlisted in the Union

[47] Dale and Rader, *Readings in Oklahoma History,* 536, 537.
[48] Gittinger, *Formation of the State of Oklahoma,* 198, 203, 204.
[49] *Statutes at Large of the United States,* XXIX, 113.

Army before the end of the Civil War, and came west to Michigan. In 1889 he was appointed first receiver for the United States land office at Guthrie. As a resident of that town in the new territory, he was elected to the house of representatives in 1894 and was chosen speaker in 1895. President McKinley named him to succeed William C. Renfrow, and he was inaugurated as governor on May 24, 1897. Barnes was an effective administrator, a good public speaker much in demand throughout the territory, and he had a wide acquaintance with the people through his work in the land office together with his private business interests. He held office until 1901 and afterward took an active interest in local affairs, serving two terms as mayor of Guthrie.

Two schools were established by acts of the territorial legislature in 1901. The University Preparatory School was located at Tonkawa and the Southwestern Normal School was finally placed at Weatherford. Instruction began at the new normal school in space provided by a church together with four small buildings in the business district. The first college building on the Weatherford campus was completed and ready for use in the spring of 1904.

The territorial clerk during the administration of Governor Barnes was William M. Jenkins. At the beginning of McKinley's second term as president in March, 1901, Jenkins was elevated to the post of governor. He served only until November 30, however. McKinley was killed by an anarchist in September, and Theodore Roosevelt became president. Governor Jenkins was under political fire in regard to care of the insane in the privately operated hospital at Norman. After the President had ordered a brief investigation which probably did not go to the bottom of charges against Jenkins, he was replaced by Thompson B. Ferguson of Watonga.

One important opening was made during the short term of Governor Jenkins when, in July, 1901, a new method of settling the Kiowa-Comanche lands was tried. Indians of the Wichita-Caddo Reservation had come to an agreement with the Jerome Commission in 1895, by which they were to receive allotments of land in severalty; and on June 6, 1900, a similar understanding was reached with the Kiowas and Comanches.[50] An allotment of 160 acres was made for each Indian, with the provision that they should

[50] Dale and Rader, *Readings in Oklahoma History*, 537–45.

not select land on sections sixteen or thirty-six in any township unless they had previously made improvements upon such property. Sections sixteen and thirty-six were to be withdrawn from entry and reserved for the support of common schools. Sections thirteen and thirty-three in each township were similarly reserved for the benefit of higher education and construction of public buildings. Another reservation was made for the use of surplus Indian livestock. This grazing land was 480,000 acres in extent—750 square miles—and was subject to reservation in one or more tracts to be selected by the secretary of the interior.[51] The United States agreed to pay the Kiowa, Comanche, and Apache Indians the sum of $2,000,000, of which $500,000 was to be delivered in cash for per capita distribution and $1,500,000 deposited in the treasury for the Indians at 5 per cent interest.

After all withdrawals from entry had been made, there remained in this vast expanse of land some 2,080,000 acres for homesteads. This land was divided into two equal districts and instead of a race for claims a lottery was held to determine the winners of homesteads. Nearly 170,000 persons registered at the land offices, one of which was established at El Reno and one at Fort Sill. The name of each person who registered was placed in an envelope and these unmarked containers were thoroughly mixed in two large boxes, each rotating on an axis and set up in a public place so that the drawing could be witnessed by all. Persons whose names were drawn from the boxes had the right to choose a claim in the district of their registration. The order of choice was the order in which the names came from the boxes, and the 6,500 names first drawn from each box were the winners of claims. Registration was open from July 9 to July 28, 1901, drawing of names from July 29 to August 5, and the actual settlement of claims began on August 6. The winner of a claim located the land of his choice, filed on his claim at the land office, and was ready to begin his term of residence for five years.

Three new counties were added to Oklahoma Territory from lands thus opened to settlement by lottery: Kiowa, Caddo, and Comanche, with county seats at Hobart, Anadarko, and Lawton. Town lots were sold at auction, and funds thus provided were used

[51] *Ibid.*, 541.

304

in each county for public purposes. At the town of Apache, lots were obtained by a run, similar to the previous town-lot races at Tecumseh and Chandler in the opening of 1891. Allotments in severalty were made to Ponca, Otoe, and Missouri Indians in 1904, and to Osages and Kaws in 1906. Also in 1906 allotments were made for Kiowa, Comanche, Wichita, and Caddo children born after 1901. In the Osage and Kaw reservations, subsurface rights were retained by the tribes—a provision which made the Osages, as a people, quite wealthy. No land was opened to white settlement in the Ponca, Otoe, Missouri, Kaw, and Osage reservations; all the land was allotted to the Indians. The share of each member of the Osage tribe was over five hundred acres.

The sixth governor of Oklahoma Territory, Thompson B. Ferguson, was born in Iowa, received his schooling in the state of Kansas, and came to Oklahoma at the time of the Cheyenne and Arapaho opening in 1892. At Watonga he established a weekly newspaper, and in 1897 was appointed postmaster by President William McKinley. He served as governor of Oklahoma under President Theodore Roosevelt from November 30, 1901, to January 6, 1906.

The seventh of the territorial governors was Frank Frantz, also appointed by Theodore Roosevelt. He was an Illinois man who settled at Enid in the Cherokee Outlet in 1893 and served with Lieutenant Colonel Roosevelt's Roughriders during the Spanish-American War. He was postmaster at Enid in 1901 and Indian agent at Pawhuska in 1903. His term as governor was brief, lasting only from January 6, 1906 until Oklahoma became a state on November 16, 1907. The important last steps in transition to statehood were taken during his term of office. Governor Frantz was an able and popular executive, the candidate of his party for first governor of the new state. But his party was in minority at the time of the election.

The society of Oklahoma Territory was characterized by simplicity, hard work, rapid changes in population, the building of towns, the development of farms, and the establishment of new industries. The people reared families, earned their livings, started schools, showed a normal interest in cultural progress, and were extremely optimistic as to the future of their section of the country.

They were inclined to speak in glowing terms of their accomplishments, too. Some of their statements in regard to Oklahoma, uttered with sober deliberation, when set down in print and viewed with the advantage of perspective, seem almost ridiculous. Most of the estimates of Oklahoma's progress, even official reports, were overflowing with confidence. Governor Seay's report to the secretary of the interior in 1892, which ended by predicting early statehood for Oklahoma, contained these lines: "The people of Oklahoma have heroically gone to work and established and are now maintaining schools in nearly every district that would be a credit to some of the old states." A few pages later he wrote: "The social and industrial progress of our people is apparent, even to the casual observer. The marks and monuments of industry meet the traveler on every hand, in town and country, and the attainments already realized are the surprise of strangers within our gates."

Five years later Governor Barnes was equally enthusiastic in his report on education. "Oklahoma may well be proud of her schools," he wrote. In a later official message he reached a climax of optimism and professional enthusiasm. "No one need have any fears in coming to Oklahoma that excellent educational advantages for his children cannot be secured, either in the country or in the cities and villages," he wrote in 1899. A year later, he had convinced himself that the goal had been reached and he wrote this astonishing statement: "The public schools of Oklahoma are the equal of those of any state in the Union. The people who settled the Territory came from sections where they had enjoyed every educational advantage, and almost their first thought, when settled in their new home was of schools for their children."[52]

By contract with Kansas, convicts were sent from Oklahoma Territory to the penitentiary of that state. Governor Barnes reported in 1897, with obvious and justifiable pride, that no mob violence had appeared in Oklahoma and that crimes against persons and property were decreasing. On June 30, 1896, there were 128 criminals from Oklahoma Territory in the custody of Kansas authorities. During the following twelve months, 61 were released and 81 committed. In view of the rapid growth of population, this record was in truth evidence of the lawful tendency of people who

[52] *Report of the Governor of Oklahoma,* 1892, p. 6, 11; 1897, p. 10; 1899, p. 9; 1900, p. 9.

tilled the soil, cared for livestock, and performed tasks necessary to the growth of towns and transportation of goods. Under its contract with Kansas, the Territory of Oklahoma paid during that year $3,599.35 for travel expenses of its convicts and $12,905 for their care in the penitentiary.

Population of the territory grew with each addition of Indian land and grew between runs by a steady flow of immigration and by natural increase of frontier families. From 61,000 in 1890 the number of residents increased to 400,000 in 1900 and to 722,441 in 1907, as shown by the special census at the time of statehood. The Indian Territory contained 197,000 in 1890 and had grown to 390,000 in 1900. At the time of statehood Indian Territory contained 691,736 population, and the combined residents of the Twin Territories was 1,414,177. Between 1900 and 1910, population of the Twin Territories more than doubled, moving up from 790,000 to 1,657,155.[53]

For Indians of the Five Civilized Tribes and those of western reservations, the territorial period meant difficult adjustments and sometimes disaster. For example, the great opening by lottery of Kiowa-Comanche and Wichita-Caddo lands in 1901, brought vice, fraud, and liquor to the Indians of the area on a scale entirely new to them. There was also an opportunity in the changed conditions for better life among the Indians. Schools multiplied, business contacts with white men increased, new markets for farm produce and livestock appeared, and the Indian citizen could try his talents in competition with white men. However, in the change from reservation life to allotments in severalty and from tribal citizenship to United States citizenship, there were many failures. In 1900, arrest of Indians for drunkenness at Anadarko was rare, in 1902 such arrests were common. At Hobart, Lawton, and other towns in the area the same period witnessed the same change in the conduct of native population; and this, in turn, was simply a repetition of the Indian's experience with European races since the beginning of white settlement in North America. Acquaintance with the white man's civilization did not prove an unmixed blessing for natives of the Plains and eastern woodlands.

[53] U. S. Census Bureau, *Thirteenth Census: Population;* Gittinger, *Formation of the State of Oklahoma,* 256, n. 43.

# CHAPTER THIRTEEN

# Statehood: Transition and Organization

## THE STATEHOOD MOVEMENT

Probably some Indian leaders of reconstruction days had in mind the creation of a state for their people as a member of the Federal Union. Excepting only location of sovereign power, the intertribal council provided by the treaties of 1866 with the Five Civilized Tribes was not essentially different from the supreme council that the Indians themselves developed in the Asbury Mission Conference of 1859 and the later joint meetings at Chahta Tamaha, Tishomingo, and Camp Napoleon. At Okmulgee in 1870 the general council of the Indian Territory met for the purpose of drafting a framework of government. The resulting "Okmulgee Constitution" was far different from the plan for a territorial government presented by Commissioner Dennis N. Cooley in 1866. Authority to make all important decisions under the Okmulgee Constitution rested with the Indians and not with the government at Washington.[1] Commissioner Cooley, on the contrary, thought in terms of a powerful governor appointed by the president, as chief executive officer of the proposed Indian Territory.

By 1900 the combined population of Oklahoma Territory and Indian Territory was more than three quarters of a million, which was larger than that of the most populous American state at the time of the first national census in 1790. The combined population of the Twin Territories was more than eight times the number of persons living in California in the year of its admission to statehood, and more than eighteen times the population of Nevada in 1900.

---

[1] Gittinger, *Formation of the State of Oklahoma*, 102 (from "Report of the Commissioner of Indian Affairs, 1870," 41 Cong., 3 sess., *House Exec. Docs.*, IV. For subsequent meetings of the Council, see *Lippincott's*, Vol. XXIV (September, 1879), 371.

Sixteen of the nation's forty-five states at the beginning of the new century were smaller in population than the Twin Territories, and twenty were less populous seven years later when Oklahoma actually attained statehood.

Party politics in Washington has often been concerned with the admission of new states. In 1864, Nevada was admitted with a population less than 40,000 to bolster the drive for ratification of the Civil War amendments to the Constitution. Nebraska was admitted in 1867 with fewer than 100,000 population in time to ratify the Fourteenth and Fifteenth Amendments. Admission of Washington, Idaho, Montana, Wyoming, North Dakota, and South Dakota, all in the first two years of Benjamin Harrison's administration (1889–93), was perhaps not altogether independent of the McKinley Tariff and the Sherman Silver Purchase Act of 1890. The six states had a combined population of about 1,200,000—approximately 300,000 fewer than the population of Oklahoma in 1907.

It is barely possible that Republican obstruction by Congress and by one or more chief executives delayed the admission of a state that was to be mainly Democratic during the first two decades of its statehood. Yet, Oklahoma did not become a one-party state, and some features of its territorial government showed a trend toward the Republican party. Of the four delegates sent to Congress by the people of Oklahoma Territory, three were Republican and only one, James Y. Callahan, was connected with the Democratic party. Perhaps the voters of Oklahoma regarded Republican delegates the best ministers to a Congress that had Republican majorities in both houses during a large part of the territorial period, 1890–1907.

Sharp disagreement of Oklahomans over the question of single or double statehood was a factor in the delay. The issue was not partisan in Oklahoma nor perhaps in the country at large except for a tendency toward opposition in the North and East, Republican strongholds, to the entry of additional states in the Southwest.[2]

The third territorial governor, William C. Renfrow, who was appointed by President Cleveland and held office from 1893 to 1897, was one of the early advocates of a single state.[3] A strong

[2] Gittinger, *Formation of the State of Oklahoma*, 238.
[3] *Ibid.*

group in Oklahoma Territory opposed Renfrow's plan, however, because it involved waiting for the newly appointed Dawes Commission to work out a revised status for Indians of the Five Civilized Tribes. At the same time a clear majority in the eastern half of the Twin Territories desired separate statehood. Nearly all Indian leaders were in favor of separate statehood. Apparently there was some fear on the east side that the people of Oklahoma Territory, with their brief experience in territorial government, would dominate a single state composed of both sections.

Creation of the Dawes Commission was authorized by an act of Congress on March 3, 1893. The law provided that three commissioners should be appointed by the president to negotiate with the Five Civilized Tribes for surrender of their tribal land titles in exchange for allotments in severalty. It was the duty of the commissioners to prepare the Indians for citizenship and their territory for statehood. In effect, the Indians were to exchange their tribal citizenship for United States citizenship.

Henry L. Dawes of Massachusetts, appointed by President Grover Cleveland to serve as chairman of the commission, had been in Congress thirty-six years, half in the House of Representatives and half in the Senate. He was seventy-seven years old, and he had refused to consider a fourth term in the Senate because of his growing tendency toward deafness; but his work was still vigorous, and it was backed by long acquaintance with Indian affairs and a sincere desire to deal fairly with native tribes.[4]

As chairman of the Senate Committee on Indian Affairs in 1887, Dawes had piloted a bill through Congress which provided for allotments in severalty to all of the civilized Indians excepting the Cherokee, Choctaw, Chickasaw, Creek, Seminole, Sac and Fox, Peoria, Miami, and Osage tribes.[5] By a supplementary act in 1889 the Peorias and Miamis were given lands in severalty; and within a period of five years all the small bands northeast of the Cherokees had received their allotments. By his ability, experience, and interest in Indian progress, Dawes was the man best fitted for the

[4] No adequate book-length biography of Henry L. Dawes has been written. The article by Claude M. Fuess in the *Dictionary of American Biography*, V, is an excellent sketch of his career.

[5] Gittinger, *Formation of the State of Oklahoma*, 169.

task assigned him by President Cleveland in 1893. Meredith Kidd of Indiana and Archibald S. McKennon of Arkansas were members of the commission with Senator Dawes when the first meeting was held at Washington in December, 1893.

News that a commission had been appointed to allot Indian lands served as a stimulant for intruders into the Indian Territory. By 1894 there were 250,000 noncitizens and a year later the Indians were outnumbered four to one in a total population of 350,000.[6] The intruders had no authority in the local governments, no schools for their children, and no legal claim upon the property they were helping to develop in growing towns. In general the towns maintained a fair degree of order, but in rural sections crimes of violence were not rare.

Tribal title to land had degenerated into a monopoly of use on the part of a few members of the tribes. Some large landholders were Indians of mixed blood and some were intermarried citizens. It was reported officially that one hundred Cherokees held about half of the tribal lands, including the best soil in the nation, and that sixty-one Creeks held 1,000,000 acres—one third of all the Creek lands. In addition to vast inequalities of tribal land occupation, the commissioners found much evidence of corrupt government. The report of 1895 stated that extinction of tribal governments would be justifiable on the ground of official corruption alone.[7] The charge has its humorous side when one considers that these officials lived in Washington and held governmental posts in the same generation with Schuyler Colfax, William W. Belknap, Stephen W. Dorsey, and Don Cameron.

The Indian tribal councils in 1894 and 1895 took a firm stand against negotiating with the Dawes Commission for allotments in severalty. Congress thereupon enlarged the powers of the commission by authorizing the making of tribal rolls as a step toward allotments. On June 28, 1898 all tribal courts were abolished by act of Congress, and United States courts were given complete jurisdiction over the Indians. The Dawes Commission was authorized to make individual allotments on the basis of tribal rolls.

[6] *Ibid.*, 226.

[7] 54 Cong., 1 sess., *House Docs.*, XV (3382), 159, 162 (report of the commission to the Five Civilized Tribes for 1895).

Provision was made for incorporation of towns in Indian Territory, and citizens of the United States as well as Indian citizens were made eligible to vote in the town elections. Three judicial districts were created for Indian Territory in 1895, and a fourth was added in 1902.[8] It was made a misdemeanor for any citizen of an Indian tribe to enclose more land than his approximate share under individual allotment.[9] Tribal citizens and others were forbidden to collect royalties for oil, coal, asphalt, or other minerals. No citizen was allowed to collect royalties or rentals on timber except on his own allotment or on such land as he already held as rental property, not to exceed a "just and reasonable share of the lands of his nation, . . . until allotment has been made to him."[10]

By specific provision of the Curtis Act, the oil, coal, asphalt, and other mineral lands in the Indian Territory were reserved for use of the respective tribes, and the secretary of the interior was made responsible for regulation of all mineral leases.[11] On March 3, 1901, Congress passed an act providing that rolls made by the Dawes Commission should be closed on a date agreed upon by the respective tribes or, in the event of failure to reach an agreement, on a date set by the secretary of the interior.[12] The same law provided that all acts passed by the Cherokee and Creek tribal councils, to be valid, must be approved by the president of the United States. Another act of the same date declared all Indians to whom allotments had been made, citizens of the United States.[13] By that time the new Indian citizens were but a small minority in the land that had been turned over to the tribes in solemn treaties, to remain in their possession forever. In 1901 the population of the Twin Territories was about one million.

While the Dawes Commission was doing its work, under the chairmanship of Tams Bixby after the death of Henry L. Dawes early in 1903, the agitation for statehood in Oklahoma continued. Two single statehood conventions held in 1900 and 1902 were

---

8 Gittinger, *Formation of the State of Oklahoma*, 230–32.

9 Clarence L. Thomas, ed., *Annotated Acts of Congress, Five Civilized Tribes and the Osage Nation*, Curtis Act, Sec. 17, p. 62.

10 *Ibid.*, Curtis Act, Sec. 16, p. 61.

11 *Ibid.*, Curtis Act, Sec. 13, p. 54.

12 *Ibid.*, 299.

13 *Ibid.*, 26, 27.

typical events of the statehood movement. The former convened at McAlester and sent a resolution to Congress asking for admission of Oklahoma as a single state. The latter met at Oklahoma City in January, 1902, and took similar action. At Eufaula in November, 1902, a convention of Indian leaders passed a resolution against union with Oklahoma Territory. These were but a few of the numerous conventions that were held during the period of territorial government in Oklahoma. In January, 1904, Judge Thomas H. Doyle of Perry, Oklahoma Territory, headed a committee in Washington that worked diligently to convince leaders of Congress that single statehood was desirable for the Twin Territories.[14] With Judge Doyle in the national capital were C. G. Jones, J. H. Maxey, Jr., Roy E. Stafford, G. A. Henshaw, Clarence B. Douglas, and A. Grant Evans. Opposed to this committee were Sidney Clarke, formerly a member of Congress from Kansas and more recently a prominent figure in the politics of Oklahoma City; J. W. McNeal, who was to become Republican candidate for governor of Oklahoma in the second state election; and Bird S. McGuire, territorial delegate to Congress.

In 1905 the Indian Territory's bid for separate statehood took the form of a constitutional convention. Principal chiefs of the Cherokee, Choctaw, Seminole, and Creek tribes sent out a call for election of delegates to a convention that would assemble in Muskogee. The Chickasaw tribe agreed to take part in the convention, and white citizens of Indian Territory were invited to participate. The delegates, 182 in number, met at the designated place on August 21 and proceeded to the organization of a constituent assembly. The Indians demonstrated their grasp of political methods by taking the lead in organization of the body and playing a dominant part in the work of writing a constitution.

Pleasant Porter, principal chief of the Creek tribe, was elected president. Five vice-presidents were chosen, one from each of the Five Civilized Tribes: William H. Murray, an intermarried Chickasaw; Charles N. Haskell, representing the Creeks; Chief W. C. Rogers of the Cherokees; Green McCurtain of the Choctaws; and John Brown of the Seminoles.

[14] Thoburn and Wright, *Oklahoma*, II, 653n.; Charles Evans, "Judge Thomas H. Doyle," *Chronicles of Oklahoma*, Vol. XXVII, No. 2 (Summer, 1949), 138ff.

313

On August 23 a committee was chosen to draft the constitution. William Wirt Hastings, a prominent Cherokee who was later to represent Oklahoma in the national House of Representatives for nine full terms, was made chairman of the drafting committee of fifty members. By September 8, 1905, the Sequoyah Constitution was ready for consideration by the voters and in an election on November 7 the people of Indian Territory accepted it by a majority of 56,279 to 9,073. In Congress, however, a bill in the House of Representatives on December 4th, 1905, to admit the State of Sequoyah was tabled, and in the Senate a later bill for the same purpose, introduced by Porter McCumber of North Dakota, met the same fate.[15] There the matter rested while the fight for single statehood was fought and won.

## THE OKLAHOMA CONSTITUTIONAL CONVENTION

On June 16, 1906, President Theodore Roosevelt signed the Enabling Act, by which Congress provided for joining the Twin Territories into a single state. Congress also made provision for admission of Arizona and New Mexico as one state, but only on condition that the voters of each territory should agree to joint statehood. A majority of the people in Arizona and New Mexico cast their ballots against single statehood, with the result that the two were admitted separately in 1912.

It was provided in the Enabling Act that a constitutional convention of one hundred and twelve delegates should be formed. Fifty-five delegates were to be elected in Oklahoma Territory, fifty-five in the Indian Territory, and two in the Osage Reservation, where allotments in severalty were still in process of being made and where no county government had as yet been established.[16]

Single-member districts were to be the rule in all elections except those of the Osage Reservation, where both were to be elected at-large. In Oklahoma Territory the governor, secretary, and chief justice had the joint responsibility of defining the dis-

[15] Gittinger, *Formation of the State of Oklahoma*, 252, 253, n. 38.
[16] *Ibid.*, 254–56.

tricts. In the Indian Territory the function was performed by a committee made up of the Indian commissioner and two federal judges designated by the President.[17] It was provided in the law that "all male persons over the age of twenty-one years who are citizens of the United States or who are members of any Indian nation or tribe in said Indian Territory and Oklahoma, and who have resided within the limits of said proposed state for at least six months next preceding the election," should be eligible to vote for members of the constitutional convention. All persons who were qualified to vote were also eligible to serve as delegates. Guthrie, the capital of Oklahoma Territory, was to remain temporary capital of the state until 1913, but in the intervening years the legislature was not to appropriate "public moneys of the state" for building a state capitol.[18] The power of Congress to bind a state by terms of the Enabling Act was challenged later in Oklahoma, and the issue was decided in the United States Supreme Court.[19]

The Oklahoma convention was required, by terms of the Enabling Act, to provide for the state a republican form of government, to establish religious liberty, to prohibit polygamous marriages, to exclude intoxicants from the Osage Reservation and Indian Territory for twenty-one years, and to assume for the state all debts of Oklahoma Territory. The convention was bound, further, to establish a system of public schools, to accept the provisions of the Fifteenth Amendment to the Constitution of the United States, and to submit the completed constitution to a vote of the people of Oklahoma.[20]

The new state was to send five members to the lower house of the United States Congress until the next regular apportionment act, as provided in the federal constitution. The sum of $5,000,000 was appropriated for Oklahoma schools in lieu of sections sixteen and thirty-six in the townships of Indian Territory, where there was no public land to reserve for public education.

On November 6, 1906, elections were held for delegates to the constitutional convention. Twelve of the men elected were

---

[17] *Statutes at Large of the United States*, XXXIV, 267.
[18] *Ibid.*, 268, 269.
[19] 57 Cong., 1 sess., *Cong. Rec.*, 5197; *Coyle* v. *Smith*, 221 U. S. 559.
[20] *Statutes at Large of the United States*, XXXIV, 269 ff.

registered as Republicans, one was an Independent, and ninety-nine were Democrats. Attorneys, merchants, real-estate dealers, farmers, cattlemen, bankers, and other occupational classes were represented in the convention. Some of the members were well-informed, and a few were men of outstanding ability. William H. Murray of Tishomingo was elected president; Peter Hanraty of McAlester, vice-president; and Charles N. Haskell of Muskogee, majority floor leader. Vice-president Hanraty was interested in the problems of labor, particularly mine labor. Robert L. Williams of Durant was a practicing attorney who had given some attention to government and party politics and who was able to make contacts in the convention which paved the way to his later political success.

Henry S. Johnston of Perry was one of the Oklahoma Territory delegates who used the convention as a stepping stone to later political prominence. James S. Buchanan of Norman was a university professor of history who was active in civic affairs but not in party politics. Haskell, Williams, Murray, and Johnston were all to be elected, within the first three decades of statehood, to the office of governor. Williams and Murray were to hold other offices of great importance and to exercise long and continuous influence in Oklahoma politics.

The Oklahoma basic law provided the traditional two-house legislature, with senators holding office for terms of four years, representatives for two years. The governor and other executives were four-year elective officers, including the secretary of state, attorney general, treasurer, auditor, commissioner of charities and correction, commissioner of labor, mine inspector, and lieutenant governor. The justices of the supreme court were also elected officers, serving terms of six years. At the beginning there were five justices of the supreme court but the number was later raised to nine.

There were many sharp differences of opinion concerning the constitution of Oklahoma. President Theodore Roosevelt was frankly critical while the convention was still in session; and in spite of some effort made by the lawmakers to meet his objections, he worked against ratification when the question was before the voters. The lengthy basic law, roughly ten times as long as the original Constitution of the United States, contained much material that might well have been left to the determination of later legislatures of Oklahoma. A great deal of space was required for definition of county boundaries, which seemed to be a necessity of the moment. Without doubt, the convention yielded to the temptation to bind future lawmakers to the peculiar views of the constituent assembly on questions such as corporate ownership of land, control of school lands, insurance, definition of "colored race" as all persons of African descent, and public revenue. Lack of confidence in future generations to make their own laws is perhaps a common weakness of constitutional conventions, but it is not consistent with a progressive concept of representative democracy.

Features of popular government that were being urged by liberals of all states in this period, such as the initiative and referendum, were put into the Oklahoma constitution. Eight per cent of the voters might initiate legislation by petition, 15 per cent might initiate constitutional amendment, and 5 per cent might obtain a referendum on an act of the legislature.

In the election of September 17, 1907, the people accepted the work of their convention by a vote of 180,333 for ratification to 73,059 opposed.[21] In the same election Charles N. Haskell was elected governor over his Republican opponent, Territorial Governor Frank Frantz, and four of the five members elected to Congress were Democrats. Both houses of the legislature were Democratic by substantial majorities, as were most other officers of the new state and county governments.[22]

The question of prohibition of intoxicants for the entire state, as well as for the Osage Reservation and Indian Territory to meet requirements of the Enabling Act, carried by a vote of 130,361 to 112,258. On November 16, 1907, President Theodore Roosevelt proclaimed Oklahoma the forty-sixth state, "on equal footing with the original states."[23]

[21] Gittinger, *Formation of the State of Oklahoma*, 257, n. 45.

[22] The Republican representative was the former territorial delegate, Bird S. McGuire, of Pawnee. The Democratic members were Elmer L. Fulton of Oklahoma City; James S. Davenport of Vinita; Charles D. Carter of Ardmore; and Scott Ferris of Lawton.

[23] *Statutes at Large of the United States*, XXXV, 2160.

## PARTY POLITICS IN THE NEW STATE

Oklahoma Territory contained a large per cent of farmers and laborers among its people who were poor—landless men who staked a claim and tried to hold it, with little capital for improvements, livestock, or implements. Agricultural discontent was sure to flourish in such a population. Radical views took root easily on the Southwestern Plains, in the wake of droughts and low prices on farm products. Agrarian radicalism took organized form in the Southern Alliance of Texas and the Northern Alliance, in which wheat farmers from Kansas to Minnesota were interested. The Populist party had many Oklahoma members in 1892 when James B. Weaver won the popular vote of Kansas, Colorado, Nevada, and Idaho, polling over a million votes for president in a national total less than twelve million.

Free silver had a strong appeal four years later when William Jennings Bryan ran against William McKinley and carried every state on the borders of Oklahoma Territory, for Populist doctrines.[24] In 1908 when the new state of Oklahoma cast its first vote for president, it gave its electoral support to Bryan over William Howard Taft. In 1910 the Socialist candidate for governor, J. T. Cumbie, held a balance with 24,707 votes between the Democratic winner, Lee Cruce, and the Republican loser, Joseph W. McNeal. In more than one instance before and after statehood, the major party candidate who had a strong appeal for the "element of discontent," had a good start toward victory.

Results of Oklahoma's first election of state officers in September, 1906, have been noted above. In the first legislature only 5 of 44 senators were Republicans and in the lower house 16 of 109 were Republicans. When the legislature met in December, 1907, it ratified the popular choices for the United States Senate, Robert L. Owen of Muskogee and Thomas P. Gore of Lawton. Actually Henry Furman was second in the voting, but withdrew to carry out an agreement among political leaders that one senator should be selected from each of the Twin Territories. As first judges of the

[24] Alley, *City Beginnings*, 102, 103.

criminal court of appeals, the highest tribunal in criminal cases, Governor Haskell appointed Henry Furman, Thomas H. Doyle, and H. G. Baker.

Governor Haskell's four years in office were occupied in organization of the new machinery of state government and adjustment to new conditions of taxation. Public buildings were needed, highways and bridges demanded attention, and the educational system was seriously handicapped by lack of funds. Every addition of land to Oklahoma Territory by run or lottery drawing had brought in many hundreds of families and literally thousands of school-age children without proportional increase in revenues to support the added educational burden.

The First Legislature, carrying out a project favored by the Governor, passed the bank-guaranty law. This act provided a fund to which each state bank contributed 1 per cent of its average daily balance for protection of depositors against losses from bank failures. The Third Legislature amended this law by increasing the deposit required of each bank; but in 1923 the Ninth Legislature felt obliged to repeal the act because the guaranty fund was exhausted.

Schools of higher learning had been in operation on the west side of Oklahoma since the early days of territorial government. The University of Oklahoma at Norman, the Agricultural and Mechanical College at Stillwater, and Central Normal School at Edmond were all holding classes by the autumn of 1892. Five years later Northwestern Normal School at Alva began its work of instruction, and in an act of March 8, 1901, the legislature made provision for a third normal school to be located in the old Cheyenne and Arapaho Reservation. The site finally chosen for Southwestern Normal School was Weatherford, in Custer County.

The University Preparatory School at Tonkawa was a territorial institution that added college courses to its original program after Oklahoma became a state, and in 1941 took the name Northern Oklahoma Junior College. Also established before statehood was the Agricultural and Normal University for Negroes at Langston in 1897. The legislature required, as a condition for the location of territorial colleges, that land and a specified sum of money be contributed by the local community.

319

Among the church schools founded in Oklahoma Territory was Kingfisher College in 1894, which was later absorbed by the University of Oklahoma. For the thirty-three years of its existence this little college maintained high standards of instruction and fought a losing battle against financial disaster. Its college farm and a variety of related industries offered students an opportunity to earn their expenses while they were in residence at Kingfisher. The faculty contained able men, capable of inspiring scholarly effort on the part of their classes.

Epworth University, founded in 1904, became Oklahoma City University in 1919. Henry Kendall College, which held its first classes at Muskogee in 1894 and moved to Tulsa in 1907, was expanded into Tulsa University thirteen years later. During the year in which Oklahoma was admitted as a state, Phillips University was founded at Enid and Oklahoma Baptist University was established in Shawnee.

Oklahoma was confronted by the problem of unbalanced distribution of state schools, since the eastern half offered very little education beyond high school. Southeastern Normal School at Durant, the first to be established in the region formerly called Indian Territory, began class work in 1909. Provision was made for opening Northeastern Normal School in the building that had housed the Cherokee Female Seminary at Tahlequah, and for establishing East Central Normal School at Ada. The Second Legislature also founded Murray State School of Agriculture at Tishomingo, Cameron State Agricultural College at Lawton, Panhandle Agricultural and Mechanical College at Goodwell, and the Oklahoma School of Mines and Metallurgy at Wilburton.

In the Enabling Act of June 16, 1906, Congress had designated Guthrie as capital of Oklahoma until 1913. The question arose, does Congress have authority to bind a state by terms of its enabling act? Governor Haskell was an advocate of removal, and on June 11, 1910, the people were given an opportunity to indicate a choice among three cities for location of the permanent capital. Perhaps many of the voters thought they were deciding the question of removal in 1913 and not immediate transfer of the capital; but with 96,261 ballots in favor of Oklahoma City, 31,301 for Guthrie, and 8,382 for Shawnee, the Governor took prompt action for removal. Without any preparations for housing the state government, Oklahoma City found itself suddenly called upon to provide space for the chief executive and other officials. W. B. Anthony, secretary to Governor Haskell, brought the great seal of the state from Guthrie to Oklahoma City in an automobile. The state supreme court continued to hold sessions in Guthrie, but found no legal means to compel the governor to return there.[25]

In the Democratic primary election of 1910, Lee Cruce of Ardmore defeated a field of candidates which included William H. Murray and other well-known men, and became the choice of his party for governor. The Republicans chose Joseph W. McNeal; and the race was close, with Cruce the choice of 120,218 voters to 99,527 for McNeal and 24,707 for J. T. Cumbie, the Socialist candidate.

By the time of this state election it had become obvious that Oklahoma was entitled by her population to more than five congressmen, the number alloted by the Enabling Act. When Congress made the new apportionment of seats after the Thirteenth Census, it was announced that Oklahoma would be represented by eight members in the House of Representatives that took office on March 4, 1913. The Republican party had provided strong opposition in every state election since statehood. Although defeated in the two races for governor, the Republicans had increased their membership in both houses of the legislature in 1908 and had carried three of five representative districts in congressional elections.[26] However, the combined pluralities of the three Republican districts was only 6,503 by comparison with 25,155 combined Democratic pluralities in the other two districts.[27] In 1910, James S. Davenport won a seat for the Democrats, displacing Charles E. Creager. There were gains for the Democrats in both houses of the state legislature, with 83 of 109 in the house of representatives and 30 of 44 in the senate.

[25] A decision was reached in the case *Coyle* v. *Smith*, 221 U. S. 559, on May 29, 1911.

[26] In 1908 the Republican members were Bird S. McGuire of Pawnee, Dick T. Morgan of Woodward, and Charles E. Creager of Muskogee. The Democrats elected Charles D. Carter of Ardmore and Scott Ferris of Lawton. See *Congressional Directory*.

[27] *Oklahoma Red Book*, II; *Directory of the State of Oklahoma*, 100.

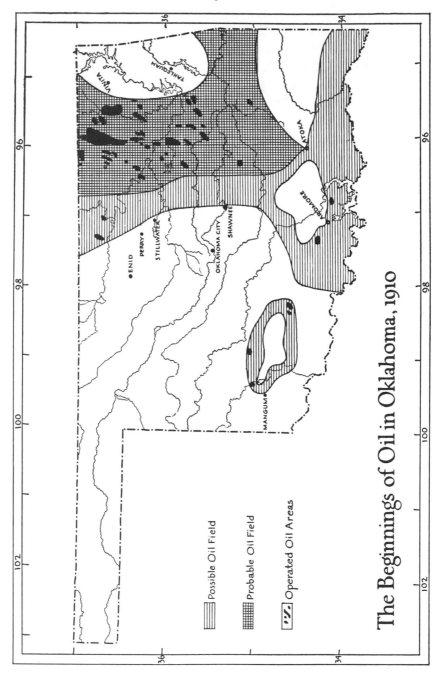

The Beginnings of Oil in Oklahoma, 1910

Possible Oil Field

Probable Oil Field

Operated Oil Areas

Instead of calling a special session of the legislature for the purpose of creating new congressional districts, Governor Cruce directed that voting should be provided for three representatives-at-large. The Democrats elected all of the new representatives: William H. Murray of Tishomingo, Joseph B. Thompson of Pauls Valley, and Claude Weaver of Oklahoma City. Three of the five districts were also carried by the Democrats while the Republicans reelected Bird S. McGuire and Dick Morgan.

In the presidential election Oklahoma voted for Woodrow Wilson. The Republican National Convention in Chicago had nominated William Howard Taft for a second term as president; but the "Bull Moose" wing of the party had bolted and nominated Theodore Roosevelt. The Oklahoma Republican Convention was controlled by Roosevelt supporters, and there was much confusion among voters, with no clear separation of the two factions on election day. Wilson held a clear plurality of 119,156 ballots to a combined vote of 83,429 for Roosevelt and Taft. Eugene V. Debs, Socialist candidate, received a vote of 41,674.[28]

Robert Owen was re-elected to the United States Senate with a plurality of 42,989 over his Republican opponent, J. T. Dickerson. The Socialist candidate, J. G. Wills, with 40,860 votes had nearly enough for a balance between the major-party candidates.[29]

## THE CRUCE AND WILLIAMS ADMINISTRATION

Governor Lee Cruce was forty-eight years of age and had been a resident of Ardmore about twenty years when he took office as governor in January, 1911. A native of Kentucky, he was educated in the common schools of that state and at Vanderbilt University Law School. He was admitted to the bar when he was twenty, and practiced law in Kentucky and in the Indian Territory. He became interested in banking and in 1901 was chosen to serve as cashier of the Ardmore National Bank. Two years later he was elected president of the same organization. His only public office

[28] Thoburn and Wright, *Oklahoma*, II, 650.
[29] *Directory of the State of Oklahoma*, 93.

before he became governor was a term as chairman of the University of Oklahoma Board of Regents from 1907 to 1910.

One of his first moves as governor was toward reorganization of the boards of regents for state colleges.[30] His purpose was to eliminate waste by avoiding duplication of courses and departments for which there was limited demand, and to consolidate control in a state board of education. The Agricultural and Mechanical College, under supervision of the Oklahoma Board of Agriculture by provision of the state constitution, was not included in Governor Cruce's plan of reorganization. The new Board of Education, composed of six members appointed by the governor, worked under the chairmanship of an elected superintendent of public instruction. Members might be removed only by the process of impeachment, and this tenure seemed to be adequate protection against frivolous tampering with state schools on political grounds.[31] In addition to control of state colleges and general supervision of the public schools, this board served as the state textbook commission. The University of Oklahoma showed immediate effects of the reorganized control. President A. Grant Evans, who had succeeded David R. Boyd in 1908, was replaced by Professor Julien C. Monnet, of the School of Law, who became acting president, a position he occupied until the selection of Stratton D. Brooks as president in 1912.[32]

Governor Cruce also gave support to establishment of a six-member supreme court commission for reduction of the state supreme court's burden. Another change, incorporated in a constitutional amendment approved by popular vote, was for reduction of the Board of Agriculture from eleven members to five, with a secretary elected by the voters and the remaining members appointed by the governor.

As highway commissioner Governor Cruce appointed Sidney Suggs, of Ardmore, who had become well known as an enthusiast for better roads in Oklahoma. He was publisher of the *Daily Ardmoreite,* and he used the newspaper as a means of building

[30] Gittinger, *The University of Oklahoma,* 71, 72.

[31] Governor Cruce attempted to remove one of the members, but the Oklahoma Supreme Court held that he could be removed only for cause and by the process of impeachment.

[32] Gittinger, *The University of Oklahoma,* 72–76.

public support for good roads. He also traveled about the state making addresses to many audiences on the subject of his greatest interest, and he became a powerful advocate of President Woodrow Wilson's federal program of grants-in-aid for highway building. With limited funds Suggs and his assistant, Clark Hudson, aided by the technical skill of W. R. Goit, highway engineer, made a good beginning in the adjustment of Oklahoma to the age of motor vehicles. The license fee for automobiles helped to meet new demands for highway support.

The early years of the twentieth century was a period in which expenses of government in all the states were steadily climbing. New services, such as hard-surface roads, required vast expenditures, and there was a general expansion in education, public health provisions, recreation facilities, and many other fields. Because Oklahoma was new and undeveloped, expenses of government were rising even faster than in the older states. A glance at the annual appropriations will show the trend. The first legislature appropriated about $3,900,000; the third, coming into office with a governor whose avowed policy was economy, appropriated twice as much. In 1913 the amount had gone up to $10,500,000 and in 1921 to $20,500,000.

The total influence of Governor Cruce in Oklahoma politics was moderate and progressive. His stand for economy was not an extreme program in which necessary services were slashed, but rather a steady pressure for efficient control of state expenditures. He was a firm friend of permanent values, such as good roads and public buildings, high quality in public service, and high standards in education. In later administrations the state schools at times became pawns in the game of politics, a development which was not a necessary outgrowth of Cruce's reorganization, but the inevitable result of mediocrity in high office. More adroit political managers have held the office of governor in Oklahoma, but few executives in any state have worked with greater zeal for the public interest.

The Democratic primary in 1914 brought a contest between strong candidates, Judge Robert L. Williams of Durant and J. B. A. Robertson of Chandler. Al Jennings, whose principal claim to distinction was the fact that he had just served a federal prison term for banditry, ran third in the primary election. Williams won the nomination with a vote of 35,605 to 33,504 for Robertson and 21,732 for Jennings.[33] In the general election Williams found himself confronted by another able opponent in the person of the Republican candidate, John Fields of Oklahoma City, who edited a farm paper. The Socialists were strong in 1914 and were not inclined to join forces with either of the major parties. In candidate John Fields they saw a man who had strong support among conservative farmers and all classes who were inclined toward Republican views in national politics. Williams they found intolerant of radical opinions, not particularly friendly either toward organized labor or toward the heirs of Populist agrarian discontent. The Socialists chose Fred Holt as their candidate for governor and threw Pat Nagle into the race against Thomas P. Gore, whose first full term in the United States Senate would expire on March 3, 1915.

The election returns gave Williams a count of 100,597; Fields, 95,904; and Holt, 52,703. In the race for the Senate seat, Gore defeated his Republican opponent, John H. Burford, by a vote of 119,442 to 73,292. Patrick Nagle for the Socialists polled 52,229 votes.[34] In the congressional elections the Republicans carried only one district, returning Dick Morgan of Woodward for a third term. The Democrats elected James S. Davenport of Vinita, William Wirt Hastings of Tahlequah, Joseph B. Thompson of Pauls Valley, Charles D. Carter of Ardmore, William H. Murray of Tishomingo, Scott Ferris of Lawton, and James V. McClintic of Snyder. For Carter and Ferris this was the fifth election to the House of Representatives.

Robert L. Williams was born in Alabama in 1868, and had been a resident of Durant for eighteen years when he was elected governor. He had served in the constitutional convention of 1906 and had been a justice of the Oklahoma Supreme Court since 1907. In public office Williams had a reputation for hard work, rigid honesty, and vigorous support for his favorite measures. He was

---

[33] Thoburn and Wright, *Oklahoma*, II, 654; *Directory of the State of Oklahoma*, 88, 89.

[34] For a short biography of Patrick S. Nagle, see Thoburn and Wright, *Oklahoma*, II, 916; the *Directory of the State of Oklahoma*, 87, gives statistics on election returns.

narrow-minded and aggressive, but he was also a man of good intentions and a tenacious champion of clean government.

Oklahoma was still in process of adjustment to the needs of statehood and at the same time was experimenting in current ideas of workmen's compensation, maximum hours of labor, and restrictions on the labor of women and children. Governor Williams worked hard at his job, and his administration adopted some of the reforms advocated by his predecessor, Lee Cruce. Penal regulations were modernized, a widows' pension act was passed, and farm legislation reminiscent of the Populist program became a part of Oklahoma's statutes. Raw agricultural products were exempted from taxation, a state bureau of weights and measures was established, and cotton gins were placed under control of the state corporation commission. A co-operative marketing act was passed, a state market commission was created, and private employment agencies were required to obtain state licenses.

A law was passed designed to protect people against insurance frauds. It provided for a state insurance board in harmony with progressive measures of other states in this period. The taxing system was revised in several important phases, including higher rates on incomes and an increase of the gross production tax on gas and oil.

A tragic accident occurred at Ardmore on September 27, 1915. Shortly after two o'clock in the afternoon, a 250-barrel tank car filled with high-gravity gasoline, standing near the Gulf, Colorado, and Santa Fe Railway station exploded, causing the loss of forty-eight lives. More than five hundred persons were injured, and the property loss was more than $1,000,000. Main Street in Ardmore extends east and west from the Santa Fe tracks. In addition to Union Depot, which was a complete wreck, business buildings along Main Street in both directions from the railroad were knocked down. A Negro poolhall and rooming house east of the tracks was demolished, and plate-glass windows for several blocks both east and west were shattered.

Many rumors were spread about in regard to cause of the explosion. According to one story, a spark from the steel hammer used by an employee of the railroad trying to stop a leak in the tank car ignited the gasoline. The Oklahoma Corporation Commission began an investigation into circumstances surrounding the accident in order to place responsibility for the explosion and to take steps for prevention of similar disasters. It was found that the tank of casing-head gasoline had been shipped to the Ardmore Refinery by the Victor Gasoline Company of Cushing, Oklahoma, for the purpose of blending it with other gasoline.

Russell Brown, city attorney of Ardmore, took steps toward placing the blame upon the Gulf, Colorado, and Santa Fe Railroad Company. He charged that the tank car was standing too near the Union Station and business district of the town, contrary to safety regulations, and that it had not been turned over immediately to the Ardmore Refining Company as that firm had asked.

It was the theory of W. B. Hassett, Ardmore Refining Company's superintendent, that the sun's ray shining upon the tank of high-gravity gasoline through several hours of midday heat, had caused the explosion. The corporation commission, state fire marshall, Ardmore City Council, and officials of the railroad company, all took part in the investigation but failed to determine with certainty the cause of the disaster.[35] President Ripley of the Santa Fe system, without waiting for damage suits to be filed, wired the mayor of Ardmore that his company would assume full responsibility in all claims for death, personal injury, and property loss. A committee of Ardmore citizens was appointed to adjust claims, and the work of determining property, personal injury, and death losses was begun. Nearly two thousand claims were settled by the committee and the adjuster for the railroad company, with total damages set at approximately $1,000,000. Perhaps railroad company officials thought that, in view of the evidence, legal battles were likely to be decided against them and that settlement out of court was the economical way. The financial condition of the Santa Fe System was good. According to President Ripley's report for 1915, net earnings for the year were $37,000,000, which gave the stockholders dividends of about 5.2 per cent. Because of the company's ready assumption of responsibility, the public was inclined to overlook charges of neglect that were made against railroad officials.

Early in the Williams administration the United States

[35] *Daily Oklahoman*, September 28, 29, 30; October 8, 10, 1915, contains an account of the disaster.

Supreme Court passed upon the "grandfather clause" of the Oklahoma constitution, an amendment which resulted from an initiated measure of 1910. The clause provided against the voting of illiterates in Oklahoma, excepting descendants of persons who were eligible to vote before January 1, 1866. The clear intention was to enfranchise illiterate white citizens and to disfranchise illiterate colored citizens. The legislature had gone to unusual lengths in obtaining passage of the measure by providing that all ballots that did not record a vote against the proposed amendment, that is the "silent vote," should be counted in its favor. The Supreme Court held that the initiated constitutional amendment was a violation of the United States Constitution, Amendment Fifteen, which provides that the right to vote shall not be denied to a citizen of the United States on account of race, color, or previous condition of servitude.

Governor Williams called a special session of the legislature to propose a new Oklahoma amendment concerning Negro suffrage. Obviously he expected to phrase the revised clause in such manner as to defeat the purpose of the Fifteenth Amendment, which was to give the Negroes equality of opportunity in the matter of voting, along with white citizens. By a special election in August, 1916, the voters of Oklahoma were given a chance to pass upon the newly devised Negro suffrage clause. The popular vote was 133,140 against the proposed measure to 90,605 in favor of its adoption.[36] Apparently toleration had made more progress at this time among the voters than among the lawmakers.

The State University Hospital at Oklahoma City, formerly housed in temporary quarters, was provided with an appropriation of $300,000 for construction of a first unit in 1917. The new hospital was ready for use in September, 1919.[37] The Sixth Legislature continued the supreme court commission and increased the number of justices in the supreme court from six to nine.

A state capitol commission had been authorized by the Fourth Legislature, which appropriated $1,500,000 for erection of a build-

[36] Thoburn and Wright, *Oklahoma*, II, 657; *Directory of the State of Oklahoma*, 157 (Initiative Petition No. 55). This proposal was that exceptions to the "literary test" should include those who served in the army or navy of the United States against Mexico or on either side in certain Indian wars.

[37] Gittinger, *The University of Oklahoma*, 104.

ing to house the state government. Governor Williams became ex-officio chairman of the commission, which was composed of William B. Anthony of Marlow, Patrick J. Goulding of Enid, and Stephen A. Douglas of Ardmore; and the work of construction, begun in July 1914, continued under its direction. Edward P. Boyd, an architect employed by the United States Treasury Department, had already designed the federal buildings in Muskogee and Oklahoma City; and at the request of the Oklahoma Capitol Commission, President Wilson granted Boyd an indefinite leave of absence in order that he might give his full attention to construction of the capitol.[38] The builders made use of materials found in the state, including Tishomingo granite.

In the national elections of 1916, in which Woodrow Wilson defeated Charles Evans Hughes for the presidency by the narrow electoral majority of 277 to 254, Oklahoma gave a clear vote of confidence to Wilson. The Socialist and other minor party candidates had very light support in Oklahoma, while Wilson received a popular vote of 148,000 to 97,000 for Hughes.[39]

The attention of all state officials during the second half of Governor Williams' administration was centered upon organization of the commonwealth's resources for the great war in Europe which had begun in 1914. The state Council for Defense, under the chairmanship of J. M. Aydelotte, was the principal civilian committee in charge of war work. Each county and school district also organized a local council to co-operate with the state council and the National Council of Defense. Stratton D. Brooks, president of the University of Oklahoma, served as secretary of the state council and also held the office of food administrator for Oklahoma in the highly important work of conserving scarce articles of food for war uses.

A democratic nation conducts a war as it conducts peacetime activities—on the basis of popular approval. A considerable part of the process whereby well-armed and thoroughly trained men are placed on the battle front is the work done by councils and committees, organized information through public addresses, activity of the press, war-loan appeals, Red Cross membership drives, and

[38] Thoburn and Wright, *Oklahoma*, II, 654.
[39] *Ibid.*, 658; *Directory of the State of Oklahoma*, 83, 84.

other civilian effort that is closely related to politics, both in method and objective. Relative freedom from partisanship is a distinguishing feature of war organization, however. Without propaganda, a representative democracy could not maintain the national unity of purpose that is necessary for conducting a war. Mechanized warfare against an autocratic power that is practically relieved of the necessity of obtaining immediate popular approval makes propaganda doubly important.

Robert L. Williams, accustomed to hard, exacting effort in the routine of his earlier public offices, made the greatest contribution of his life in his final years as governor. He directed the work of all major councils, drove himself to the limit in supporting the Oklahoma Speakers' Bureau, Red Cross, Y. M. C. A., Salvation Army, Knights of Columbus, Liberty Loans, and countless related services.

Congress decided upon a process of selective service in building the national Army in 1917. A force composed of National Guard units had been sent to the Mexican border by President Wilson in 1915. The Oklahoma National Guard, as a part of this army, served under Colonel Roy Hoffman in the Mexican expedition and after the trouble on the border subsided was sent to Europe. Colonel Hoffman became a brigadier general in the army of the United States. Volunteer enlistments for military service were accepted also, but the federal government depended principally upon the draft. Registration and recruiting in Oklahoma came under the direction of Major Eugene M. Kerr. Under three draft acts, 435,688 men were registered in the state, and 90,126 served in the armed forces. Of this number more than 1,000 were killed in action, and 6,286 were listed as killed or wounded.

Camp Doniphan, near Fort Sill in Comanche County, became a famous center for training American soldiers in the use of artillery. Many Oklahomans received instruction there, a large number were sent to Camp Bowie, Texas, where the Thirty-sixth Division was in training, and another group was sent to the Ninetieth Division at Camp Travis, Texas. Both divisions took part in major campaigns in Europe.

One political effect of the war was decline of the Socialist party in Oklahoma, along with the rest of the nation. Opposition to the war by extreme pacifists discredited all organizations to which the objectors belonged. The "Green Corn Rebellion" which took the form of antidraft agitation among tenant farmers was clearly related to agrarian discontent that had been so large a factor in radical politics of Oklahoma.

With the coming of peace, two important boundary settlements were made with Texas in 1919. When oil was discovered in northern Texas, that state claimed the southern half of the Red River bed and made leases on it to drilling companies. Oklahoma, relying upon provisions of the Adams-Onís Treaty of 1819, sued in the United States Supreme Court to prevent drilling under the Texas leases.[40] Actually, there were three claimants: Oklahoma, claiming the entire river bed on the basis of the Spanish treaty which specified that Red River should lie within the limits of the United States, that the boundary line should follow the south bank; Texas, which claimed the southern half of the river bed; and the United States, which had an interest in the case through its relations with the Indian tribes of Oklahoma.

The Supreme Court decided that the boundary of Texas was still determined by the Treaty of 1819, and that the line followed the southern bank of Red River. Three commissioners were appointed to run the boundary, subject to approval of the court. Where sudden changes had taken place in the river bank through the action of flood waters in cutting a new channel, the commissioners were ordered to observe the principle: "Such avulsive action does not carry the boundary with it, but leaves it where it was before." On the other hand, where change had resulted from the gradual process of "erosion and accretion, the boundary follows the varying course of the stream." (*Arkansas* v. *Tennessee*, 246 U. S., 158, 173; *Nebraska* v. *Iowa*, 143 U. S., 359, 368).[41] Parties claiming avulsive changes in the channel were required to prove their contention and survey of the river bed, particularly in oil-producing areas, was sharply contested. The Supreme Court sustained the claim of Texas to land cut off from the south bank, after 1902, and changed to an island in the river bed by avulsive action, near the boundary between Hardeman and Wilbarger counties.

[40] *Oklahoma* v. *Texas*, 260 U. S., 606.
[41] *Oklahoma* v. *Texas*, 260 U. S., 636.

In other cases, claims of changes in the channel of Red River were denied by the court, for want of conclusive evidence.[42]

An error in the survey of the Texas Panhandle caused another suit in 1919, which Texas began as a counter claim against Oklahoma's action in the Red River case. The Panhandle boundary was finally settled in 1926 and the corrected line, eighty rods east of the previous boundary, gave Texas possession of about 23,000 acres of land along the western borders of Ellis, Roger Mills, Beckham, and Harmon counties.

The Williams administration is difficult to appraise in terms of Oklahoma's development, because of concentration by state officials upon the war program. Governor Williams was conservative in many of his policies; in a few items he was a reactionary. On Negro suffrage his attitude was approximately the same as that of Alabama at the time of his birth—during the bitterness of Reconstruction in the South. He approved tax measures that were fairly progressive, such as increase in the gross-production tax on oil to 2 per cent, the new inheritance tax ranging upward from 1 per cent on $25,000 estates to 4 per cent on estates worth $100,000 or more, and the sharp increase in motor-vehicle tax. His influence was in favor of economy even at the sacrifice of badly needed services, and some of the state's progress in building received only reluctant support from the Governor. His war record was superb. His co-operation with the national government was complete, his efficiency was remarkable, and his energetic drive was matchless.[43]

[42] *Oklahoma* v. *Texas,* 260 U. S., 632, 638.
[43] Dale and Rader, *Readings in Oklahoma History,* 751, 752.

# CHAPTER FOURTEEN

# The Era of Impeachments, 1919-1931

## THE ROBERTSON ADMINISTRATION

During the autumn months of 1918, Germany and her allies in the European War, in spite of external appearance of great strength, were about to collapse. In Oklahoma, the Democratic primary brought victory to J. B. A. Robertson as candidate for governor. Robertson had run a close second to Robert L. Williams in the primary election of 1914.[1] His principal opponent in the primary of 1918 was William H. Murray, and Robertson's margin was decisive, 48,568 to 24,283. He then defeated Horace G. McKeever, Republican candidate for governor, by a vote of 104,132 to 82,865. The popularity of men who had supported the war against Germany is evident in the prestige Robertson gained as law partner of Oklahoma's only high-ranking military officer, Brigadier General Roy Hoffman.

On the other side of the picture the Socialist party was practically wiped out. The antidraft agitation of 1917 reacted strongly against all organizations of radical political tendencies. Patrick S. Nagle, who had once scored above 50,000 votes in a three-cornered race for a seat in the United States Senate, received only 7,438 for governor in 1918. Robert L. Owen, a strong supporter of President Wilson's war program, was re-elected to the United States Senate. The defeat of Thomas P. Gore in his bid for re-election to the Senate two years later is further evidence of popular disapproval of pacifism. Senator Gore had opposed the declaration of war, sharply criticized the Wilson administration for its farm policies, and helped to defeat United States membership in the League of

---

[1] Results of the Democratic primary election in 1914: Williams, 35,605; Robertson, 33,504; Al Jennings, former bank robber, 21,732. Dale and Rader, *Readings in Oklahoma History*, 750.

Nations. Oklahoma Democrats in the 1920 primary election chose Representative Scott Ferris over Gore to make the race for the Senate. However, the Republican congressman, John W. Harreld of Oklahoma City, who had been elected after Joseph B. Thompson's death in September, 1919, to fill his place in the House, announced himself as a candidate for the United States Senate. He received determined support from sundry groups: Republicans, Socialists, opponents of the war, and anti-Wilson Democrats. Harreld won over Scott Ferris by a plurality of 30,000.[2]

In the same election Warren G. Harding, Republican candidate for the presidency with Calvin Coolidge as his running mate, defeated James M. Cox and Franklin D. Roosevelt by an overwhelming majority. Oklahoma voted for Harding 243,464 to 215,808 for Cox, and with its new Republican senator, J. W. Harreld, sent five Republican representatives to Washington: Thomas A. Chandler of Vinita, Joseph C. Pringley of Chandler, Alice Robertson of Muskogee, L. M. Gensman of Lawton, and Manuel Herrick of Perry. The Democrats elected only Charles D. Carter, J. V. McClintic, and Fletcher B. Swank.

James Brooks Ayres Robertson, a native of Iowa and fourth governor of the state of Oklahoma, took office in January, 1919, in his forty-eighth year. He was the first chief executive to be elected from the west side of the state and he had lived in Chandler since 1893, as a practicing attorney since 1898. Before his election as governor he had held office as county attorney of Lincoln County, state district judge, and member of the supreme court commission. He had also served for a time on the state capitol commission and had been a delegate to the Democratic National Convention in 1908.

When Governor Robertson took office in 1919, Oklahoma was enjoying a period of high production that was gratifying but deceptive for most of the people. Prices were high, especially on scarce goods. In 1920 Oklahoma produced 106,206,000 barrels of crude oil ( 4,460,652,000 gallons ), which was more than either California or Texas produced in that year. With war restrictions removed, the price of oil soared from $2.25 per barrel in the fall of 1918 to $3.50 by March 1, 1920.[3] Farm prices were high, too, during

[2] *Ibid.*, 755.    [3] *Ibid.*, 755.

the year after the end of the war. Then came a period of sharp decline, first in cotton and corn, then in wheat. With declining prices of grain, livestock prices suffered a collapse also. During the war, unproductive land had been put into cultivation of wheat and other crops. This marginal land was dependent upon abnormally high prices for a return sufficient to give the farmer a living income. Often this unhealthy economic situation was complicated by farm mortgages and machinery bought at high prices and on credit. The depression of 1920–21 was felt earlier and more keenly by farmers than any other part of the population. Second to mineral production in total value of output, agriculture was of great importance to Oklahoma prosperity.

Oil declined as rapidly in price as it had risen. From a top price of $3.50 a barrel on March 1, 1920, it moved down to $1.75 in less than a year.[4] Wages of laborers were reduced without a corresponding drop in the cost of goods other than raw farm products, and two large classes of Oklahoma voters were ready for political revolt.

In addition to electing Senator Harreld and the five congressmen mentioned above, the Republicans scored heavily in state political races, electing four of nine justices of the supreme court, one justice of the criminal court of appeals, and one of three corporation commissioners. In the legislature a Republican majority was returned in the house of representatives, but the Democrats still held a majority of twenty-seven to seventeen in the senate, where only twenty-two seats were filled by the election.

A major item of Governor Robertson's executive program was his better-highways campaign. The seventh legislature, at his request, submitted to the voters an amendment to the constitution providing a bond issue of $50,000,000 for highways. This measure was defeated by an overwhelming margin of more than 100,000 negative votes.[5] The license tax on automobiles was raised, however, with a minimum rate of $10 for cars valued at $500 or under.

The Seventh Legislature passed a state budget law intended to provide systematic control of state expenditures by executive planning. As in the case of national budget legislation enacted shortly afterward, the changes effected by Oklahoma's budget law

[4] *Ibid.*, 756.
[5] *Ibid.*, 755; *Directory of the State of Oklahoma*, 158.

have not proved revolutionary. Certainly the trend toward higher cost of state government was not reversed; but probably a more reasonable distribution of state funds among various departments and institutions has been secured. The Seventh Legislature appropriated $18,913,121.39 for all purposes. Three hospitals for tubercular patients were included in the expansion of state institutions. At Miami a school of mines was established, which became the Northeastern Junior College six years later and in 1943 was changed again to the Northeastern Oklahoma Agricultural and Mechanical College. It is governed by the nine-member Board of Regents for Agricultural and Mechanical colleges, of which the president of the state board of agriculture is a member, ex officio.[6]

The Eighth Legislature, with a Republican majority in the house of representatives and a Democratic majority in the senate, devoted a great deal of time and energy to party conflict. At the end of the sixty-day regular session, the appropriation bills were still subjects of bitter dispute, and the legislature adjourned without passing necessary money bills. Governor Robertson called a special session to continue work on appropriations, and the bills were finally passed.[7] In spite of partisan conflict, delay, and reduction of the Governor's requests, the total amount appropriated was the largest in the history of the state up to that time, $20,416,100.23. Included among other money bills was an appropriation of $100,000 for weak school districts, a beginning of the movement directed toward equalizing educational opportunity in different parts of the state. State aid for all primary schools and for secondary schools unable to support a minimum term grew rapidly from that beginning, and by 1937 the state appropriation reached the sum of $12,800,000 a year.[8]

The Eighth Legislature authorized a commission of educational survey. Governor Robertson appointed five men, including State Superintendent Robert H. Wilson as chairman, as members

[6] Presidents of the Oklahoma Board of Agriculture have been: J. P. Connors, G. T. Bryan, F. M. Gault, J. A. Whitehurst, Harry B. Cordell, Joe C. Scott, and Harold P. Hutton.

[7] Dale and Rader, *Readings in Oklahoma History*, 757.

[8] The Twenty-fourth Legislature in 1953 appropriated $29,515,000 for school aid during each of the following two years. Approximately $3,185,000 additional is expected to be available for school aid in each of the two years.

of the commission.[9] William T. Bawden of the United States Bureau of Education was secured to direct the survey, together with nineteen other educators from outside of Oklahoma as his assistants. In its report the commission recommended state aid as a means of equalizing educational opportunity, a nine-month term in every school district, and development of a system of rural high schools. There were other proposals dealing with textbooks, methods of selecting school officials, and other problems. Some of the recommendations have not been followed, but a large part of Oklahoma's progress in public education since 1921 has been in harmony with the findings of the survey commission.

There was a great deal of impeachment talk in the Eighth Legislature. Oklahoma banks had been hit hard by the financial depression of 1920–21, and the bank-guaranty fund had proved but slight protection for depositors. Governor Robertson's political opponents tried to connect him with failure of the Bank of Commerce at Okmulgee as a basis for impeachment proceedings, but were unable to make a case.

An incident of the Robertson administration that brought much unfavorable publicity to Oklahoma was the race riot at Tulsa on May 31 and June 1, 1921.[10] The affair started with the arrest of Dick Rowland, a Negro charged with assault on a white girl. Rowland was placed in a cell on the upper floor of the courthouse, and about dark a crowd of white men gathered around the place. A large number of Negroes in cars came to the courthouse and paraded around the block several times, apparently with the idea of preventing the lynching of Rowland. The crowd of whites broke into hardware and sporting-goods stores, helped themselves to guns and ammunition, and became an uncontrollable mob. Shortly after dark a police officer stopped a Negro to disarm him, the man resisted, and the policeman shot him.

Armed men of both races appeared on the streets, and soon shooting became general. Outnumbered, the main body of whites at the courthouse scattered, and the Negroes fired upon them as

[9] In addition to Superintendent Wilson, the survey commission included Cyrus S. Avery of Tulsa, George F. Southward of Enid, Charles L. Brooks of Sapulpa, and J. A. Duff of Cordell.

[10] New York Times, June 2, 3, 4, 5, 1921; Tulsa Daily World, June 1, 2, 3, 4, 1921; Tulsa Tribune, June 1, 2, 3, 4, 1921; Daily Oklahoman, June 1, 2, 3, 4, 1921.

they ran. One white man was killed in this phase of the battle. The whites returned in larger force and the Negroes fell back. Skirmishes took place from time to time, and in one instance a car of armed white men driving rapidly through the streets and mistaking one of their own number for a Negro shot him to death. Fires were started in the Negro section, and firemen were prevented by the mob from fighting the flames. Shooting and incendiary fires continued throughout the night.

City authorities had called upon Governor Robertson for military help at eleven o'clock in the evening, and Adjutant General Charles F. Barrett took charge of the National Guard at Tulsa. By midnight, officers mobilized Company B, surrounded the courthouse with soldiers, and began the difficult task of restoring order. Several thousand Negroes had fled from the city and several thousand more were given protection in detention camps. At the time when shooting was at its worst, a passenger train on the St. Louis and San Francisco Railroad was hit by many bullets as it passed the scene of the rioting. Passengers left their berths and stretched out in the aisles to escape from the danger of stray bullets. In spite of the best efforts of National Guard units, scattered firing continued throughout the afternoon of June 1.

When rioting ended it was found that 33 persons had lost their lives by gunfire or in the burning buildings, and 240 were wounded. City officials of Tulsa were blamed by many citizens for permitting the affray to gain momentum, and there was some inclination on the part of Democrats to blame the Republican police department and on the part of Republicans to blame the Democratic sheriff's office. Actually there was enough blame for all concerned, and the good citizens of Tulsa were heartily ashamed of the entire affair.


## The Administration of J. C. Walton

By 1922 a large number of Oklahoma citizens were keenly dissatisfied with the discrepancies between campaign promises of 1920 and lack of prosperity in the following months. The Farmer-Labor Reconstruction League, organized at Shawnee in February,

339

1922, was the group that gathered into its membership a large part of the discontented, both in rural areas and in towns. A political platform was adopted, and the League was soon in a position to throw decisive strength to the major party candidate who promised co-operation with its radical program. This minority, following methods and to a large extent the platform of the Non-Partisan League in the Northwest, dominated the Democratic primary election. League members succeeded in nominating John C. Walton, mayor of Oklahoma City, for the governorship. Mayor Walton defeated such opponents as Judge Thomas Owen of Muskogee and Robert H. Wilson, the able and popular superintendent of public instruction.

To run against Walton the Republicans nominated John Fields, a candidate who had come close to defeating Robert L. Williams in 1914. In that earlier election Williams was the conservative candidate, Fields the progressive; but now the Democratic candidate had accepted the radical platform and partisan support of the Reconstruction League along with the major party machine, and Republicans were on the defensive.[11] The campaign speeches of John Fields were dignified assaults upon the principles of Socialism and the dangers of untried, left-wing theories of government.

The Constitutional Democratic Club, taking a stand against radical policies of the Farmer-Labor Reconstruction League, declared themselves opposed to Walton and in some cases gave active support to his Republican opponent. The Democratic candidate accepted the entire platform of the Reconstruction League, including a state bank, state insurance, free textbooks in the public schools, state warehouse inspection, a liberal soldiers' bonus, state officials to grade cotton, state grain inspection, community marketing co-operatives, and extension of the state's control over cotton ginning.

Results of the election show clearly the depth of discontent in Oklahoma during 1922. In spite of the wide acquaintance of John

[11] Dale and Rader, *Readings in Oklahoma History*, 758; *Daily Oklahoman*, November 1–30, 1922. A full account of the candidates and the election appeared also in the *Tulsa Tribune* and the *Tulsa Daily World*, November 1–30, 1922. For statistics on the election see *Directory of the State of Oklahoma*, 71–76.

Fields, through his work as director of the experiment station at the Oklahoma Agricultural and Mechanical College, as author of a widely used textbook on agriculture, and as editor of the *Oklahoma Farmer,* in spite of his excellent record as a liberal Republican and support obtained through opponents of the Democratic party's coalition with the Farmer-Labor Reconstruction League, Jack Walton won the election by fifty thousand votes. Walton discovered in this campaign the effectiveness of a jazz band for arousing enthusiasm and found among his own talents new tricks of the demagogue in appealing to the voters. His was the largest majority given to any candidate for governor up to that time; and most of the other Democratic candidates won by similarly wide margins.

The Democrats placed substantial majorities in both houses of the legislature, elected the entire slate of state executive officers, and chose seven of the eight members of Congress.[12] In this election the element of discontent was decisive. Many of the same voters who cast their ballots for Warren G. Harding and John W. Harreld in 1920 were now ardent supporters of John C. Walton and the Farmer-Labor Reconstruction League.

Governor Walton was a native of Indiana. He lived for a time in Kansas City, Missouri, and came to Oklahoma Territory in 1904. At Oklahoma City he engaged in civil engineering and contracting, and was elected mayor in 1919 largely on his spectacular appeal to the common man, his vociferous support of public charities, and his resounding platitudes. He began his career as governor on January 9, 1923, with a gigantic barbecue on the state fair grounds and ended it less than ten months later as a result of impeachment and conviction on eleven charges of high crimes and misdemeanors.[13]

In 1923 Oklahoma was ready to resume the progressive tendency that was interrupted by the Harding revolt of 1920, after a great world war. A majority of the legislature were not in sympathy with the program of the Reconstruction League in its entirety, but were ready to adopt reform measures in harmony with current

[12] *Congressional Directory.* The Republican member, elected in the eighth district, was Milton C. Garber of Enid. The Democratic members were: E. B. Howard of Tulsa, W. W. Hastings of Tahlequah, Charles D. Carter of Ardmore, T. D. McKeown of Ada, F. B. Swank of Norman, J. V. McClintic of Snyder, and J. W. Elmer Thomas of Medicine Park.

[13] Ernest T. Bynum, *Personal Recollections of Ex-Governor Walton.*

changes in other western states. The principle of state aid for school districts that were financially unable to meet a minimum standard made notable progress when the legislature appropriated $650,000 for that program. State warehouse inspectors under a superintendent, grain inspection by state officers, cotton grading under supervision of the state board of agriculture, and revision of the workmen's compensation law with higher pay for injuries and death benefits were all quite acceptable to the Reconstruction League. In addition to these measures, the legislature gave recognition to co-operative marketing by providing for community marketing associations under the state market commission, provided free textbooks for public school children of the first eight grades, and gave the corporation commission increased authority in regulating cotton gins. City planning commissions authorized by the ninth legislature, along with regional planning groups, made a beginning in an important field of municipal progress. Tax assessments for paving were also authorized at this time.

An early law of the new state, denounced by its opponents from the first as socialistic, was not functioning successfully. The bank-guaranty act of C. N. Haskell's administration, which had been amended by the third legislature to provide a larger guaranty fund for protection of depositors, was still unable to maintain an adequate guarantee against losses. The fund was bankrupt, and the Ninth Legislature, after a sharp debate, repealed the law.

New tax laws were necessary to meet rising expenses of government, especially in the building and maintenance of highways. Unexpected increase in the gross revenue receipts of 1922 had made the ad valorem levy for general expenses of government unnecessary for that year. But the Ninth Legislature levied a state tax of one cent per gallon on retail sales of gasoline and a new tax on busses and trucks employed as common carriers.

Perhaps it was inevitable that Governor Walton should clash with conservatives and even with many prominent liberals and radicals. He was inexperienced in politics and unable to adjust his policies to the necessity of dealing with men of many views, conflicting interests, and a great variety of aims. His quick rise to a position of power, the ridiculously high estimate placed upon his services by uninformed followers, his own marked inclination toward vanity and lack of poise, all contributed to his downfall. It is fair to say that Governor Walton did not possess the intellect to comprehend the nature of his problems, nor the character to stand against the temptations of a governor.

The Ku Klux Klan, modeled in part upon the organization of the same name that flourished in the South immediately after the Civil War, had grown up suddenly in Oklahoma and other states after the end of World War in 1918. Although the Oklahoma Ku Klux Klan contained members who were innocent of any intention to engage in lawless violence, the central idea of the organization was basically unsound, in that it did recognize the use of force unsupported by law. That self-appointed enforcers of regulations agreed upon secretly by themselves can administer justice, when courts and legally chosen executive officers have failed, is a fantastic concept. The Klan was a fad which held the interest of immature adults through secret rituals and robed, spectacular night assemblies. It offered an opportunity for professional organizers who were intent upon obtaining quick financial rewards, often by fraud or by theft from the organization's treasury, and for a few lawless persons who used the secret order for violent revenge or other criminal designs. At best, it was an outlet for overgrown juveniles who had been denied the privilege of membership in more respectable secret orders; at worst, it practiced brutal violence upon persons who had not been adjudged guilty of any crime by regularly constituted courts. If social order based upon law is right, then the Ku Klux Klan was wrong.

Governor Walton seized upon the Klan in Oklahoma as an excuse to abuse executive power. Within a few months after his term began, he had become involved in contests with various political leaders and with state school officials whose long records of service should have warned the brash executive that he was venturing beyond his depth.

Within two months after his inauguration, Governor Walton began a series of changes in the boards of state schools with the obvious intention of building partisan support for his position in Oklahoma politics. Before the end of the spring semester in 1923, he had removed five members of the University Board of Regents and appointed five new members.[14] A sixth member resigned, and

343

only George L. Bowman of Kingfisher, who had served since 1919, remained of the old board. Changes were made about the same time in the board of agriculture which resulted in removal of President J. B. Eskridge of the Agricultural and Mechanical College at Stillwater and the appointment of George Wilson, a former instructor in the college and a leader of the Reconstruction League, to serve as president. A storm of protest from alumni and other interested groups caused the Governor to make another quick shift; and before he was fairly settled in his new office, George Wilson was removed and the place was filled by Bradford Knapp, dean of the School of Agriculture at the University of Arkansas.

Stratton D. Brooks, who had been president of the University of Oklahoma since May 1, 1912, probably could have made a successful fight against removal. However, he had just declined an offer of the presidency of the University of Missouri; and when he was assured by the Missouri regents that he could still have that position, he resigned, with his resignation to take effect on July 1, and moved his household to Columbia, Missouri. The loss of President Brooks was a blow to the cause of education in Oklahoma. His undergraduate preparation in the University of Michigan and his graduate degree at Harvard, together with a varied experience in educational work, had provided him with an excellent background. Six years as superintendent of the Boston city schools had given him a working acquaintance with actual problems of large-school administration. He had given eleven years of able and energetic leadership to the University of Oklahoma; and with that experience, his wide acquaintance in the state, and his prestige as a writer and scholar, he was in a position to make an even greater contribution. The peculiar twist that was given to the principle of executive responsibility in Oklahoma, together with the rise of John C. Walton, resulted in educational disaster.

Gradually the tide of public disapproval against the Governor grew. In his zeal to marshal his political forces, he could not refrain from attacking institutions that were not political by their nature. The University of Oklahoma and its president were special objects of his bitterness. After the resignation of President Brooks, the Governor revealed in a speech before a group of farmers at Shaw-

14 Gittinger, *The University of Oklahoma,* 122, 127, 224.

nee the pattern of his thinking on educational institutions. Brooks was more of an organizer than an educator, Walton declared. He charged that the university president had built up an alumni organization, "30,000 or 40,000 strong, and he hit me square in the face with the whole bunch when I came out for office."[15]

Disorder appeared in various parts of the state, and the Ku Klux Klan added to the general confusion by attempting to take the law into its own corrupt and incompetent hands. Governor Walton tried to make it appear that all the opposition to him was the work of the Klan. After the whipping of a man by a masked band in Okmulgee and similar mob violence in Tulsa, the Governor placed those cities under martial law.[16]

Lawlessness in Oklahoma and other states during the decade after World War I was bad, but not so terrible as to demand either irresponsible vigilance committees on the one hand or long-continued martial law on the other. There were labor fights, clashes between racial groups, bank robberies, train robberies, mob whippings, and many other kinds of criminal disorder. On August 14, Governor Walton issued his proclamation of martial law in Tulsa:

"By virtue of the authority conferred upon me by the constitution and laws of Oklahoma as chief executive of the state and as commander-in-chief of its military forces, I, J. C. Walton, Governor of Oklahoma . . . being apprised that a state of lawlessness and disorder amounting to a state of insurrection against the civil law now prevails in the city of Tulsa, and local officers of the law either cannot or will not suppress the breeches of the peace, I hereby declare martial law throughout the area of the city of Tulsa."

Later the area of control by troops was extended to include the towns of Red Fork, Bixby, and the entire southern portion of Tulsa County. Investigations of the numerous whippings in the area were conducted by Adjutant General Baird H. Markham, with the assistance of Colonel Charles F. Barrett, Colonel Paul F. Walker, and Major Turner Roark. By a military order General Markham stopped an "indignation meeting" of Tulsa citizens, but was unable to control the newspaper criticism of martial law.

[15] *Tulsa Daily World*, August 22, 1923.

[16] For an account of martial law in Tulsa, see files of *Tulsa Daily World*, August 14–31, 1923.

Attorney General George E. Short, who accompanied Markham to Tulsa, came near breaking with Governor Walton over the question of keeping 150 national guardsmen in Tulsa for an extended period.[17]

During the days of martial law in Tulsa, newspapers carried an announcement that the University of Oklahoma regents had offered to employ as president Dr. A. Ross Hill, formerly president of the University of Missouri. An agreement was not reached, however, with the Missouri man whose eminence might have saved to some extent the face of Governor John C. Walton. No permanent president for the University of Oklahoma was employed until 1925, when William B. Bizzell took the position.

On August 18, 1923, the Oklahoma Supreme Court rendered a decision in regard to the university which affected other state schools as well. The governor had reduced the appropriation of the legislature for university maintenance from $700,000 to $500,000. The court held by a five-to-three decision (one justice being absent) that executive reduction of the appropriation was unconstitutional and ordered that the amount appropriated be devoted to university expenses.[18]

On August 21 a band of outlaws held up an M. K. & T. train near Okesa in Osage County, looting the mail and express cars. The bandits escaped in three automobiles, but were captured later and brought to trial.

In the meantime, General Markham at Tulsa found evidence of many mob whippings and ample reason to suppose that local Ku Klux Klan organizations were responsible for the violence. On August 24, Ben F. Sikes and Earl Sack, charged with participation in rioting, were convicted in a district court on evidence brought to light by Markham and on their own plea of guilt. They were sent to the state penitentiary for two years; their testimony implicated six other persons and further prosecutions followed.

The man whipped by this Ku Klux Klan unit at Broken Arrow was a hard-working German farmer of sixty, head of a household consisting of a wife and eight children. Apparently he was innocent of any offense against the peace and dignity of Tulsa County other

---

[17] *Tulsa Daily World,* August 16, 17, 1923.
[18] *Tulsa Daily World,* August 19, 1923.

than failure to make himself understood. In asking the court for clemency, the attorney for Earl Sack and Ben Sikes remarked that his clients were not nearly so guilty as officials of the Ku Klux Klan. Before he left the courtroom at the trial, Ben Wagner, the farmer who had been whipped, rather timidly offered his hand to the convicted men.

"I'm sorry it happened this way," he told them.

"So are we," answered Sack. "Some day we'll come back and we'll all be neighbors again—and we'll understand each other better."[19]

The *Tulsa Tribune* took the lead in advocating impeachment of the chief executive; and when a grand jury was called in Oklahoma County to investigate charges of misconduct against state officers, including Walton himself, the Governor placed the entire state under martial law. With machine guns in the hands of national guardsmen covering the door of the jury room, the Governor forbade the session of the grand jury.

Members of the legislature attempted to meet in the Capitol on September 26, but Governor Walton again used the military arm to prevent the meeting. The Governor had called for a special election on October 2 to place before Oklahoma voters a proposed bonus for veterans. Campbell Russell prepared petitions for an initiated measure to legalize meeting of the legislature in special session without a call by the governor.

Unable to prevent submission of the initiated measure by leaving it off the ballots, the Governor tried to stop the election. But election officials opened the polls and the people voted. Affirmative votes numbered 209,452; negative votes, 70,638.[20] The bond issue for a veterans' bonus was defeated.

W. D. McBee, new speaker of the house of representatives, called the legislature into session for October 17. The Governor, thereupon, called a special session for October 11, asking that the Ku Klux Klan be outlawed. The legislature met in response to the Governor's call but immediately adjourned to meet again on October 17.

One of the complaints against Governor Walton was that he

19 *Tulsa Daily World*, August 26, 1923.
20 Dale and Rader, *Readings in Oklahoma History*, 761.

objected to the death sentence as punishment for murderers and that he used the pardoning power to excess. While it is not unreasonable to suppose that he sincerely regarded the death penalty a relic of barbarism, the assertion that he freed dangerous criminals to prey upon society was hard to disprove and constituted one of the factors that led to his downfall. Newspapers of the period are filled with accounts of the Governor's clemency, and in some instances the pardons and paroles are hard to explain. The record for August 30, 1923, was two full pardons and nine paroles. In addition, an investigator found that Jim Baldwin, sentenced in 1919 to serve thirty years for bank robbery at Lindsay, Oklahoma, was out of the penitentiary "on leave of absence." The Governor's clemency record on August 31 was five paroles and two pardons—one for a merchant who had been convicted of receiving stolen goods and one for an armed robber. One of the paroled prisoners that day was Roy Carr, who had served eight years of a twenty-one-year sentence for manslaughter.

The house of representatives considered twenty-two charges against the Governor presented by W. E. Disney as chairman of an investigating committee. While these were before the house, it was rumored that Walton was planning a wholesale delivery of criminals from the penitentiary by exercise of the pardoning power. The house quickly impeached the Governor on two charges and sent them to the senate, which determined by a vote of thirty-eight to one to suspend him pending the outcome of his formal trial. Lieutenant Governor Martin E. Trapp then became acting governor.

The house sent other charges to the senate, and Walton's trial proceeded with Chief Justice J. T. Johnson presiding. The accused chief executive withdrew early in the hearings with the statement that he did not expect a fair trial by that senate. Eleven of the charges were sustained by votes considerably over the two-thirds majority required for conviction. With more than three years of the term remaining, Martin E. Trapp became governor.

The charges on which the Oklahoma Senate convicted Governor Walton included: excessive and illegal expenditures in his primary campaign; illegal collection of campaign funds; the padding of state payrolls; use of the National Guard to prevent meeting of an Oklahoma County Grand Jury; placing his private chauf-

348

feur upon the payroll of the state health department; illegal issuance of deficiency warrants in order to place unauthorized employees on the state payrolls; suspension of the writ of *habeas corpus;* excessive use of the pardoning power; and general incompetency.[21] The senate vote on overuse of the pardoning power was unanimous. Campbell Russell, who circulated the petitions that were instrumental in bringing about Governor Walton's downfall, was awarded the distinction of being voted "most useful citizen" of Oklahoma City in 1924.[22]

## THE TRAPP ADMINISTRATION

Martin E. Trapp was a native of Kansas, where he lived until he was twelve years old. In 1889 his father made the run into Oklahoma and succeeded in staking a claim about seven miles west of Guthrie in Logan County. Here Martin grew up, attending the local schools and obtaining a certificate to teach at the age of twenty-one. His early career was varied: two years as a teacher, four years on the road as a salesman, and three years as county clerk of Logan County. In 1907 he was elected first state auditor of Oklahoma and held that office until 1911.[23] In that year he opened a bond office in Guthrie but in 1913 moved his business to Muskogee. He was elected three times as lieutenant governor: in 1914 as the running mate of Robert L. Williams, in 1918 with J. B. A. Robertson, and in 1922 with John C. Walton. His nine years of experience in the practical working of politics was a far more extensive apprenticeship than that of either Governor Robertson or John C. Walton. Furthermore, he was a man of simple, straightforward bearing, keen perception, and outstanding ability as an organizer of work. More or less by political accident the state discovered a good man for governor in a difficult situation.

[21] *New York Times*, November 20, 1923; Howard A. Tucker, *Governor Walton's Ku Klux Klan War.* The legal limit for campaign expenses in the primary election was $3,000. Governor Walton was convicted on the charge of spending $30,000.

[22] The *Daily Oklahoman*, January 3, 1929, contains pictures and record of four "most useful citizens," selections to that date.

[23] *Directory of the State of Oklahoma*, 101.

Early in the Trapp regime, careful investigations led to a few removals of state officials. John A. Whitehurst, president of the Board of Agriculture, was impeached but acquitted by the senate. In a special session the legislature passed an act designed to check disorderly activities of the Ku Klux Klan by prohibiting the wearing of masks on streets or highways of Oklahoma and requiring registration of the names of members.

The special session of 1924 also passed an act that provided for a three-member highway commission and raised the gasoline tax to two and one-half cents per gallon. Governor Trapp appointed Cyrus S. Avery, Roy M. Johnson, and F. G. Gentry commissioners. As part of his economy program, Governor Trapp reduced the number of state employees and cut down the building program for 1924. A major item of reorganization changed the terms of county officers from two years to four years: sheriffs, court clerks, county attorneys, county treasurers, and superintendents of schools, beginning with the officers elected in November, 1924; county weighers, judges, assessors, surveyors, and county clerks, beginning with those elected in 1926.

Robert L. Owen, who had been in the United States Senate since 1907, announced that he would not again be a candidate, and John C. Walton immediately came out for nomination as the Democratic candidate. Results of the primary election proved that former Governor Walton still had a following in Oklahoma. In a field of five he received 91,510 votes; E. B. Howard of Tulsa, 83,922; Thomas P. Gore, 52,249; C. J. Wrightsman, 51,291; and F. P. Freeling, 15,384. Howard was serving his second term in Congress; and Gore, who had been defeated in the primary election of 1920, had a record of fourteen years in the United States Senate. The Republicans nominated W. B. Pine of Okmulgee, and a spectacular contest took place between Walton and Pine. Disagreement among the Democrats in regard to their candidate for the United States Senate was the only serious break within party ranks. The legislature was Democratic in both houses by large majorities, all state executive officers were of the same party, and Oklahoma elected her ten presidential electors for John W. Davis over Calvin Coolidge by a substantial plurality.[24] In the senate campaign, however, W. B. Pine was the beneficiary of a Democratic split. John C. Walton's supporters were enthusiastic, and the former Governor was an effective campaigner; but anti-Walton Democrats were equally aroused, and their numerical strength combined with that of the Republicans was too great to be denied, in spite of the tuneful efforts of Walton's jazz band. Women voters came to the polls in large numbers, and more than 500,000 ballots were cast in the senatorial race. W. B. Pine, the second Republican to be sent to the United States Senate by Oklahoma, received a majority vote of 339,646 to Walton's 196,417.[25]

In the Tenth Oklahoma Legislature J. B. Harper was elected speaker of the House, and William J. Holloway of Hugo, president of the senate. The emphasis of party leaders was still upon economy, and the administration was committed to the same policy. The free-textbook law was repealed, the prison farm at Aylesworth was sold and state aid for weak schools was reduced from $650,000 to $500,000. In their zeal to curb extravagance, perhaps state officials cut expenditures for development that was sorely needed. In other fields there were some constructive measures. A bureau of criminal identification was established, and commissions responsible to the governor were provided in such important areas as conservation, fish and game protection, real estate, and forestry. Tax laws were revised, with 20 per cent increase on automobile licenses and retail sales of gasoline.

The supreme court ruled that Governor Trapp, although he had served less than a full term, was not eligible to succeed himself. In the Democratic primary on August 3, 1926, Henry S. Johnston of Perry won by a small plurality over a field which included W. M. Darnell and O. A. Cargill, mayor of Oklahoma City. The combined vote for Darnell and Cargill was higher by thirty thousand than the vote cast for Johnston. Furthermore, the winner's minority was composed of fairly definite groups within the Democratic party, and these groups were sometimes hard to hold together. On the liquor question Johnston was known as a dry and might expect support from the temperance organizations. He had a wide follow-

---

[24] *Daily Oklahoman*, November 7, 1924. The popular vote gave Oklahoma to the Democratic candidate, 259,798 to 226,242. Robert La Follette, running as a Progressive, received 41,141 votes in Oklahoma.

[25] *Directory of the State of Oklahoma*, 67.

ing of personal friends, dating back to territorial days, and they were men of somewhat diverse political views. The Republicans named Omer K. Benedict, Tulsa postmaster, to run against Henry S. Johnston for the governor's office.

Fewer than 384,000 voters cast their ballots in this election—approximately 127,000 short of the total number who voted when Walton was elected governor over John Fields in 1922. Johnston won by a count of 213,167 to 170,714 for Benedict, but 25,000 Democrats who voted in the primary election did not cast their ballots for the winner in the general election. For the seat in the United States Senate held by J. W. Harreld, the Democrats elected Elmer Thomas of Medicine Park by a vote of 195,312 to 159,287. State executive officers were again Democratic, together with strong majorities in both houses of the legislature, as was the lieutenant governor, William J. Holloway. Of eight members elected to seats in the national House of Representatives, the Republicans placed but one, Milton C. Garber of Enid.

## THE JOHNSTON ADMINISTRATION

In the Eleventh Legislature D. A. Stovall of Hugo became speaker of the house and Mac Q. Williamson president of the senate.[26] In addition to these men the legislature contained some very able members, such as E. P. Hill, Tom Kight, Jim Nance, Tom Anglin, R. L. Graham, W. J. Otjen, and Tom Johnson, who were all leaders of public opinion in the sections where they lived. By comparison with some of these men the new governor, Henry S. Johnston, had but a feeble grasp of political affairs. Born in Indiana in 1869, he was an older man than either Trapp, Walton, or Robertson, the three who preceded him in office. He had been an attorney in Perry since early territorial days, had served in the convention of 1906, and had been president pro tempore of the first state senate. His record in the Oklahoma Masonic Lodge, of which he had been grand master, was excellent, and his wide acquaintance in fraternal work was undoubtedly a strong factor in his political support. He

[26] *Ibid.*, 128, 140.

also enjoyed the confidence of Oklahoma drys, of many churchmen who were believers in prohibition, and of many active Ku Klux Klan leaders who were still vital forces in state politics.

A progressive measure on which the Governor and legislature co-operated was the appropriation of $1,500,000 for the aid of elementary schools. Another act provided for building a crippled children's hospital, and a third established a fund for medical treatment of those children. As a party measure, two-year terms for county officers were restored to guarantee more frequent political activity with the incentive of elections.

Hostility on the part of legislators and many citizens toward Governor Johnston began early in the administration. A part of this opposition was on trivial grounds. Some men of influence in the Eleventh Legislature resented the prominence of Mrs. O. O. Hammonds, confidential secretary of the Governor, who, it was said, made executive decisions of far-reaching importance. In truth, the Governor was not at his best under the pressure of executive duties at his advanced age, and it is quite possible that Mrs. Hammonds possessed better judgment on some political problems than the Governor himself. There is no evidence of undue influence by her upon affairs of state. The highway commission, with a strong preference for asphalt over cement as a material for state road building, also aroused the hostility of some Oklahomans and opened the way for charges of corruption. In the fall of 1927 many members of the legislature were ready to make use of the remedy that had proved so successful in the case of Walton—impeachment.

A great deal of confusion surrounded the first attempt to remove Governor Johnston by impeachment. An attempt to get action in a special session, meeting without the Governor's call, was held unconstitutional by the state supreme court. The initiated measure of October 2, 1923, under authority of which the legislature convened, had not been legally submitted to the voters, in the court's opinion; and the legislature, under a constitution which provided that special sessions should be held upon call of the chief executive, did not have an inherent right to meet in special session.[27] The legislature met, however, and with a quorum in both houses took the necessary steps to bring impeachment charges

[27] *Ibid.*, 160, 161 (Initiative Petition No. 79).

353

against the Governor. The house replaced D. A. Stovall with E. P. Hill as speaker and named Tom Kight to head a committee of investigation. On authority of the supreme court decision, concerning the special session not called by the Governor, the district court of Oklahoma County issued a writ of injunction against the meeting of the legislature. Members denied that the writ was valid, however, on the ground that the legislature was above the supreme court when the two houses were exercising the function of impeachment.

On the strength of the supreme court's decision and the injunction issued by the lower court, Governor Johnston prevented meeting of the legislature in the Capitol by the use of National Guard units. But members of the house of representatives, meeting in the Huckins Hotel, voted impeachment charges against Governor Johnston, Chief Justice Fred P. Branson, and Harry B. Cordell, chairman of the Board of Agriculture.[28] The senate, also meeting in a hotel room, organized as a court and received the impeachment charges. The situation was surrounded by grave constitutional questions to which there was no clear solution, either in the language of the law or by precedent. Perhaps legal doubts would not have stopped the legislators; but there were also political problems to consider. Election time was less than a year away, and many leaders of the legislature had political ambitions which might be set back by undue haste or a serious blunder in regard to Henry S. Johnston. The senate still declared its authority superior to that of the supreme court, but ruled that house action had been illegal and that no properly drawn articles of impeachment were ready to be tried. Then the senate adjourned.[29]

Impeachment of Governor Johnston was now definitely postponed until after the national elections of 1928. The Governor and his associates who were under fire had their chance to build up public support and official support against charges that were sure to be in a large measure inspired by partisan considerations. Perhaps in the case of the Governor that chance was a slender one. He was peculiarly unfortunate in his contacts with the Democratic National Convention, which met in Houston. The Democratic

28 *Daily Oklahoman,* December 14, 1927.
29 *Daily Oklahoman,* December 27, 28, 29, 1927.

candidate for president, Alfred E. Smith of New York, could not command solid support from Protestants and drys of the South, since it was well known that he was a member of the Roman Catholic Church and an opponent of prohibition. Governor Johnston's delegation at the Houston convention, faced with the problem of going along with their party or bidding for anti-Catholic and dry support in Oklahoma, voted for Smith. The choice of Joseph T. Robinson of Arkansas as Smith's running mate was expected to make the New York Catholic acceptable to southwestern Democrats. It did in Arkansas but not in Oklahoma or Texas. Oklahoma voted for Herbert Hoover and Charles Curtis over Smith and Robinson, 394,046 to 219,174. In the congressional election, Carber of Enid was re-elected, and two districts that were normally Democratic voted for Republican candidates—Charles O'Connor of Tulsa defeating E. B. Howard, and U. S. Stone of Norman defeating F. B. Swank. Fred P. Branson, Democratic chief justice of the Oklahoma Supreme Court, lost to Thomas G. Andrews by a large majority; and the popular Democratic justice of the criminal court of appeals, Thomas H. Doyle of Perry, who had served more than twenty years, was defeated by W. G. Chappell.[30]

The Oklahoma Ku Klux Klan, with its strong anti-Catholic inclination, was disappointed in Governor Johnston, as were the drys and many Protestant churchmen who were among his active support. These men were devoted to the cause of prohibition, and it cannot be doubted that most of them were sincere in their belief that dry laws constituted the great issue of the day. It must be admitted, however, that in the gangsters and the criminal element of Ku Klux Klan, the churchmen had "strange bedfellows."

The Twelfth Legislature had fifty-seven Democrats and forty-seven Republicans in the house and a larger Democratic majority in the senate, thirty-two of forty-four.[31] The Governor had but little support in either house and the expected blow was not long in coming. Leaders of the antiadministration group in the senate included Tom Anglin of Holdenville, Paul Stewart of Haworth, Jess Pullen of Sulphur, and J. O. Ferguson of Pawnee. The house im-

---

[30] Dale and Rader, *Readings in Oklahoma History*, 766; *Daily Oklahoman*, November 7, 8, 9, 10, 1928.

[31] *Daily Oklahoman*, November 7–10 and December 30, 1928.

peached Johnston on eleven charges, and the senate on January 20 suspended him from office. William J. Holloway became acting governor.

The trial lasted two months and hinged principally on the eleventh charge, general incompetency. Much was said about the use of asphalt instead of concrete in Oklahoma highway building, but no positive evidence of corruption was brought into the hearings. It boiled down to a question of political power. Competency is a relative term: all officials are more or less incompetent as also, obviously, are all the senators who are empowered by the constitution to sit in judgment upon them. The question was: Will senators vote for conviction of the chief executive when no crime can be proved against him? On March 20, 1929, the yeas and nays were taken on the Governor's incompetency, he was adjudged unfit to hold the office on that eleventh charge by a vote of thirty-five to nine, and acquitted on the other ten charges.[32]

Henry S. Johnston's administration, like the Walton regime, was a low point in Oklahoma politics. There were many able men in public life at the time, but to a great extent their efforts toward progress were nullified by clashing interests, vicious partisan contests, and bungling in state affairs. The Governor was not an able administrator. Some of his activities suggest senility. He showed an excessive interest in discussions of the mystic, the occult. His grasp of the duties of his high office was never strong. One of his pardons was for a murderer who had previously been paroled and had broken his parole. After he had been returned to the penitentiary, Governor Walton had granted an "informal leave," and he simply remained outside and appeared on the penitentiary records as a fugitive. When Johnston learned details of the fugitive's record he attempted to revoke the pardon by which he had granted the man his freedom, but found that he could not legally withdraw clemency after a complete pardon.[33] The Governor was neither a criminal nor a statesman. His impeachment and conviction, however, were dangerous precedents.

The senate also suspended three justices of the supreme court who were impeached. Before the end of the session, however, two

---

[32] *Daily Oklahoman,* March 21, 1929.
[33] *Daily Oklahoman,* January 1, 1929.

were acquitted, one was dismissed on demurrers to the charges made against him, and all resumed their seats in the court.

## The Administration of William J. Holloway

Entering upon his duties shortly after the middle of the four-year term, Governor Holloway wisely determined to concentrate upon efficiency and economy, rather than an extensive building program.

William J. Holloway was born in Arkansas in 1888 and received an elementary education in the public schools of that state. He graduated from Ouachita College at the age of twenty-two, moved to Hugo, Oklahoma, and was employed as principal of the high school. He studied law at Cumberland University and was admitted to the practice of law at Hugo. He became county attorney of Bryan County in 1916, was elected a member of the state senate in 1920 and 1924, served as president pro tempore of the senate, and was elected lieutenant governor with Henry S. Johnston in 1926.

Holloway was quiet and unassuming, his manner was brisk, he received visitors with courtesy and all due consideration but without waste of time, and the governor's office was characterized by a businesslike administration of the state's affairs. The financial panic of 1929 and the long depression that followed it make estimates of financial measures peculiarly difficult. Governor Holloway did not succeed in erasing the state's deficit as he had planned, but he did help to inaugurate some measures of permanent value. Improvements were made in the Oklahoma child-labor restrictions, and a new coal mining code was passed.

As chairman of the state highway commission, Governor Holloway appointed a Republican, Lew Wentz of Ponca City.[34] The state elections of 1930 brought some new men to the attention of Oklahoma voters and in two instances marked the beginning of new careers for men who were already well known. William H.

[34] *Daily Oklahoman*, December 2, 1928. Lew Wentz was a wealthy oilman, at one time considered a possible choice for a cabinet position by President Herbert Hoover.

Murray, colorful and resourceful president of the Oklahoma Constitutional Convention and member of Congress for two terms, came back from South America, after spending several years in Bolivia, in time to make the race for governor; and Thomas P. Gore, United States senator from 1907 to 1921, came out of a ten-year period of retirement to defeat the Republican senator, W. B. Pine.

In the Democratic primary election seven well-known politicians ran for nomination to the governor's office. William H. Murray, past sixty years of age, had been longest before the public, often in the headlines. E. B. Howard of Tulsa, representative from the first district in the Sixty-sixth, Sixty-eighth, and Seventieth Congresses, had powerful support. Frank Buttram of Oklahoma City, who had made himself a leading figure in the oil industry, had little political experience, but held the confidence of many citizens.

Murray made Buttram the second candidate in the field, perhaps deliberately, by concentrating his campaign against him as a representative of great wealth. Martin E. Trapp, who was now eligible to run for another term as governor, announced himself as a candidate. Judge Frank M. Bailey of Chickasha, state senator; Jess Pullen of Sulphur; and the state auditor, A. S. J. Shaw, were all in the race. All of the candidates had blocs of support of varying strength and several were men of sufficient ability to be taken seriously as material for the governorship.

Murray was first in the voting and Buttram second. Howard and Trapp followed in order with the others scattered over the remaining positions. Murray showed almost twice as much strength as Buttram in the first primary and in the runoff drew 220,250 votes to 125,838 for Buttram. Ira Hill won the Republican nomination, with O. O. Owens as his running mate. James E. Berry of Stillwater, making his first race for lieutenant governor in the Democratic primary, lost to Robert Burns.

Democratic voters gave their candidate upward of 300,000 ballots and a majority of 93,000.[35] Thomas P. Gore, bidding for a return to the United States Senate, defeated W. B. Pine by a much smaller margin, 255,838 to 232,589.[36]

[35] *Directory of the State of Oklahoma,* 55; Gordon Hines, *Alfalfa Bill, an Intimate Biography,* chap. XIII.

[36] *Daily Oklahoman,* November 5, 6, 7, 30, 1930.

# CHAPTER FIFTEEN

# Contrasts in Governors, 1931-1943: Murray, Marland, Phillips

## THE NINTH GOVERNOR

William H. Murray was born in Texas in 1869. His early life was filled with hardship, and he made a precarious living by means of a great variety of occupations. His mother died when he was two, and his grandfather took him in. As soon as he was big enough to handle a light hoe, he worked in the fields, chopping cotton in the spring and helping to harvest the crop in the fall. He was a fast worker, and even after he began other occupations he returned at intervals to cotton picking, in which the laborer was paid by the pound. He tried his hand at selling goods, teaching, news reporting, and the practice of law.

In 1898 he came to Tishomingo where he met the Hearrell sisters—Alice, Daisy, and Ada—and promptly fell in love with Alice. The mother of these girls was Martha Walker Hearrell, one-eighth Chickasaw and one-eighth Choctaw, the niece of Tandy Walker, Choctaw principal chief, and the half-sister of Douglas H. Johnston, who was soon to be elected governor of the Chickasaw Nation. J. B. Hearrell, Alice's father, was a blacksmith from Tennessee who became an intermarried citizen of the Chickasaw Nation.[1]

Mary Alice Hearrell, born in Pontotoc County, Chickasaw Nation, in 1875, was twenty-three years old when the young Texas attorney William H. Murray came to Tishomingo. The Hearrell sisters all attended Bloomfield Academy while their uncle, Douglas H. Johnston, was head of the school. Although Bloomfield was noted for its achievements in the fine arts—oil painting, music, drama, and elocution—Superintendent Johnston warned young

[1] Hines, *Alfalfa Bill*, chap. VIII.

359

ladies of the academy against being "high toned" when they returned to their simple homes. "A snob is an inferior person trying to assert his superiority," he told them once in an address to the school assembly.

Tishomingo, where Bill Murray served his apprenticeship as an attorney, was a rough frontier town and capital of the Chickasaw Nation. Its main street was ankle-deep in dust during dry weather, in mud when it rained. In 1898 seven lawyers were already practicing there, including J. S. Maytubby, Nick Wolf, Madison Lucas, and Buck Garrett. Some of these men had been trained in law schools (Maytubby was a graduate of the University of Texas and of Vanderbilt), and some had attended school but little, obtained their knowledge of law in the office of a practicing attorney, and had been admitted to the bar without being required to submit to rigorous tests or annoying regulations.

Dave Irwin, Tishomingo blacksmith, fashioned "handsome" walnut coffins at a price ranging from $5 to $10. John Irwin, who fell in a well as a child "and who stayed a child," was treated with kindness by all the people. Mike Hickman published a little weekly newspaper, and his father preached at the Methodist Church. Bill Mickle ran a poolroom and refreshment parlor called, locally, the Honky Tonk.[2]

Bill Murray made a reputation among the Chickasaws as an attorney who could get results in court. He defended Gray, a little man who was accused of assault with a dangerous weapon, a fence rail. The plaintiff was a large man and Murray won his case by posing the little man with the fence rail upraised in front of the big one. The jury decided it was ridiculous to suppose that a fence rail was a dangerous weapon in the hands of a man as small as Gray. An Indian charged with killing a white man who was courting his daughter, had a case so weak that the attorney decided upon a plea of insanity. The jury, however, declared the Indian father "sane but innocent."

Bill Murray was employed to rewrite the Chickasaw statutes, to meet the supercilious criticism of Ethan A. Hitchcock, secretary of the interior. "I am returning certain papers, purporting to be bills," wrote Hitchcock, and the implied rebuke for Chickasaw

[2] *Ibid.,* 112.

usages in lawmaking wounded Governor Douglas H. Johnston deeply. Murray rephrased the statutes and at the same time studied the Chickasaw tax system, with the result that he was able to suggest certain measures for equitable distribution of taxes.[3] During this time his law practice was steadily growing, and he began to receive lucrative fees. One fourth was a customary payment in the settlement of land-title and citizenship cases. Early in his practice at Tishomingo, one of his land settlement cases brought a fee of $7,500. For defending a gang of cattle thieves, he received only a broncho, Bullet.

In 1905, Bill Murray represented the Chickasaws in the Sequoyah convention at Muskogee, where he was elected one of the five vice-presidents. In 1906 he became president of the Constitutional Convention at Guthrie. He served as speaker of the state house of representatives and in 1912 and 1914 was elected to represent his district in Congress. In the primary election of 1918 he was defeated by J. B. A. Robertson as Democratic candidate for governor.

He traveled in Latin American countries and formed the plan of leading a band of agricultural colonists to Bolivia. The project was organized, and Murray's neighbors at Tishomingo held a farewell party for him on May 3, 1924. After five years he returned to Oklahoma. The colony was not an unqualified success, and great differences of opinion have been expressed in regard to the blame for its failure.[4]

William H. Murray returned to Tishomingo at a fortunate time for his political ambitions. As noted above, he displayed skill in his campaign against Frank Buttram for nomination, and in the later race against Ira Hill for the governorship. The homespun manners of the small-town lawyer appealed to many voters of Oklahoma who sprang from pioneer stock. His attack on wealth was pleasing to liberals, his defense of business enterprise calmed the fears of capital, and his broadsides against monopolists struck a welcome note in many quarters. He combined the effective methods of the experienced politician with a sincere interest in his

---

[3] *Ibid.,* 132, 133.
[4] *Ibid.,* 248–61. Hines is a friendly critic who gives Murray a great deal of credit for his efforts in the Bolivian colony.

fellow citizens, and he displayed no small ability as a manager of political forces.

A short selection from one of his speeches will serve to illustrate his style: "I've been called a radical. Mr. Webster says that radical means 'proceeding from the root or foundation; essential, fundamental.' If that's what my critics mean, I'm complimented. I'm not an extremist. I believe firmly in our capitalistic plan—if capitalism can be forced to restrain its ungodly greed and to serve the needs of humanity. But I do despise the wicked machinations of the monopolists who believe the masses should . . . starve in a land of plenty while their hefty carcasses smother in their own fat."

His announcement for the governorship in 1930 had been met with "tolerant amusement" by Oklahoma newspapers.[5] He had borrowed forty dollars at a Tishomingo bank in order to finance his economical campaign, during which he regularly lunched on cheese and crackers, carried with him in a paper bag. A cheese manufacturer, sensing the publicity value of the gesture, made him a present of a large cake of cheese. Most newspapers took a stand against him, and a part of the press resorted to tactics intended to make him ridiculous in the public view. A woman columnist wrote that he dressed in "two pairs of pants in cold weather and dirty underwear." With similar coarseness but keener sense of amusement value, Bill answered, "How'd she know? I stay in an Oklahoma City hotel once in a while—but I sleep alone. Maybe she works in a hotel laundry."

Sam Hawks, Murray's campaign manager, purchased the *Blue Valley Farmer* at a bargain and moved it from Roff to Oklahoma City. Advertising helped to pay expenses of the little paper, and it became a major factor in the political campaign.

In it Bill Murray appealed to the "common folks" for a majority of 100,000 and they came close to giving it to him. As governor he advocated rigid economy, the establishment of a tax commission, and equalization of tax assessments. He set forth a program which included substantial increase in the gasoline tax and the gross-production tax, revision of the inheritance tax, a new corporation license tax, an increased income tax, free textbooks in the elementary grades, and a budget reform that would increase the authority of the chief executive in directing state finances.

362

The Thirteenth Legislature was organized with W. G. Stigler as president pro tempore of the senate and Carlton Weaver of Wilburton, as speaker of the house of representatives.[6] The deficit had grown from $2,000,000 at the beginning of Governor Holloway's administration to about $5,000,000 in 1931. It was necessary for Murray's aides to find a market for $6,000,000 in state warrants. Generally, the new house of representatives was in agreement with the Governor's program, while the senate was more inclined to bargain, particularly in regard to executive appointments; but Murray was no novice to be dominated by men of little political weight. In an angry session with a senate committee, he gave its members his view concerning separation of legislative and executive powers.

A tax commission was created and the Governor appointed Melvin Cornish chairman. The equalization board was authorized to conduct hearings on tax assessments, and the new tax commission had the function of supervising valuation of property. One result of Murray's efforts to equalize the tax burden in Oklahoma was reduction of small home owners' valuations by $141,000,000 and increase of corporation property values by $65,000,000.[7]

The corporation license tax brought in new revenues of about $800,000, and the tax on corporation incomes added another substantial amount. Confronted with the argument that business would be driven out of Oklahoma, Governor Murray answered, "Well, I guess they won't take any oil wells . . . out of the state." The new motor-fuel and gasoline tax resulted in revenues of about $2,000,000. Thus, the legislature gave limited support to one of the two major promises of Murray's campaign. He had given assurance that he would try to equalize the tax burden and to cut down total costs of government.

On the question of appropriations there was a sharp clash between the Governor and senate leaders. Threatened with impeachment, Murray told the senators: "I've heard about your threats. I've even been reminded that Jim Ferguson was impeached in Texas for vetoing a university appropriation bill. You fellows go

[5] *Ibid.*, 271, 272.
[6] *Directory of the State of Oklahoma*, 130, 144.
[7] Hines, *Alfalfa Bill*, 283.

ahead and pass these appropriations as you have them outlined and I'll veto every damned one of them. And if you've got any impeachment ideas in your heads, hop to it. It'll be like a bunch of jack-rabbits tryin' to get a wild cat out of a hole."[8]

Governor Murray accepted an invitation to deliver an address at a Lincoln's birthday banquet in Springfield, Illinois, on February 12, 1931. On that occasion his friends persuaded him to wear formal attire, which he did reluctantly, apparently with the feeling that it was a surrender of democratic principles. There were many listeners who thought his speech a good one for the occasion.

In spite of a federal court injunction obtained by toll-bridge operators at Red River crossings, Governor Murray succeeded in opening the free bridge between Denison, Texas and Durant, Oklahoma. Governor Ross Sterling of Texas, under authority of a ruling by Texas courts, proposed to barricade the Texas free-bridge entrance and to guard it with rangers. Murray called out an Oklahoma National Guard unit, ordered it to the bridge on U. S. Highway 69, claimed control of both ends of the structure, and opened it to traffic on July 25, 1931.

Governor Murray called the National Guard into service again as a means of stopping oil production. Prices of all commodities were in a serious slump. The enormous volume of oil produced by the East Texas field and other new supplies had forced the price of crude oil below fifteen cents a barrel. Oklahoma revenues, with strong reliance on the gross-production tax, were sharply reduced. Nine states had joined in organizing the Oil States Advisory Committee, which selected as its chairman Cicero Murray, a distant relative of the Governor. William H. Murray advised oil producers to set a price of one dollar per barrel; but some of the companies were interested in filling their tanks with low-priced oil and their officers would not voluntarily curb production. Under authority of the Oklahoma proration act, the Governor declared that an emergency existed, placed the state under martial law and used troops to close down the wells on August 4, 1931. Governor Sterling of Texas also employed National Guard units to stop production in the East Texas fields, and the results of combined action in the two states were gratifying. By November 1 the price had gone up to

[8] *Ibid.*, 285.

eighty-three cents a barrel and soon afterward reached one dollar.[9]

The legislature neglected a part of Governor Murray's proposed reforms. Free textbooks—enacted and repealed by former legislatures—new income taxes, and executive control of the budget were not enacted into law. Another measure advocated by Governor Murray was escheat of corporation land to the state. When these proposals were carried to the people by initiated measures, they were all voted down. Reduced appropriations for state institutions, reduced salaries for state employees, and other items of Murray's economy program had proved unpopular, although as campaign promises they had been acceptable to the voters.

The state elections of 1932 reflected the Governor's declining political strength.[10] Forty house members were avowed opponents of Murray's policies. His followers numbered a few more but did not constitute a clear majority. About twenty who regarded themselves as independents held a balance of power in the house. The senate was still inclined to oppose major plans of the administration, although Murray did succeed in making one important compromise with them.

The Governor had been in sharp conflict with Lew Wentz, appointed by Governor Holloway as chairman of the state highway commission. Under the law creating a three-man commission, Murray found that he could not dismiss Wentz. By giving the senate more authority in highway policies, the Governor obtained a reorganization of the commission, with four members and a new chairman.

In the national elections of 1932, Oklahoma voted for Franklin D. Roosevelt and John N. Garner over Herbert Hoover and Charles Curtis by an overwhelming majority. The vote was 516,468 for Roosevelt to 188,165 for Hoover. In the United States Senate race, Elmer Thomas was a candidate for re-election. In the second primary he won the nomination over Gomer Smith of Oklahoma City, and in November defeated the Republican candidate, Wirt Franklin.[11] E. W. Marland ran for Congress as a Democrat in the "Repub-

[9] *Ibid.*, 294–96.

[10] *Daily Oklahoman, November* 9, 10, 13, 1932.

[11] *Daily Oklahoman,* November 9, 10, 13, 1932; *Directory of the State of Oklahoma,* 52, 54.

365

lican" Eighth District and won over the incumbent, Milton Garber of Enid.[12] John C. Walton, still eager to serve in public office, ran for a place in the corporation commission and was elected.

The stature of William H. Murray in Oklahoma is a subject on which there will always be disagreement. To some observers, his manners were offensive; to others they were of no consequence, trivial details of a rugged frontier character. He was lacking in polish, deficient in education for the chief executive post in a modern state, opinionated, and overconfident. But he had courage, intellectual power, and constructive ability as a party leader. He put a solid floor under Oklahoma economy, reversed the low trend of crude-oil prices, and gave common citizens the advantages of more equitable taxation. He broke the Oklahoma legislature of the bad habit of impeaching political nonconformists, a habit which might develop, in the hands of incompetent men, toward complete subjection of the executive power to factional combinations of the house and senate. Impeachment of Governor Robertson by the Eighth Legislature, discussed but not effected, was preposterous; impeachment of Jack Walton by the Ninth was inevitable and probably the best solution for a bad situation; attempts to impeach Henry S. Johnston by the Eleventh and his impeachment by the Twelfth were in the nature of political wrongs. The old gentleman would have been happier and the state better off if he had never been put up by political managers as a candidate for governor. His removal on the ground of incompetency was an admission by Oklahoma of failure to make a written constitution work effectively. But when the Thirteenth Legislature would have strengthened the precedent of impeaching governors who dared to disagree with them by an attack on Bill Murray, they met their match.

After three years of the nation's worst depression, Oklahoma had voted in 1932 almost three to one against President Hoover and his party. Both of Oklahoma's members in the United States Senate and all its members in the lower house of Congress were Democrats at the beginning of Franklin D. Roosevelt's first term as President. During the second half of William H. Murray's governorship, relief legislation of the New Deal had some effect in Oklahoma. Over

[12] John Joseph Mathews, *Life and Death of an Oilman: The Career of E. W. Marland*, 203–18.

ninety thousand persons received direct relief and a large number of work projects furnished employment for a great variety of laborers, office workers, and others. Schoolhouses, armories, municipal buildings, sidewalks, boulevards, and park improvements were constructed. The Civilian Conservation Corps began its great work of relief, conservation of natural resources, and social rehabilitation. It was inevitable, from the experimental nature of New Deal projects, that many errors should be made, both in the field of economics and in politics. By the time of state elections in 1934, Oklahoma Democrats included many citizens and a few leaders, including Governor Murray, who were not friendly to the New Deal.

For governor of Oklahoma in the election of 1934, Murray gave his support to Tom Anglin of Holdenville. Anglin was in accord with some Murray policies and an especially strong advocate of economy. On the other hand, he supported phases of the New Deal program with which Murray had gone out of his way to disagree. Probably most people regarded Murray as anti-New Deal, Anglin as middle-of-the-road, and Representative E. W. Marland as a full-fledged advocate of the New Deal. Anglin's well-known support of revised workmen's compensation laws, old age pensions, and exemption of homesteads from land taxes gave him powerful support among the common people. From the beginning of the campaign it was clear that Anglin and Marland were the outstanding Democratic candidates. There were other strong campaigners, however, including former Governor John C. Walton, Lieutenant Governor Robert Burns, Attorney General J. Berry King, and Gomer Smith.

Results of the Democratic primary election were as follows: E. W. Marland, 165,885; Tom Anglin, 101,689; J. C. Walton, 85,616—and the others in descending order. Under the primary law a second contest between Marland and Anglin was expected, but Anglin decided to withdraw and give Marland a clear field. The Republican primary named W. B. Pine of Okmulgee over Rex Craig and Ray Ferrell. Pine had served as United States Senator from 1925 to 1931. In the November election Marland won by a large majority, receiving 363,992 votes to 243,841 for Pine. Nearly 100,000 more voters went to the polls than in any previous election for governor of Oklahoma. Again the Democrats succeeded in electing all the members of Congress, with Philip Ferguson taking Marland's place in the Eighth District.

### ERNEST WHITWORTH MARLAND, TENTH GOVERNOR OF OKLAHOMA

The Ponca City oilman was a new kind of political figure in Oklahoma. Perhaps the contrast is greatest when he is considered by the side of William H. Murray, his predecessor. Certainly it would be hard to find two men more sharply different in personal characteristics than the ninth and tenth governors. Ernest Whitworth Marland was born to wealth and reared in a city where his father was a man of consequence.[13] He had nothing in his background to give him an understanding of pioneers like Murray, or rough, tough, gouging, biting, partisan fighters like Jack Walton.

Alfred Marland, Ernest's father, was a native of Scotland. He came to America in 1862 and enlisted in the Confederate Army to "aid Southern gentlemen fighting for their culture against hordes of Northern tradesmen." Apparently Alfred showed more talent as a tradesman than he did as a soldier, for the end of the war found him settled in Pittsburgh, where he set up a mill to manufacture flat metal bands, his own invention for binding cotton bales. He was elected to the Pennsylvania Legislature and served also for a period of twenty years in the Pittsburgh Select Council. His business ventures included extensive holdings in city real estate, with a large building project for steel-mill workers. According to the Marland tradition he rented these houses as cheaply as possible and sold them with the smallest margin of profit.[14] He built a fine twelve-room house in the part of Pittsburgh known as South Hills, and there his family grew up.

As a boy, Ernest Whitworth Marland was a dreamer with no interest in rough competitive sports common to the youth of his time. His biographer states that he was interested in playing mar-

---

13 *Ibid.*, Part I, "The Age of Freedom."
14 *Ibid.*, Part I.

bles "for keeps," however, and that he carried his winnings in a large bag, intent upon accumulating them but never counting his marbles. He attended private schools and the University of Michigan, where he received a law degree in 1893 at the age of nineteen.

After he grew up he showed a keen interest in promoting various business enterprises. He took risks, made large profits, and lost heavily in a variety of schemes for developing gas and oil properties in Ohio, West Virginia, and at Pittsburgh. In 1903 he married Mary Virginia Collins, a woman of superior intelligence and beauty who was employed as a court stenographer in Philadelphia.

Five years later he came to Oklahoma and considered the problem of developing oil and gas on Miller Brothers' 101 Ranch. This opportunity had come to Marland through his nephew Franklin Kenny, a young man of his own age who had lived in Alfred Marland's home at Pittsburgh. Ernest Marland and his brother-in-law, Sam Collins, took steps to finance the drilling venture on Miller Brothers' property. As a last resort Marland probably got a loan from his father in Pittsburgh and received small sums from former business associates. He struck oil and within a few years was directing a prosperous drilling and refining enterprise from his headquarters in Ponca City. His sister Charlotte came to live with Ernest and Virginia Marland. Alfred Marland came to visit his son and remained as a permanent guest in the household. The Ponca City home of the Marlands had numerous visitors and a rather large family. The oilman adopted little George Roberts and his sister Lydia in 1916.

The Marland Oil Company expanded steadily, and by 1920 the holdings of E. W. Marland were valued at $85,000,000. The new office building in Ponca City contained lecture rooms, recreation facilities, lockers and showers, and many other conveniences for employees. In a period of twelve years Marland became known as an employer with advanced ideas concerning relations of labor and business enterprise. Marland insisted that working men were entitled to more than a living wage. To insure sound national economy, he thought, the employer should pay not only a living wage "but a saving wage."[15]

"There are three interested parties in every industrial dispute,"

[15] *Ibid.*, 138, 139.

369

Marland said: "labor, the employer, and the public. Some may think industrial progress depends upon the activity of labor leaders and the strength of the union; others may think that such progress depends upon the enterprise and cunning of the employer. There is ample evidence in our industrial history to justify the belief that sound progress depends upon neither of these two great forces, but rather upon public opinion, which demands that both forces pull in the same direction and in the interest of the community."[16]

In this sage and penetrating observation he was paraphrasing, consciously or unconsciously, the words of the late Theodore Roosevelt.

The liberality of E. W. Marland extended to other interests besides his employees. He supported local charities and a Mississippi plantation which he turned over to the 250 families that performed its labor.[17] He also gave large sums to political campaign funds. In 1920 he contributed to Warren G. Harding's campaign for president, although Marland described himself as an Oklahoma Democrat. With associates from *Roxana* and *Dutch Shell* oil companies, he gave $73,000 to the Democratic state campaign fund in 1922 and later contributed to Jack Walton's personal expenses in the campaign, although Marland had been opposed to Walton's election in the primary and had no personal liking for the political adventurer. Later, since there was no official governor's mansion in this period, Walton needed a place of residence near the Capitol. He purchased one for $48,000 from Walter D. Caldwell, paying $18,000 in cash and giving a note for $30,000, which was purchased by E. W. Marland. This transaction became a subject for investigation during Walton's impeachment trial, since Marland had large transactions in oil leases with the School Land Commission, of which the Governor was ex-officio chairman.[18] Marland explained his purchase of the notes simply as a business transaction. He received 5 per cent on the loan, and at the same time had the satisfaction of seeing that Oklahoma's governor lived in a decent house, he said.

At the greatest extent of his holdings with oil properties in

16 *Ibid.*, 139.
17 *Ibid.*, 177–84.
18 *Ibid.*, 140, 141, 142.

West Texas, at Seal Beach in California, in New Mexico, Mexico, and elsewhere, Marland found it necessary to travel widely. He used his private car when the journey was by rail and his yacht, the seagoing *Whitemarsh*, on water trips to New Orleans, Louisville, and along the Gulf Coast. He took an ocean liner when he visited London, which was quite often. Frequently he took parties of friends on his trips abroad, in addition to Mary Virginia and his adopted son and daughter, George and Lydia.

His desire for business expansion brought Marland into contact with Charles Sabin of the Guaranty Trust Company in New York, J. P. Morgan and George Whitney, partners in a powerful banking firm, and W. C. Potter, president of the Guaranty Trust Company. Beginning with a sale of stock amounting to $12,000,000 in 1923, the Marland Company eventually sold to Morgan and his associates 3,000,000 shares of stock at $30 a share and an option on 335,000 additional shares at $39, to run until February 10, 1925.[19] Marland's associates were much impressed by the resources of Morgan and his associates, and by a gradual process the New York financiers were permitted to gain control of the oil company. Marland was prevented from building a pipe line connecting his West Texas field with the Gulf Coast at a cost of $5,000,000 which would have saved him $3,000,000 a year in freight charges. Similarly, the new owners of majority stock in his company blocked all his efforts to construct pipe lines from Ponca City to Chicago and from southeastern New Mexico to the Gulf. That proposed line, had it been constructed, would have run through the East Texas field soon to be opened, which proved to be the greatest oil-producing area in the United States. The Santa Fe Railroad Company collected $1,013,060 in freight charges from Marland's Ponca City plant in 1921; his proposal to construct a railway line from Ponca City to Billings and a pipe line for gasoline to Chicago was protested by the Santa Fe, opposed by the Chicago, Rock Island, and Pacific (which had a line running through Enid, Blackwell, and Billings), and vetoed by the Interstate Commerce Commission.[20]

During 1927 and 1928, the Marland Company suffered heavy losses. Production in 1926 at Ponca City was 13,137,048 barrels of

[19] *Ibid.*, 165, 169.
[20] *Ibid.*, 146, 147.

crude oil, but at the end of the year 5,603,117 barrels had not been sold. Supply of oil was increasing faster than demand. Pressure was put upon Marland to cut expenses by reducing salaries, particularly of the young men who had been trained as executives in his methods.

D. J. Moran became president and general manager at Ponca City, and Marland resigned as chairman of the board. "The old Marland Oil Company was a thing of the past. The House of Morgan had merged it out of existence," said the Ponca City oilman, in regard to his experience with the New York banking firm.[21]

In 1929, Marland borrowed $850,000 in order to pay his income tax and used his home at Ponca City as security. At that time he was trying to recover $1,600,000 from the federal government as an income tax refund, but received less than one tenth of the amount he claimed after a suit that lasted four years. The Ponca City Oil Company, started by Marland in 1929 with the young executives from his former company as its principal officers, was born to misfortune. The great depression was beginning, and the price of Oklahoma oil was to descend until it reached a level of fifteen cents a barrel.

In 1931 the Marland estate at Ponca City was sold to satisfy the owner's debts. W. H. McFadden, an old business associate, bought the property with the expectation that Marland would recover his footing in business and redeem the estate. He was no more insolvent than he had been in 1908, when he first came to Oklahoma, and he had a host of friends, well-understood business connections, and vast experience in the production of oil. The depression was on, however, and E. W. Marland was twenty years older than the driving young oil promoter who had built the Ponca City plant when Oklahoma was a new state.

His election to Congress in 1932 was the beginning of a new career. He made his campaign without any loss of dignity. His private grudge against the "wolves of Wall Street" made good material for bridging the gap between Marland and the common man, in spite of his vagueness about the offences of those wealthy enemies of society. The Oklahoma voter was not clear on the subject either, and Marland was not asked to explain the distinction

[21] *Ibid.*, 197.

between his methods in building a little oil empire and Morgan's methods in building a great financial empire.

In Congress, Marland proposed to separate the buying and selling of securities for profit from the management of corporate organizations. His bill would have divorced J. P. Morgan and Company from Standard Oil, United States Steel, Humble Oil Company, and Conoco, with which Marland Oil Company was merged. He carried his grievances into the halls of Congress, but made little headway against the great capitalists who were financing oil production in Oklahoma.

The slogan for Marland's campaign for the governorship of Oklahoma, "Elect me and bring the New Deal to Oklahoma," showed a keener sense of political values in 1934 than that of "Alfalfa Bill" Murray.

As governor, Marland proposed an extensive four-year program of reform. He wanted a planning board of fifteen members, a highway commission of three, and a flood-control board of three. He asked for a state highway patrol, extension of the classified civil service, and a tenure law for teachers. State indebtedness in 1935 was $20,000,000, and it was Governor Marland's purpose to pay it off at the rate of $2,500,000 a year, meeting deficiency warrants by means of short-term notes. He asked for a severance tax of two cents a barrel on petroleum, two cents per one thousand cubic feet on natural gas, and one cent a gallon on gasoline. He also asked the legislature to lay an increased weight of taxes on cigarettes, rentals, insurance premiums, inheritance, and incomes. He wanted an increase in property taxes for the benefit of destitute people. In general, he hoped to take schools out of politics, provide an equal educational opportunity for every child in the state, develop better housing facilities for the lowest income group, establish a pension for the aged, and attract new industries to Oklahoma.

The Fifteenth Legislature passed a sales tax of 2 per cent for support of blind, dependent, and aged persons who were destitute. It raised the gross-production tax from 3 to 5 per cent and passed a homestead exemption act, based on the constitutional amendment of 1935, which gave the legislature authority to set the amount exempted from ad valorem tax, above a minimum limit of $500. At Marland's request the legislature also provided for a state

373

highway patrol, a planning board, and state aid to weak schools in the amount of $8,200,000.

Governor Marland used his influence for establishment of the Interstate Oil Compact Commission, which was devoted to the conservation of oil and gas and stabilization of prices. Governor Allred of Texas and Alfred M. Landon of Kansas were opposed to control of production, on principle; but Harold Ickes of the Interior Department was suggesting the necessity of federal control, and the governors disliked state restriction less than the exercise of authority from Washington. As a matter of choice, Marland succeeded in committing these men to a policy of state control of production. He was the first chairman of the Interstate Commission, and under his leadership six states ratified its conservation compact. By 1947 the number of member states had grown to nineteen.

In the national elections of 1936 the Democratic candidate, Franklin D. Roosevelt, was elected over Alfred M. Landon by the largest electoral vote in the history of the United States and by a popular majority of 10,797,090, also the largest in the nation's history.[22] Oklahoma voted more than two to one for Roosevelt and gave the administration further support by electing a full slate of Democratic congressmen. Josh Lee of Norman, who had served one term in the House of Representatives, won Thomas P. Gore's seat in the United States Senate, defeating the Republican candidate, Herbert K. Hyde, by a vote of 493,407 to 229,004.

The Sixteenth Legislature devoted a great deal of attention to reorganization of the planning board and appropriated liberally to match federal grants-in-aid. Work on expansion of state parks and recreation centers, in a period of serious unemployment, served as a measure of relief for many workers and furnished demand for a variety of Oklahoma materials. This legislature also increased state aid for schools to $12,800,000 per year. In spite of powerful opposition to Governor Marland's tax program and economic depression which brought acute distress to thousands of citizens, the administration was a period of constructive achievement. In the

[22] Presidents George Washington and James Monroe in the early years of the Republic received electoral votes of larger per cent. From 132 electors, Washington received 132 votes. Monroe received 231 votes, to 1 in opposition. Franklin D. Roosevelt's electoral vote in 1936 was 523 to 8 for Governor Landon.

Fifteenth Legislature, Speaker Leon Phillips of the house and President Pro Tempore Claud Briggs of the senate were outspoken leaders against increased taxes. In the Sixteenth Legislature the Governor's influence was strong enough to get J. T. Daniel elected over Phillips and A. G. Nichols over Briggs. The press and a large part of the public, however, along with the legislature, refused full support for Marland's tax proposals during his entire term of office.

Marland had an ambition to return to Washington as a senator from Oklahoma. He made his bid for the seat vacated by Senator Gore in the election of 1936 and for Senator Elmer Thomas's place in 1938. In each case President Roosevelt gave his support to the man who beat Marland—in 1936 to Josh Lee, who won over the governor in a second primary, and in 1938 to the incumbent, Elmer Thomas. Marland was offered by the chief executive a place in the Civil Aeronautics Authority, which he declined.

In addition to Senator Thomas, the Democrats elected all the members of the lower house from Oklahoma in 1938. The men elected to Congress were Wesley E. Disney of Tulsa, Jed Johnson of Anadarko, Sam Massingale of Cordell, Lyle H. Boren of Seminole, Phil Ferguson of Woodward, Jack Nichols of Eufaula, Wilburn Cartwright of McAlester, Mike Monroney of Oklahoma City; and as representative-at-large, Will Rogers of Oklahoma City.

At the time of this election Governor Marland was adding to the strong tide of opposition that had developed against him. With approval of the pardon and parole board, he paroled Philip Kennamer from the penitentiary for a period of six months. The prisoner was the son of Federal Judge Franklin E. Kennamer and had been sentenced in 1935 to twenty-five years in the state penitentiary for killing another youth, the son of Dr. John Gorrell of Tulsa. Members of the parole board who signed the petition for his release included the chairman, Jim Hatcher, Clarence E. Page, Charles Knight, C. A. Schweinlie, and Robert S. Kerr. Bitterly opposed to the parole were Dixie Gilmer, Tulsa County attorney, and Fred Cunningham, parole board attorney. Dr. John Gorrell, called before the board by Dixie Gilmer, protested the freeing of young Kennamer. Governor Marland, after some hesitation, ordered a sanity examination for the prisoner and when he was pronounced sane, granted the parole. Oklahoma citizens, perhaps oversensitive on the subject of pardons and paroles because of Governor Walton's record, received the news of Kennamer's release with bitter hostility. In his protest against clemency, Dixie Gilmer had not failed to emphasize the need of equal justice to all.[23]

Governor Marland also took a stand for modified federal control of oil and gas production. He thought the amount allowed for each state should be set by Congress. Each state, in turn, should maintain control of actual production through its own governing body.[24] This new position of a former oilman was not popular in Oklahoma and it gave his opponents a convenient point of attack.

E. W. Marland's rise and decline in Oklahoma politics are not to be explained by rational judgment of the voters. He made an earnest effort for better schools, efficiency in handling state finances, humane provision for aged citizens, rehabilitation for all handicapped persons, and planning for the best use of the state's resources. When Marland was accused of being inconsistent he admitted the charge. It was pointed out to him that he had tried to organize an oil company powerful enough to challenge the greatest competitors and then as a member of Congress had proposed restrictions upon the management of oil production. As an independent producer he had defended free enterprise and then had helped to organize the Interstate Oil Compact. "I'm governor of the state," he answered his critic. "I'm not an oilman any more."[25]

In spite of his penetrating analysis of major trends in politics, Governor Marland was not always a skilled politician. That was to be expected since he had not devoted many years to the practice of campaigning, compromising, yielding at one point in order to gain an advantage in another quarter. The great energy of his life had been spent in building his private enterprise, the Marland Oil Company. If he had plunged into politics in 1908 instead of 1932 he would have understood the game better. As congressman and governor, he was not an effective public speaker; his audiences did not feel the dynamic, convincing power that had made him a successful oil promoter; his leadership did not inspire people. He never quite grasped the essential differences between managing an oil

23 *Daily Oklahoman,* November 1, 1938.
24 *Daily Oklahoman,* November 13, 1938.
25 Mathews, *Life and Death of an Oilman,* 241, 242.

company and directing the activities of a political party; but he left a deep impression upon the public affairs of his adopted state. Many of his reforms were permanent improvements.

## THE ELEVENTH GOVERNOR OF OKLAHOMA

Leon C. Phillips was born in Missouri in 1890 and came to Oklahoma Territory at an early age. He attended public schools, studied for the ministry at Epworth University and for law practice at the University of Oklahoma. He served in the army against Germany, and in 1918 returned to practice law in Okemah. In 1932 he was elected to the lower house of the legislature from Okfuskee County, was re-elected in 1934 and 1936, and served as speaker in the Fifteenth Legislature (1935-37).[26]

Phillips made economy the theme of his campaign for the governorship, as he had done in his race for the legislature. Economy had a powerful appeal for the voters during the depression, particularly in the term of E. W. Marland, who was a "spending governor." Nine candidates for governor entered the Democratic primary election, and five of them received substantial backing: Leon C. Phillips, 179,139; W. S. Key, 176,034; William H. Murray, 148,395; Jack Walton, 45,760; and Ira M. Finley, 37,107. It was pointed out by Democrats who opposed the winner that he was nominated by about 30 per cent of the voters who took part in the election, with no opportunity for a runoff election between Phillips and Key. Withdrawal of the fourth and fifth names in the primary, or either of them, probably would have changed the entire complexion of the contest and might well have reversed the choice. Certainly, a runoff primary would have been more satisfactory to the supporters of Key, Murray, Walton, and Finley; and the results of the general election seem to justify the criticism of the method used in nominating Phillips.

In November, the Republican candidate, Ross Rizley, received nearly 100,000 more votes than the entire number of registered

[26] *Directory of the State of Oklahoma,* 144. A brief biography of Governor-elect Phillips appeared in the *Daily Oklahoman* in November, 1938.

Republican voters in the primary election.[27] The results seem to indicate that a large number of Democrats voted for the Republican candidate, and a considerable number neglected to cast ballots at all, rather than cast them for their party's choice. Phillips received 355,740 votes to 148,861 for Rizley. The total ballots cast was not unusually light, but the winner did receive fewer than the number of Democrats who voted in the primary, by 240,000.

Between election and inauguration Phillips repeated his plea for economy and a balanced budget, along with other recommendations which would have a tendency, however, toward defeat of the major aims of his campaign program. A *Daily Oklahoman* headline gave one version of his attitude: "Governor-elect warns state jobholders to avoid deficits or write their resignations."[28] The new governor proposed to the Seventeenth Legislature, however, larger expenditures for farm-to-market roads, co-operation with the federal relief program, and aid for weak schools, all of which were seriously needed in Oklahoma. This legislature and the one which followed it increased the tax on tobacco, raised the gasoline tax to five cents a gallon, the cigarette tax from three cents to five cents a package, and changed the state highway commission from four to three members. Other executive boards were reorganized, including the tax commission and the Grand River Dam Authority. State aid for elementary schools was reduced from $12,800,000 to $11,500,000, per year.

Early in the Phillips administration the legislature passed a law providing for a council of twenty-five members—ten senators and fifteen representatives—to meet between sessions, compile information relative to current problems, study the operation of executive agencies, and plan legislation for the following session. In theory, this legislative council was to provide continuing organization with quarterly meetings and its program might be accepted or rejected. Nine states had previously established such a council, beginning with Kansas in 1933 and including Michigan, Virginia, Kentucky, Nebraska, Illinois, Connecticut, Rhode Island, and Maryland. Wisconsin and some other states had tried similar devices for increasing legislative efficiency.[29] In Oklahoma, as in

27 *Directory of the State of Oklahoma,* 38, 39, 41.
28 *Daily Oklahoman,* November 13, 1938.

some other states, the experiment suffered at first for want of financial support.

In the national election of 1940, Oklahoma was carried by Franklin D. Roosevelt and Henry A. Wallace over Wendell Willkie and Charles McNary, by a vote of 474,313 to 348,872.[30] The war against Nazi Germany, creating an abnormal demand for American goods, had broken the hold of the great depression; and Oklahoma again saw rising prices and a higher per cent of employment. The Democrats elected their candidate as representative-at-large and seven other members of the national House of Representatives. In the Eighth District Ross Rizley defeated the Democratic candidate, Phil Ferguson, by a vote of 48,738 to 41,417.[31] Representative Sam Massingale of Cordell died in January, 1941; and Victor Wickersham, of Mangum, was elected to his seat in the House of Representatives.

The second world war within a single generation had arisen out of the aggression of Adolph Hitler's Germany, between 1936 and 1939. The entrance of Japan into the conflict and involvement of the United States came at the end of 1941. Thus, the last year of Leon C. Phillips' term as governor found the United States again engaged in foreign war. At the beginning of his law practice, military duties had changed Phillips' personal plans and perhaps completely altered the pattern of his life; and at the end of his term as governor, political events in Oklahoma were dominated by the state's part in the great war machine. Mobilization of troops and production of war materials—petroleum, coal, lead, zinc, food supplies, cotton, and many other products—became the chief objectives of citizens and officials. The emphasis on economy, declining gradually as business and employment recovered, disappeared entirely with the coming of war.

President Franklin D. Roosevelt's appeal on December 8, 1941, the day after Pearl Harbor, for unity in the effort to defeat

[29] Frederic H. Guild, "The Development of the Legislative Council Idea," *Annals of the American Academy of Political and Social Science*, Vol. CXCV (January, 1938), 146.

[30] *Directory of the State of Oklahoma*, 34.

[31] *Ibid.*, 35. In districts one to seven, the Democratic candidates elected to Congress were Wesley E. Disney, Jack Nichols, Wilburn Cartwright, Lyle H. Boren, Mike Monroney, Jed Johnson, and Sam Massingale.

Hitler and his allies, found enthusiastic response throughout the nation. As in the first world war, Oklahoma took a creditable part. The numerical strength of the United States Army grew from 500,000 at the end of October, 1940, to 8,000,000 at the end of December, 1944. The Navy personnel, including the Naval Reserve, had reached approximately 3,000,000 by 1945. Enlistments in the army during the period of four years and two months totaled 9,957,693. Of that number Oklahoma supplied 144,533 in addition to approximately 60,000 enlistments in the Naval Reserve and 7,500 in the Marine Corps.

A large number of military and naval training bases were established in Oklahoma. Fort Sill, already famous for its Artillery School of Fire, continued the tradition and developed the greatest of all the schools for training soldiers in that branch of warfare. Twenty-eight army camps and thirteen naval bases were established in the state, as a part of the enormous training program provided by the nation for giving technical instruction that has become necessary in modern warfare. Convenience in transportation, central location, and a large per cent of flying weather were advantages possessed by Oklahoma in the location of these training bases. Tinker Air Field at Oklahoma City, Will Rogers Field at the same place, large naval air stations at Clinton and Norman, a naval hospital at Norman, and the air training centers at Miami and Ponca City were among the important establishments for the armed forces.

State colleges of Oklahoma were active in the technical training of soldiers and sailors. College classrooms were filled, too, with young men in uniform who were looking forward to a future of peace and were utilizing such time as the army or navy allowed them for studying English, government, economics, history, and other subjects of the liberal arts curriculum.

In addition to its common soldiers and sailors, Oklahoma supplied many officers of various ranks in all branches of the armed forces. Veterans like Major General William S. Key, who commanded the Oklahoma National Guard, were soon joined by many young officers who, under the pressure of war conditions, rose rapidly in rank. Ira C. Eaker, Lucian K. Truscott, Jr., and Raymond S. McClain held the rank of lieutenant general at the end of the war. Major General Clarence L. Tinker, for whom the air base at Oklahoma City was named, was an Osage Indian who was killed in a bombing raid against the Japanese over the Pacific. Patrick J. Hurley, who had been secretary of war under President Herbert Hoover, also became a major general.

Mark A. Mitscher of Oklahoma City received an appointment as admiral in the United States Navy on March 21, 1944. At the end of the war two Oklahomans, J. J. Clark of Pryor and A. S. Soucek of Medford, had achieved the rank of rear admiral. Many other men and women of the armed forces had gained distinction in rank, citations, or other forms of recognition for unique service, to continue Oklahoma's tradition for outstanding performance in national defence.

As in the first world war, civilian organization played a large part in the national unity that made the war effort effective. Organization for the sale of war bonds and war saving stamps, the U S O (United Service Organizations), the American Red Cross, and many other groups helped directly or indirectly in financing the war and keeping up the morale of civilians and men and women of the army, navy, and marine corps.

State elections in 1942 included the executive and legislative officers, three justices of the state supreme court, and one judge of the criminal court of appeals. Josh Lee was about to complete his term in the United States Senate and was a candidate for re-election. As a result of apportionment for the House of Representatives following the United States census of 1940, Oklahoma was entitled to eight congressmen instead of nine, which had been its quota since the election of 1932. In the United States Senate race the Republicans showed unexpected strength by electing E. H. Moore, millionaire oilman of Tulsa, over Josh Lee by a vote of 204,163 to 166,653. Senator Lee had received 20,000 more votes in the Democratic primary election, held on July 14, than he received in the November election.[32] He did not campaign actively, and his principal rivals in the primary, Orel Busby and William H. Murray, apparently did little to promote party unity. The Democrats succeeded in electing seven of the eight congressmen, losing only in the Eighth District, where Ross Rizley was elected for his second term.

[32] *Ibid.*, 31, 32, 33, 34.

The Democrats also elected an overwhelming majority in the state house of representatives and forty of forty-four state senators. In the judicial branch the Democrats elected Bert Barefoot for his second six-year term as judge of the criminal court of appeals, and for the supreme court elected Wayne W. Bayless, Thurman S. Hurst, and Fletcher S. Riley. This was justice Riley's fourth election to the Oklahoma high court.[33]

Seven candidates made the race for governor in the Democratic primary, and thirteen candidates sought nomination as lieutenant governor. Robert S. Kerr, Gomer Smith, and Frank Douglas were the leading candidates for governor, and Kerr won the nomination with a vote of 147,169. The combined vote of his six opponents was 100,000 more; but with no runoff primary provided by law, he became the candidate of his party. In a listless primary election the Republicans chose William J. Otjen to make the race against Kerr. For lieutenant governor the Democrats named James E. Berry of Stillwater, and the Republicans chose Harry E. Ingram.

Again the Republicans displayed unexpected vigor in the general election on November 3. Final results gave Robert S. Kerr, 196,565 to 180,454 for William J. Otjen.[34] The entire number of votes cast for governor in this election, for candidates of both parties, was approximately equal to the vote for E. W. Marland alone in 1934, and a quarter of a million under the total vote in that election. Absence of men in the armed forces of the United States accounts in part for the shortage of voters in 1942; perhaps, too, there was some loss of confidence among common people because of mediocre leadership in the Seventeenth Legislature and in the chief executive office.

[33] *Ibid.*, 31, 32, 132, 133, 148–51.
[34] *Ibid.*, 31.

# CHAPTER SIXTEEN

# Politics and Economics at Mid-Century, 1943-1953

## THE ADMINISTRATION OF ROBERT S. KERR

Robert Samuel Kerr was born near Ada, Indian Territory, on September 11, 1896. He was the twelfth governor of the state and the first who was born in Oklahoma. His grandfather was killed by Quantrill's raiders during the Civil War in Missouri, and Robert's father, W. S. Kerr, left the state at the age of seventeen. Apparently his reason for leaving Missouri was to avoid contact, after the war years, with men who were his avowed enemies and determined to kill or be killed. The young emigrant went to Ellis County, Texas, where he worked as a share-cropper, raised cotton, and married.

From Texas he moved to Ada in the Chickasaw Nation, built a log cabin, and farmed 160 acres of land. As his family grew up, W. S. Kerr tried various occupations—ranching, teaching in a rural school, retailing goods, and cotton-buying. The log cabin where Robert was born is still standing. Robert attended public school in Ada, the East Central State Normal School, Oklahoma Baptist University at Shawnee for a year, and the University of Oklahoma Law School for a year. He continued the study of law in the office of B. Robert Elliott at Webb City, Missouri. He entered military service in 1917 and emerged from the war a second lieutenant of field artillery.

After the war he entered the produce business at Ada and had the misfortune to lose a warehouse by fire. Other reverses were to follow. Six years after he returned from France as a young military officer his business ventures had lost money steadily and his debts amounted to $10,000. He had also lost his wife.[1]

[1] Accounts of Robert S. Kerr's life have appeared in *Current Biography*; Mar-

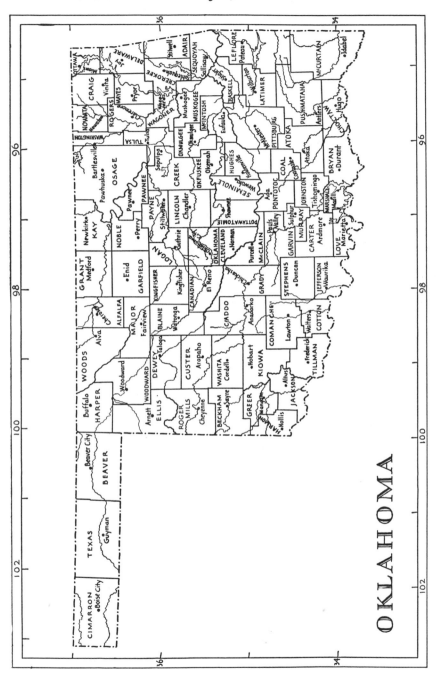

In 1925 Kerr was elected American Legion commander for Oklahoma. He took a second wife, Grayce Breene of Tulsa, and worked as an attorney for her brother who was engaged in oil drilling. He entered the oil business in a small way, became a partner in the Kerr-McGee Oil Company, and prospered. In the course of years his holdings grew to extensive properties in Oklahoma, Texas, Wyoming, and the Louisiana tidelands.[2] His law practice was successful also, and in 1930 he moved from Ada to Oklahoma City.

Since the United States was in the midst of a great war when Kerr became governor, his first two years in office were shaped largely by war needs. He was an ardent supporter of Franklin D. Roosevelt's foreign policies, and he proved to be a strong executive in carrying out the complicated war program in Oklahoma. Almost without experience in politics when he became governor in 1943, he showed aptitude and a growing interest in the give and take of party contests. In the course of his campaigns he admitted that his oil properties had reached a value of $10,000,000, but seemed to take more pride in his frontier background, particularly the fact that he was born in a log cabin, than in his business success. He was an effective public speaker, not perhaps with the polished oratory of Josh Lee, but with a hearty manner, good nature that was hard to resist, and a keen sense of humor.

Governor Kerr advocated reform measures in three fields: education, pardon and parole, and state finances. He wanted a fundamental change in the status of University of Oklahoma regents and the regents of the Oklahoma agricultural and mechanical colleges. For school districts that were unable to maintain a term of nine months, he proposed additional state aid. He advocated a revision of the pardon and parole regulations, in line with the best state laws on the subject. Finally, he was in favor of measures to reduce the bonded indebtedness of the state.

Constitutional amendments adopted by the voters provided

---

quis W. Childs, "The Big Boom from Oklahoma," *Saturday Evening Post,* Vol. CCXXI, No. 41 (April 9, 1949), 22–23, 118–20; and Robert T. Elson, "If Not Truman, Who?" *Life,* Vol. XXXII, No. 12 (March 24, 1952), 126–28.

[2] Elson, "If Not Truman, Who?" *Life,* Vol. XXXII, No. 12 (March 24, 1952), 126–28.

the type of control requested by the Governor for Oklahoma's largest schools, making the boards of regents constitutional instead of statutory. One amendment created a board of seven regents for the University of Oklahoma, with the provision that members in office should hold their places to the end of their current terms. The members were to be appointed by the governor with the advice and consent of the senate and were removable only for cause "as provided by law for elective officers not liable to impeachment."[3] Another amendment of the same date, July 11, 1944, created a board of regents for the agricultural schools and colleges of the state, with eight members appointed by the governor and removable only for cause as provided by law, and the ninth member, ex officio, president of the state board of agriculture.[4]

The seven-year terms and the restrictions upon removal seem to be adequate safeguards against frivolous party politics in the management of state schools and weird concepts of executive responsibility. Governor Jack Walton would have been far less dangerous if he had been controlled by a constitutional provision of this nature.

During the last year of Governor Kerr's administration the campaign for better common schools, in which he had the support of school officials and many other citizens, resulted in adoption of four amendments to the state constitution. One of these provided per capita aid at the minimum rate of $42 for each pupil in the elementary schools;[5] a second raised the maximum ad valorem levy from ten mills to fifteen mills in all districts voting for the higher tax;[6] a third amendment provided for an additional levy of one mill, in any county "upon certification of the need therefor by the governing board," for building separate schools for white and Negro children;[7] and the fourth established free textbooks for elementary school children.[8] Of these the third, recognizing the fact of racial segregation, was intended to remedy the general defect of inferior buildings in the Negro schools. Actually, the whole idea

[3] *Directory of the State of Oklahoma,* 172. Legislative Referendum No. 88.

[4] *Ibid.,* 172, Legislative Referendum No. 87.

[5] *Ibid.,* 173, Initiative Petition No. 225, November 5, 1946.

[6] *Ibid.,* 173, Initiative Petition No. 224, November 5, 1946.

[7] *Ibid.,* 173, Initiative Petition No. 226, November 5, 1946.

[8] *Ibid.,* 173, Initiative Petition No. 228, November 5, 1946.

of segregation has changed completely since the Supreme Court, on May 17, 1954, ruled that the principle of segregation in American public schools violates the Fourteenth Amendment of the federal Constitution.[9] Governor Kerr's administration, however, in its broad effects upon education in the state, was a period of outstanding progress.

The governor's plan in regard to tenure of office for members of the pardon and parole board was adopted. This measure required the chief executive to report all acts of clemency to the legislature and limited reprieves and leaves of absence to sixty days.[10] Governor Kerr's reform in state finances, adopted eighteen months after he took office, provided for placing accrued surplus of the state general revenue fund at the end of each month in the sinking fund "to be used solely to pay the state's bonded indebtedness." This measure gave his administration the advantage of sound economy in a period of general employment and good incomes. The debt of the state was reduced by $40,000,000 without neglect of current needs.[11]

Senate Bill No. 1 of the Nineteenth Legislature, re-establishing the runoff primary election for Oklahoma, was submitted to the people on July 11, 1944, and approved by a majority of 37,000.[12] The Twentieth Legislature revised the income tax law, permitting separate returns by husband and wife. This revision has the effect of lowering surtax assessments. Those who favored the law, including the Governor, argued that it had the advantage of increasing the charm of Oklahoma for persons in the higher income brackets.

In the national elections of 1944, with a considerable part of the state's eligible voters serving in the armed forces of the United States and absent from Oklahoma, the vote was light.[13] Franklin D. Roosevelt, running for a fourth term as president, received 401,549 votes in the state, to 319,424 for Thomas E. Dewey of New York.

[9] Article XIV, Amendments to the Constitution. Section I provides that "No State shall make or enforce any law which shall abridge the privileges or immunities of citizens of the United States."

[10] *Directory of the State of Oklahoma,* 172.

[11] Elson, "If Not Truman, Who?" *Life,* Vol. XXXII, No. 12 (March 24, 1952), 126–28.

[12] *Directory of the State of Oklahoma,* 172, Legislative Referendum No. 89.

[13] Oklahoma soldiers were permitted to send absentee ballots, but the number who thus cast their votes was relatively small.

Dewey thus polled 30,000 fewer votes than Wendell Willkie's ballots of 1940; but President Roosevelt received 70,000 fewer than his own vote in 1940. Elmer Thomas was re-elected to the United States Senate over his Republican opponent, William J. Otjen, by a vote of 390,851 to 309,222.[14] In the elections for congressmen, the Republicans re-elected Ross Rizley of Guymon in the Eighth District and added a new member, George B. Schwabe of Tulsa, in the First. The Democrats returned the other six members: W. G. Stigler of Stigler in the Second District, Paul Stewart of Antlers in the Third, Lyle H. Boren of Seminole in the Fourth, Mike Monroney of Oklahoma City in the Fifth, Jed Johnson of Anadarko in the Sixth, and Victor Wickersham of Mangum in the Seventh.[15]

In twenty general elections since the beginning of statehood in 1907, the Democrats had won 127 seats in the lower house of Congress, the Republicans, 29. Except in the northwestern part of the state (the Eighth District from 1914 to 1950), Republican candidates who won seats usually held narrow pluralities in the general election. Three Republicans had been elected to the United States Senate, each for a single term. No Republican candidate had been elected governor. Thus, the state was regarded normally Democratic in politics, but usually with strong Republican opposition and occasionally a major upset, such as the election of Senator J. W. Harreld in 1920, Senator E. H. Moore in 1942, and Senator W. B. Pine in 1924. Also the Republicans named Oklahoma's presidential electors in 1920 and 1928, a political phenomenon that was to be repeated in 1952.

In the state elections of 1946, nine entered the Democratic primary as candidates for governor. Four of them were strong contenders—Roy J. Turner, Dixie Gilmer, H. C. Jones, and William O. Coe. James E. Berry, running for his fourth term as lieutenant governor, had seven competitors in the primary. Turner and Gilmer led the field, and Turner won in the runoff by a majority of 25,000. The Republicans nominated Olney J. Flynn, the son of a well-known territorial delegate to Congress, Dennis Flynn. Nominated by a vote of 30,000 in the Republican primary election, Flynn showed surprising strength in the regular election. The final vote

[14] *Directory of the State of Oklahoma,* 28.
[15] *Ibid.,* 28.

was as follows: Turner, 259,491; Flynn, 227,426. James E. Berry won his fourth race for the office of lieutenant governor. Mickey Harrell, the first woman to try for the chief executive office in Oklahoma, ran as an independent and received over 7,000 votes.[16] Two Republicans were elected to Congress, George Schwabe of Tulsa for his second term, Ross Rizley of Guymon for his fourth. In the other districts the Democrats won by comfortable majorities except in the fifth, where Representative Mike Monroney was hard pressed to defeat Carmon C. Harris by a vote of 47,173 to 43,508.[17]

The twenty-first legislature had 7 Republicans in a membership of 44 in the senate and 22 Republicans in a membership of 118 in the house of representatives. C. R. Board of Cimarron County was elected speaker of the house and James C. Nance of Purcell, president pro tempore of the senate.[18]

## THE TURNER ADMINISTRATION, 1947–1951

Roy J. Turner was the second native Oklahoman to hold the office of governor. Born in Lincoln County in the third year after the opening of the Sac and Fox Reservation, he attended public school in Oklahoma Territory and graduated from Kendrick Highschool four years after Oklahoma became a state. A short period of study in Hill's Business College at Oklahoma City completed his formal schooling. In 1911 he began work as a bookkeeper for Morris Packing Company, and in 1916 served for a time as salesman for the Goodyear Rubber Company. He entered the army as a private soldier during World War I. He was a dealer in real estate, principally in Oklahoma, Florida, and Texas, and by 1928 had become an independent oil producer in the firm of Harper and Turner at Oklahoma City. In 1933 he established the Turner Ranch at Sulphur, mainly devoted to raising fine Hereford cattle. From 1939 to 1946 he served on the Oklahoma City Board of Education.

As a corollary of his economy program, Governor Turner

[16] *Ibid.,* 24.
[17] *Ibid.,* 25.
[18] *Ibid.,* 132, 133, 148–51.

worked for reduction of taxes. The state legislative council was in agreement with the governor on tax reduction, and the Twenty-first Legislature quickly passed the measure reducing income taxes. This legislature also effected the reorganization of several boards and commissions. The Oklahoma Planning and Resources Board was made up of five members appointed by the governor together with four ex officio members: Harold P. Hutton, president of the state board of agriculture; H. E. Bailey, director of the state highway commission; Kelly De Busk, director of the state game and fish commission; and Governor Turner. Clarence Burch of Norman was named chairman of the nine-man board.[19] The Oklahoma Tax Commission was reorganized with three members serving staggered terms of six years. The state highway commission was composed of eight members, one from each congressional district, under a salaried director. Governor Turner appointed H. E. Bailey of Oklahoma City as the first director of the reorganized board.

The state legislative council was composed of all members of both houses with Senator Bill Logan, of Lawton, chairman and Representative Walter Billingsley, of Wewoka, vice-chairman. Ten senators and fifteen representatives made up the executive committee. The legislative council began a study of the Oklahoma Public Welfare Commission, the Children's Code Commission, and the Crippled Children's Commission. The Public Welfare Commission in 1949, under the direction of Virgil Stokes, administered five divisions of social service—child welfare, aid for crippled children, old-age assistance, aid for the blind, and aid for dependent children. Funds for these services are derived in part from the federal government. The Twenty-first Legislature made some progress in the consolidation of rural schools.

In 1948, after serving as president of the United States following the death of Franklin D. Roosevelt on April 12, 1945, Harry S. Truman was his party's candidate for a full term. The Republicans chose Thomas E. Dewey of New York, their unsuccessful candidate against Roosevelt in 1944. Truman won the full term by an electoral vote of 303 to 189 for Dewey. President Truman had the support of important farming states of the Mississippi Valley, such as Illinois, Iowa, Missouri, and Wisconsin. He carried California with its 25

[19] *Ibid.*, 9–14.

electoral votes, Ohio with an equal number, and all states of the former Confederacy excepting South Carolina, Mississippi, Louisiana, and Alabama, which cast their votes for James S. Thurmond.[20]

Oklahoma voted for President Truman and his running mate, Alben W. Barkley of Kentucky, by the substantial margin of 452,782 votes to 268,817 for Thomas E. Dewey and Earl Warren. The state's total vote was light, as in 1944—short of the ballots cast in 1940 by nearly 100,000. Former Governor Robert S. Kerr, running for the United State Senate against the Republican member of Congress from the Eighth District, Ross Rizley, won by a decisive majority.

Kerr had adopted a platform style that made him an effective campaigner and gave him an acquaintance far beyond the state's borders. He had some ability in the making of epigrams, and his spontaneous humor appealed strongly to audiences. His campaign quips were widely quoted by radio speakers and others. When an opponent called attention to his wealth he replied, "I'm a millionaire now, but you should have seen me back in Hoover's day."

While he was governor he had made a wager with Dwight Griswold of Nebraska, a barrel of Oklahoma sorghum against a fat Nebraska hog, that Oklahoma would run ahead of Nebraska on a war-bond sales drive. He won the hog and of course brought much publicity to the sale of bonds, to Oklahoma, and to Robert S. Kerr. Upon the request of a Brooklyn family for a gallon of Oklahoma sorghum, he delivered the molasses in person—with resulting news stories in light and humorous vein. Because of his large scale advertising in political campaigns, his opponents began referring to him as "Billboard Bob." It was claimed that his primary campaign for the United States Senate seat cost $62,000 more than the $3,000 limit provided by law, but no legal charges grew out of the accusation.

Senator Kerr's religious activities appealed strongly to a large part of the voters in Oklahoma. A member of the Baptist Church, he took a vigorous part in the organization, teaching a Sunday School class and performing other active duties. On prohibition in Oklahoma, he was an ardent dry; and unlike some of the political enemies of liquor, he had the advantage of being a teetotaler.

[20] Tennessee cast one of its twelve electoral votes for Thurmond.

In the primary election of July 6, 1948, a measure was adopted by the voters creating a board of regents for the six state colleges, at Edmond, Ada, Weatherford, Alva, Tahlequah, and Durant, defining their duties, providing compensation, and effectively removing those colleges from the field of partisan politics.[21] In another legislative referendum the people approved a salary of $100 per month for members of the legislature, and "in lieu thereof," payment of $15 per day during regular and special sessions.[22] This progressive measure was passed by a very narrow majority of the voters. An initiative petition (No. 248) providing repeal of prohibition in Oklahoma was defeated by a majority of 55,000.

In the Democratic primary election of July 5, 1950, candidates for governor included Johnston Murray, son of former Governor William H. Murray, William O. Coe, Frank B. Douglas, and Philip Ferguson. Murray and Coe led the field and neither had a majority of all the votes cast. In the runoff, held on July 25, Murray was declared winner by a small margin after a bitter contest. Coe demanded a recount, and the result was a gain of 128 votes for Murray. The Republican choice was Jo O. Ferguson, and in the November election results were close again: Murray, 322,282; Ferguson, 304,367. The vote for Murray was not the largest ever cast for a candidate in Oklahoma, but the sum of the ballots, 626,649, was the largest vote of the two major parties for governor up to this time.[23] Representative Mike Monroney won the Democratic nomination for the seat in the United States Senate held by Elmer Thomas, and in the general election defeated Bill Alexander, the Oklahoma City preacher, by a vote of 338,630 to 277,358. The Republicans sent George Schwabe to Congress from the First District and Page Belcher of Enid from the Eighth District. The other six districts returned Democrats to Congress, and the Twenty-third state Legislature contained a substantial Democratic majority in both houses.

The administration of Governor Johnston Murray is too close

[21] *Ibid.*, 174.

[22] *Ibid.*, 174, Legislative Referendum No. 94. The vote was 165,953, "yes"; 159,225, "no."

[23] National elections have brought out more voters in Oklahoma, in 1940, 1944, 1948, and particularly in 1952, when 948,984 Oklahomans voted.

for evaluation. Perspective is lacking for other recent governors, in varying degrees; but measures of the current chief executive, such as completion of the Turner Turnpike and other proposed turnpike construction, are not so simple as to lend themselves to easy judgment by a voter of the present decade.

With little political experience, Johnston Murray has shown a strong aptitude for the techniques of campaigning. Not a constant source of copy for newspapers, he does occasionally get his name in the headlines, and apparently the publicity thus obtained does no political damage. For example, open house once a week at the Governor's Mansion and in his office at the State Capitol was a gesture of hospitality which was liked by many of the common people and not actively resented by anyone.[24] Governor Murray was extremely frank in his public contacts. In an address before a Tulsa medical association, he berated the physicians for losing public confidence through pursuit of wealth. Strongly opposed to any form of socialized medicine, he was ready to blame the doctors themselves for growth of sentiment in favor of that approach to public health.[25] Many of Oklahoma's older citizens have thought that the Governor showed a strong resemblance to his father, William H. Murray, in his direct approach to current problems and his bluntness in dealing with men of diverse opinions.

In the presidential election of 1952 Oklahoma cast its electoral vote for the Republican candidate, Dwight D. Eisenhower. Adlai E. Stevenson of Illinois, the Democratic candidate, received the very creditable popular vote of 430,939 to 518,045 for Eisenhower. The total popular vote was 948,984, by far the largest in the state's history.[26]

---

[24] *Life*, Vol. XXXI, No. 25 (December 17, 1951), 131.

[25] *Time*, Vol. LXIX, No. 4 (January 28, 1952), 49.

[26] The national vote of 1952 was the largest on record in actual number of votes cast, in per cent of the total population, and per cent of the population over twenty-one years of age. Oklahomans who cast their votes, either for Eisenhower or for Adlai Stevenson, constituted 68.66 per cent of the population over twenty-one. The national vote, 61,637,951, was 63.28 per cent of the population over twenty-one. The states varied greatly in actual exercise of suffrage, from Utah, Connecticut, Delaware, Idaho, New Hampshire, Rhode Island, Nevada, Indiana, and Illinois—all over 75 per cent—down to Virginia, South Carolina, Georgia, Alabama, and Mississippi—all under 35 per cent. Mississippi was lowest in percentage voting, with 23.6 per cent of the population over twenty-one.

## RECENT HIGHWAY DEVELOPMENT IN OKLAHOMA

A significant development in the state's highway system is in progress at mid-century. Governors Kerr, Turner, and Johnston Murray in succession have used their influence to extend hard-surfaced roads in Oklahoma. Roy J. Turner was the first to advocate an extensive toll-road project, in 1947. His specific proposal was a turnpike to connect Oklahoma City and Tulsa, with toll gates near the terminal cities and additional entries along the way at Chandler, Stroud, Bristow, and Sapulpa. Opposition to the project, largely from local interests in by-passed towns, delayed beginning of construction until Governor Turner's administration was almost ended.

Governor Turner won his first fight in the legislature and obtained a law authorizing the highway on April 29, 1947. The act provided that toll-road bonds should not be a part of the state's debt, and it became the governor's task to borrow $30,000,000 with this legal restriction. The market for toll-road bonds was not good, the law authorizing the road was limited to two years, and there were many times when the entire project seemed likely to be defeated. In May, 1949, work had not begun because funds were still lacking and the legislature, after another hard fight, voted to extend the time for beginning construction. In November of that year Governor Turner got his loan.[27] Two New York firms and a San Antonio firm united in a syndicate which purchased the Oklahoma Turnpike Authority's first issue of bonds in the amount of $31,000,000. The rate charged was 3.413 per cent. The first contract for grading was awarded during the next month.

The old contest between cement and asphalt interests in Oklahoma had to be fought out. The Turnpike Authority considered the problem for several months before reaching a decision and in July, 1951 agreed to use twelve-inch sub base, and then took bids on five separate specifications for surfacing the highway. In the end it was decided to use asphaltic concrete for the entire job.

The work proceeded with the new governor, Johnston Murray, serving as ex officio member of the board, along with J. Wiley

[27] *Daily Oklahoman*, March 1, 1953.

Richardson, chairman; Glen Key, R. P. Matthews, and Joe Jarboe, members; and H. E. Bailey, formerly director of the state highway commission, manager.

Cost of building the turnpike ran higher than the estimates, because materials and labor steadily rose in price and also because law suits over land values on the right of way were unexpectedly expensive. Sapulpa citizens fought to route the turnpike along a line that had been surveyed for a new section of U. S. Highway 66. The Turnpike Authority finally settled upon a more direct route which cost less but involved new surveys for the Sapulpa interchange.

A new loan of $7,000,000 was obtained on June 3, 1952, at the rate of 3.84 per cent. The Turner Turnpike was completed and opened to public use as a toll road on May 17, 1953. The road is 88 miles long, from Wicher toll gate on the west to the Tulsa terminal on the east. The distance from Main and Broadway, Oklahoma City to Third and Boston, Tulsa is 106 miles, approximately 14 miles shorter than the old highway. The turnpike consists of two asphaltic concrete roadways separated by fifteen feet of turf. Each roadway is twenty-four feet wide with paved shoulders twelve feet wide, and no grade over 3 per cent. Cross traffic is entirely eliminated by underpass and overpass construction.

At the end of 1953 the political contest in regard to Oklahoma toll roads was still going strong. Those who advocate toll roads urge the need of better highway facilities, including the safety factor included in newer types of highway building, the desirability of taxing those who use the road as a means of paying for its construction, and the saving involved in shorter distances between towns and smoother road surfaces. Opponents of the road argue that collection of tolls is a regressive tax, tolls will not pay the cost of construction, the right of way cuts farm property and reduces its value, and routing traffic past retail establishments will cause loss of business for the towns.

In addition to the Turner Turnpike other important roads have been built, and many attractive improvements of older highways have been made during the administrations of Kerr, Turner, and Johnston Murray. Paving has replaced gravel in many places, including Oklahoma State Highway 21, from Beaver Bend State

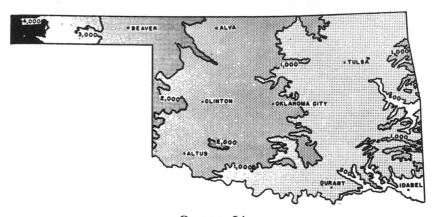

*Contour Lines*

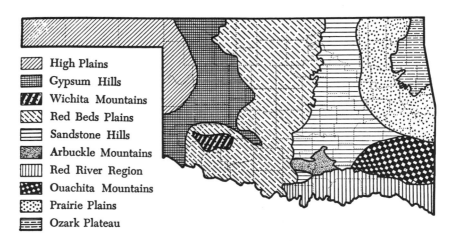

High Plains
Gypsum Hills
Wichita Mountains
Red Beds Plains
Sandstone Hills
Arbuckle Mountains
Red River Region
Ouachita Mountains
Prairie Plains
Ozark Plateau

*Geographical Regions of Oklahoma*

Park to Broken Bow; over forty miles of Oklahoma State Highway 9, between Eufaula and Earlsboro; about forty miles on U. S. 270 west of Fort Supply; over twenty miles on U. S. 64 southwest of Boise, and on other substantial sections of roadway in different parts of the state. In 1953, Governor Murray estimated that new highway construction during his administration would cost $166,000,000 and that the state actually needed about $740,000,000 for new hard-surfaced roads.

### OKLAHOMA AGRICULTURE IN 1950

In many respects Oklahoma had developed, by mid-century, into an average farming state. In 1945 the value of farms, land and buildings, in the United States was set by the Census Bureau at $46,388,925,560; and in Oklahoma at $1,106,153,826. In the entire nation, farm values stood at approximately $40 per acre; in Oklahoma, at $31 per acre. In 1950 the per acre value of Oklahoma farms had increased sharply to $51.42, a change that was due in part to general rise in prices.[28] Nine states had greater acreage in farms than Oklahoma—Arizona, Colorado, Kansas, Montana, Nebraska, New Mexico, North Dakota, South Dakota, and Texas. The other thirty-eight states had smaller acreage, in some instances smaller than the farm land of a large Oklahoma county.

The native Americans on the "buffalo plains" had farmed Oklahoma soil before the coming of the first Europeans. Indians from the region east of the Mississippi River had brought their methods of cultivation into Indian Territory and had farmed as much or as little fenced ground as they pleased, raising their livestock on the open range without serious restriction by the tribal government. Men who had occupied large areas in Mississippi or Alabama, with slaves to perform the heavy labor of clearing timber from the fields, breaking the soil, planting and harvesting, did the same thing in the new land. Livestock remained an important factor in the economy of each tribe, and some Indians became wealthy in their possession of cattle, horses, and swine, with an

[28] U. S. Bureau of the Census, *Agriculture: 1950*, Vol. I, Part 25, p. 581.

almost unlimited range for their support. The Indian who performed all of his own labor usually cleared a small space for his field and raised stock on a moderate scale. Occupation of large areas by relatively few persons was one of the principal arguments used to justify allotments in severalty.

White settlers of the Indian Territory, tilling the soil as crop-renters from Indian landlords, did not have the incentive nor the knowledge to farm the land with careful attention to conservation of soil. Many fields became less productive from year to year, and in regions of loose, sandy soil erosion took a heavy toll. White homesteaders in Oklahoma Territory, the western half of the Indian lands, came in sudden spurts of settlement as a result of opening reservations or unoccupied areas. Land was plowed with the immediate needs of the homesteader and his family in mind, with the scant supply of implements at hand, and with little concern for future fertility of the soil. Most people who settled the territory had little advance knowledge of the best methods to employ in planting crops, of means for restoring fertility to the ground, or of devices for preventing erosion. After a few years the homesteader brought new ground into use, clearing off timber in the wooded areas and simply breaking new land in the prairies. Unfortunately, the first plots brought under cultivation were frequently ruined by the treatment they had received. Too often they were simply abandoned. Denuded of their timber or of prairie grass, fields became barren wastes, scarred by gullies and incapable of producing any crop or furnishing pasturage for livestock.

As an area for crops and livestock, Oklahoma has peculiar need for scientific adaptation to conditions of soil and climate. In large areas the top soil is thin and subject to rapid erosion. Sudden changes of temperature, long periods without rain, and wind storms sweeping the level plains with long continued violence, combine to make the Southwest a difficult region to farm.[29] On the other hand, careful adjustment to conditions set by nature results in fine crops and excellent returns from livestock. The United States Department of Agriculture began to solve the problems of dry-land

[29] Debo, *Oklahoma: Foot-loose and Fancy-free*, Chapter VII. Miss Debo estimated in 1949 that one-third of Oklahoma's top soil had been removed by erosion and over one-third of the nitrogen and organic matter lost in the remainder. *Ibid.*, 75.

farming, particularly under the administrations of Secretary James Wilson (1897–1913) and Secretary David F. Houston (1913–20). Gradually Oklahoma developed more progressive methods in soil cultivation, returning fields to pasturage, and attention to livestock industries. Experiments at Oklahoma Agricultural and Mechanical College at Stillwater and the dry-farming experiments at Lawton and Woodward, especially fitted to conditions within the state, have proved especially useful to Oklahoma farmers.

In some parts of Oklahoma, solution of the erosion problem seems to be returning the land to grass. With 2,000,000 acres of ground that was formerly cultivated fields abandoned because of reduced fertility or erosion, and with 8,000,000 acres of marginal farm land in the state, the need for prompt and drastic action would seem to be clearly indicated.[30] By 1946 the tendency toward reckless waste of fertile soil by bad farming methods had been checked. In that year it was estimated that 8,880 acres of soil in Oklahoma were broken for crops that should have been left in grass, for best permanent results; but in the same period a larger area was recovered from waste land and planted in grass.[31]

In 1949 the total value of all farm crops in Oklahoma was $346,355,739 and the total value of all livestock was $300,241,879.[32] The largest single item was cattle, with a value of $272,691,555. Other important items included wheat, $145,666,119; cotton, $66,294,000; dairy products, $54,289,000; hogs, $37,528,000; eggs, $31,255,000; corn, $22,912,308; alfalfa, $15,314,058; and peanuts, $9,610,163. The total for all farm products was $646,597,618. By way of comparison, California, Texas, and Iowa each produced crops and livestock more than three times as valuable in 1949; Pennsylvania farm products were valued at $768,348,000, more than $100,000,000 above Oklahoma production; and South Dakota farms yielded $550,407,000, nearly $100,000,000 less than the farms of Oklahoma.

[30] Total area of Oklahoma is 44,179,840 acres, of which approximately 36,000,000 acres are in farms. U. S. Bureau of the Census, *Agriculture: 1950*, Vol. I, Part 25, p. 58.

[31] Debo, *Oklahoma: Foot-loose and Fancy-free*, 83.

[32] U. S. Bureau of the Census, *Agriculture: 1950*, Vol. I, Part 25, p. 82. In 1952 the total farm income for the state was $673,251,000 divided as follows: crops, $296,378,000; livestock, $376,873,000.

In 1880 tenants operated 25.6 per cent of all the farms in the United States. From that time until 1930 farm tenantry steadily increased to 42.4 per cent. In a single decade, 1920 to 1930, tenantry grew by more than 3 per cent. During the following twenty years the trend was in the opposite direction. By 1945 farm tenantry had moved downward to 31.7 per cent and at mid-century about 70 per cent of all farm operators were owners.[33]

In Oklahoma Territory there was a brief period following the run of April 22, 1889, when practically every occupant of a farm home was an owner or in the process of becoming an owner. By 1900 tenants operated about 40 per cent of the farms.[34] This was a higher figure than the national average in 1900, which stood at 35.3 per cent. In 1910 nearly half of the farm operators in Oklahoma were tenants and in 1920, 51 per cent. In 1935 Oklahoma farms were 61 per cent tenant-operated, placing the state among the worst in the nation. During the following ten years farm tenantry dropped to 40 per cent, a change directly traceable to greater rural prosperity and to the national farm-credit acts of 1933 and 1934, the Farm Security Administration, and the Bankhead-Jones Farm Tenant Act of 1937.

In 1935, tenant operated farms in Oklahoma had an average value of $2,809. Owner-operated farms at the same time had an average value of $3,915. The sections of the state where farm tenantry was highest in per cent also had the highest rate of illiteracy. For example, illiteracy in the Panhandle counties ranged from .3 per cent to .6 per cent; in Okfuskee County, 7.8 per cent; and in Choctaw County, 8.5 per cent. Farm tenantry was also at its lowest in the Panhandle, ranging from 27 to 37 per cent. In Okfuskee County tenants operated 78 per cent of the farms; in Creek County, 78 per cent; and in the lower Red River Valley, from 71 to 75 per cent. For any person who will take the trouble to study conditions of tenant cotton farmers, the relation between tenantry and child labor, low school attendance, poverty, and misery is too obvious to require explanation.

The wide variety of soil and climate in Oklahoma accounts for

[33] *United States Economic Almanac, 1950.*
[34] This figure applies to the "West Side" (Oklahoma Territory) only. Later figures are for the state of Oklahoma.

the considerable range of its crops. In the Panhandle, which lies west of the 100th meridian, annual rainfall is frequently as low as 15 inches. In the southeastern part of the state, forty-five inches is a common annual precipitation. Since rainfall steadily increases from northwest to southeast, the middle portion of the state has an annual supply that ranges from twenty-five to thirty-five inches.

Along the Red River in the old coastal plains region, a strip thirty miles wide and extending west from the boundary of Arkansas to the 98th meridian, 230 days per year on the average are free from killing frost. On the high plateau at the western extremity of the Panhandle, usually not more than 180 days are without frost —roughly half the days in the year. The elevation of Black Mesa Butte in northwestern Cimarron County is 4,700 feet above sea-level. The ground slopes gradually to the southeast and the longer streams flow in the same general direction. At the southeastern corner of McCurtain County the elevation is less than 400 feet.

The Ouachita Highlands of southeastern Oklahoma extend northward from the coastal plains to the Arkansas Valley. Well-defined ranges of mountains are to be found in various parts of this area. The Kiamichi Range extends from the upper waters of Little River northeast to the Arkansas border. The Winding Stairs lie a few miles farther north, beyond the headwaters of the Kiamichi River. Other ranges are the San Bois, halfway between the Winding Stairs and the Arkansas River, and the Jack Fork Mountains, northwest of the Kiamichi. To the west this hilly section extends to the 96th meridian, gradually sloping off to the Boggy River Valley.

The Arbuckle Mountains, centering in western Murray County and the northwestern arm of Carter County, are approximately forty miles north of the Red River and midway between the eastern and western borders of the state. The Wichita Mountains, eighty miles farther west and about twenty miles farther north, are the most striking elevations of western Oklahoma. This rugged area extends from Fort Sill and Lawton on the east, across North Fork to the vicinity of Mangum on the west.

In the northeastern section of the state the Ozark Plateau extends eastward from the Grand River and northward from the Arkansas Valley, beyond the borders of Arkansas and Missouri.

This is one of the most productive areas of Oklahoma. Limestone is abundant here, which accounts in part for the high yield of grain, clover, alfalfa, and other crops. The timber is of good quality and the region produces excellent apples.

Five extensive plains cover portions of the state not included in the Ouachita, Arbuckle, Wichita, and Ozark uplands. West of the Ozarks is a wide expanse of territory called by geologists the Sandstone Hills Region. West of it lie the Redbeds Plains, then the region of the Gypsum Hills, and in the extreme northwest the High Plains, including Harper, Ellis, and Roger Mills counties in addition to the Panhandle. Along two hundred miles of the Red River below the 98th meridian lies the coastal plain, previously described.

## MINERAL PRODUCTS IN OKLAHOMA

The mineral that has produced the highest cash return in Oklahoma has been petroleum. Beginning with wildcat wells before statehood, production rose above 1,000,000 barrels in 1904. Between that year and the admission of Oklahoma as a state in 1907, new oil fields were opened near Okmulgee, a great new development was begun at Glenn Pool in Tulsa County and another at Wheeler Pool in Carter County. By 1907, Glenn Pool wells were yielding more than 100,000 barrels a day and production for Oklahoma in that year reached 43,500,000 barrels.[35]

During the following twenty years, oil production in Oklahoma moved steadily higher. New fields were discovered in Osage, Kay, and Seminole counties, the Cushing fields were opened in Payne County and the Healdton fields in Carter County, and finally in 1928 a great new development was begun at Oklahoma City. Oil wells were sunk on city lots and eventually on the grounds of the State Capitol. Peak production in 1927 was 278,000,000 barrels. For ten years Oklahoma ranked near the top among oil-producing states and for nearly fifty years has been among the first three or four states.[36] It ranked first in production in 1920 and first in value of petroleum products during five of the next ten years.

[35] Debo, *Oklahoma: Foot-loose and Fancy-free,* 57.

Oklahoma is also high among the states that produce natural gas and natural gasoline. Natural gas, which is usually found in the same regions that have resources in oil, has become the principal fuel of Oklahoma. As a by-product of petroleum, its value was not recognized in the early days of drilling; but as knowledge of the industry grew, means were developed for preventing waste of gas and for transporting it to places where it was in demand as a fuel. During the first year of statehood, sales of natural gas in Oklahoma were about $500,000, and waste was still enormous. Probably nearly forty cubic feet were allowed to escape for every cubic foot sold to consumers.[37] In 1929, Oklahoma marketed 357,893,000,000 cubic feet of natural gas, of which approximately 90,000,000,000 cubic feet were transported out of the state by means of pipe lines. Ten years later production had dropped back to 294,124,042,000 cubic feet,[38] and in 1943 was approximately the same.

Natural gasoline, or casing-head gasoline, produced from "wet gas," is an important by-product of the petroleum industry. Production began in Oklahoma shortly after statehood and grew into a $30,000,000 industry by 1920. High point in volume of production and value was 1929, before limits on production had seriously checked the flow of petroleum. Total production in 1929 was 676,000,000 gallons, valued over $40,000,000. During the years of depression the output diminished, and in 1939 natural gasoline production in Oklahoma stood at 428,107,437 gallons, valued at $16,392,872.[39] This was approximately one sixth of the total output of the United States. Casing-head gasoline is used principally as a blend for obtaining a desired quality in motor fuels.

Less important than petroleum products, but at the same time a substantial part of Oklahoma's mineral wealth is coal. In the last year before statehood, Indian Territory produced 2,500,000 tons, roughly 1 per cent of the coal production for the United States in

---

[36] Since 1940, California has produced far more petroleum than Oklahoma, and Texas has become the top producer with an average far above both Oklahoma and California. In 1951, Texas produced five times as many barrels as Oklahoma, and in the same year California produced nearly double the Oklahoma yield. Louisiana passed Oklahoma in 1950.

[37] Debo, *Oklahoma: Foot-loose and Fancy-free*, 68–71, 105.

[38] U. S. Bureau of the Census, *Sixteenth Report: Mineral Products*, I, 157.

[39] *Ibid.*, 212.

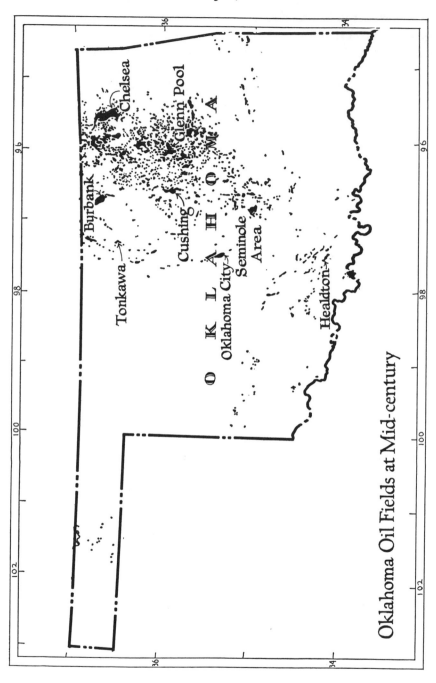

Chelsea

Glenn Pool

Burbank

Cushing

OKLAHOMA

Tonkawa

Oklahoma City

Seminole Area

Healdton

Oklahoma Oil Fields at Mid-century

Boomers at Caldwell, Kansas, 1883–84

*Courtesy Muriel H. Wright*

Buffalo Springs, afternoon before the Run of 1889

The Run, Cherokee Outlet, 1893

Guthrie, April 22, 1889

Oklahoma City, April 24, 1889
showing jog, Robinson and Grand

El Reno City Lot Arbitration Board, May 31, 1889

Tulsa, 1897

CHARLES N. HASKELL
*first Governor of Oklahoma after statehood*

Altus-Lugert Dam in the Hobart-Altus-Mangum area confines one of the
many man-made lakes in the state which have contributed immensely to
Oklahoma's water resources since the 1930's.

*Oklahoma Planning and Resources Board*

Keystone Dam, on the Arkansas northwest of Tulsa, is a part of the great inland water navigation project on the Arkansas River and its tributaries. It will control floods and silt on the Arkansas and provide power and water for Oklahomans.

*Oklahoma Water Resources Board*

Eufaula Dam and Reservoir, near the forks of the Canadian, will control floods and silt on that river in addition to providing hydroelectric power.

Great Salt Plains Lake, near Cherokee and Jet in the northwestern part of the state, lures fishermen and water skiers to a once arid area.

*Oklahoma Planning and Resources Board*

1906. Production in Oklahoma had increased to 4,849,228 tons by 1920, and in that year the United States produced approximately 400,000,000 tons of bituminous and 90,000,000 tons of anthracite coal. Thus, Oklahoma coal was still about 1 per cent of national production. With the growth of natural-gas consumption, coal mining decreased in the state. However, the outbreak of war in Europe brought increased demands for coal, and the industry revived, reaching 3,000,000 tons during the last year of the war.

In lead and zinc the Oklahoma mines, located principally in Ottawa County, were among the largest producers of the nation for many years. The Tri-State area, consisting of southwestern Missouri, southeastern Kansas, and northeastern Oklahoma, produced about one billion dollars worth of lead and zinc in one hundred years following discovery of the first important mines at Oronogo, Missouri, in 1849.[40] Production on a large scale began in Oklahoma about three years before statehood; and by 1914 zinc mined in Oklahoma was valued at $3,500,000. During the next eleven years production steadily grew to an annual value of nearly $44,000,000. After 1925 there was a period of decline and the Tri-State area saw years of poverty during the great depression, 1929–39. Again war orders brought revival of mining, with subsidies from the government for production of lead and zinc. After the war ended, subsidies were discontinued and Oklahoma mining slumped. By 1950, Idaho, Montana, Arizona, and New Jersey had passed Oklahoma in production of zinc. Missouri still ranked first in lead production with Idaho, Utah, and Colorado following. Oklahoma reached its peak in both lead and zinc in 1925, with production of more than 283,000 tons of zinc and nearly 80,000 tons of lead in that year. Production of lead and zinc concentrates in 1952 totaled 139,008 tons.[41]

Other mineral products in Oklahoma, small in cash value by comparison with petroleum, gas, and coal, are yet important in their aggregate contribution to the state's wealth. Building stone, in which the resources of the Wichita Mountains, Arbuckles, Kiamichi, and Ozarks are enormous; clay products, with practically unlimited resources; glass sand and building sand; gypsum, tripoli,

[40] *American Dictionary of History*, III, 181.
[41] *Oklahoma Business Bulletin*, Vol. 19, No. 12 (December, 1953). This bulletin is published by the Bureau of Business Research, University of Oklahoma.

salt, and many other minerals have a part in the economic development of Oklahoma.

Of all the building material that has been found in Oklahoma, limestone is first in importance. Limestone areas are extensive and widely spaced. The entire Ozark Plateau in the northeast, the Arbuckle and Wichita Mountains, and a belt north of the Red River from the borders of Arkansas westward to the 97th meridian are large segments of the state that contain much limestone. Another extensive area is the great triangle marked by the 37th parallel on the north, down the Arkansas River to its junction with the Grand, and up that stream to the northern state boundary. A region smaller in extent but containing stone of excellent quality lies east of Pontotoc, across southern Coal County and central Atoka County. From this area of limestone another belt extends northwest through the Jack Fork Mountains to Wilburton.

Limestone is used for a great variety of purposes—crushed rock for concrete blocks and all kinds of concrete building, including road construction; with shale, for the making of cement; for manufacturing lime, stucco, paint, and glass; and, as building stone. Lime is an important factor in commercial soil building on many Oklahoma farms. Crushed limestone is one of the best materials for railroad-bed construction. Rock wool, used for insulation, is a limestone product, manufactured by a process recently devised. One plant for rock wool manufacture was established at Sand Springs in 1940, a second at Ada in 1946.[42]

Limestone production has increased steadily in Oklahoma since territorial days. In marked contrast to zinc and lead, which are largely mined out, and even natural gas, in which a definite limit to production can be seen, limestone in Oklahoma appears almost inexhaustible. Granite is another important building stone of Oklahoma. The Wichita and Arbuckle Mountains and a small area in the Ozark Plateau produce granite of excellent quality.

In 1939, Oklahoma ranked fifth among the states in total value of mineral products, with more than a quarter of a billion dollars of income from mineral sources. By 1950, it stood sixth among the states, after Texas, Pennsylvania, California, West Virginia, and

[42] Debo, *Oklahoma: Foot-loose and Fancy-free*, 108; U. S. Bureau of the Census, *Sixteenth Report: Mineral Industries*.

Louisiana, in that order.[43] The cash value of Oklahoma mineral products more than doubled between 1940 and 1950; but other states, too, were making rapid progress, and part of the increase in all states resulted from general rise in prices.

## OKLAHOMA MANUFACTURING AT MID-CENTURY

Manufacturing in Oklahoma has been disappointing to some observers and to some towns that have tried to attract industry to the state. Progress has been slow but substantial. Ten years after the run of 1889 there were 495 establishments for manufacturing in Oklahoma Territory, which included besides the counties of the original Unassigned Lands, the Panhandle, Lincoln and Pottawatomie counties, lands of the Cheyenne and Arapaho Reservation, the Cherokee Outlet, and old Greer County. Persons engaged in manufacturing numbered 2,650 and the value added to raw goods by manufacturing processes totaled just over $2,700,000.[44]

At the end of World War I in 1919, Oklahomans who lived by means of manufacturing had increased to 35,445, and the value added to goods was $87,551,000. The average wage earned by workers in Oklahoma manufacturing plants was just over $1,300 a year. During the following decade, which was a prosperous period for manufacturers, the number of workers in Oklahoma increased slightly, their wages increased in the aggregate by $11,000,000 a year, average wages grew to almost $1,500, and the total value added to goods came up to $149,404,000, or nearly $62,000,000 above the amount added in 1919.[45] The fundamental weaknesses of the decade (1919–29) in national economics is clear in Oklahoma manufacturing: labor did not receive a sufficient part of the general prosperity to maintain a healthy purchasing power. With steadily rising prices, laborers were not so well off in 1929 as they were in 1919. This condition of laborers in manufacturing

---

[43] *Statistical Abstract of the United States: 1952.* Bureau of the Census.
[44] U. S. Bureau of the Census, *Manufacturing: 1947*, III, 495.
[45] *Ibid.*

affected a relatively small fraction of Oklahoma's population; but unfortunately the same trend was apparent in the relation between cost of living and income of farmers, farm laborers, retailers and their employees, secretaries and clerks, teachers, preachers, mail carriers, and common people in general. The "prosperity" of the period was a fiction and the errors in national policies, with respect to production and distribution of goods, were to be followed presently by the tragedy of depression on a large scale.

The years between 1929 and 1939 were marked by the nation's greatest depression, not only among farmers and the lowest groups of unorganized laborers, but among nearly all classes. Furthermore, it was a depression that extended around the world. The number of persons engaged in manufacturing fell off slightly in Oklahoma, their annual wages decreased by more than $10,000,000 and the value added to manufactured goods dropped to $101,782,000, a decrease of $48,000,000 by comparison with 1929.[46]

Emergence from the depression was painfully slow during the early months of recovery. Many capable workers were unemployed and many thousands of children were undernourished. War orders for Oklahoma goods in Europe, followed by vigorous preparation for national defense at home brought increased employment, new investments, higher prices, higher wages. The number of Oklahomans engaged in manufacturing rose above 55,000 in 1949, their aggregate wages grew to $143,605,000—an average income of $2,592 per person. Value added to goods by the processes of manufacturing reached $341,027,000 in 1949. This figure was nearly $240,000,000 above the value added by manufacturing in 1939, and almost $100,000,000 above the total amount paid out for wages and salaries.[47]

The largest manufacturing interests of Oklahoma are the petroleum refineries and other industries connected with oil production. These plants are situated in Tulsa, Ponca City, Oklahoma City, Enid, Duncan, Cushing, and many other towns of the state. The vicinity of Grand River Dam is making notable progress in development of its industries, while towns in the wheat belt have established flour mills of some importance, others have found it

[46] *Ibid.*
[47] *Ibid.*

convenient to manufacture cottonseed products, some have developed limestone products, a great many have printing industries, and a few have extensive lumber mills. Muskogee, Ada, Ardmore, Bartlesville, Shawnee, and McAlester are among the towns that produce manufactured goods beyond the needs of local consumption.

Refining is followed, in varying order of importance from year to year, by products of the meat packers, flour mills, zinc smelters, lumbering industries, bakeries, stone, clay, and glass enterprises, newspaper and book publishers, ice manufacturers, makers of cottonseed products, oil-field machinery and tool manufacturers, and other industries. The rank of Oklahoma among the manufacturing states is low, since there are only fifteen states that add less to the total value of manufactured goods and pay less in wages and salaries for industrial workers in the field of processing. The comparatively recent settlement of Oklahoma, its serious lack of transportation facilities, and its distance from ports and populous trade centers are handicaps in the development of manufacturing. Its abundant supply of fuel in the form of natural gas and coal, the availability of certain raw materials, such as petroleum, wheat, cotton, hides, lumber, and limestone, and the high per cent of good flying days in each year, are among the advantages. Probably manufacturing will continue to show steady growth. At present mineral and agricultural products furnish about four fifths of the state's revenues; manufacturing, about one fifth. More manufactured products for Oklahoma would mean greater concentration of population, better markets for raw materials, and greater prosperity for the state as a whole.

In 1953 the largest industrial employer in Oklahoma was the Tinker Air Force Base. The Tinker Base was established in 1942 under Colonel William Turnbull as commander. Its principal activity in the period since war began in Korea in the summer of 1950 has been the overhaul and repair of jet engines for the armed forces of the United States. It employs 23,650 workers and has an annual payroll of $84,000,000.[48] About two thirds of the employees live in Oklahoma City, and several thousand commute from near-by counties.

[48] *Daily Oklahoman*, March 1, 1953.

One of the unique industries connected with petroleum is the Halliburton Oil Well Cementing Company, at Duncan. This firm in 1952 employed 1,662 persons and maintained a payroll of $7,800,000. The largest single item in the ad valorem taxes of Stephens County in 1952 was the sum paid by Halliburton Company, which amounted to $72,700.

As in other parts of the West, population trends in Oklahoma have shown rapid increases in urban population and corresponding decline in per cent of rural dwellers. In 1890, 3.7 per cent of Oklahoma Territory's people lived in the towns, 96.3 per cent on farms and ranches. In 1900 the urban population was 7.4 per cent, in 1920 it was 26.5 per cent, and in 1940 it had grown to 37.6 per cent. Up to 1950 the Bureau of the Census listed as urban population all residents of incorporated places with 2,500 inhabitants or more, and in addition a few areas defined as urban under special rules. A new definition of urban population in the latest census includes "the densely settled urban fringe" around cities of 50,000 or more and "unincorporated places of 2,500 inhabitants or more outside any urban fringe." Under the new definition Oklahoma's population in 1950 was 51 per cent urban. Maine and New Mexico had approximately the same division of population, in 1950, as Oklahoma.[49]

[49] U. S. Bureau of Census *Seventeenth Report: Population.*

# CHAPTER SEVENTEEN

# Mid-Century and Afterwards, 1954-1964

## INDUSTRIAL REVOLUTION

Most fundamental of the changes in Oklahoma since mid-century is the trend toward concentration of population in towns and cities. This urban trend is simply an acceleration of a movement that started before statehood. During the decade 1950 to 1960, the population of the state increased by 4 per cent, farm residents continued a steady decline in number, cities ranging from 7,000 to 15,000 population increased by 31 per cent, and cities over 15,000 increased by 35 per cent. By 1960 over half of the people lived in thirty-three cities with populations above 6,000, more than one-third lived in two of the seventy-seven counties, and more than one-fourth lived in two cities—Oklahoma City and Tulsa.

During the decade, Tulsa gained 72,682 inhabitants—nearly 40 per cent—and Oklahoma City added 74,140—an increase of 30 per cent. Lawton grew from 34,754 to 60,806, and Atlus increased its population almost 125 per cent, from 9,735 to 21,840. Six other Oklahoma towns doubled their populations between 1950 and 1960.

Incorporation of large areas adjacent to cities is a major factor of urban growth in Oklahoma. By November 1, 1961, Oklahoma City had annexed industrial sites which raised the total incorporated area to 304,352 acres, making it larger in area than any other city in the United States. At the same time it ranked thirty-seventh in population.

The expansion of business enterprises—stores, factories, and others—along the highways beyond city limits resulted in a new development, the strip town. Dealers in farm machinery, requiring space for effective display of their merchandise, were among the first to utilize the highway strips. Restaurants, taverns, furniture stores, lumber yards, feed stores, groceries, motels, laundries, and filling stations were eager to take advantage of the market provided by Oklahomans and visitors traveling by automobile. The strip town, as the name indicates, is a narrow belt of business houses along the highway, with perhaps a few residences on the same row or a short distance back of it. A heterogeneous group of business and professional people have found the strip town attractive, so that one finds barbershops, doctors' offices, veterinarians' offices, and small-animal hospitals among its establishments.

The movement of farmers to the cities has been accompanied or perhaps prompted by an increase in the use of farm machinery. Large-scale farming with tractors and combines, cotton pickers and terracing machinery, the use of airplanes for crop dusting, and the application of modern chemical fertilizers and time-saving methods have made possible greater production per man hour and have contributed to the reduction in the amount of farm labor required. Livestock raising is more and more dependent upon the investment of capital, with extensive fencing, facilities for growing and storing large crops of hay, and great ponds for the storage of water or deep wells for bringing water to the surface. Some of the outstanding farmers and livestock producers of the state are also prominent in oil production or other business enterprises. Some, such as Roy Turner and the late Robert S. Kerr, have been distinguished in public office.

The development of manufacturing is an important part of the trend toward urban residence. As noted above, recovery from the great depression of 1929–39—when manufacturing declined in Oklahoma—included a steady rise in wages, profits, and value added to goods. The number of persons employed in manufacturing rose from 55,403 in 1947 to 77,222 in 1952, and to 93,337 in 1961. The following table shows the trend:

| Value added by m'f'g. | Average annual wages | No. of employees | Payroll |
|---|---|---|---|
| 1947 $341,027,000 | $2,592 | 55,403 | $143,605,000 |
| 1952 493,379,000 | 3,455 | 77,222 | 266,783,000 |
| 1961 724,998,000 | 4,909 | 93,337 | 458,183,000 |

Thus the average wages of persons engaged in manufacturing industries nearly doubled in fourteen years, and the number of employees increased more than 68 per cent. Perhaps the family incomes of one-fifth of Oklahoma's population were directly affected by the rise of wages in the manufacturing industries. Certainly the general structure of the state's economy was changed by the addition of nearly three-fourths of a billion dollars to the value of manufactured goods.

The completion of Turner Turnpike and Will Rogers Turnpike, with expressways at Tulsa and Oklahoma City and hard-surfaced roads connecting the turnpikes with near-by towns, gave Oklahoma an enormous impulse toward an efficient transportation system. The addition of the H. E. Bailey Turnpike from Oklahoma City through Lawton to a point just north of the Texas line near Walters in the spring of 1964 was another forward step in highway construction. With a central location between the Texas Gulf Coast and the St. Louis–Kansas City trade area, transportation has become increasingly important to Oklahomans. The rapid increase of truck tonnage and passengers transported by common carriers, including airplanes, is matched by the growth of travel by privately owned automobiles. In 1960 the number of automobile registrations in Oklahoma reached 1,183,550, which was 508 per thousand population, by comparison with 412 per thousand in the nation at large.

Since the Korean war the development of engineering techniques for successful application of secondary recovery methods in oil fields has caused a great extension of water-flooding and other forms of secondary recovery. In essence, these methods have not only resulted in the continued successful extraction of oil from many of the older fields of the state, but have set aside earlier estimates of oil reserves, increasing them significantly. Almost equally important has been the new exploration of older fields, where deeper oil horizons have been tested and proved. In some instances shallower oil horizons, penetrated but never produced under techniques previously used, have also been opened to production by secondary recovery methods. The consequences of these developments to Oklahoma's industrial potential and mineral reserves have been of almost inestimable value in the past decade.

The Democratic choice for governor in the primary election of 1954 was Raymond Gary of Madill. William O. Coe again contested strongly for the nomination, receiving 233,079 votes to Gary's 251,920 in the run-off election. Gary defeated the Republican candidate, Reuben K. Sparks, in the general election by a majority well over 100,000. Senator Robert S. Kerr was re-elected over the Republican challenger, Fred Mock, and the Democrats won five of the six seats in Congress. The Twenty-fifth Legislature contained 39 Democratic and 5 Republican senators, while the House of Representatives was made up of 104 Democrats and 19 Republicans.

Raymond Gary had served in the state senate since 1940 and was president pro tempore when he became candidate for governor. His election as governor occurred in a period of decline in the prices of crops and livestock and reduced employment in manufacturing and transportation. Employment in building increased in 1954, however, and retail sales were up. The average weekly earnings of employees in the manufacturing industries grew from $54.14 in 1948 to $59.33 in 1950 and to $71.86 in 1954.

The year 1954 was a high point in the development of Oklahoma's educational system. Financial support for the public schools had grown steadily during the administration of Kerr, Turner, and Murray, and in 1954 the expenditure per pupil reached $245.78, with funds from all sources totaling $105,425,091. Local sources provided $53,347,540; state, $47,883,266; and federal 4,194,283.

The Turner Turnpike, which had been constructed at a cost of $38,000,000, brought a net revenue of $1,599,594 during its first year of operation (May 17, 1953, to May 17, 1954). The Twenty-fourth Legislature authorized the issuance of bonds for three new turnpike projects: (1) From Tulsa to a connection with Joplin, Missouri; (2) from Oklahoma City to a connection with Wichita, Kansas; and (3) from Oklahoma City to a connection with Wichita Falls, Texas. The estimated cost of all three of the roads totaled $220,000,000.

Existing laws prohibiting manufacturing, transportation, and sale of intoxicants received much attention during the Gary administration. A newspaper estimate placed the illegal sales of tax-paid liquor in Oklahoma City at 48,000 pints a week, or 2,496,000 pints a year. Annual sales in Oklahoma County amounted to $10,000,000 and in the state to $100,000,000. In addition to the tax-paid intoxicants imported illegally from other states, there was still a brisk trade in corn whiskey manufactured without payment of federal revenue in remote mountain regions and other places—including the larger cities. Thus the liquor traffic in Oklahoma, carried on in violation of the law, in 1955 amounted to approximately twice the total value of the wheat crop and nearly one-fourth of the entire farm income, which stood at $477,146,000.

The presidential election of 1956 was a contest between the candidates who had run in 1952. President Eisenhower had conducted his administration with due regard for the Truman diplomatic program of collective security and with no outright declaration for the tariff policies of the Harding-Coolidge-Hoover era. He had succeeded in holding the support of the divergent wings of his party, with the possible exception of extreme isolationists.

At Chicago on August 13, 1956, the Democratic National Convention, after nominating Adlai Stevenson as their candidate for President, followed his suggestion that the convention itself, rather than Stevenson, would select the candidate for Vice-President. Five Democratic leaders sought the support of the delegates, but the contest narrowed down to Estes Kefauver and John F. Kennedy, with the Tennessee man finally winning by a narrow margin.

Senator Joseph McCarthy of Wisconsin had received a severe rebuke from the upper house of Congress after a committee hearing of his charges against officers of the United States Army Signal Corps. President Eisenhower's secretary of the army, Robert F. Stevens, filed counter-charges against Senator McCarthy, and before the televised hearings were completed, it had become clear to Republican leaders that the chief proponent of wild disloyalty charges—as a political technique—had become a liability to the administration.

The Senate created a special committee to investigate McCarthy's conduct. Upon hearing the report of Arthur V. Watkins of Utah, the committee chairman, the Senate voted a resolution of censure against the Wisconsin member. The resolution was not partisan: twenty-two Republicans and one Independent joined the Democrats to carry it by a majority of sixty-seven to twenty-two.

Vice-President Nixon had gained distinction by his part in the disloyalty investigations and was well aware of their political effects. With the recent action of the Senate fresh in his mind, however, and the trend of public opinion clearly turned toward sane evaluation of disloyalty charges, the Vice-President conducted his campaign with admirable restraint. President Eisenhower, recovering from a severe illness, was as popular as he had been in 1952.

Again the electoral majority for Eisenhower and Nixon was decisive—457 to 73. Stevenson carried Missouri, but lost Kentucky, Virginia, and Louisiana, which he had won in the previous election. The Democrats also carried Alabama, Arkansas, Georgia, Mississippi, North Carolina, and South Carolina.

Oklahoma voted for the Eisenhower ticket, with approximately the same majority as in 1952. Stevenson carried 41 of 77 counties, but the vote of the industrial areas, such as Oklahoma, Tulsa, Garfield, and Washington counties, was overwhelmingly Republican. Muskogee County voted for Eisenhower by a small majority and Kay County by a majority that was almost two to one.

## THE EDMONDSON ADMINISTRATION

The state elections of 1958, especially the primaries, were interesting political fights. Toby Morris defeated Victor Wickersham for the nomination in the Sixth Congressional District by a slim plurality, and in November won from his Republican opponent by a much larger margin. In the First District, traditionally Republican, Page Belcher was hard pressed by the Democratic challenger and barely won a majority in the general election. A. S. J. Shaw, state auditor, was defeated for the Democratic nomination by William A Burkhart.

Of the long list of men who filed for governor in the Democratic primary, W. P. Atkinson of Midwest City and J. Howard Edmondson of Tulsa qualified for the run-off. Edmondson won the race by a majority of two to one, the largest ever recorded in an Oklahoma run-off election. The Republicans nominated Phil Ferguson, former Democratic congressman from the old Eighth District. On November 4 the Oklahoma voters elected Edmondson by a majority of more than a quarter of a million votes—also the largest in the state's history. George Nigh of McAlester had defeated "Cowboy" Pink Williams, the incumbent lieutenant governor, for the Democratic nomination, and won the office in the general election. The Democrats also seated a complete list of state administrative officers, 109 of 119 representatives and 21 of the 22 state senators who were due to be elected. In six Congressional districts, only Page Belcher won for the Republicans.

The question of prohibition repeal was submitted to the voters on April 7, 1959. Again a new record was established, the largest special-election vote in Oklahoma up to this time: for repeal, 396,-845; against repeal, 314,380. In this election county option on the sale of intoxicating beverages was defeated by a substantial majority, 469,503 to 221,404. During the first two months of legal sales of liquor, state revenues were as follows: licenses, $460,656.56; refunds, $57,651.29; net, $403,006.27. The initial sales of stamps, as of August 31, 1959, brought in $3,985,100.82. By November 3 the stamp sales had reached $5,186,655.40, and the net returns from licenses and stamps was $5,589,661.67.

The national election of 1960 emphasized the political revolution in Oklahoma that had been in the making for ten years. The state had never been strictly a one-party unit of government. It has many citizens of southern background and unadjustable political loyalty who suppose that the Confederacy of 1861–65 was the creation of the Democratic party—an assumption that is inaccurate but persistent. Many of these persons vote the Democratic ticket, especially in state elections, with the idea of taking a stand for justice, liberty, and state's rights. They cast their votes, one hundred years after the secession of the southern states, against the dominance of Yankee Republicans.

Many wheat-raising Oklahomans, who are descendants of farmers from the old Northwest Territory or from New England, cast their votes at four-year intervals for the current successor of Abraham Lincoln. Thus they support the party name that was accepted (for one term) by the foremost advocate of Union in 1860, the Great Emancipator. This is done without a thought for the northern Democrats of 1860 who made Lincoln's task possible of achievement, or for the southern Whigs who clung to the principles of their section and made the task of maintaining the Union doubly hard. These votes are cast as a matter of habit by citizens who do not realize that the issues which carried Lincoln and the Union Whigs and Union Democrats through four terrible years of war came to an end with the surrender of Lee and Johnston; or that the Stalwart Republicans of the following decade abandoned the ideals and the humane moderation of the Civil War President, who insisted upon adoption of the name "Union party."

As in other states, neither intelligent self-interest nor high ideals completely dominate Oklahoma voters, but a clear pattern of support for Republican policies has emerged in the industrial areas. The people who are engaged in manufacturing—petroleum, machinery, food products, transportation equipment, printing and publishing, lumber, furniture, pulp and paper, leather products, the industries connected with stone, clay, and glass, and miscellaneous manufactures—have largely cast their lot, since 1950, with the Republican party. In the state elections, party names have little meaning as far as political issues are concerned. Many thousands have regularly voted for Democratic state officers who have also supported Republican electors of the President.

In the Democratic National Convention at Los Angeles in the summer of 1960, John F. Kennedy of Massachusetts was nominated for President on the first ballot. At the Republican Convention in Chicago, later in July, Richard Nixon was nominated for President, also on the first ballot and with but ten dissenting votes. Henry Cabot Lodge, Jr., of Massachusetts was chosen by the Republicans to make the race for Vice-President. Senator Kennedy selected, and the Democratic Convention confirmed, Lyndon Johnson of Texas as Kennedy's running mate.

Kennedy's choice of his strongest Democratic rival was indicative of deep understanding of his party's composition. He knew that he would have to overcome prejudice against his affiliation with the Roman Catholic church in some parts of the rural South and elsewhere in order to obtain normal party support in those areas. Perhaps no man in the Democratic party could have served the purpose better than Lyndon Johnson. Texas alone, with twenty-four electoral votes, had a large number of voters who would need special attention in the area of religious tolerance.

The Nixon-Kennedy debates, broadcast by the major television and radio networks on September 26, October 7, 13, and 21, brought the rival candidates face to face on the main issues of the campaign. Both had established previously that they were effective public speakers, and the people listened eagerly to their views of desirable American policies. In his rebuttal speeches, the Republican candidate seemed to view Senator Kennedy's criticism of the Eisenhower administration as an attack upon the United States—a species of "national self-disparagement." Kennedy was quick to recognize the fallacy of Nixon's stand and to point out its similarity to the Federalist party's attitude in passing the Alien and Sedition laws of 1789. "I do not equate criticism of Republican leadership with criticism of our country," Senator Kennedy declared.

In view of the small pluralities by which the Democrats won some of the states and the slender margin of 112,801 votes out of 68,838,005 in the nation, the statement made by many listeners—that Kennedy won the election in the debates—is perhaps defensible. Of the electoral votes, Kennedy received 303 to Nixon's 219. Senator Harry F. Byrd received six of Alabama's eleven ballots, the eight electoral votes of Mississippi, and one of Oklahoma's electoral ballots. The odd Oklahoma elector was chosen by Republican voters, and while he had a clear understanding of the fact that he was not bound by the Constitution to vote for the convention choice, he apparently was confused about everything else.

Oklahoma gave its support to Richard Nixon by a popular majority of 162,928—nearly double the margin of Eisenhower over Stevenson in 1952 and in 1956. In addition to the industrial counties carried by Eisenhower in the earlier elections, Nixon won such Protestant strongholds as Atoka, Beckham, Caddo, Comanche, Garvin, Grady, Haskell, Hughes, Kiowa, LeFlore, McClain, Okfuskee, Pushmataha, Sequoyah, Stephens, and Washita counties. In a few regions, such as Seminole, Pottawatomie, and Comanche counties, both urbanization and the Protestant bias of many lifelong Democrats were factors in favor of the Republican candidate. Nixon carried fifty-nine of seventy-seven counties. His majorities were over two to one in Garfield, Washington, Woods, Woodward, Blaine, and Texas counties, and nearly two to one in Beaver, Cimarron, Kay, Tulsa, and Oklahoma counties.

The following tabulation shows presidential election results in Oklahoma since statehood:

| *Democratic Candidates* | | *Republican Candidates* | |
|---|---|---|---|
| 1908 William Jennings Bryan | 122,363 | William Howard Taft* | 110,474 |
| 1912 Woodrow Wilson* | 119,156 | William Howard Taft | 90,786 |
| 1916 Woodrow Wilson* | 148,113 | Charles E. Hughes | 97,233 |
| 1920 James M. Cox | 215,808 | Warren G. Harding* | 243,464 |
| 1924 John W. Davis | 259,798 | Calvin Coolidge* | 226,242 |
| 1928 Alfred E. Smith | 219,174 | Herbert Hoover* | 394,046 |
| 1932 Franklin D. Roosevelt* | 515,468 | Herbert Hoover | 188,165 |
| 1936 Franklin D. Roosevelt* | 501,065 | Alfred M. Landon | 245,122 |
| 1940 Franklin D. Roosevelt* | 474,313 | Wendell Willkie | 348,872 |
| 1944 Franklin D. Roosevelt* | 401,549 | Thomas E. Dewey | 319,424 |
| 1948 Harry S. Truman* | 452,782 | Thomas E. Dewey | 268,817 |
| 1952 Adlai Stevenson | 430,979 | Dwight D. Eisenhower* | 518,045 |
| 1956 Adlai Stevenson | 385,581 | Dwight D. Eisenhower* | 473,769 |
| 1960 John F. Kennedy* | 370,111 | Richard Nixon | 533,039 |

*Winner in the national election.

In fourteen presidential elections, Oklahoma has given a majority to the Democratic candidate nine times and to the Republican candidate five times. Four of the departures from Democratic support have been phases of a national trend; that is, Oklahoma was in the current of a strong Republican surge that swept the nation. In the fifth Republican victory in Oklahoma, that of 1960, two powerful forces combined to make Richard Nixon's margin overwhelming. In eleven of the fourteen elections, Oklahoma has voted for the winner. In three, the state has cast its vote for the loser—one Republican and two Democrats.

In spite of the strong evidence of Governor Edmondson's popularity in Oklahoma, his administration became a period of unusual political turmoil. Some of his principal objectives were opposed by determined groups on grounds completely apart from party issues. The result was defeat for his reform program in phases where change was long overdue. The longest legislative session in the history of Oklahoma ended on July 29, 1961, after defeating all efforts to obtain equitable reapportionment of the legislature on the basis of population shifts to the cities.

Tulsa and Oklahoma counties were still limited by a provision of the original constitution which sets the maximum number of representatives from any county at seven. On the population basis, Tulsa County would be entitled to eighteen representatives and Oklahoma County to twenty-three. A by-product of the fight between the executive and legislative branches of the government was the refusal of the lawmakers to pass needed appropriations and a consequent shortage in some vital services of the state. The Governor had limited success in expanding the merit system for state employees.

## POLITICS, 1962–1964

For the first time in the state's history, a Republican governor was voted into office in 1961. Henry Bellmon defeated Democrat W. P. Atkinson in the November election, but the Democrats carried all other major state offices. The Republicans seated one congressman, Page Belcher, in the First District; the Democrats seated five congressmen: Ed Edmondson, Carl Albert, Tom Steed, John Jarman, and Victor Wickersham. After a bitter fight, A. S. (Mike) Monroney was re-elected to the United States Senate. Upon the death of Senator Robert S. Kerr, J. Howard Edmondson resigned as governor, and was succeeded by Lieutenant Governor George Nigh, who then appointed Edmondson to Kerr's seat in the Senate.

Thus, at the end of 1963, Oklahoma had a Republican governor, two Democrats in the United States Senate, one Republican congressman, Democratic majorities in both houses of the legislature, and a full slate of Democratic officers under the chief executive.

At the same time, a growing tendency toward secret interparty exchange of influence was becoming obvious. "You help our man, we'll help yours." Republicans who registered as Democrats and took an active part in the choice of candidates for both parties became an accepted feature of Oklahoma politics. "Democrats for Ike" and "Democrats for Richard" reduced the programs of both parties to empty declamations of platitudes. Certainly, this was not new in Oklahoma politics—or in the nation at large—but in a period that had some appearance of two-party politics, the bad features of solid partisanship were emphasized. Intrigue replaced the healthy atmosphere of party competition, and it was inevitable that the voters should lose confidence in the weight of their influence in public affairs.

In July, 1963, the federal court declared that the legislature of Oklahoma had not met the ultimatum on reapportionment given by judicial decree a year earlier. That decree had set the final date for a legislative plan as March 8, and prior to that time a measure had been pushed through both houses; but the court labeled the proposal "a patchwork of political maneuvering and manipulation to perpetuate the same invidious apportionment which prevailed under the antecedent laws."

Judge Alfred Murrah of the Tenth U. S. Circuit Court of Appeals wrote the opinion, Judges Ross Rizley and Fred Daugherty joining in the unanimous decision. The plan ordered by the court provided a Senate of 44 members with 8 allotted to Oklahoma County and 7 to Tulsa County. House membership might vary from 107 to 109, with 19 representing Oklahoma County and 15, Tulsa County. "We are convinced," the court declared, "that the legislature, as now constituted, is either unable or unwilling to reapportion itself, in accordance with our concept of the requirements of the equal protection clause of the 14th Amendment."

Through January and February, 1964, the struggle against reapportionment of the Oklahoma legislature continued. The state attorney general, Charles Nesbitt, had asked the United States Supreme Court for a stay of the federal court order of July, 1963; and on February 6, Justice Byron White ordered the stay. With three appeals from the lower court's order awaiting a ruling by the United States Supreme Court, the state election board announced that for the legislative elections of 1964 it would be guided by an apportionment plan advanced by the Oklahoma Supreme Court. The Oklahoma high court's plan provided an increase for the Senate members from Oklahoma and Tulsa counties, but no increase in the representation of those counties in the lower house.

EDUCATION SINCE 1960

In public education Oklahoma has made steady progress toward adequate financial support. The School Land Commission collected a record sum during the fiscal year, 1960–61, from which the common schools received $2,334,943.74. From all sources the educational funds totaled $115,432,000. School districts were reduced by consolidation from 4,450 in 1948 to 1,274 in 1961. The number of one-room schools fell below 300 during 1961. On December 1, 1960, the total number of high schools in the state was 620, and of this number 187 had some measure of racial integration. Integration had also been accomplished without serious difficulty in 102 junior high schools and 196 elementary schools. Governor Edmondson's Committee on Human Relations, under the chairmanship of Harvey P. Everest, did notable work in extending integration into other areas besides the public schools. Certain Oklahoma City restaurants, after long adherence to segregation, announced the abandonment of racial barriers. Hotels and other establishments in Oklahoma City, Tulsa, Okmulgee, Henryetta, and other Oklahoma towns joined the movement, which seems to be general.

Theoretically, the schools of Oklahoma had adopted complete racial integration. Pupils are listed without racial designation, and the school records do not show the percentage of Negroes in the various institutions. Residential distribution still accounted for some all-Negro schools, however; and during 1963 there were instances of refusal by all-white school boards to enroll Negro pupils. A suit was begun on September 12 in a federal court to open the New Lima School in Seminole County to Negro pupils. In Tillman County, Negroes were refused admission to all-white schools. On the reverse side of the integration picture, the state board withheld allocation of state funds to schools that refused obedience to the law. In February, 1964, the Board of Regents of the University of Oklahoma extended anti-discrimination to approved private housing for students. Landlords for approved student housing are required to agree in writing that no student shall be refused available space on the sole grounds of race, nationality, or national origin.

A plan for modernizing the physical plant of the University of Oklahoma School of Medicine was taking shape at the end of 1963. The legislature passed a bill authorizing a bond issue of $7,-000,000, subject to approval of the voters on December 3, for buildings to be constructed in the medical center. The measure was approved by a margin of approximately three to one. In the same election a proposal that the terms of legislators should be lengthened—from two to four years in the house of representatives, and from four to six years in the senate—was defeated, almost four to one. Probably many voters regarded the plan as simply a last-ditch stand to defeat or delay equitable apportionment.

During the fiscal year 1962–63, Oklahoma expended $202,-553,538 for the support of its common schools, approximately $10,-000,000 above that for 1961–62. The average salary of school teachers was $5,257; and the average cost per pupil, which was $36 in 1940 and $246 in 1954, had grown to $325 in 1962.

During the decade, 1953–63, enrollments in the colleges of Oklahoma grew from 39,236 to 67,420. Major increases in November, 1963, were most in evidence on the main campus of the University of Oklahoma, where enrollment was up by 887 over the number in November, 1962; Central State College, which grew by 767 in one year; Northeastern State College, up 508; and Southeastern State College, up 357. Oklahoma State University added 162 students on its main campus and 196 students at the Okmulgee Technological branch, from November, 1962, to November, 1963.

## Development in Roads and Water Resources

The first leg of the third Oklahoma turnpike, the H. E. Bailey Turnpike, running from Oklahoma City to Lawton, was opened on March 1, 1964; the last portion, to the Texas line, a few weeks later. This toll road is 84.6 miles in length with 26.6 miles of freeway connecting roads built by a state bond issue of $56,500,000. The four-lane bypass at Oklahoma City, seven miles in length, connects Interstate Highway 35 with the toll road entrance.

This southwestern turnpike, with the earlier toll roads—the

Turner and the Will Rogers—completed a continuous four-lane express highway across the state for 337.6 miles from a point near Joplin, Missouri, to the Texas line north of Wichita Falls. Tulsa, Oklahoma City, and Lawton are thus connected by highways of limited access with Missouri on the northeast and Texas on the southwest.

Inland water projects for Oklahoma, based on plans that grew out of an act of Congress in 1946, have developed rapidly. Reservoirs at Oologah on the Verdigris, Keystone on the Arkansas-Cimarron, and Eufaula, at the forks of the Canadian, are among the most notable additions to the state's struggle for an adequate supply of water. The late Senator Robert S. Kerr envisioned a series of dams that would create some four hundred miles of navigable water by 1972 along the Arkansas River and its tributaries between Catoosa and the Mississippi.

Construction began on the Eufaula project in 1958; and on February 10, 1964, Senator Kerr's widow took part in the ceremony of closing the last sluice gate in the Eufaula Dam.

Another important water project, an Atoka–Oklahoma City pipe line one hundred miles in length with six pumping stations, was ready for its first test in February, 1964. Water from Atoka in southeastern Oklahoma is pumped to Elm Creek Reservoir to supplement the water supply of Oklahoma City.

# CHAPTER EIGHTEEN

# The Culture of Oklahoma

## GENERAL CHARACTERISTICS

In a broad sense all the preceding chapters have dealt with the development of culture in Oklahoma. The background of primitive Indian life, the transformation of Indian culture through contact with white men—explorers, traders, missionaries, government agents, politicians, educators, intermarried citizens, and others perhaps less worthy—the farming, mining, building, educational, and religious activities of settlers in every stage of Oklahoma's growth—all these and many more items make up the culture of the state. In this chapter it is our purpose to deal with culture in a narrower sense.

What have been the contributions of Oklahoma to public education, literature, the fine arts? In what respects and in what degree is American civilization richer, better, or different from the culture of earlier times as the result of ideas or things developed in Oklahoma? In short, to what extent has the state added directly to the enlightenment and refinement of the present century?

A considerable part of the interest to be found in regional studies lies in the differences between people of separate geographical areas. The focus of attention upon distinguishing traits has led to neglect of an obvious and important fact: the culture of an American state is simply a part of national development. There is no such thing as a segregated culture, for the factors of unity far outweigh the items of difference. Particularly in the era of rapid transportation, easy access to news reports, common acquaintance with books and periodicals, motion pictures, and television, the culture area is far wider than the state. Even in earlier days, moreover, the tendency was strong for usages, conveniences, and beliefs to spread. The pre-Caddoan culture of Oklahoma was related to

426

that of the Tombigbee Valley. Later, a mission of the Going Snake District of the Cherokee Nation was constantly engaged in the introduction of New England life to Indian pupils. The writer of editorials for an Indian newspaper at Park Hill or Atoka used the techniques employed in Washington and Atlanta.

Yet it is obvious that the environment of the Cherokee and Choctaw Indians before the Civil War was vastly different from that of the citizens in eastern seaboard towns. Furthermore, the primitive and vigorous traits of that Indian and pioneer society have placed their mark upon every generation of Oklahomans. Their culture is not an isolated development, but it has in it peculiar elements of distinction which belong to the Indian, the cattleman, the tiller of the earth, and the free western plainsman.

Kenneth Kaufman, who lived forty-seven years of his life in Oklahoma, was a product and an enduring factor of its peculiar culture. In *Level Land*, a book of verse published in 1935, he wrote:

*"But I, who never have been anywhere,*
*But opened first wide eyes on waving grass,*
*Can bring you but the love of this wide land*
*Whose beauty sometimes has caught me unaware;*
*Sunrise and starshine, and the winds that pass*
*Over the plains; and you will understand."*[1]

In an address delivered at the dedication ceremony for Kaufman Hall on the University of Oklahoma campus in 1949, Savoie Lottinville touched upon some traits of Kenneth Kaufman which help to explain the paradox of a culture area that is common, yet distinct, unique, yet part of an uniform pattern.

"He was forever curious, forever observant, not merely with his mind but with his poet's eye and from the heart: the golden plover coming down to the fresh furrow behind the plow, the curlew's distant cry at dusk, the full baying of a hound dog in the valley below, sun and the odor of saddle leather on the long drive with a trail herd—these, as well as Homer, Cervantes, Goethe, Molière, and Shakespeare, were well-beloved elements in Kenneth Kaufman's world."

[1] Kenneth Kaufman, *Level Land.*

In the present era an Oklahoma writer of fiction or drama addresses his words to a public much wider than his state. He understands this wider audience and they understand him, because his people are like the people of other areas in the nation. However, the interest that he arouses may spring in part from the fact that his background, his people, the scenes he has witnessed, and the folklore he has heard are different from all others. His region has shades of color, designs and patterns of culture, ideas and attitudes which help to shape his product.

In tracing the development of the Creek Indians in Oklahoma, a study of their Alabama background, early towns, the roofs and walls that protected them, their food, clothing, and means of living is necessary for an understanding of the people. Similarly the sod house, log cabin, or frame shanty of the settler who took a claim is a significant part of his story; but the separate study of a thousand one-roomed shanties as examples of regional architecture would reach, perhaps in the second unit, the point of diminishing returns. The same principle holds for many other phases of Oklahoma culture. A significant contribution has not been made by every person who has published a story with its setting in the Cherokee Outlet or who has borrowed a hillbilly tune, adapted it to a cowboy song, and had it recorded for a million victims of the juke-box.

The culture of Oklahoma is made up of items that have proved good enough to be permanent or that give promise of permanence. Will Rogers was not great because he chewed gum and twirled a rope, but because he looked straight at the contemporary scene and told the truth about what he saw. He was a reflective Cherokee-American, and the rope was simply background for his frank, good-humored observations. If one small trace of the braggart had marred his humor, its spell would have been broken. But life in Oologah, where the men he respected laughed at swashbuckling, left him capable of enjoying a joke on Will Rogers. His newspaper column was good in Washington, New York, Colorado Springs, and Claremore.

The civilization of the Chickasaw Nation in the era of Governor Douglas H. Johnston (1898–1902; 1904–1906) included the native Indian culture, modified by contacts with Europeans in the Mississippi homeland of the tribe. Included also were the patterns of culture brought from colleges of Connecticut and Massachusetts to the Chickasaw and Choctaw academies. Music and drama at Bloomfield were phases of culture which had a lasting influence on Indian life, and indirectly on the entire future of Oklahoma.

The culture of Oklahoma Territory at the time of Governor Thompson B. Ferguson (1901–1906) was not exclusively the pursuit of knowledge in books and laboratories, emphasized by President David Ross Boyd at the University or by President Angelo C. Scott at the A. and M. College. Nor did the culture of the territory consist entirely of rural festivals, Indian dances, wildcat drilling, young metropolitan newspapers, or the opinions of the territorial supreme court. It was a combination of all these items and a multitude more. It was big and complex, filled with variety and incongruity but also with vigor and power, running over with optimism and good humor.

The population of Oklahoma Territory and Indian Territory was approximately 270,000 in 1890.[2] Ten years later the official census placed population of the two territories at 790,000—nearly a three-fold increase in one decade. Obviously the people in 1900 were more than half newcomers and their culture was that of the regions from which they came. That is to say, it was the culture of Kansas, Texas, Arkansas, Missouri, and many other states in widely separated geographical areas. The ideas and practices of these people were added to the basis of culture already present in the Twin Territories. The new citizens influenced and in turn were shaped by the environment in which they settled.

By 1910 the number had gone up to 1,657,155—more than double the last previous count—in 1920 the population was over 2,000,000, and in 1930 it had reached 2,396,040. During the next two decades population in Oklahoma decreased slightly, to 2,233,351 in 1950. After 1945, however, the population trend seems to be slightly upward at the rate of about 28,000 per year. The estimate for July, 1952 was 2,260,487.[3] Indian population in 1945

[2] Population of the Indian Territory was 197,000, including the freedmen, the small tribes in the northeast, and white intruders, along with the Five Civilized Tribes. The new settlers in Oklahoma numbered 61,000 and the Indians of Oklahoma Territory, 13,167. U. S. Bureau of the Census, *Eleventh Report: Population.*

[3] Bureau of Business Research, University of Oklahoma, *Oklahoma Business Bulletin,* August, 1953.

was 110,864—also an increase over previous census figures for Oklahoma Indians.[4] Of the total population, the fraction born in Oklahoma steadily increased from 1890 to 1950, and the foreign-born population decreased, falling from 40,084 in 1910 to 18,906 in 1950.[5] Negro population in 1950 was 145,469 or approximately one sixteenth of the total.

Early in the period of rapid settlement of Oklahoma, notable differences appeared among the people in separate sections of the state. The possibilities of cotton growing in the southwestern and central portions attracted farmers from Texas, Mississippi, and Arkansas. A considerable part of these people, farming cotton for a share in the crop, were retarded by their hard economic lot; but they were also made keen to recognize the natural rights of man and humble with the philosophy of adversity. As conditions of public education improved, illiteracy among them decreased; but the cultivation and harvesting of cotton continued as a cause for poor attendance in elementary schools for many years. Considerable areas in southwestern Oklahoma are still dominated by cotton production, although the acreage varies widely from year to year. Livestock and diversified farming have increased the prosperity of the entire section, and cultural differences from other parts of the state, dependent upon material progress, have shown a corresponding change.

The coal-mining regions, no longer active as in times past, have in their population large elements descended from European miners transplanted in America one or more generations ago. In Ottawa County the lead and zinc mines have created a society distinct from the rest of Oklahoma. Wheat farming in north central and northwestern Oklahoma is responsible for culture traits that are in some respects peculiar. Although the differences between sections are often overestimated, the trade centers of this area have obvious traits in their appearance which distinguish them: towering grain elevators, neat business blocks, substantial school buildings, wide streets, and well-kept lawns. In common with most

[4] Wright, *Indian Tribes of Oklahoma*, 4.

[5] U. S. Bureau of the Census, *Seventeenth Report*, Vol. II, Part 36. *Oklahoma*, 38 (Table 24).

430

American towns, less desirable features may be seen in these progressive communities, such as unpainted huts used as human habitations, dirty taverns, and lots filled with the unsightly wrecks of automobiles. In some degree, Oklahoma towns in all sections have a brightness of appearance that arises from the presence of new buildings, generous use of paint, and a large per cent of fair weather.

Among the outstanding contributors to Oklahoma culture, some have found subjects for their work on the western frontier and their principal inspiration within the borders of the state. Will Rogers, although he discovered materials for his humorous philosophy in Washington and Hollywood, Bluefield, West Virginia, and Houston, Texas, was still as much a part of the Sooner State as an oil well in the shadow of the Capitol or a Wichita grass house. Edward Everett Dale, born in a neighboring state, trained in research and distinguished for his histories and his lectures on a wide variety of subjects, yet belongs to the soil and people of Oklahoma as the Cimarron River belongs. Alexander Posey, member of the Creek tribe and resident of the Indian Territory, was an Oklahoman in lineage, background, and the character of the poetry he wrote.

Other persons who have helped to shape the culture of the state have done so by bringing to it some notable phase of outside development to link Oklahoma with the best in modern civilization. The medical practices of Vienna, the common law as it is taught at Oxford, English composition in the Harvard manner, botany in the best traditions of Germany, and mathematics as the subject is presented in Belgium—none of which are native to Oklahoma—have yet been made a part of its culture. All the men of medicine and music, art, physics, and architecture, geology and journalism who were trained elsewhere and labored effectively in Oklahoma were contributors to the state's culture—in some instances, large contributors.

Samuel Austin Worcester, a son of New England who was educated for the ministry, came to Georgia in 1825 at the age of twenty-seven and reached Park Hill in the western Cherokee Nation ten years later. His contribution was in the field of religion, use of the printing press, and the steady pressure that he exerted, as a man of character and learning, toward adjusting Indians to the civilization of white men. His preparation for ministry on the Indian frontier included a term in the Georgia penitentiary where he was sent by state authorities in violation of a Cherokee treaty and held in violation of a decision by the United States Supreme Court. Because of his courage in maintaining the cause of justice for the Cherokees, Worcester held a place of peculiar honor among them. He was the advance agent of many able men who came to introduce in Oklahoma the culture of other regions.

## EDUCATION IN OKLAHOMA

From the start Oklahoma drew upon the educational experience of older communities, and its schools are largely the product of men who received their training elsewhere. Educational trends at various levels of instruction cover the nation from coast to coast. Like other states Oklahoma has embraced new and improved methods of teaching, reforms in curriculum, and new standards of educational equipment, along with many fads that sweep the country like new styles in hairdressing, or in the case of some ill-considered changes, like minor pestilences. Because the region is newly settled and its people have contained a large element of youth, Oklahoma has been enthusiastic in its exchange of the old for the new. Hence, educational experiments have been plentiful, progress has been marked, and blunders have been many.

By comparison with educational systems of older states and particularly wealthier states, Oklahoma has never ranked high in its educational program. In struggling upward from the discouraging poverty of territorial schools, when buildings, equipment, and books were inadequate, Oklahomans have generally viewed their schools with extreme optimism. But in spite of confident claims by territorial governors and many grades of educational leaders, the state still has libraries and laboratories that are not the best, examples of low standards in teacher preparation, and perhaps its full share of current educational quackery.

In 1949, Oklahoma expended $167.03 per pupil in the public

432

schools. Thirty-four states and the District of Columbia invested more money per pupil, thirteen states invested less. The average national expenditure for each person in school was more than thirty dollars higher than that of Oklahoma. The liberal and progressive trend in Oklahoma may be seen, however, in the fact that its expenditure per pupil rose during the period 1944 to 1949 by 73 per cent. The national average for the same period rose by approximately 58 per cent.[6]

Another hopeful tendency in the education of Oklahoma is the high per cent of its total income that is devoted to schools—a condition that has been persistent since early territorial days. The national expenditure for education in 1944 was 1.53 per cent of total income; in Oklahoma the figure was 1.92 per cent. Only nine of the states ranked higher.[7]

Some of the ablest schoolmen of Oklahoma, particularly in the early days of statehood, have encountered the opposition of strong political factions. President David Ross Boyd of the University of Oklahoma was released in the conflict of transition from territorial government to statehood. Thirteen members of his teaching force were removed, or resigned as the result of political pressure in this period. Most of them were men of considerable ability, difficult to replace; and among them was Vernon Louis Parrington, perhaps the most talented teacher and writer who ever lived in Oklahoma.[8] Stratton D. Brooks, employed in 1912 to remedy the bad situation created by partisan politics over the state university, held the presidency for eleven years and was forced out during the brief and stormy career of Governor Jack Walton. In the departure of Brooks, the state lost another schoolman of rare ability.

President Angelo C. Scott of A. and M. College at Stillwater survived the political ordeal of statehood, but was forced into political fights in his efforts to provide the growing college with adequate libraries, laboratories, and teaching staff. Henry G. Bennett, a later president at the A. and M. College, and William B. Bizzell at the University of Oklahoma were more successful in

6 *Statistical Abstract of the United States, 1952.*

7 United States Bureau of Education, *Biennial Survey, 1944–46.*

8 Gittinger, *The University of Oklahoma.* 54, 196.

bridging the gap between political interests and educational progress.

The current trend in regard to support of schools in Oklahoma is upward. State aid for school districts that were unable to maintain a full term of instruction was voted by the legislature for the first time in 1921. The appropriation at that time was $100,000, the Ninth Legislature raised the amount to $650,000, and during Governor Trapp's economy program the annual aid was reduced to $500,000. Under the influence of E. W. Marland the Fifteenth Legislature appropriated annual aid in the amount of $8,200,000 and the Sixteenth Legislature raised the amount of $12,800,000.

With the principle of state responsibility for adequate child training firmly established, progress has been rapid. The Twenty-fourth Legislature in 1953 appropriated $29,515,000 per year for school aid and made additional funds of more than $3,000,000 available for elementary schools. The evidence is persistent that Oklahomans believe strongly in public education and that the basic principles advocated by educators such as Stratton D. Brooks and state officials like E. W. Marland have not been lost.

## LITERATURE

The writing of books has become a major factor in the culture of Oklahoma. The range covered by Oklahoma writers is enormous, and of course the variation in the quality of product is wide. Since a survey of the field is impossible within the limits of this discussion, a few representative authors will be presented to indicate the character of the work done by Oklahoma poets, humorists, and historians.

Alexander Lawrence Posey was a Creek poet whose verses had unique character and lasting charm. He was born in the Creek Nation in 1873. His father was an intermarried white citizen and a cattleman. His mother was fullblood Indian, and Alex spoke only the Creek language until he was twelve years old.[9] He attended

[9] Minnie L. Posey, ed., *The Poems of Alexander Lawrence Posey;* Debo, *Oklahoma: Foot-loose and Fancy-free,* 232, 233.

434

Bacone Indian University at Muskogee, wrote for the *Baconian*, and made a start in his writing of poems and other literary efforts. Later, he became editor of the *Indian Journal* at Eufaula. His life was cut short in 1908, when he was drowned in the North Canadian River. His tragic end has drawn the attention of many readers to his little poem, "My Fancy," written but a short time before his death:

> *Why do trees along the river*
> *Lean so far out o'er the tide?*
> *Very wise men tell me why, but*
> *I am never satisfied;*
> *And so I keep my fancy still,*
> *That trees lean out to save*
> *The drowning from the clutches of*
> *The cold remorseless wave.*

Other poems by Posey reveal the Indian's close contact with nature, his dependence upon the elements, his feeling of intimacy with natural forces. "Coyote," "The Mocking Bird," "To a Robin," "My Hermitage," "The Flower of Tulledega," and "The West Wind" have in them the sentiment of a people for the land that gave them nurture.

His "Chitto Harjo," written upon the occasion of Crazy Snake's imprisonment in 1900, is different in tone.[10] The chief of the "Crazy Snake Rebellion" was leader of a fullblood group who simply were unable to adjust themselves to the inevitable absorption of Indians into the white man's society. Alex Posey was a leader of those Creeks who believed strongly in the education of Indians, individual landholding, and United States citizenship for members of his tribe. In spite of their opposite stand on Creek policy, the poet understood his fellow Indian's point of view, as the final lines of the poem clearly show.

> *A traitor, outlaw—what you will,*
> *He is the noble red man still.*
> *Condemn him and his kind to shame!*
> *I bow to him, exalt his name.*

[10] Debo, *The Road to Disappearance*, 376.

435

Yet another mood is found in Posey's letters of "Fus Fixico," a mood of whimsical, mild satire. The author lapsed into the Creek-English dialect easily because in conversation with fullblood Indians he heard it spoken and used it himself. He had the love of laughter that is common to the Indian's nature and the quaint sense of humor that appears so often in the Indian's speech. One of the short poems will serve to illustrate his use of dialect.

### Hotgun on the Death of Yadeka Harjo

"Well so," Hotgun he say,
  "My ol' time frien' Yadeka Harjo, he
Was died the other day,
  An' they was no ol'-timer left but me.

"Hotulk Emathla he
  Was go to be good Injun long time 'go,
An' Woxie Harjoche
  Been dead ten years or twenty, maybe so.

"All has to die at las';
  I live long time, but now my days was few;
'Fore long poke-weeds an' grass
  Be growin' all around my grave-house too."

Wolf Warrior he listen close,
  An' Kono Harjo pay close 'tention, too;
Tokpafka Micco he almos'
  Let his pipe go out a time or two.

Other Oklahoma Indians have shown talent in poetry and various forms of creative writing. John Rollin Ridge, who went from the Cherokee Nation to California after his father was killed in 1839, wrote under the nom de plume Yellow Bird. His collected poems, like those of Alexander Posey, made a small but extremely interesting volume, with many touches that reveal the thought and sentiment of the Indian. John Joseph Mathews, a living member of the Osage tribe, has written books of distinction: *Wah'kon-tah, Sundown, Life and Death of an Oil Man,* and *The Osages.*[11]

[11] *Wak'Kon-Tah* (Norman, 1932); *Sundown* (New York, 1935); *Talking to the Moon* (Chicago, 1945); *Life and Death of an Oilman* (Norman, 1951); *The Osages: Children of the Middle Waters* (Norman, 1961).

Will Rogers, Oklahoma's best-known humorist, was born on a ranch twelve miles north of Claremore on November 4, 1879. His father, Clem V. Rogers, was a mixed-blooded Cherokee who served with Stand Watie's forces during the Civil War. His mother was one-fourth Cherokee, "an old-fashioned woman named Mary," as Will described her. Will grew up in the Verdigris country, attended school at intervals, and spent much time hunting and exploring the area around Dog Iron Ranch, his father's home.

Clem Rogers sent the lad to school at several places—Neosho, Missouri, "Drumgoul," near Chelsea, Indian Territory, Kemper at Boonville, Missouri, and elsewhere. "In some of them I would last for three or four months," he recalled. He always started in the fourth grade when he enrolled in a new school. "I had that education thing figured down to a fine point," he wrote in his *Autobiography*. "Three years in McGuffey's Fourth Reader, and I knew more about it than McGuffey did."[12]

Will worked as a ranch hand in western Oklahoma, wrangling ponies, branding calves, learning to handle range livestock. Eventually Clem Rogers gave him the Dog Iron Ranch; but Will was more interested in country dances, horse races, and roping contests than in the serious business of ranching. He fiddled for dances, roped steers at the Elks' Carnival in Springfield, Missouri, entered as many roping contests as possible, and acquired a remarkable cow pony, Comanche. At the Rough Riders' Reunion in Oklahoma City he contested with the best of the performers—Clay McGonnagill, Tom Vest, Abe Wilson, Booger Red of San Angelo, Texas, and many others. "I broke my rope and old Jim O'Donnell won," Will recorded. "He'd of beat me anyhow."

Will started as a professional entertainer with Colonel Zack Mulhall's Wild West Show. As a cowboy comedian he was in great demand and he traveled to many lands—England, the continent of Europe, New Zealand, Australia, and Africa. Back in New York he played at Hammerstein's and in Ziegfeld's Follies, and appeared on occasions where a single well-known performer was desired, such as important political banquets. He appeared at the unveiling of the Pioneer Woman statue, in Ponca City, Oklahoma; and he tried his hand at motion-picture acting in Hollywood. He wrote a news-

12 Rogers, *The Autobiography of Will Rogers*, 3.

paper column that was used by a large number of metropolitan papers, devoting his space largely to current political events. Nominating conventions of the major political parties always caught his attention, but he wrote comments on a wide range of subjects. He abused politicians without rancor, because there was no bitterness in him. They enjoyed his "attacks" and the public loved them.

In regard to the settlement of peace terms with Germany in 1919, Will wrote: "One thing we got to be thankful for our soldiers can win wars faster than our diplomats can talk us into them."[13] He called attention to the length of the peace terms—eighty thousand words he said—"only thing ever written longer than a LaFollette Speech." Will referred to President Calvin Coolidge as "my genial competitor for the nation's ear." After a gallstone operation, he had many observations to make concerning surgery in general and gallstone removals in particular. What were the causes of the malady? "Republicans staying in power too long will increase the epidemic; seeing the same ending to Moving Pictures is a prime cause; a wife driving from the back seat will cause Gastric juices to form an acid, and that slowly jells into a stone as she keeps hollering."[14]

Will Rogers wrote a great deal and appeared before many audiences, generally under the pressure of a heavy schedule of work. He was expected to start roars of laughter in his audiences and he usually did. Not all of his humor was equal to that of Mark Twain at his best; for that matter, neither was Mark Twain's. But there is unique quality in the observations of the ranch boy from Oologah. Simplicity, directness, and honesty were there, along with belief in people and understanding of their human weaknesses. Much of his life was occupied with work in which the greatest threat to his success was in the peril of egotism. If he had seen himself as a romantic daredevil during his reckless youth, he might have survived, but not as a legend of humorous philosophy. He was honest in his appraisal of opponents, frank in his estimates of his own skill as a roper and trick rider, humble in the face of evidence that vast numbers of people regarded him highly, and generous in his estimates of other men. He knew his limitations, he was

[13] *Ibid.*, 56.
[14] Rogers, *Ether and Me, or Just Relax,* 65.

genuine, and he summed up the wisdom of a large section of Oklahoma society.

Histories by Oklahomans cover a wide range of material, including subjects far removed from the state. Some of the historians have devoted themselves chiefly to Oklahoma subjects—the American Indian, the range cattle industry, the formation of the forty-sixth state. Since space does not permit an adequate coverage of all the historians of merit, our purpose shall be to give a brief account of a few historians who have written about Oklahoma.

Best known of this group is Edward Everett Dale, whose range of interest is wide and whose special fields of research are the American Indian and the cattle industry of the Southwest. He was born in Texas in 1879. He lived in southwestern Oklahoma and worked as a cowboy and ranchman from the age of sixteen until he was twenty-two. He taught a country school, attended the Central Teachers College at Edmond, and took his B.A. degree at the University of Oklahoma in 1911. His graduate work was done at Harvard, where he received the M.A. degree in 1914 and the Ph.D. in 1922.

He began his work as a teacher of college classes at the University of Oklahoma in 1914. In ten years he became professor of history and head of the department. In 1943 he became research professor of history and in 1952, research professor emeritus. In 1953 and 1954 he served for a year as Fullbright Lecturer at the University of Melbourne in Australia. During his teaching career, Professor Dale has been in demand for addresses and seminars in many colleges throughout the United States. He is widely known also for his occasional lectures, on a variety of subjects. His whimsical humor gives a special charm to his speeches, both in the college classroom and on the public platform. Many hundreds of students have become absorbed in the study of history through his inspiring work as a teacher, and many thousands through his books.

Among his histories are the following: *The Range Cattle Industry* (Norman, 1930); *Readings in Oklahoma History* (ed., with Jesse L. Rader, Evanston, Ill., 1930); *History of Oklahoma* (with James S. Buchanan, Evanston, Ill., 1935); *Cherokee Cavaliers* (ed., with Gaston Litton, Norman, 1939); *Cow Country* (Norman, 1942); *History of Oklahoma* (with Morris L. Wardell, New York,

439

1948); *History of the United States* (with D. L. Dummond and E. B. Wesley, New York, 1948); *The Indians of the Southwest* (Norman, 1949).

Joseph B. Thoburn, who served for many years as secretary of the Oklahoma Historical Society, was a prolific writer. His most useful study is the four-volume history which he published in 1929 with Miss Muriel Wright as coauthor: *Oklahoma, a History of the State and Its People.*[15] This work contains a great deal of the historical record that is not available elsewhere. Miss Wright is still actively engaged in writing and is on the editorial staff of the *Chronicles of Oklahoma,* official publication of the Oklahoma Historical Society. One of her best books is the latest, *A Guide to the Indian Tribes of Oklahoma.*[16]

Grant Foreman is an important name in the field of Indian history, early Oklahoma history, and related frontier subjects. For twenty years he produced a steady stream of articles and books. He read widely, traveled far in search of records, worked diligently in the archives of this and other countries, and made valuable contributions in the discovery and preservation of source materials. Throughout his long life, assisted by his wife, Carolyn Thomas Foreman, a historian in her own right, he maintained an unwavering flame of interest for finding and recording facts of historical significance. In some of his works, the dry and dusty records have been woven into narratives of fascinating interest. The Grant Foreman books include the following: *Pioneer Days in the Early Southwest* (Cleveland, 1926); *A Traveler in Indian Territory* (Cedar Rapids, Iowa, 1930); *Indians and Pioneers* (New Haven, 1930; Norman, 1936); *Indian Removal* (Norman, 1932); *Advancing the Frontier* (Norman, 1933); *The Five Civilized Tribes* (Norman, 1934); *Down the Texas Road* (Norman, 1936); *Fort Gibson* (Norman, 1936); *Adventure on Red River* (Norman, 1937); *Marcy and the Gold Seekers* (Norman, 1939); and *A History of Oklahoma* (Norman, 1942).

Angie Debo is the historian of the Choctaws and the Creeks, among other fields of research. She combines a high grade of

[15] Thoburn and Wright, *Oklahoma: A History of the State and Its People* (4 vols., New York, 1929).

[16] Wright, *A Guide to the Indian Tribes of Oklahoma* (Norman, 1951).

scholarship with a command of the English language which gives her work distinction. Her books are readable, filled with interesting, vital subject matter, and they show meticulous care in their accuracy. Among her principal works are the following: *The Rise and Fall of the Choctaw Republic* (Norman, 1934); *And Still the Waters Run* (Princeton, 1940); *The Road to Disappearance* (Norman, 1941); *Tulsa: From Creek Town to Oil Capital* (Norman, 1943); *Prairie City* (New York, 1944); *Oklahoma: Foot-loose and Fancy-free* (Norman, 1949); and *The Five Civilized Tribes* (Philadelphia, 1951).

Roy Gittinger has published two books on Oklahoma history. The quality of the work compensates, in a measure, for the relatively small volume, although it is regrettable that his long service as an administrator and teacher did not afford him more time for writing. Each of his two books is definitive in its field. All students of Oklahoma history are indebted to Dean Gittinger for his thorough, well-balanced, and scholarly treatise, *The Formation of the State of Oklahoma.*

Roy Gittinger was first employed to teach history in the preparatory department at the University of Oklahoma in 1902, when he was twenty-four years of age. He was a fine instructor and his advancement was rapid. He received the M.A. degree at the University of Chicago in 1906 and the Ph.D. degree at the University of California in 1916. He became professor of English history in 1905, dean of undergraduates in 1915, dean of admissions in 1926, and regents' professor of history in 1946. In 1954 he is still teaching classes in English history. His twenty-seven years of administrative duties combined with classroom work, from 1915 to 1941, covered a period when the University of Oklahoma was growing rapidly. The office of admissions was undermanned, and the duties of the dean were heavy, but he could not be spared entirely from the work of class instruction. One of the remarkable facts of his career is that he found time to write two books of high quality. His second book was *The University of Oklahoma,* published in 1942 by the University of Oklahoma Press at Norman.

Stanley Vestal's writing covers a wide range of subjects and a considerable variety of literary forms: verse, essays, fiction, history, and biography. His treatises on the technique of writing have had a wide influence, best confirmed by the quality and amount of the work published by his students. His titles indicate the nature of his interests in biography and history: *Kit Carson, Sitting Bull, Warpath, King of the Fur Traders, Bigfoot Wallace, Jim Bridger, The Old Santa Fe Trail, New Sources of Indian History, Mountain Men, Warpath and Council Fire,* and *Dodge City.*

*Warpath and Council Fire* deals with the Plains Indians from Montana to Texas, over the forty years from 1851 to 1891.[17] "The Plains Indians put up a great fight, inflicting five casualties on the troops for every one they suffered," the author wrote in his preface. "And the best of them were no mean diplomats. This book is the story of their struggle, in war and in diplomacy, to keep their country from the whites." When Stanley Vestal tells the story of Black Kettle's disaster in the Battle of the Washita, he is in a familiar setting. As a boy he played over the ground—hunting rabbits, following his dogs, racing his pony against the mounts of Indian boys, some of them descended from the survivors of Black Kettle's band. He knows his recorded sources, too—War Department reports, letters of men who fought in the battle, and other accounts of contemporaries. Best of all, he knows the people who fought over the Southwestern Plains—not only Custer and his men but also the people who were encamped along the Washita, and were awakened, belatedly, by the "negligent sentinel, Double Wolf." One phase of the battle, Major Elliott's pursuit of the fleeing Cheyennes as a part of the "mopping up" action after the main clash at dawn, Stanley Vestal heard from the Indian warrior Roman Nose Thunder forty-five years after the battle and pieced it together with Custer's account.

The historian of the Cherokees in Oklahoma is Morris L. Wardell.[18] Many other writers have dealt with portions of Cherokee history, and some of them have made notable contributions. Marion L. Starkey, for example, has traced the history of the tribe in Georgia, the Carolinas, and Tennessee, prior to their westward removal, and she has written with skill and understanding of the people.[19]

[17] Vestal, *Warpath and Council Fire.*
[18] Morris L. Wardell, *A Political History of the Cherokee Nation, 1838–1907* (Norman, 1938).
[19] Starkey, *The Cherokee Nation* (New York, 1946).

Grant Foreman and Carolyn Thomas Foreman have treated some phases of Cherokee history and have preserved important portions of the record. But the thorough, comprehensive work on the Cherokee Nation in its western home is that of Professor Wardell. It is scholarly, readable, and is a book of such importance as to give its author a secure place among the historians of Oklahoma.

## VERNON LOUIS PARRINGTON, SOJOURNER IN OKLAHOMA

Vernon Louis Parrington was born at Aurora, Illinois, in 1871. His father was a New England man who graduated at Colby, became a captain during the Civil War, and served as a public-school principal in New York and Illinois. The family moved west again, this time to Kansas, where Vernon attended public school and after graduation from high school, entered the College of Emporia. Returning to his father's section of the country for more advanced education, he was admitted to Harvard as a junior, and after graduation he returned to Emporia to teach English and French in the College. In 1897 he came to the University of Oklahoma, where he taught classes in English composition and literature for the next eleven years. He also demonstrated his versatility by coaching the football team until a full-time instructor in that sport could be obtained. In 1901, Parrington married Julia Rochester Williams of Norman, Oklahoma.[20]

The transition from territorial government to statehood involved no little partisan conflict in the colleges of the forty-sixth state. In the words of Henry Steele Commager, Parrington was "blown from Oklahoma to the Pacific coast" by a "political cyclone," in 1908.[21] His great books on the cultural history of America were developed and written after he moved to Seattle; but his keen analysis of literary product, his grasp of the forces that made colonial and national politics, even the polished sentences in which he set forth his views, were the daily intellectual diet spread before

[20] *Dictionary of American Biography*, IV, 253, 254 (article by George Harvey Genzmer); Henry Steele Commager, *The American Mind*, 293–309.
[21] Commager, *The American Mind*, 298.

his students of literature at the University of Oklahoma. His sharp mind was grappling with the political doctrines of Roger Williams as he sought to introduce the thought of that freethinking early American to young Democrats, Republicans, and Populists from the farms, ranches, and towns of Oklahoma Territory. He was fighting the battle of popular liberties and the right of people to control their own destinies when he presented to his classes the mind of Thomas Jefferson, as he was later when he wrote of Jeffersonianism, "Government from the grave is a negation of the inalienable rights of the newborn"; and in another passage, "The love of profits is always seeking to overthrow the rule of justice."[22]

*Main Currents in American Thought,* in three volumes, was the work which won a Pulitzer Prize for Parrington and brought him wide recognition from American scholars. *The Colonial Mind, 1620–1800; The Romantic Revolution in America, 1800–1860;* and *The Beginnings of Critical Realism in America, 1860–1920,* are the titles of his three volumes.

Parrington was at his best when he dealt with a Tory like Thomas Hutchinson of Massachusetts, or when he analyzed the work of an intellectual liberal like William Cullen Bryant. When he failed to sound the depth of a character or to estimate accurately the total influence of a person, it was generally the result of the agrarian liberalism that colored the politics of Illinois, Kansas, Oklahoma, and Washington in his day. His estimate of John Marshall shows clear evidence of the tendency. "Masterful" and "tenacious" are the only descriptive terms in which reluctant admiration for the "judicial sovereign," Marshall, can be discerned. "No man in America was less democratic in his political convictions," he wrote, of the great Virginia jurist who held the chair of chief justice for one third of the nineteenth century. The prejudice in this view may be tested by comparing it with the opinions of John Marshall's contemporaries. Extreme partisans among the Federalists regarded him lukewarm in his support of their party; he was a moderate Federalist by every test that includes historical perspective. Parrington accepts the view of the political antagonist who contested every point with Marshall for thirty years—Thomas

[22] Parrington, *Main Currents in American Thought* (3 vols., New York, 1927–30), II, 12.

Jefferson. The liberal opinions of Jefferson were acceptable to the region of agrarian discontent—the middle western states, where Parrington was born and where he received his early education and his first opportunity to instruct youth. During the administrations of Benjamin Harrison, Grover Cleveland, and William McKinley, the Populists furnished much of the impulse toward liberal thinking in this area and to some extent Parrington shared their prejudices. His estimate of the Federalist chief justice was a partisan valuation. "Of social and humanitarian interests he was utterly devoid," Parrington wrote. "One might as well look for the sap of idealism in a last year's stump as in John Marshall."[23]

## CONCLUSION

The contributions of Oklahoma in architecture, mechanical invention, the printing of newspapers, periodicals, and books, painting, sculpture, and music, all contain elements of distinction. Treatment in detail of these cultural developments cannot be attempted in this survey. The work of Oscar B. Jacobson at the University of Oklahoma School of Art, in discovering talent in young painters and helping them to develop their skill, would have a special place in an extensive treatise upon culture in Oklahoma. The Indian painters, many of whom were students of Professor Jacobson, would also receive, in a detailed study of the state's development in fine arts, more space than can be devoted to them in this survey.

Musicians and musical organizations have made notable contributions in every decade since statehood. Bohumil Makovsky built a fine tradition for good music at the Oklahoma A. and M. College; and, it may be added that there was a sound basis of music appreciation in the community, developed in territorial and early statehood days by such enlightened leaders as President Angelo C. Scott. Makovsky served as director of the college band and head of the music department, under a variety of titles, for thirty-five years,

[23] *Ibid.,* II, 22.

445

and left behind him a permanent impression upon the musical taste of the Southwest.

Dean Frederick Holmberg at the University of Oklahoma early established the precedent of high-grade instruction in the music department, and his successors have maintained high standards of excellence. The bands directed by Leonard Haug and the choruses of Chester Lee Francis rank high among the nation's musical organizations. The Oklahoma City Symphony Orchestra, of late years under Victor Allesandro and more recently under Guy F. Harrison, has given performances of outstanding quality.

Newspapers of Oklahoma have made significant contributions to the culture of the state. However, a steady trend toward editorial sterility, together with marked partisanship in the reporting of news, have brought decline of newspaper influence in Oklahoma, as in other parts of the nation, during the second quarter of the present century. The independence and courage of men like Sidney Suggs of Ardmore, Freeman E. Miller of Stillwater, and John Fields of Oklahoma City in early Oklahoma are scarcely matched by the editorial policies of current newspapers. Vigorous and competent editorial leadership in line with the public interest has become rare but has not disappeared. For example, Luther Harrison, after more than thirty years of service on the staff of the *Daily Oklahoman,* is not only skilled in his profession but is keenly awake to public welfare and is not bound by narrow partisan interests.

The University of Oklahoma Press is comparatively new in the field of books. The first director was Joseph A. Brandt, who served from 1929 until 1938, when he was succeeded by Savoie Lottinville, his former assistant. Both directors received their early schooling in Oklahoma and both attended Oxford University as Rhodes scholars.

It is impossible for a contemporary to estimate with certainty the total influence of the University of Oklahoma Press. Many Oklahomans of scholarly tastes have been stimulated to literary efforts by its existence and in some instances their work has been good. Emphasis upon regional studies of the Southwest is clearly indicated by such books as: *A Guide to the Indian Tribes of Oklahoma,* by Muriel Wright; *The Indians of the Southwest,* by Edward Everett Dale; *Deserts on the March,* by Paul B. Sears; *The Ten*

*Grandmothers,* by Alice Marriot; and *Fort Worth,* by Oliver Knight.[24] The field of attention has widened, however, during recent years. William E. Livezey's book, *Mahan on Sea Power,* was published in 1947; *Mark Twain as a Literary Artist,* by Gladys Bellamy, was published in 1950; and *The Writing of American History,* by Michael Kraus, in 1953.[25] Further evidence of the expanded scope of publication by the University of Oklahoma Press may be seen in a recent release, *The Case of Mrs. Surratt,* by Guy W. Moore.[26]

Savoie Lottinville, director since 1938, was born in Idaho in 1906. As a boy he lived in Tulsa, where he attended public school. After graduation from the University of Oklahoma he went to England on a Rhodes Scholarship award and was graduated from Oxford in 1932. Upon his return to the United States he worked for a brief period as a reporter for the *Oklahoma City Times,* served as business manager and assistant editor for the University of Oklahoma Press, and succeeded Joseph A. Brandt as director. Since 1938, Professor Lottinville has maintained a high standard of scholarship in his editorial staff, which has included the talented art editor, Will Ransom, and the equally able associate editor, Mary Stith.

A periodical of unique interest published by the University of Oklahoma Press is the quarterly, *Books Abroad,* founded by Roy Temple House in 1927 and edited under his direction for twenty-two years. This great editor and teacher was born in Nebraska in 1878. He studied modern languages at Miami University and did graduate work at the University of Michigan, at the University of Montpelier in France, and at the University of Chicago, where he received the Ph.D. degree in 1914. He served as head of the modern language department in the Southwestern Normal School at Weatherford, Oklahoma, from 1905 to 1910. During the following

[24] Sears, *Deserts on the March* (Norman, 1935); Marriott, *The Ten Grandmothers* (Norman, 1945); Knight, *Fort Worth, Outpost on the Trinity* (Norman, 1953); Dale, *The Indians of the Southwest* (Norman, 1949).
[25] Livezey, *Mahan on Sea Power* (Norman, 1947); Garel Grunder and William E. Livezey, *The Philippines and the United States* (Norman, 1951); Bellamy, *Mark Twain as a Literary Artist* (Norman, 1950); Kraus, *The Writing of American History* (Norman, 1953).
[26] Guy W. Moore, *The Case of Mrs. Surratt* (Norman, 1954).

447

year he was an exchange teacher in Magdeburg, Germany. His work at the University of Oklahoma began in 1911 and continued until 1954. For more than two decades he carried the load of serving as head of the modern language department and during a large part of that time was also editor of *Books Abroad*.

The reviews of foreign publications written by Professor House and his associates brought national recognition for their quarterly publication and distinguished citations for the editor from many parts of the world. No man of outstanding talent has maintained a more humble bearing than Roy Temple House. Widespread acclaim from the scholars of his generation and extravagant praise from thousands who stand in awe of his learning, have left him entirely unimpressed with his own greatness.

This attempt to present an estimate of Oklahoma culture, by the use of examples and general observations, can do no more than to point out traits and call attention to their kinship. Many notable men and women of the state have been omitted for the obvious reason that space is limited. It is hoped that the careers selected as examples of cultural growth will prove suggestive, and perhaps useful to the reader in forming a broader concept of Oklahoma's contribution to modern civilization.

# Bibliography

### I. MANUSCRIPTS

Acts, Bills, Resolutions, etc. of the Choctaw Nation (25 vols., 1869–1910), Phillips Collection, University of Oklahoma.

Draper Collection (Tecumseh Manuscripts, Vols. IV and X), Phillips Collection.

E. C. Boudinot Letters (3 vols.), Phillips Collection.

Stand Watie Letters (11 vols.), Phillips Collection.

Union Agency Files, Office of the Superintendent of the Five Civilized Tribes, Muskogee, Oklahoma.

Indian-Pioneer Papers (116 vols. and Table of Contents), Phillips Collection.

### II. FEDERAL AND STATE DOCUMENTS

*American State Papers.* 38 vols. Washington, 1832–61.

Bureau of American Ethnology. *Fourteenth Annual Report.* Washington, 1900.

———. *Forty-second Annual Report.* Washington, 1928.

———. *Bulletin No. 103.* Washington, 1931.

Commissioner of Indian Affairs. *Annual Reports* (1836, 1841, 1842, 1847, 1859, 1861, 1864, 1865, 1870, 1871, 1882, 1897).

*A Compilation of All the Treaties between the United States and the Indian Tribes.* Washington, 1873.

Congress of the United States. Documents and Records:

    23 Cong., 1 sess., *Sen. Doc. 512, III.*

    27 Cong., 3 sess., *House Exec. Doc. 219.*

    41 Cong., 3 sess., *House Exec. Docs., IV.*

    48 Cong., 1 sess., *Sen. Exec. Doc. 54, IV.*

    49 Cong., 1 sess., *Sen. Reports,* Vol. VIII.

    52 Cong., 1 sess., *Cong. Rec.*

    54 Cong., 1 sess., *House Docs., XV.*

57 Cong., 1 sess., *Cong. Rec.*

61 Cong., 2 sess., *Sen. Doc. 357.*

Kappler, Charles J. *Indian Affairs: Laws and Treaties.* 3 vols. Washington, 1904.

Malloy, William M., ed. *Treaties, Conventions, International Acts, Protocols, and Agreements between the United States and Other Powers.* Washington, 1904. Also, in 61 Cong., 2 sess., *Sen. Doc. 357.*

Marcy, Randolph B. *Exploration of the Red River.* 32 Cong., 2 sess., *Sen. Exec. Doc. 54.*

Oklahoma: *Directory of the State of Oklahoma.* Issued by the Oklahoma Election Board. Oklahoma City, 1949.

Oklahoma: *Officers and Members of Oklahoma State Offices and Boards.* Prepared by Ralph Hudson, state librarian, 1953.

Oklahoma Geological Survey
*Bulletin No. 1* (C. N. Gould and others.) Norman, 1908.
C. W. Shannon. *Handbook on the Natural Resources of Oklahoma.* Norman, 1916.
*Bulletin No. 4. Coal in Oklahoma.* (C. W. Shannon and others.) Revised and edited by C. L. Cooper. Norman, 1926.

*Opinions of the Attorneys General of the United States.* Vols. IX–XII (ed. by J. Hubley Ashton); Vols. XIII–XIX (ed. by A. J. Bentley). Washington,1852–19–.

Secretaries of the Interior. *Annual Reports:* 1865, 1866, 1870, 1872, 1885, 1895.

*Statistical Abstracts of the United States, 1952.* Washington, 1953.

*Statutes at Large of the United States of America.* Washington, 1887–1904.

Territorial Governors of Oklahoma. *Annual Reports to the Secretary of the Interior,* 1891–1907.

United States Bureau of the Census, *Eleventh, Twelfth, Thirteenth, Sixteenth,* and *Seventeenth Reports;* United States Bureau of the Census, *Manufacturing; 1947,* Vol. III. Washington, 1948.

United States Bureau of Education. *Biennial Survey, 1946–47.*

United States War Department. *The War of the Rebellion: a Compilation of the Official Records of the Union and Confederate Armies.* 130 volumes. Washington, 1880–1901.

III. OTHER COLLECTIONS OF DOCUMENTS, LETTERS, AND PAPERS

Adams, John Quincy. *Memoirs of John Quincy Adams* (ed. by Charles Francis Adams). 12 vols. Philadelphia, 1874–77.

Bureau of Business Research, University of Oklahoma. *Oklahoma Business Bulletin,* Vol. 19 (December, 1953), No. 12. Norman, Okla.

Coues, Elliott. *The Expedition of Zebulon M. Pike.* 2 vols. New York, 1895.

Dale, Edward Everett, and Rader, Jesse Lee. *Readings in Oklahoma History.* Evanston, Illinois, 1930.

Hart, Albert Bushnell. *American History Told by Contemporaries.* 4 vols. New York, 1897–1901.

Jefferson, Thomas. *The Writings of Thomas Jefferson* (ed. by Paul L. Ford). 10 vols. New York, 1892–99.

Madison, James. *The Writings of James Madison* (ed. by Gaillard Hunt). 9 vols. New York, 1900–10.

Monroe, James. *The Writings of James Monroe* (ed. by Stanislaus Hamilton). 7 vols. New York, 1898–1903.

Richardson, James D., ed. *A Compilation of the Messages and Papers of the Presidents, 1789–1902.* Washington, 1896–99.

Thomas, C. L., ed. *Annotated Acts of Congress, Five Civilized Tribes and the Osage Nation.* Columbia, Mo., 1913.

IV. MISCELLANEOUS SOURCES

Aldrich, Gene. "A History of the Coal Industry in Oklahoma to 1907." (Unpublished Ph.D. dissertation, University of Oklahoma, 1952.)

*Cambridge Modern History.* 13 vols. and atlas. New York and London, 1902–12.

*Current Biography.* New York, 1950.

*Dictionary of American Biography.* (ed. by Allen Johnson, Dumas Malone, and H. E. Starr). 21 vols. New York, 1928–36.

*Dictionary of American History* (ed. by James Truslow Adams). 6 vols. New York, 1940.

*Encyclopaedia Britannica.* 11th edition. 29 vols. New York, 1910–11.

Folsom, Joseph P. *Constitution and Laws of the Choctaw Nation.* New York, 1869.

Hopkins, J. C. "James G. Blunt and the Civil War." (Unpublished master's thesis, University of Oklahoma, 1952.)

*Niles' Weekly Register,* 1831ff.

*Oklahoma Red Book.* 2 vols. Oklahoma City, 1912.

*United States Economic Almanac, 1950.* New York, 1950.

*World Almanac, 1954.* New York, 1954.

V. CASES CITED

*Cherokee Nation v. Georgia.* 5 Peters, 1.

*Worcester* v. *Georgia.* 6 Peters, 515.
*United States* v. *Texas.* 162 U. S., 1.
*Coyle* v. *Smith.* 221 U. S., 559.
*Oklahoma* v. *Texas.* 260 U. S., 606.

VI. DAILY NEWSPAPERS

*Daily Oklahoman.*
*New York Times.*
*Oklahoma City Times.*
*Tulsa Daily World.*
*Tulsa Tribune.*

VII. ARTICLES

Blunt, James G. "General Blunt's Account of His Civil War Experiences," *Kansas Historical Quarterly,* Vol. I, No. 1 (1932).

Carr, Susan. "Bloomfield Academy and Its Founder," *Chronicles of Oklahoma,* Vol. II, No. 4 (December, 1924), 366–79.

Childs, Marquis W. "The Big Boom from Oklahoma," *Saturday Evening Post,* Vol. CCXXI, No. 41 (April 9, 1949), 22–23, 118–20.

Dale, Edward Everett. "History of the Range Cattle Industry in Oklahoma," The American Historical Association, *Annual Report, 1920,* p. 309–22.

Debo, Angie. "Southern Refugees of the Cherokee Nation," *Southwestern Historical Quarterly,* Vol. XXXV (April, 1932), 255–66.

Elson, Robert T. "If Not Truman, Who?" *Life,* Vol. XXXII, No. 12 (March, 1952), 126–28.

Evans, Charles. "Judge Thomas H. Doyle," *Chronicles of Oklahoma,* Vol. XXVII, No. 2 (Summer, 1949), 138–44.

Foreman, Carolyn F. "The Choctaw Academy," *Chronicles of Oklahoma,* Vol. VI, No. 4 (December, 1928), 453–80.

Foreman, Grant. "Early Post-Offices in Oklahoma," *Chronicles of Oklahoma,* Vol. VI, Nos. 1–4 (March, June, September, December, 1928), 4–25, 155–62, 271–98, 408–44.

Guild, Frederic H. "The Development of the Legislative Council Idea," *Annals of the American Academy of Political and Social Science,* Vol. CXCV (January, 1938), 146ff.

McCurtain, B. F. "The Indians of Oklahoma," *Sturm's Oklahoma Magazine,* Vol. XI, No. 3 (1910), 23ff.

Orr, Kenneth G. "The Archaeological Situation at Spiro," *American Antiquity,* Vol. XI, No. 4 (April, 1946), 228–56.

Peery, Dan W. "Col. Crocker and the Boomer Movement," *Chronicles of Oklahoma*, Vol. XIII, No. 3 (September, 1935), 273–96.

——. "Captain David L. Payne," *Chronicles of Oklahoma*, Vol. XIII, No. 4 (December, 1935), 438–56.

Wardell, Morris L. "Protestant Missions among the Osages," *Chronicles of Oklahoma*, Vol. II, No. 3 (September, 1924), 285–97.

Wicks, Hamilton S. "The Opening of Oklahoma," *Cosmopolitan*, Vol. VII (September, 1889).


VIII. Books

Abel, Annie Heloise. *The American Indian as Slaveholder and Secessionist.* Cleveland, 1915.

——. *The American Indian as Participant in the Civil War.* Cleveland, 1919.

——. *The American Indian under Reconstruction.* Cleveland, 1925.

Abernathy, Thomas P. *Western Lands and the American Revolution.* New York, 1937.

Adair, James. *The History of the American Indians.* London, 1775. A later edition was published at Johnson City, Tennessee, in 1930.

Adams, Henry. *The History of the United States During the Administrations of Jefferson and Madison* (ed. by Herbert Agar). 2 vols. 1947.

——. *History of the United States of America, 1801–1817.* 9 vols. New York, 1889–91.

——. *The Life of Albert Gallatin.* New York, 1879.

Alexander, Holmes. *Aaron Burr: The Proud Pretender.* New York, 1943.

Alley, John. *City Beginnings in Oklahoma Territory.* Norman, 1939.

Alvord, Clarence W. *The Mississippi Valley in British Politics.* 2 vols. Cleveland, 1917.

Babcock, Kendrick C. *The Rise of American Nationality.* New York, 1906.

Baldwin, Leland D. *Whiskey Rebels: The Story of a Frontier Uprising.* Pittsburgh, 1939.

Barbé-Marbois, François de. *Histoire de la Louisiane.* Paris, 1829. (English translation, 1830.)

Bartram, William. *Travels through North and South Carolina, Georgia, East and West Florida, the Cherokee Country . . . and the Country of the Choctaws.* London, 1792.

Bassett, John Spencer. *The Federalist System.* New York, 1906.

Bellamy, Gladys Carmen. *Mark Twain as a Literary Artist.* Norman, 1950.

453

Bemis, Samuel Flagg. *Pinckney's Treaty.* Baltimore, 1926.

Benton, Thomas Hart. *Thirty Years' View.* 2 vols. 1854–56.

Billington, Ray Allen. *Westward Expansion.* New York, 1949.

Bolton, Hebert E., ed. *Athanase de Mézières and the Louisiana-Texas Frontier, 1768–1780.* 2 vols. Cleveland, 1914.

————, ed. *Spanish Explorations in the Southwest, 1542–1706.* New York, 1916.

————. *The Spanish Borderlands,* New Haven, 1921.

————, and Thomas M. Marshall. *The Colonization of North America.* New York, 1922.

Bourne, Edward Gaylord, ed. *Narratives of the Career of Hernando de Soto.* 2 vols. New York, 1904.

————. *Spain in America.* New York, 1904.

Bradbury, John. *Bradbury's Travels in the Interior of America.* Vol. V of Reuben Gold Thwaites, ed., *Early Western Travels* (q.v.).

Brant, Irving. *James Madison.* 4 vols. 1941–50.

Brooks, Stratton D. *English Composition.* 2 vols. New York, 1911–12.

Brevoort, J. C. *Verrazano the Navigator.* Albany, 1874.

Britton, Wiley. *The Civil War on the Border.* 2 vols. New York, 1890–99.

————. *The Union Indian Brigade in the Civil War.* Kansas City, Mo., 1922.

Buchanan, James Shannon, and Edward Everett Dale. *A History of Oklahoma.* Evanston, Ill., 1935.

Bynum, Ernest T. *Personal Recollections of Ex-Governor Walton.* Oklahoma City, 1924.

Catlin, George. *The North American Indians.* 2 vols. London, 1876.

Chambers, Henry E. *Mississippi Valley Beginnings,* New York, 1922.

Channing, Edward. *History of the United States.* 6 vols. New York, 1905–25.

————. *The Jeffersonian System.* New York, 1906.

Charlevoix, Pierre François Xavier de. *History of New France* (ed. by John G. Shea), 6 vols. New York, 1900.

Chinard, Gilbert. *Honest John Adams.* Boston, 1933.

Chittenden, Hiram M. *The American Fur Trade in the Far West.* 3 vols. Elmira, N. Y., 1935.

Clark, Daniel. *The West in American History.* 1937.

Commager, Henry Steele. *The American Mind.* New Haven, 1950.

Connelley, William E. *Quantrill and the Border Wars.* Cedar Rapids, Iowa, 1910.

Cox, Isaac J. *The Early Exploration of Louisiana.* Cincinnati, 1906.

454

Culin, Stewart. *Games of the North American Indians.* Bureau of American Ethnology *Twenty-Fourth Annual Report.* Washington, 1907.

Cushman, H. B. *History of the Choctaw, Chickasaw, and Natchez Indians.* Greenville, Texas, 1899.

Dale, Edward Everett, with James Shannon Buchanan. *A History of Oklahoma.* Chicago, 1924.

———, ed. *Letters of Lafayette.* Oklahoma City, 1925.

———, with Meriam and others. *The Problem of Indian Administration.* Baltimore, 1928.

———, and Jesse L. Rader. *Readings in Oklahoma History.* Chicago, 1930.

———. *The Range Cattle Industry.* Norman, 1930.

———, ed. *Frontier Trails.* Boston, 1930.

———. *Grant Foreman: a Brief Biography.* Norman, 1933.

———, ed. *A Rider of the Cherokee Strip.* Boston, 1936.

———, and Gaston Litton. *Cherokee Cavaliers.* Norman, 1939.

———. *Cow Country.* Norman, 1942.

———, Dwight L. Dumond, and Edgar B. Wesley. *History of the United States.* Boston, 1948.

———, and Morris L. Wardell. *History of Oklahoma.* New York, 1948.

———. *Oklahoma: The Story of a State.* Evanston, 1949.

———. *The Indians of the Southwest.* Norman, 1949.

Debo, Angie. *The Rise and Fall of the Choctaw Republic.* Norman, 1934.

———. *And Still the Waters Run.* Princeton, 1940.

———. *The Road to Disappearance.* Norman, 1941.

———. *Tulsa: From Creek Town to Oil Capital.* Norman, 1943.

———. *Prairie City.* New York, 1944.

———. *Oklahoma: Foot-loose and Fancy-free.* Norman, 1949.

———. *The Five Civilized Tribes.* Philadelphia, 1951.

De Costa, B. F. *Verrazano the Explorer.* New York, 1880.

Dobie, J. Frank. *Coronado's Children.* New York, 1931.

Doyle, J. A. *English Colonies in America.* 5 vols. New York, 1889–1907.

Duffus, Robert Luther. *The Santa Fe Trail.* New York, 1930.

Folsom, Joseph P. *Constitution and Laws of the Choctaw Nation.* New York, 1869.

Foreman, Carolyn Thomas. *Indians Abroad.* Norman, 1943.

———. *Oklahoma Imprints, 1835–1907.* Norman, 1936.

———. *Park Hill.* Muskogee, 1948.

Foreman, Grant. *Pioneer Days in the Southwest.* Cleveland, 1926.

———. *A Traveler in Indian Territory.* Cedar Rapids, Iowa, 1930.

———. *Indians and Pioneers.* New Haven, 1930.

————. *Indian Removal.* Norman, 1932.

————. *Advancing the Frontier,* Norman, 1933.

————. *The Five Civilized Tribes.* Norman, 1934.

————. *Fort Gibson.* Norman, 1936.

————. *A History of Oklahoma.* Norman, 1942.

————. *Muskogee: The Biography of an Oklahoma Town.* Norman, 1943.

————. *Sequoyah.* Norman, 1938.

Foster, George. *Se-quo-yah, the American Cadmus and Modern Moses.* Philadelphia, 1885.

Fowler, Jacob. *The Journal of Jacob Fowler* (ed. by Elliott Coues). New York, 1898.

French, Benjamin F. *Historical Collections of Louisiana.* 5 vols., New York, 1846–53.

————. *Historical Collections of Louisiana and Florida.* New York, 1875.

Fuller, Hubert Bruce. *The Purchase of Florida.* Cleveland, 1906.

Gilbert, E. W. *The Exploration of Western America, 1800–1850.* New York, 1933.

Gittinger, Roy. *The Formation of the State of Oklahoma, 1803–1906.* Norman, 1939.

————. *The University of Oklahoma: A History of Fifty Years, 1892–1942.* Norman, 1942.

Goebel, Dorothy Burne, and Julius Goebel, Jr. *Generals in the White House.* New York, 1945.

Grant, A. J. *The French Monarchy, 1483–1789.* 2 vols, New York, 1905.

Gray, Lewis C. *History of Agriculture in the Southern United States to 1860.* 2 vols. New York, 1933.

Gregg, Josiah. *Commerce of the Prairies.* Parts I and II, in volumes XIX and XX, respectively, Reuben Gold Thwaites, ed., *Early Western Travels.* (q. v.).

————. *Diary & Letters of Josiah Gregg* (ed. by Maurice Garland Fulton). 2 vols. Norman, 1941, 1944.

Hafen, LeRoy, and Carl Coke Rister. *Western America.* New York, 1941.

Haley, J. Evetts. *Charles Goodnight: Cowman and Plainsman.* Norman, 1949.

Hayes, Carlton Joseph H. *A Political and Cultural History of Modern Europe.* 2 vols. New York, 1936.

Henderson, Archibald. *Conquest of the Old Southwest, 1740–1800.* New York, 1920.

Hines, Gordon, *Alfalfa Bill.* Oklahoma City, 1932.

Hinsdale, Burke Aaron. *The Old Northwest.* 2 vols. New York, 1891.

Hodge, Frederick Webb, ed. *Handbook of American Indians North of*

*Mexico*. Bureau of American Ethnology *Bulletin No. 30.* 2 vols. Washington, 1907, 1910.

Hollon, W. Eugene. *The Lost Pathfinder: Zebulon Montgomery Pike.* Norman, 1949.

Hosmer, J. K. *The Louisiana Purchase.* New York, 1915.

Irving, Washington. *A Tour on the Prairies.* New York, 1885.

———. *The Western Journals of Washington Irving* (ed. by John Francis McDermott). Norman, 1944.

James, Edwin. *Account of an Expedition from Pittsburgh to the Rocky Mountains* Vols. XIV–XVII of Reuben Gold Thwaites, ed., *Early Western Travels* (q. v.).

James, J. A. *The Life of George Rogers Clark.* Chicago, 1928.

Jefferson, Thomas. *The Writings of Thomas Jefferson* (ed. by Paul L. Ford). 10 vols. New York, 1892–99.

Johnson, Allen. *Jefferson and his Colleagues.* New Haven, 1921.

Johnston, Mary. *Pioneers of the Old South.* New Haven, 1921.

Kaufman, Kenneth. *Level Land.* Dallas, 1935.

Latrobe, Charles Joseph. *The Rambler in North America, MDCCCXXII–MDCCCXXXIII.* 2 vols. London, 1836.

Lewis, Anna. *Along the Arkansas.* Dallas, 1912.

Livezey, William E. *Mahan on Sea Power.* Norman, 1947.

———, with Garel A. Grunder. *The Philippines and the United States.* Norman, 1951.

Lyon, E. Wilson. *Louisiana in French Diplomacy, 1759–1804.* Norman, 1934.

Malone, James H. *The Chickashaw Nation.* Louisville, 1923.

Margry, Pierre. *Découvertes et établissements des Français.* 6 vols. Paris, 1879–88.

Masterson, V. V. *The Katy Railroad and the Last Frontier.* Norman, 1953.

Mathews, John Joseph. *Wah'Kon-Tah: The Osage and the White Man's Road.* Norman, 1932.

———. *Sundown.* New York, 1935.

———. *Talking to the Moon.* Chicago, 1945.

———. *Life and Death of an Oilman: The Career of E. W. Marland.* Norman, 1951.

McCoy, Joseph G. *Cattle Trade of the West and Southwest* (ed. by Ralph P. Bieber). Glendale, Calif. 1940. Vol. VIII of *The Southwest Historical Series.*

McMaster, John B. *A History of the People of the United States from the Revolution to the Civil War.* 8 vols. New York, 1883–1913.

Meriam, Lewis, and others. *The Problem of Indian Administration.* Baltimore, 1928.

Mohr, Walter H. *Federal Indian Relations,* Philadelphia, 1933.

Moorhead, W. K. *The American Indian,* Andover, Mass., 1914.

Morison, Samuel Eliot, and Henry Steele Commager. *The Growth of the American Republic.* 2 vols. New York, 1950.

Munro, William Bennett. *Crusaders of New France.* New Haven, 1921.

Myer, William P. "Indian Trails of the Southeast." Bureau of American Ethnology *Forty-second Annual Report.* Washington, 1928.

Nevins, Allan. *America Through British Eyes.* New York, 1948.

Nuttall, Thomas. *Nuttall's Journal of Travels into the Arkansa Territory, October 2, 1818–February 18, 1820.* Vol. XVIII of Reuben Gold Thwaites, ed., *Early Western Travels* (q. v.).

O'Beirne, H. F., and E. S. O'Beirne. *The Indian Territory: Its Chiefs, Legislators, and Leading Men.* St. Louis, 1892.

Ogg, Frederick Austin. *The Opening of the Mississippi.* New York, 1904.

———. *The Reign of Andrew Jackson.* New Haven, 1919.

Oskison, John M. *Tecumseh and His Times: the Story of a Great Indian.* New York, 1938.

Parish, J. C. *The Man with the Iron Hand.* New York, 1913.

Parkman, Francis. *Montcalm and Wolf.* 2 vols. New York, 1884.

———. *The Pioneers of France in the New World.* Boston, 1903.

———. *La Salle and the Discovery of the Great West.* Boston, 1902.

———. *The Conspiracy of Pontiac.* New York, 1927.

Parrington, Vernon Louis. *Main Currents in American Thought.* 3 vols. New York, 1927–30.

Parrish, Randall. *The Great Plains.* Chicago, 1915.

Parton, James. *Life of Andrew Jackson.* 3 vols. New York, 1860.

Paxson, Frederick L. *The Last American Frontier.* New York, 1911.

———. *History of the American Frontier.* Boston, 1924.

Pelzer, Lewis. *Marches of the Dragoons in the Mississippi Valley.* Iowa City, 1917.

Phelps, Albert. *Louisiana.* New York, 1905.

Pitkin, Timothy. *A Statistical View of the Commerce of the United States.* New York, 1816.

Pratz, Le Page du. *History of Louisiana.* London, 1774.

Prescott, William H. *History of the Conquest of Mexico.* 3 vols. New York, 1901.

Rister, Carl Coke. *Land Hunger: David L. Payne and the Oklahoma Boomers.* Norman, 1942.

Rogers, Will. *How We Elect Our Presidents.* Boston, 1926.

458

——. *Ether and Me, or Just Relax.* New York and London, 1929.

——. *The Autobiography of Will Rogers.* Boston, 1949.

Royce, Charles C. *Indian Land Cessions in the United States.* Bureau of American Ethnology *Eighteenth Annual Report,* Part II. Washington, 1900.

——. *The Cherokee Nation of Indians.* Bureau of American Ethnology *Fifth Annual Report.* Washington, 1887.

Seybert, Adam. *Statistical Annals of the United States of America, 1789–1818.* New York, 1818.

Starkey, Marion L. *The Cherokee Nation,* New York, 1946.

Stith, William. *History of Virginia.* Williamsburg, 1747. Reprinted in London, 1753.

Stuart, James. *Three Years in North America.* 2 vols. Edinburgh, 1833.

Swanton, John R. *Early History of the Creek Indians and Their Neighbors.* Bureau of American Ethnology *Bulletin No. 73.* Washington, 1922.

——. *Source Material for the Social and Ceremonial Life of the Choctaw Indians.* Bureau of American Ethnology *Bulletin No. 103.* Washington, 1931.

——. "Social Organization and Social Usages of the Indians of the Creek Confederacy." Bureau of American Ethnology *Forty-second Annual Report.* Washington, 1928.

——. "Aboriginal Culture of the Southeast." Bureau of American Ethnology *Forty-second Annual Report.* Washington, 1928.

Terrage, Villiers du. *Les dernières années de la Louisiane française.* Paris, 1903.

Thoburn, Joseph B., ed. *History of Oklahoma.* 5 vols. New York and Chicago, 1916.

——, and Muriel H. Wright. *Oklahoma: A History of the State and Its People.* 4 vols. New York, 1929.

Thomas, Alfred Barnaby, ed. *Forgotten Frontiers.* Norman, 1932.

——, ed. *After Coronado: Spanish Exploration Northeast of Mexico.* Norman, 1935.

Thwaites, Reuben Gold, ed. *Early Western Travels, 1784–1897.* 32 vols. Cleveland, 1904–1907.

——. *France in America.* New York, 1905.

Tixier, Victor. *Tixier's Travels on the Osage Plains* (ed. by John Francis McDermott). Norman, 1940.

Tracy, Joseph. *History of American Missions.* Worcester, Mass., 1840.

Tucker, Howard A. *Governor Walton's Ku Klux Klan War.* Oklahoma City, 1923.

Turner, Frederick Jackson. *The Rise of the New West*. New York, 1906.

———. *The Frontier in American History*. New York, 1920.

———. *The Significance of Sections in the United States*. New York, 1932.

Vestal, Stanley. *Sitting Bull, Champion of the Sioux*. Boston, 1932.

———. *Warpath, the True Story of the Sioux Wars*. Boston, 1934.

———. *New Sources of Indian History*. Norman, 1934.

———. *The Old Santa Fe Trail*. Boston, 1939.

———. *Jim Bridger*. New York, 1946.

———. *Warpath and Council Fire*. New York, 1948.

Wakeman, H. O. *Europe, 1598–1715*. New York, 1904.

Wallace, Ernest, and E. Adamson Hoebel. *The Comanches: Lords of the South Plains*. Norman, 1952.

Wandell, Samuel H., and Meade Minnigerode. *Aaron Burr*. 2 vols. New York, 1925.

Wardell, Morris L. *A Political History of the Cherokee Nation 1838–1907*. Norman, 1938.

Whitaker, Arthur P. *The Mississippi Question, 1795–1803*. New York, 1934.

Winship, George Parker, ed. "The Coronado Expedition." Bureau of American Ethnology, *Fourteenth Annual Report*, Part I. Washington, 1896.

Wright, Muriel H. *A Guide to the Indian Tribes of Oklahoma*. Norman, 1951.

Wrong, George M. *The Conquest of New France*. New Haven, 1918.

———. *The Rise and Fall of New France*. New York, 1928.

# Index

(For authors cited, consult Bibliography.)

461